THE ATROCITY PARADIGM

The Atrocity Paradigm

A Theory of Evil

CLAUDIA CARD

OXFORD
UNIVERSITY PRESS

2002

OXFORD
UNIVERSITY PRESS

Oxford New York

Auckland Bangkok Buenos Aires Cape Town
Chennai Dar es Salaam Delhi Hong Kong Istanbul Karachi
Kolkata Kuala Lumpur Melbourne Mexico City Mumbai Nairobi
São Paulo Shanghai Singapore Taipei Tokyo Toronto
and an associated company in Berlin

Published by Oxford University Press, Inc.
198 Madison Avenue, New York, New York 10016

www.oup.com

Library of Congress Cataloging-in-Publication Data
Card, Claudia.
The atrocity paradigm : a theory of evil / Claudia Card.
p. cm.
ISBN 0-19-514508-9
1. Good and evil. I. Title.
BJ1401 .C29 2002
170—dc21   2001036610

9 8 7 6 5 4 3 2 1

Printed in the United States of America
on acid-free paper

To my teachers,
whose example and encouragement have elicited my best efforts:

Ruby Healy Marquardt (1891–1976)

Marjorie Glass Pinkerton

Marcus George Singer

John Rawls

Lorna Smith Benjamin

Preface

Four decades of philosophical work in ethics have engaged me with varieties of evil. It began with an undergraduate honors thesis on punishment, which was followed by a Ph.D. dissertation on that topic; essays on mercy and retribution, and a grant to study the U.S. penitentiary system. Besides "Crime and Punishment" courses, I also teach or have taught Kant, Schopenhauer, Nietzsche, and the philosophy of religion, all with a central focus on evil.

The mid-1970s brought an encounter with the radical feminist essays of Marilyn Frye, which worked a revolution in my approaches to everything. I affiliated with Women's Studies and developed three courses in feminist philosophy. My research interests expanded to take in rape, atrocities of domestic violence and child abuse, histories of slavery, lynching, and segregation, and, thanks to pioneering work by Andrea Dworkin and Mary Daly, histories of witch burnings, foot binding, sati, and the imposed female genital surgeries of clitoridectomy and infibulation.

For a decade I taught a multicultural Women's Studies course on lesbian culture from Sappho to the present. (One could do that in the late '70s and early '80s before research in the field mushroomed.) I began work on horizontal violence in my *Lesbian Choices* (1995) and on the impact of social institutions and intimate relationships on moral character development and was struck, even more than in my work on mercy, by the pervasiveness of what Bernard Williams and Thomas Nagel taught us to call "moral luck." My book *The Unnatural Lottery: Character and Moral Luck* (1996) initiated a struggle to come to terms with the idea of moral responsibility under oppression. That struggle continues in this book, especially in chapters 3, 4, 9, and 10.

When a colleague who taught environmental ethics left my department in the late 1980s, I affiliated with the university's Institute for Environmental Studies. For a decade I taught a large cross-listed course that included attention to environmental racism, pesticides, factory farms, global warming, and destruction of natural habitats. Evils, I became convinced, are done to many living beings, not just people or even just sentient beings. The theory of evil offered in this book is intended to accommodate that idea, although I do not here develop the wider applications.

This coming fall I will teach for the second time my newest course, "Moral Philosophy and the Holocaust," cross-listed with Jewish Studies. This course returns me to issues of punishment and such related matters as restitution, reparations, apology, forgiveness, and mercy. But now they are contextualized in large-scale international atrocities rather than in the more manageable framework of a single state or institution dealing with simpler deeds and remedies.

After years of reflecting on different evils, it seemed finally time to confront the concept of evil head-on. I wanted to articulate an ethical analysis of what makes deeds, people, relationships, practices, intentions, and motives evil and use that analysis to begin a more general pursuit of ethical questions regarding what to do about evils and how best to live with them. These are the ambitious projects of this book. As the reader can see by now, my background for undertaking them, besides decades of work in ethical theory, is acquaintance with issues raised by particular sets of evils: crime and punishment, past and present misogyny and anti-Semitism, some forms of racism and of slavery, hatred of homosexuals, violence in the home, cruelty to animals, environmental assault and neglect, war rape (and other torture and terrorism), and genocide. Atrocities from that list have become my paradigms of evils. A similar acquaintance with other evils might expand my paradigms and possibly lead to modifications in my theory.

Many kinds of support eased the writing of this book and helped greatly with its completion. I thank the University of Wisconsin Graduate School Research Committee for summer salary support in 1999 and 2000 and a sabbatical leave during the spring of 2001. The sabbatical is especially appreciated, since I had to reapply after declining it the year before in order to accept a Senior Fellowship from the American Council of Learned Societies and a Resident Fellowship at the Institute for Research in the Humanities at the University of Wisconsin. These fellowships, for which I am deeply grateful, enabled me to produce a complete draft during 1999–2000, which I was then able to rework during 2001.

Parts of many chapters draw on work begun in short articles. All previously published material is thoroughly rewritten, rethought in the context of the theory developed in this book, revised in substance, and greatly expanded with completely new material. The Nietzsche chapter got a jump start from "Genealogies and Perspectives," presented to the North American Nietzsche Society and published in *International Studies in Philosophy* (28, 3 [1996]). The last part of chapter 3 grew from "Stoicism, Evil, and the Possibility of Morality," presented to the Illinois Philosophical Association and published in *Metaphilosophy* (29, 4 [1998]). Parts of chapter 5 draw on parts of "Evils and In-equalities," presented at a Feminism and Law conference at the University of San Diego and published in the *Journal of Contemporary Legal Issues* (9 [1998]). Portions of chapters 6 and 7 draw on portions of essays published in *Hypatia*, "Against Marriage and Motherhood" (11, 3 [1996]), "Rape as a Weapon of War" (11, 4 [1996]), and "Addendum to 'Rape as a Weapon of War,'" (12, 2 [1997]). An ancestor of part of chapter 10 appeared in the introduction to my edited collection *On Feminist Ethics and Politics* (University Press of Kansas, 1999) as "Groping Through Gray Zones" and another in *Metaphilosophy* (31, 5 [2000]) as "Women, Evil, and Gray Zones." For permission to draw freely on these materials, I am grateful to the journal publishers and the University Press of Kansas.

Many readers and audiences provided stimulating questions, comments, advice, and support. Marcus G. Singer, Van Rensselaer Potter, Paula Gottlieb, David Weberman, Robin Schott, Hilde Lindemann Nelson, and anonymous reviewers read drafts of many chapters, commenting helpfully and in detail. The Nietzsche chapter benefited from suggestions also by Lynne Tirrell, Paul Eisenberg, Ivan Soll, and Lester Hunt and from discussions with audiences at the University of Copenhagen, Dalhousie University, and Washington University-St. Louis. Chapter 4 on Kant was read and discussed helpfully by a faculty seminar at Colgate University. Chapter 5 benefited from comments by Angelika Krebs and discussions with audiences at Moorhead State University and the University of Wisconsin. Chapter 6 on war rape was improved by comments from Bat-Ami Bar On and Hilde Lindemann Nelson. Chapters 6 and 7 profited from discussions with audiences at the International Association of Women Philosophers Seventh Symposium in Vienna (1995), the Graduate Student Philosophy Conference at Washington University-St. Louis (1996), the University of Chicago, and the University of Cincinnati. Chapter 10 benefited from discussions with audiences at the International Association of Women Philosophers Eighth Symposium in Boston (1998), the Feminist Ethics Revisited Conference in Tampa (1999), the Philosophy Institute at the Goethe University in Frankfurt, the Economics Institute at the Albert-Ludwigs University in Freiburg, Bryn Mawr College, Dalhousie University, Florida Atlantic University, the University of Georgia, the University of Wisconsin, Colgate University, and the Women in Philosophy Group at the University of Chicago, as well as from comments and suggestions by Lisa Tessman, Bat-Ami Bar On, Marilyn Friedman, Marcia Homiak, Paula Gottlieb, David Weberman, and many contributors to *On Feminist Ethics and Politics*.

For bringing valuable materials to my attention or helping me track them down, I am grateful to Marcus G. Singer, Lorna Smith Benjamin, Carol Quinn, Angelika Krebs, Suzanne Solensky, Steven Nadler, Kenna Del Sol, Elizabeth

Heaps, and Maudemarie Clark. Support of many kinds also came from Martha Nussbaum, Sandra Lee Bartky, Michael Stocker, Norman Care, Axel Honneth, Alison Jaggar, Marilyn Frye, Wendy Lee-Lampshire, Virginia Held, Jean Rumsey, Chris Cuomo, Victoria Davion, Kate Norlock, Tracy Edwards, Steven Whitton, David Concepcion, Ruth Ginzberg, William McBride, Dan Hausman, Steven Nadler, Robert Skloot, Fran Schrag, Terry Penner, Harry Brighouse, Dan Wikler, Bruce Suttle, Elton Tylenda, and Josephine Pradella, as well as graduate students in my seminars on evil and on Kant's ethics. Shelley Glodowski, Nancy Le Duc, Patty Winspur, and Lori Grant in the philosophy department office provided a level of backup and support that made my own office a great environment for writing.

For long-term support and inspiration by their example, I am forever indebted to the teachers to whom I dedicate this book. Ruby Healy Marquardt, my seventh-grade teacher at Pardeeville High School (Wisconsin), never let me get away with "I don't know" but insisted that I think until I found an answer. It got to be a habit. Often, when I'm not really sure, I still reach for an answer anyway. I could hardly have had the audacity to venture a book on so awesome a topic as the nature of evil without that old habit.

Madison, Wisconsin   C. C.
May 2001

Contents

Abbreviations, xiii

1. Introduction: The Atrocity Paradigm, 3

2. Nietzsche's Denial of Evil, 27

3. Utilitarian Attack and Stoic Withdrawal: Two Extremes, 50

4. Kant's Theory of Radical Evil, 73

5. Prioritizing Evils over Unjust Inequalities, 96

6. Rape in War, 118

7. Terrorism in the Home, 139

8. The Moral Powers of Victims, 166

9. The Moral Burdens and Obligations of Perpetrators, 188

10. Gray Zones: Diabolical Evil Revisited, 211

Notes, 235

Index, 265

Abbreviations

CPrR   Kant, *Critique of Practical Reason*

G   Kant, *Groundwork*

L   Mill, *On Liberty*

LE   Kant, *Lectures on Ethics*

MM   Kant, *The Metaphysics of Morals*

R   Kant, *Religion within the Boundaries of Mere Reason*

U   Mill, *Utilitarianism*

THE ATROCITY PARADIGM

Introduction:
The Atrocity Paradigm

A philosophical theory of evil can be expected to address many questions of meaning and value: Is "evil" a concept worth preserving? In what ways does evil exceed the merely bad or wrong? When is a person evil? An intention or motive? A deed? An institution? Are we all potentially evil? What is the role of suffering in evil? What is the role of culpability? Is hatred necessarily evil? How can we resist evils without doing evil in the process? Are there evils we should tolerate? Are some unforgivable? What can make evils difficult to recognize? Is evil an inevitable aspect of the human condition? Responses to some of these questions are sketched in this chapter, to be developed further later, and others are explored in later chapters.

Philosophy and Evil

Philosophical theories address questions of meaning and value in the attempt to clarify fundamental or important concepts. One way to go about this is to identify commonly asked questions, such as these, and use them to develop an analysis. The theory of this book begins with a simple abstract definition, not expected to be controversial, and develops it by amplifying its basic concepts, addressing such questions as these, placing the theory in relation to others influential in the history of moral philosophy, and considering some case studies. Briefly, the theory of this book is that evils are foreseeable intolerable harms produced by culpable wrongdoing. On my theory, the nature and severity of the harms, rather than perpetrators' psychological states, distinguish evils from ordinary wrongs. Evils tend to ruin lives, or significant parts of lives. It is not surprising if victims never recover or are never quite able to move on, although sometimes people do recover and move on. Evildoers, however, are not necessarily malicious. Oftener they are inexcusably reckless, callously indifferent, amazingly unscrupulous. Evildoers need not be evil people, although they may become so over time.

Evils, on this view, have two basic components: (intolerable) harm and (culpable) wrongdoing, neither reducible to the other. Sometimes we identify evils by the deed, as with the term "genocide," and other times by the harm, as in "mass death." The nomenclature easily creates the impression that the evil is simply the deed in the first case, or the suffering in the second. But neither wrongdoing nor suffering alone is sufficient for an evil. The nomenclature simply reveals one's focus of attention.

By itself the abstract definition is not illuminating. It requires interpretation, and interpretation is gained not only by amplifying the basic concepts and addressing such questions as those of the opening paragraph of this chapter but also by comparing and contrasting this theory with others in the history of moral philosophy and by considering examples of evils. Historically important conceptions of evil have focused on either the harm or the culpable wrongdoing, to the relative neglect of the other component, or have collapsed the two into one. Two extreme views of evil influential in the history of moral philosophy are those of utilitarianism and stoicism (discussed in detail in chapter 3). Utilitarians regard all harm as evil, regardless of its source, and maintain that some evils are justified. Stoics focus on the human will and find all wrongful uses of the will evil. For stoics, what exceeds the will's control is neither good nor evil. It follows that suffering, insofar as it is beyond one's control, is not an evil. My atrocity theory is intermediate between these two theories. It combines features of both but is more specific than either. It makes both harm and wrongful willing essential to evils, but finds neither all harms nor all wrongful uses of the will evil. It presupposes that wrongdoing is not defined simply by the harm that it does or risks, which differentiates it importantly from the utilitarian view. Nor is the harm that evil does accidental, which importantly differentiates the atrocity theory from stoic theories, such as that of Immanuel Kant (chapter 4). In partial agreement with Kant, however, it treats evil as an ethical concept, presupposing culpability. Agreeing in part also with the utilitarian tradition, the theory treats (real or risked) suffering or harm as a necessary element, even the most outstanding element, of evil. Victims are not accidental to it.

More than one understanding of evil floats in prephilosophical everyday thinking. My theory does not attempt to capture them all. It is secular, for example, although many conceptions of evil are religious. As Nietzsche saw, judgments of evil have evolved historically and embody certain perspectives. Evil may be what Ludwig Wittgenstein called a "family resemblance" concept.[1] If so, not all the family members are equally, or even ethically, interesting. To borrow John Rawls's distinction between the (general) concept of something and a (particular) conception of it, the theory of this book might be regarded as a conception of evil, not the only conception, much as Rawls has claimed to offer a particular conception of justice, not the only one.[2] My aim, however, is to articulate a conception of evil that captures the ethically most significant, most serious publicly known evils of my lifetime.

Natural events—earthquakes, fires, floods—not brought about by or preventable by moral agency are not evils. Catastrophes are not the same as atrocities. Nor is death itself an evil, although the manner of death can be, and it can be an evil to be robbed of the opportunity to live out a meaningful life. Those who attribute natural disasters to the activity of a supreme being might meaningfully wonder whether they were evils, which they would be if they were lacking in moral justification. My theory presupposes no such agency, but can be adapted for those who do. When not guided by moral agents, forces of nature are neither goods nor evils. They just are. Their "agency" routinely produces consequences vital to some forms of life and lethal to others.

A significant part of the shock produced by an atrocity is due to the perception that human agents either engineered it or failed to intervene to prevent it when they could and should have. The epidemic of a fatal disease becomes an evil when human beings wrongly fail to prevent or alleviate it (as in the case of the Tuskegee syphilis experiments) or were wrongly behind the spread of the disease in the first place.[3] The distribution by the British to Native Americans of blankets infected with the smallpox virus was an atrocity. The Black Death in fourteenth-century Europe was not (although anti-Semitic propaganda portrayed it as such).[4] The point is not that it is more important to alleviate suffering initiated by human beings than to alleviate that caused by natural catastrophes. Rather, human failure to respond can turn a natural catastrophe into an atrocity. Much of the involvement of human agency in atrocities is a matter of aggravating the suffering brought about by nonhuman causes or tolerating it unnecessarily

We need to be able to make judgments of right and wrong in order to apply the atrocity theory of evil, as harm is not evil unless aggravated, supported, or produced by culpable wrongdoing. The atrocity theory is meant to be compatible with many understandings of the distinction between right and wrong, as long as they neither define "wrong" as "harmful" nor equate "wrong" with "evil." It is compatible, for example, with W. D. Ross's or H. A. Prichard's intuitionism, with John Rawls's principles of justice and natural duties, with Kant's Categorical Imperative.[5] It is not my intention to offer a new theory of right and wrong.

To illustrate the theory I take up three case studies, with a chapter on each. First are the relatively public atrocities of mass rape as a weapon of war and related forms of sexual slavery (chap. 6). Second are the private atrocities of domestic violence: severe, prolonged, and often fatal spousal battering and the comparably severe abuse, including sexual abuse, of children (chap. 7). The last are the complex and troubling forms of complicity that exist in what Holocaust survivor Primo Levi called "gray zones," in which victims of oppression are used to maintain and administer the very machinery of oppression (chap. 10).

A philosophical theory of evil leaves unanswered empirical questions of history, psychology, and sociology that are apt to have aroused one's interest in the subject in the first place: statistical questions regarding the prevalence and distribution of evil, questions regarding its psychological roots and proximate or situational causes, and questions regarding the efficaciousness of various means of resistance and attempts at prevention. Is evil on the rise? Is the contemporary Western developed world less evil than, say, Rome was under the caesars? How often are evildoers themselves survivors of prior evils? Are the causes of evil primarily situational, as suggested by social psychologist Stanley Milgram's obedience experiments and the Stanford prison experiments of his colleague (and former high school classmate) Philip Zimbardo?[6] Is gradual desensitization to others' sufferings a significant cause, as Ervin Staub's examination of group violence suggests?[7] Is punishment an effective deterrent? Do rewards work better, as B. F. Skinner argued?[8] Philosophy alone cannot answer these questions. But the empirical inquiries necessary to answer them can benefit from philosophy in gaining greater clarity about what counts as evil, what the phenomena are that we should want to explain.

Still, it is not always easy or even possible to keep philosophical and empirical inquiries distinct. Questions regarding human nature are bound to be both psychological and philosophical. Chapter 4 on Kant's theory of radical evil, for example, draws on work in interpersonal psychology and attachment theory, a branch of psychoanalysis, to supplement and deepen Kant's account of how ordinary people can become capable of great evils. Although not quite a causal theory (if one retains, with Kant, belief in the agent's freedom of choice), it suggests ways, other than by prioritizing prudence, that choices to do what is evil can become attractive, while preserving something from Kant's sense that we do not choose evil simply for its own sake.

Until the past two decades, surprisingly few secular moral philosophers have attended specifically to the concept of evil. The traditional problem of evil (to be discussed shortly) addressed by theologians and philosophers of religion has been of interest primarily to those who accept the metaphysical presuppositions of theology.[9] Most twentieth-century moral philosophers do not mention evil very often. Hastings Rashdall's two-volume classic *Theory of Good and Evil* mentions evil only in the second volume and gives it nothing like the extended attention he has given to such concepts as "right" and "good."[10] The index to W.D. Ross's *The Right and the Good* does not mention evil.[11] Nor is evil mentioned in the index to Henry Sidgwick's *The Methods of Ethics*.[12] Rawls's *A Theory of Justice* has one mention of "the evil man," who, he says, is moved by "love of injustice."[13]

When moral philosophers do mention evil, they often treat it as loosely equivalent to "immoral" when applied to conduct and even more loosely as equivalent to "undesirable" when applied to experience. In *Wickedness* British philosopher Mary Midgley treats evil as roughly equivalent to wrongdoing, in that the questions she asks about it might be asked about most wrongdoings.[14] Laurence Thomas, however, writing on American slavery and the Holocaust, offers a commonsense counterexample to the equation of evil with wrongdoing: subway riders who do not pay their fare do wrong, but not evil.[15] Midgley's examples also reveal her awareness that not all wrongdoing but only very serious wrongdoing is evil. We need a theoretical account of what makes wrongdoing serious enough to count as evil or in what ways it is serious. "Evil" is a heavy judgment. Much that is bad is disappointing, undesirable, inferior, even unjust or unfair, but not evil. Many wrongdoings are trivial. Evils never are, even if their perpetrators are ordinary people and their motives not unusual. The nontriviality of evil may account for some widespread resistance to Hannah Arendt's idea of the banality of evil.[16] As Nietzsche saw, what one judges to be evil engages one's attention profoundly.[17] One takes it seriously. One may doubt the humanity of those who do not. There is a risk of becoming obsessed with it. What is merely poor or inferior is less engrossing. According to Nietzsche, one aims to rise above it, not take it too seriously.

On a practical level, there has been international interest in preventing atrocities. Philosophers have been consulted in formulating such major documents as the Universal Declaration of Human Rights, proclaimed by the U.N. General Assembly in 1948.[18] The concept of human rights began from concerns that motivate interest in evil but became more comprehensive. The Universal Declaration includes rights basic to a tolerable and decent life, such as freedom from torture and slavery and rights to a standard of living adequate for health, as well as others critical to escaping evils, such as rights to change one's nationality or religion. Unlike torture and slavery, the lack of an adequate standard of living is not always due to wrongdoing and therefore is not ethically always an evil. Further, the declaration includes rights that easily exceed what is needed for a tolerable or decent life, such as the right "to enjoy the arts and share in scientific advancement and its benefits."[19] Interestingly, Harvard law professor Mary Ann Glendon discovered that widespread consensus among nations on lists of specific human rights was not matched by agreement on underlying philosophical reasons, not even approximately.[20]

Works published or translated in the latter decades of the twentieth century that really do treat evil as a topic worthy of philosophical investigation in its own right include, in addition to cited works by Thomas and Arendt, Primo

Levi's *The Drowned and the Saved*, portions of Ronald Milo's *Immorality* and of Stanley Benn's "Wickedness," Nel Noddings's *Women and Evil*, John Kekes's *Facing Evil* and *Against Liberalism*, Susan Neiman's essay on Rousseau's hypotheses regarding the origins of evil, and Robin Schott's reflections on war rape.[21] Jonathan Glover's *Humanity: A Moral History of the Twentieth Century*, issued in the United States in the year 2000, is in some ways the most ambitious recent contribution to the topic by a philosopher, discussing in detail both world wars, as well as Nazism, Stalinism, Vietnam, the Cuban missile crisis, and Rwanda.[22] It helpfully elucidates concepts involved in the thinking that can dispose perpetrators toward mass killings. His paradigms of evil, like mine, are atrocities.

The Atrocity Paradigm

Concern about large-scale and in some cases unprecedented atrocities during my lifetime motivates my own interest in evil: the Holocaust; the bombings of Hiroshima, Nagasaki, Tokyo, Hamburg, and Dresden; the internment of Japanese Americans and Japanese Canadians during World War II; the My Lai massacre; the Tuskegee syphilis experiments; genocides in Rwanda, Burundi, and East Timor; the killing fields of Cambodia; the rape/death camps of the former Yugoslavia; and the threat to life on our planet posed by environmental poisoning, global warming, and the destruction of rain forests and other natural habitats. Such a litany seems to confirm the view of Arthur Schopenhauer, (in)famous as the philosopher of pessimism, that human conduct produces far more suffering and harm than joy and happiness.[23] Historians and psychologists justifiably probe the causes of evildoing, with the aim of helping future generations avert some of the worst consequences of past errors and ignorance. But if Schopenhauer really is right, if it is unrealistic to expect that within our future as a species there will be no more atrocities, it is all the more important that philosophers also consider how we may better live with that knowledge and with the aftermath of evils we fail to prevent or escape.

Well-known kinds of atrocities include genocide, slavery, torture, rape as a weapon of war, the saturation bombing of cities, biological and chemical warfare unleashing lethal viruses and gases, and the domestic terrorism of prolonged battery, stalking, and child abuse. Some are highly visible (bombings), others can be difficult to detect (environmental poisoning). Atrocities do not always have special names (Stalin's murders at Katyn in Poland, the slow deaths by labor and starvation in the Gulags, mass starvation induced by Mao's policies in the cultural revolution). Most of these examples are uncontroversial as paradigms of evil.[24] Some would add capital punishment, especially when indigence of the accused makes wrongful convictions likely. My own list includes evils done to animals who are raised on factory farms and butchered in mass-production slaughterhouses.[25] I do not regard only human beings as victims of evil, although in this book I consider primarily human victims (and only human perpetrators).[26]

Why take atrocities as paradigms? Many evils lack the scale of an atrocity. Not every murder is an atrocity, although murder is also a paradigm of evil. Atrocities shock, at least when we first learn of them. They seem monstrous. We recoil from visual images and details. Many think no one should have to suffer them, not even evildoers. It is not for their sensationalism, however, that I choose atrocities as my paradigms. I choose them for three reasons: (1) because they are uncontroversially evil, (2) because they deserve priority of attention (more than philosophers have given them so far), and (3) because the core features of evils tend to be writ large in the case of atrocities, making them easier to identify and appreciate.

Atrocities are both perpetrated and suffered. There is no such thing as an atrocity that just happens or an atrocity that hurts no one. These facts yield the two basic elements of my theory: wrongdoing and harm. A focus on atrocities also gets us to attend to evils, plural. Evil, in the singular, suggests to some ears a metaphysical force. I wish to avoid that suggestion. It suggests to others a demonic psychology. Yet atrocities are recognizable without our knowing the perpetrators' states of mind. Often we wonder what the motives could have been. The atrocity paradigm reveals a concept of evil that is not defined by motive, although it implies culpability.

Because it does not define evil by motive, the atrocity paradigm encourages a focus first on suffering. Harm is what is most salient about atrocities. Questions that arouse interest in atrocities are those likely to be asked by victims, potential victims, survivors. The very naming of an atrocity as such suggests identification with victims. The terms "victims" and "perpetrators" mislead, however, if they suggest that individuals are simply one or the other, if either. For it is not unusual for victims of some evils (perhaps as a result) to perpetrate others.

Perpetrators commonly do not understand their deeds as atrocities. Psychologist Roy F. Baumeister calls the discrepancy between perpetrators' and victims' perceptions "the magnitude gap," noting that the importance of what takes place is almost always greater for the victim.[27] Summarizing the results of an experiment that concluded that "victims and perpetrators distorted the facts to an equal degree" although "the distortions were systematically different," he says that victims "reshuffled and twisted the facts to make the offense seem worse than it was" whereas "perpetrators reshuffled and twisted things to make it seem less bad."[28] Thus, it appears that victims overestimate and perpetrators underestimate the offense. With the atrocity theory, we can conjecture, more specifically, that perpetrators are likely to underestimate the harm, whereas victims are likely to exaggerate the reprehensibility of the perpetrators' motives. Thus, they would not be overestimating and underestimating exactly the same thing. Belonging to different ethnic, religious, or racial groups (or species) exacerbates the magnitude gap. Consequently, many evils are not perceived as such by the general public, while other things are wrongly feared as evils. Hunting animals for sport is an evil widely not recognized as such. Until recently, the mass rape of women in war was not publicly denounced, either. Infamous mis-attributions of evil include the libelous anti-Semitic *Protocols of the Elders of Zion* and the "blood libel."[29]

To begin with a focus on suffering is not to assume that those who self-identify as victims are necessarily right or that real victims are accurate in what they attribute to perpetrators. Levi found depriving prisoners of food, water, and sanitation on the transport trains an instance of "useless violence," sheer sadism.[30] Yet it is possible that those policies were motivated partly by cold economics, like the National Socialist "euthanasia" program, under which the aged, mental patients, the terminally ill, and the disabled were killed as "useless eaters." Why "waste" food and sanitation on people who will die soon (perhaps sooner without)? Livestock animals have been managed on similar principles, and those in charge need not have been sadists. Drafters and implementers of transport policies may have given little if any thought to what it would actually feel like to be inside the transport cars. Even if Levi's diagnosis of sadism exaggerated the reprehensibility of the perpetrators' motives, the evil was in no way excusable. Nor does the possibility of that distortion count against the view that evil's importance is best revealed by the suffering of victims. Since my object in calling attention to the relatively neglected experience of victims is not to support their specific accusations but to enlarge the body of data that a theory of evil should organize, I do not say much about how to correct likely errors, although my view is that such corrections are, in principle, possible, and I make a few suggestions in later chapters.

Since World War II, social psychologists, psychoanalysts, and psychiatrists have approached evil usually with a focus on the perpetrator, inquiring into how human beings can reach the point of knowingly inflicting terrible harm on others. In the 1990s others have begun to address survivors' responses to trauma.[31] The atrocity paradigm attempts to broaden our theoretical interests still further by giving victims' perspectives more of their due and considering how perpetrators might respond to what they have done and to the continuing needs of victims.

A major source of knowledge regarding the harm of atrocities is victim testimonies. This source is often lost with the victims' deaths. Many articulate narratives have been published, however, by survivors of twentieth-century atrocities. These survivors are not on the whole preoccupied with the motives of perpetrators. (Where they do speculate about that, they often get it wrong.)

Rather, they raise such questions as how to live with the effects of trauma, how to resist oppression, how to keep one's sanity under oppression, how to avoid being victimized, and what attitudes to take toward perpetrators (whether to reconcile, forgive, ignore) and toward humanity in general. Martha Minow has recently explored many kinds of initiatives (truth commissions, seeking reparations, education, memorials), lying between vengeance and forgiveness, that nations, and groups within nations, can take in response to atrocities they have suffered from others with whom they must now somehow continue to live and interact.[32] Chapters 8 and 9 take up ethical issues of attitudinal response that arise for victims as individuals who must occupy the same territory as former evildoers and issues that arise for victims, perpetrators, and their descendants who must live with the legacies of evils. These issues—forgiveness, mercy, gratitude, guilt—take on special interest in the case of atrocities, given the limits of punishment.

In beginning with the victim's perspective, the atrocity approach also differs from the approaches of most recent philosophical work on evil. Kekes, for example, in his absorbing and thoughtful treatise *Facing Evil,* understands evil as the infliction of undeserved suffering. But instead of focusing on the suffering or the victim, he focuses on the tragedy of becoming an evildoer. Evil is a problem, he writes, "because it jeopardizes our aspirations to live good lives."[33] His interest is especially in the jeopardy to the perpetrator. In a subsequent book *Against Liberalism,* however, he works with an understanding of "moral evil" that appears very much in the spirit of mine.[34] Midgley's *Wickedness* also focuses on perpetrators, taking up responsibility, aggression, free will, and a variety of motives. S. I. Benn's "Wickedness" offers a very helpful taxonomy of perpetration, as does Ronald Milo's *Immorality.*

Noddings's *Women and Evil* departs substantially from this tradition. She begins with an enumeration of evils from a sufferer's point of view, although her sufferer need not be a victim of wrongdoing, and takes women's experiences as paradigms. She reduces evils to three basic kinds: pain, separation, and helplessness. Yet in the end, she, too, focuses her practical proposals on potential perpetrators and how they might avoid actualizing their potentiality for doing evil.

Evil can be resisted and sometimes averted not only by potential evildoers but also by potential victims. Many survivors avoid the term "victim" because of its suggestion of passivity and embrace the term "survivor" instead. From respect for victims who do not survive, however, I prefer to emphasize that victims are also, often, capable of agency. The perpetrator questions that trouble me most are those that arise for victims who find themselves drawn into complicity with the very evils they have suffered. As Kekes appreciates, a major evil is the corruption of the character of victims. Chapter 10 of the present work treats the knowing or deliberate corruption of the character of victims as a case of diabolical evil, thereby giving philosophical and traditional sense to a notion that Kant, who understood it differently, found inapplicable to human beings. Levi was acutely sensitive to complicity issues in his reflections on death-camp prisoners who performed services for captors in exchange for "privileges" that often consisted in little or nothing more than a delay of their murder. He found the creation of the *Sonderkommando,* special squads of prisoners charged with running the crematoria, "National Socialism's most demonic crime."[35]

Perhaps the best argument against modern warfare is that it cannot be conducted without atrocities. Although premodern warfare was also regularly accompanied by atrocities, they were less inevitable and tended to be on a lesser scale. In June 1999 the *New York Times* published an extensive article in its science section on the military stockpiling of the smallpox virus and on the impossibility of controlling the spread of infection once the virus is unleashed in a dense and vulnerable population.[36] The evil use of such a virus today can be extended even further and more rapidly, with modern technology, than in previous centuries.

Atrocities reveal evil to be a higher order moral concept. Evil presupposes culpable wrongdoing in a moral agent as the source of the harm that it does or risks. Higher order moral concepts presuppose others, more basic. Although evil is of fundamental importance, it is not, logically, a basic concept. There may be no absolutely basic moral concepts in the sense of concepts making no reference any other moral concept. Yet some have a greater complexity than others in what they presuppose. The Kantian concept of the moral worth of an action is higher order in that its definition makes reference to the more basic concept of duty, obligation, or right, defined independently of moral worth. Actions have moral worth when done for the reason that they are right, from the motive of duty, the sense of obligation. Likewise, in defining evil, it is necessary to refer to the more basic concept of wrongdoing, to distinguish evils from other horrors. Intolerable harm is an evil when it results foreseeably from culpable wrongdoing.

This complexity in the concept of evil is what gives the classical theological problem of evil its ethical interest. In this problem, the question is raised how a supreme being could permit human injustice and allow such natural catastrophes as fires and floods to fall on the guilty and innocent alike. How could an omnipotent, omniscient, and provident creator of the world, who supremely exemplifies goodness, permit the innocent to suffer? As David Hume and John Stuart Mill observed, an omnipotent being who wanted to prevent that surely would be *able* to, and a supremely good being who was able would surely *want* to.[37] Why, then, do the innocent suffer?

Construed simply as a metaphysical conundrum, this problem does not, strictly speaking, require the concept of *evil*. An *imperfect* world suffices to generate the question. Why would a perfect being create a flawed world? Citing the existence of evil in the creator's world goes further than necessary for the merely logical puzzle, threatening to cast major aspersions on the character of the supreme being. The problem's enduring interest stems not from mere flaws but from what appear to be truly gross defects that produce intolerable harms.

The specifically moral challenge for theists has been to argue that a supreme being is not culpable in bringing about (or failing to prevent) intolerable harms—that is, to show that the supreme being is not an evildoer. Some conclude with Mill that the existence of evils proves there is no supreme creator who is both omnipotent and perfectly good. William James opted for belief in a finite supreme being, rather than an omnipotent, omniscient one. The most popular response has been the free-will defense, which argues that a world where creatures freely shun evildoing is better than one where they have no choice, and that evil is then the responsibility of those who freely choose it, not of their creator. This response addresses only evils perpetrated by human beings, not the fires and floods, for which no divine justification or excuse is apparent. Believers are ultimately left with the faith that there must be some justification, unfathomable to mere humans. The atrocity paradigm thus makes sense of what is morally at stake in the theological problem of evil, but without solving it and without presupposing either theism or atheism.

In contrast to the classical treatments of the theological problem of evil, however, the atrocity paradigm does not focus on victims' deserts or innocence. Innocence is neither necessary nor sufficient for suffering to count as evil. It is not sufficient because the suffering may not be intolerable. It is not necessary because the perpetrator's culpable wrongdoing does not presuppose innocence in the victim. There are special evils in harming the innocent, who are commonly defenseless and naive. Yet there is no general presumption of innocence among atrocity victims, who may include habitual criminals, as they commonly do in the case of genocide. The presumption is, rather, that no one should have to suffer atrocities, regardless of individual character or deserts, a matter that gives many pause regarding the character of a supreme being who consigns sinners to eternal hellfire. Innocence is relevant to the justice of particular punishments. But those who find the death penalty an atrocity do so irrespective of the victim's guilt. Abolitionists readily concede the guilt of many, perhaps even most, victims.[38]

Not only are evils worse than other wrongs (such as minor injustices), but some evils are worse than others. Yet comparing atrocities is a morally sensitive issue. A theory of evil should be able to make sense both of degrees of evil and of the resistance we may feel to making the comparisons that degrees suggest. The atrocity paradigm does this. First, we can distinguish dimensions along which one atrocity may be worse than another, even though it may not be easy, or even possible, to reach an *overall* judgment about which was worse. Second, by way of its identification with victims' positions, the atrocity paradigm encourages us to consider the impact on victims of making comparisons. This consideration argues against gratuitously ranking atrocities, out of respect for all victims.

One approach to distinguishing degrees of evil is by grading the severity of the harm. "Severity" is more complex than one might initially expect. For harm has many aspects, and "degrees" is a metaphor. What is at stake is not entirely quantitative. As with Aristotle's "doctrine of the mean," which is not the merely quantitative idea that the mathematical mean suggests, we have a multifaceted notion with no common denominator, which makes levels of severity not reducible to quantities of anything.[39] Severity of harm is a function of such factors as (1) intensity of suffering, (2) effects on one's ability to function (to work, for example) and (3) on the quality of one's relationships with others, (4) how containable the harm is (what Bentham quaintly called its "fecundity"), (5) how reversible, (6) possibilities of compensation, and also (7) duration and (8) the number of victims. Not all of these factors are quantifiable (most clearly, the first three), nor is it clear how to weight them. Factors 4 and 5 lead many to find widespread use of organic pesticides and production of nuclear power especially profound evils. Food chains and groundwater spread pesticide contamination beyond anything controllable by current technology.[40] A major problem with nuclear power is the absence of any currently known safe way to store radioactive wastes, such as plutonium with a half-life of 24,000 years (dangerous for 250,000 years), or iodine-129, which has a half-life of 16 million years (dangerous for 160 million!).[41]

Another way to distinguish "degrees" of evil is by dimensions of culpability, as is commonly done in criminal courts, at least at sentencing. Some motives are worse than others: sadism is more reprehensible than greed (although its consequences are not necessarily worse). Culpable wrongdoing in the atrocity paradigm need not be sadistic. As noted, it can take the form of unscrupulousness in the pursuit of interests not themselves bad. There are also "degrees" of voluntariness, which yield "degrees" of ignorance and "degrees" of duress. And there are "degrees" of inattentiveness: recklessness is grosser than neglect or carelessness. To say that one evil is worse than another is thus multiply ambiguous and therefore apt to mislead. There are no simple correlations among the dimensions along which different evils might be compared.

In sum, the atrocity paradigm discourages broad comparisons in at least three ways, at the same time that it allows, theoretically, for comparisons that are relatively specific and limited. First, because of the ambiguities of "worse" just enumerated, there is the likelihood that comparative evaluations, if not highly qualified, will be misleading. Second, incommensurability of dimensions makes broad comparisons extraordinarily difficult if not impossible.

Charles Larmore argues convincingly that incommensurability need not imply incomparability.[42] We can judge one headache worse than another without being able to measure, quantitatively, how much worse. But the complexity of atrocities, in contrast to the relative simplicity of headaches, may often in fact be an obstacle to meaningful broad comparisons. Third, because the atrocity paradigm highlights suffering and harm, it encourages us to think of the impact on victims and their families of making such comparisons. No doubt some atrocities really are worse than others, even in an overall sense. Historian Michael Burleigh notes, for example, that the atrocities of the Nazi "euthanasia" program were not as great as those of Hitler's Final Solution.[43] Yet an atrocity is already so evil that in some contexts it seems disrespectful of victims to point out that another was even worse. For the individual, intolerable is intolerable.

Another fact about such large-scale atrocities as American slavery or the European witch burnings that makes them difficult to assess overall is that they consist of multiple activities extending over major stretches of time, often with interruptions. They are perpetrated by many players in various roles who have different degrees of knowledge of the enterprise. How is one to reach summary judgments that might be compared? There may be no good reason to try.

When there are questions of punishment for someone's part in an atrocity, it is important to distinguish degrees of responsibility. Some persons may be relatively unwitting instruments manipulated by others. Such judgments, however, neither yield nor require a comparative judgement about the value of the atrocity as a whole.

The atrocity paradigm is compatible with the idea that some evils are worse than others without committing us to the idea that, even in principle, large-scale atrocities can always be ranked. It enables us to explain both a moral reluctance to rank them, if we could, and our sense of the impossibility in many cases of doing so, even if we would. Steven Katz examines the Holocaust in historical context, comparing and contrasting that atrocity with others involving mass death, such as the witch burnings in Renaissance Europe, slavery in ancient Rome, and the decimation of native populations in the Americas and Australia. In so doing he distinguishes between appreciating what is, in a nontrivial sense, unique to a particular atrocity and ranking that atrocity on a scale of values.[44] His defense of the uniqueness of the Holocaust aims to do only the former, to set out what he finds unique without making an overall judgment of whether that atrocity was worse than others with which he compares it. Still, in making specific comparisons and contrasts, he does not avoid making, or implying, more limited value judgments. Some atrocities had more victims, for example, and *in that respect* were worse. Such limited judgments do not have the same impact on victims and their families as broad rankings.

Laurence Thomas likewise is at pains to explain, in his examination of American slavery and the Holocaust, that in finding some things true of one atrocity but not the other, he is not implying that it was worse.[45] He notes, for example, that Hitler's Final Solution, unlike American slavery, was shrouded in secrecy, whereas American slavery produced a more extreme alienation from kin and culture ("natal alienation") among victims and their descendants than was produced by the Final Solution.[46] Neither observation implies that either atrocity was worse on the whole.

The Theory: Basic Concepts and Distinctions

The two basic concepts of intolerable harm and culpable wrongdoing need interpretation and the relationship between them needs to be clarified. To elaborate the initial definition a bit, with that end in view, an evil is harm that is (1) reasonably foreseeable (or appreciable) and (2) culpably inflicted (or tolerated, aggravated, or maintained), and that (3) deprives, or seriously risks depriving, others of the basics that are necessary to make a life possible and tolerable or decent (or to make a death decent). Such basics include uncontaminated food, water, and air; sleep; freedom from severe and prolonged pain and from debilitating fear; affective ties with other human beings; the ability to make choices and act on them; and a sense of one's own worth as a person. Severe and unremitting pain or humiliation, debilitating and disfiguring diseases, starvation, extreme impotence, and severe enforced isolation are evils when they are brought about or supported by culpable wrongdoing. This is not to say that those whose lives are already wretched cannot become victims of evil. For even they ordinarily have some (although not enough) of the basics that make a life tolerable or decent, and their lives may yet sustain hope. Evildoers can rob them of the little that they have and remove what hope remained.

I understand "tolerable" as a normative concept, not entirely subjective, although some subjective elements may be inevitable. A "tolerable" life is at least minimally worth living for its own sake and from the standpoint of the being whose life it is, not just as a means to the ends of others. If we can meaningfully consider what is tolerable and decent for other forms of life and living systems in general, the atrocity paradigm can make sense of ecological evils the victims of which include trees and even ecosystems, although I do not attempt that application here.

We are not infallible judges of what is necessary to make even our own lives tolerable or decent. Pain, however, can make life intolerable when it is so intense and unremitting that it absorbs one's attention to the exclusion of nearly everything else. Consensual euthanasia of the ill or injured whose terrible sufferings cannot be tolerably alleviated is not an evil, even if it is (as some believe) wrong. It is certainly not an atrocity. It is not an evil because, when consensual, it enables sufferers to have a decent death where a decent life seems impossible. The term "murder" should not be applied to it. But involuntary "euthanasia" (a euphemism for murder)—terminating without their consent the lives of sufferers who still have and can express a will—is a great evil in that it robs sufferers of the autonomy that could make their lives minimally worth living.[47] What can make an extremely painful existence tolerable is precisely the sufferer's will to embrace it.

In an earlier work, I treated basic harms as themselves evils.[48] I did not then include wrongdoing as a source of the harm in the concept of an evil. That approach has proved theoretically less fruitful than the present one. If "evil" means only "basic harm," there is no reason for an atheist not to consider the devastation of cities by an earthquake an evil. I also proposed, at that time, a theory of "basic evils," inspired by Rawls's theory of "primary goods," which he initially defined as what everyone can be presumed to want, whatever else they might want.[49] Analogously, my proposal was that we understand "basic evils" as what everyone can be presumed to shun, whatever else they might want—that is, the sort of thing it would not be reasonable to endure voluntarily for the sake of something else. Rawls's "primary goods" make no essential reference to right or wrong conduct, and neither did my "basic evils."

Yet another formula for "basic evils" that I used at the same time, without appreciating its difference from the formula modeled after Rawls's idea (what everyone can be presumed to shun), was "what no one should be made to suffer, no matter what it does for anyone else." This second formula differs significantly from the first and is closer to my current view, for in the phrase "be *made to* suffer" it implies a reference to what should not be done.[50] This formula suggests that evils do presuppose wrongdoing, and that is the idea I wish to preserve here.

There is, to be sure, a popular sense of "evil" used to refer to even minor wrongs and merely undesirable or unpleasant experiences. This loose conception is invoked in everyday contexts when people justify an option as "the lesser of two evils." Common sense here is not philosophically deep. Unlike most contemporary ethical theories, it does not distinguish among such concepts as "unjustified," "wrong," "culpable," and "harmful." Consequently, it flounders logically in the idea that it is not necessarily evil to do evil. More distinctions are needed. The atrocity paradigm, distinguishing among the concepts of wrong, culpability, and harm, enables us to say, coherently, that it need not be evil (because not wrong or not culpable) to do what has undeserved harmful consequences.

In something like the popular, loose sense of "evil," the concept of punishment has been defined by utilitarian thinkers as the infliction of an evil upon an offender. Following Jeremy Bentham, who wrote in the early nine-teenth century that "all punishment in itself is evil,"Anthony Flew writes, "I *propose* . . . that we take as parts of the meaning of 'punishment,' in the pri-mary sense, at least five elements. *First*, it must be an evil, an unpleasantness, to the victim," and he goes on to explain that he says "evil" rather than "pain" to avoid the suggestion of "floggings and other forms of physical torture."[51] Yet it is important in designing and maintaining criminal justice institutions that we *not* allow them to become evil. The loose understanding of "evil" as merely "undesirable" is not helpful for making this point but makes it seem self-contradictory. Punishment is truly an evil when the indigent innocent ac-cused are imprisoned or executed as a result of wrongfully tolerated police and prosecutor incompetence and corruption.[52] Nor does the loose sense of "evil" do justice to atrocities. On my theory, there is no such thing as being justified in committing the lesser of two atrocities. If the deed is morally justified, it is not culpable and therefore does not produce an evil, even if others suffer undeservedly.

Yet there is the well-known problem of "dirty hands." This is not an everyday, commonsense issue but arises usually in difficult political contexts. Dirty hands seem inevitable when it appears that one cannot avoid doing evil, at any rate, bringing about major undeserved suffering (not just something unpleasant or undesirable), because in order to prevent some evils, it appears that one must perpetrate or condone others. Again, more distinctions are needed. There are situations where, no matter what we do, we wrong some people in the sense that they do not deserve the harms we cause them. It does not follow that we are culpable. To be culpable, we ought to have acted differ-ently. That a deed inflicts a wrong, even an injustice, however, does not imply that the doer had a better alternative. Sometimes the best we can do is try to identify the least unjust option. Being confronted only with unjust options is commonly a result of someone's prior wrongdoing (perhaps evil). But noncul-pable agents are not evildoers, even when they are used as instruments by oth-ers who are culpable.

Because it is important to be able to make such distinctions, it is theoreti-cally more fruitful to understand evils as including a reference to culpable wrongdoing as their source and not to understand basic harms as in them-selves evils. This more complex concept of evil is also found in everyday moral consciousness, alongside the loose sense of "evil" as "unpleasant," and is apt to be invoked when what has been done is horrifying, as in the case of atrocities.

The basic elements of intolerable harm and culpable wrongdoing give us two roles associated with an evil: perpetrators and victims, doers and suffer-ers. Clearly, there can be multiple perpetrators and multiple victims in what is commonly identified as a single evil, such as a mass murder. But can one person be both perpetrator and victim? I tend to characterize evils as inflicted on *others*. Is that overly narrow? Can one do evil to oneself?

One can certainly deprive oneself of basics that make life worth living, however perverse that may seem (or be). But is doing so culpable? The same thing done to others, without consent, would clearly be evil. Many modern moral philosophers have been reluctant to acknowledge the possibility of treating oneself immorally. If one cannot wrong oneself, the harms one could suffer by one's own hand would not count as evils. Marcus Singer, for example, argues that there can be no moral duties to oneself because if there were, one could release oneself from them at will, but any duty from which one can release oneself at will is not a genuinely moral duty.[53] Thomas Hobbes, in *De Cive*, offers basically the same argument against the idea of being obligated to oneself: "Nor can he be obliged to himself; for the same party being both the obliged and the obliger, and the obliger having power to release the obliged, it were merely in vain for a man to be obliged to himself, because he can release himself at his own pleasure; and he that can do this, is already actually free."[54] Aristotle argued that one can neither treat oneself unjustly nor be willingly treated unjustly.[55] In *The Doctrine of Virtue* Kant was able to make sense of duties to oneself, but only by bifurcating the self into noumenal (real) and phenomenal (apparent) aspects, which has its own problems.[56] And in *On Liberty* John Stuart Mill held that the so-called self-regarding vices "are not properly immoralities and to whatever pitch they may be carried, do not constitute wickedness"; he allows that "they may be proofs of any amount of folly, or want of personal dignity and self-respect" but "they are only a subject of moral reprobation when they involve a breach of duty to others."[57] They may be imprudent, he thought, but not immoral.

Yet failures of self-respect are no more reducible to imprudence than are violations of obligations to others. Demands of self-respect, like those of duties to others, can conflict deeply with one's interest, as civil rights protesters and lesbian and gay activists have discovered.[58] Mill may be right that for failures of self-respect no one is *accountable* to others. Yet self-respect provides a moral basis for change, and its absence provides a basis for moral criticism. If disrespect for oneself can be culpable, there may be no logical barrier to suffering evils by one's own hand. Perhaps ruining one's future at a young age through drugs is (sometimes) a self-inflicted evil. Further, if the self is not unified, what is to prevent one part from inflicting an evil on other parts? Multiple personality survivors have testified to the fear of such "suicides." The evils that motivate my interest in this book, however, are not self-inflicted.

Still, the concepts of "perpetrator" and "victim," or "doer" and "sufferer," sound deceptively simple. There are many "degrees" (kinds) of involvement in perpetrating an atrocity and many ways in which suffering extends to others than those most directly victimized. Bystanders become doers, in the relevant sense, if they choose to do nothing when they could have done something that might have made a constructive difference. Survivors' children can suffer serious effects of atrocities perpetrated against their parents.

Taking "an evil," as the root concept, we can clarify a series of concepts pertaining to the perpetration of evil. We can distinguish evil intentions from evil motives and evildoers from evil persons. We can show how each is related to such things as evil deeds and institutions. To review, an evil is a reasonably foreseeable harm (which need not be highly probable) that falls within a certain range of magnitude and importance and is brought about, seriously risked, sustained, aggravated, or tolerated by culpable wrongdoing.

Without the foreseeability qualification, moral analogues of "felony murder" pose a problem. Culpable wrongdoing can accidentally cause intolerable harm. Suppose a thief steals a briefcase for the money it contains from a young woman whose heart is weak, triggering a fatal heart attack, or suppose the briefcase also contains medications not recognizable to the average person as vital. However culpable the deed, it is problematic to count it as evil or regard the thief as a murderer (which the law may do if the money is sufficient to make the theft a felony). Some might do so on the ground that the thief could be expected to foresee the possibility of intolerable consequences—a matter on which there might be reasonable disagreement. The point is that it is not reasonable to expect even culpable perpetrators to foresee freak accidents.

To build on this idea, an evil *intention* is a culpable intention to do someone intolerable harm, or to do something with that foreseeable result, even if the intention does not succeed. In an evil *deed*, the intention succeeds. An evil intender may not foresee harm, owing to culpable recklessness, negligence, or even a choice to ignore. But the harm must be foreseeable if one were to attend with reasonable care. Culpability in an evil intention can take many forms, such as (1) the aim to bring about intolerable harm, (2) the willingness to do so in the course of pursuing an otherwise acceptable aim or in adhering to some other value or principle, or (3) the failure to attend to risks or take them seriously. The intention to inflict torture is evil because of its aim, even if the motive was not sadism. The intention to sell automobiles that one knows are unsafe is evil for its unscrupulousness, even if the seller aims to become a philanthropist. Promiscuity plus ignoring issues of safer sex in an era of HIV is evil for its recklessness, regardless of aims or motives.

Analogously, an institution, law, or practice is evil not only when its purpose is inhumane (as with bullfighting) but also when it is reasonably foreseeable by those with power to change it that intolerably harmful injustices will result from its normal or correct operation (as many believe true of capital punishment). Were it reasonably foreseeable that the laws of marriage and divorce would facilitate major domestic abuse and spousal murder, that would be reason to consider those laws evil, even if their purpose were not to facilitate such things. The purposes of the laws of slavery were, presumably, to secure cheap labor and protect slave owners, not to make slaves suffer horribly and die young. Yet those harms to slaves were reasonably foreseeable.

An agent's *motive* is evil if it is no accident that, when the motive is efficacious, evil results—that is, the agent would bring about harm that makes or threatens to make someone's life intolerable. It is no accident that evil results from efficacious sadistic desires. This understanding of an evil motive is inspired by Kant's understanding of a virtuous motive, although it is not Kant's own understanding of an evil motive (for that, see chapter 4). In Kant's ethics, the good will is the motive of morally worthy conduct. It is no accident that one who acts with goodwill acts rightly.[59] A person of goodwill is committed to acting on the Categorical Imperative, and the Categorical Imperative defines what is right. Analogously, we may regard a motive as evil when it is no accident that, if efficacious, it results in evil. Loyalty is not an evil motive, even though much evil has been done from loyalty. Malicious envy is an evil motive, if understood as the desire for major harm to those who are better off, just because they are better off.[60] But, arguably, jealousy—the desire not to lose to others what one regards as one's own—is not. Perhaps hatred is not, either (a question taken up in chapter 2), even though much evildoing is fueled by hatred.

Someone may be rightly judged an evil person on the basis of persistent and effective evil motives or intentions (or both) or on the basis of persistent gross negligence or recklessness. Adolph Eichmann is rightly judged an evil man on the basis of his persistent and effective evil intentions, regardless of the banality of his motives. He persistently and effectively intended to send masses of defenseless people to their deaths, to be a major instrument in the Nazi genocide against the Jewish people. Given such intentions, his motives scarcely matter. Of course, people can change over time. Good people can be corrupted. After becoming evil, some repent and regenerate. Eichmann did not.

Because people who participate in an institution do not all have the same knowledge or ability to foresee or confront the same options, some participants may be evil and others not. (Arendt reports that on Eichmann's visits to Minsk, Treblinka, and Auschwitz, he saw "just enough to be fully informed of how the destruction machinery worked" and that it was in operation.)[61] Among participants who are evil, culpability takes different forms. Some do not know because they do not want to and so refuse to think or inquire. Others know but also refuse to think about it because they are not sadistic—or they are squeamish—and thinking about it could produce major internal conflict. (Eichmann was, apparently, squeamish). Or they look on the bright side, or tell themselves that if they didn't do it, others would and might do it worse.

Some participants may fail to identify a better alternative, despite a genuine will to do so.

One whose evil intentions are ineffective can also be an evil person, if the intention persists. In an illuminating article on punishment for intentions, Ronald Dworkin and David Blumenfeld contrast two would-be assassins. One fails because the alarm clock fails to sound that morning. In the other case, the alarm sounds, the person gets up, loads the gun, gets into position for the shot, aims, pulls the trigger and misses, owing to the intervention of unforeseeable outside forces.[62] If the agent successfully takes all but the last step, leaving no opportunity for a change of mind, and then is prevented by sheer luck from succeeding in that last step, the commitment to evil is clearly there. Having in addition some good intentions is insufficient to distinguish those who are not evil from those who are. If an evil person must be utterly devoid of good intentions, or be the authors of no good deeds whatever, then, of course, there are no evil people.

Although unsuccessful evil but persistent intentions can make the intender an evil person, one who successfully resists evil motives is not (yet) an evil person, however persistent the attractions may be. The successful resister is better regarded as potentially evil but so far winning the battle against temptation. One way to distinguish motives from intentions is to regard an intention as a choice to act and a motive (such as a compassionate or sadistic desire) not as a choice but as providing a basis for possible choices.[63] Motives incline us, but not necessarily all the way. They influence but do not ordinarily determine our choices. Under moderately favorable circumstances, we can resist an inclination, feel the attraction of a possible choice without forming the intention to act on it.

It follows from these distinctions that evil people need not be evildoers (intentions may fail) and that evildoers need not be evil people (evil intentions or gross oversights may be anomalous). If we are interested primarily in the evils that people suffer and do, our focus should not be too much on evil people. To call someone evil without qualification is to imply that the person's character is evil. We are not all potentially evil simply because we are human beings, although many of us might acquire that potentiality under circumstances we would not choose. To be potentially evil is to have more than the mere logically possibility of becoming evil and more than the mere capacity to experience the attraction of evil incentives or even to form evil intentions. It is to have something real (a persistent desire, habits of gross inattention) in one's character, in virtue of which one's evildoing would be no accident. To be human is not necessarily to have such desires or habits. But even though people are not all potentially evil, there may be families and communities whose practices really do have the potential to inculcate evil desires and habits among many of their members.

Preview

I have referred in the foregoing sections to matters discussed in various chapters. In the rest of this chapter I sketch a more systematic overview of the chapters to come.

For much of the twentieth century, evil has been an unpopular concept among intellectuals in Europe and North America. The reasons appear to be that thinking in terms of evil tends to demonize others instead of understanding them and that demonizing is counterproductive, that it stirs up destructive hatreds. When radical feminist philosopher Mary Daly spoke at a feminist conference in 1977 at the University of Wisconsin's Madison campus on the history of female genital mutilation (clitoridectomy and infibulation), practiced as a religious ritual in some countries of Africa, a common reaction among women who did not want to hear it was to accuse her of "hate mongering."[64] Treating hatred as the problem conveniently deflects attention from what evokes it. Hatred can be easier to stifle than the evils that evoke it are to address.

Unfortunately, Nietzsche's approach to evil in his *Genealogy of Morality* has been successful, in secular circles, in effecting a general shift away from questions about evildoing and evil practices to psychological questions about why people have wanted to use the concept of evil, what hidden agendas they may have, and how they can thereby manipulate others. The shift is from a distrust of evildoers to a distrust of critics who rail against evils. It is time to reassess this shift, stop blaming the messenger, and restore the ethical focus to its rightfully primary target: evils. The critic is often not the problem. "Evil" may seldom mark monsters. But it often enough marks monstrous deeds, wrongs that deserve priority of attention from political resistance movements, such as feminism and antiracism. With the aim of such reassessment, chapter 2 considers what is sound and what is not in Nietzsche's genealogy of evil. It defends the atrocity theory against his suggestions that dishonesty and envy are embedded in the concept of evil by way of the distorted perspectives of impotent victims.

In their accounts of evil, the most historically influential ethical theories in modern philosophy, Kantian and utilitarian, are each in different ways incomplete, on one hand, and too inclusive, on the other. Yet both philosophies had humane aims. Bentham's utilitarianism was motivated by the desire to reduce or eliminate evils in nineteenth-century English criminal law, such as hanging for petty theft.[65] Kant produced a major analysis of the corruption of moral character and argued that evil in human beings, even at its worst, is never diabolical. Why neither utilitarianism nor Kant's theory of radical evil yields an adequate conception of evil is the subject begun in chapter 3. If utilitarianism is too focused on the sufferer, to the relative neglect of culpability, stoicism neglects most of the harm to victims. The extreme stoicism of some ancients, discussed by Martha Nussbaum, ultimately makes morality, and by implication evil, impossible.[66]

The stoic influence is prominent, albeit less extreme, in Kant's theory, the subject of chapter 4. Kant locates evil exclusively in the perpetrator's character. He presents radical evil as the overarching choice to subordinate morality to self-interest. Evil, on his view, has no essential connection with harm; victims are incidental. Still, Kant is worth study for his structuring of degrees of culpability and for his reasons for thinking that we never do evil for its own sake. Chapter 4 extends his analysis of moral psychology, building on Christine Korsgaard's critique and making use of recent psychoanalytic work by Lorna Smith Benjamin in attachment theory. In doing so, it reexamines the question of whether human beings can do evil for its own sake.

Chapter 5 argues that genuine evils are not reducible to unjust inequalities and that, morally and politically, movements for social justice and liberation should prioritize addressing evils over correcting unjust inequalities. If evils are not reducible to unjust inequalities, it is not surprising that Kant's ethics, which analyzes wrongdoing as making an irrational exception for oneself, is unable to give a satisfactory account of evil. Taking feminism as an example of resistance to oppression, chapter 5 argues that the focus of mainstream American feminism on gender equality fails to target evils as such and that feminists would do better to target such misogynous practices as war rape and domestic battery, the subjects of chapters 6 and 7.

Chapter 6 takes up war rape as a major evil that has only recently been publicly recognized and officially acknowledged as a war crime. Drawing on recent work on the rape/death camps in Bosnia-Herzegovina and Rwanda and on the Korean "comfort women" enslaved by the Japanese military during World War II, this chapter considers why that recognition took so long, why the practices have been so difficult to eliminate, and what might be done about them. War rape is a crime in which the perpetrators are almost exclusively male and most immediate victims female. The combination of a focus on the perpetrator's point of view, with insufficient attention to victims, and the absence of women's voices from the arenas where crimes are defined have contributed to widespread ignoring and erasure of the evils of war rape. Another difficulty is common also to many practices of torture: those who execute the deed and are punished (if anyone is) are seldom those with power, those most responsible for the existence of the practice.

Rape, I have argued elsewhere, is not just an individual act and a form of torture but also a terrorist institution.[67] One reason that many evils go unrecognized is that the source of harm is an institution, not just the intentions or choices of individuals (many of whom may not share the goals of the institution, even when their conduct is governed by its norms). Another is that the harm is the product of many acts, some of which might have been individually harmless in other contexts. Victims are more likely than perpetrators to appreciate the harm. But when the source is an institution, even victims can be hard-pressed to know whom to hold accountable. .

Chapter 7 takes up domestic violence to expose evil in the social institutions of marriage and motherhood. It argues that these institutions support terrorism in the home. Trapping victims in enforced cohabitation with perpetrators who have the power to prevent access by potential witnesses and rescuers, these institutions facilitate the perpetration and cover-up of severe and prolonged child abuse, as well as severe and prolonged partner rape and battering. Both evils often enough lead to murder or to killing in self-defense. Instead of taking up responses to individual perpetrators or focusing on choices made by individuals within the frameworks set by the norms of marriage and motherhood as institutions, this chapter considers responses at the level of change in the institutional norms. It argues for the abolition of marriage and motherhood (as institutions), in favor of alternative forms of durable intimate partnership and child rearing.

Past evils leave legacies that pose ethical questions for individual survivors, perpetrators, and their descendants. Chapters 8, 9, and 10 are about living with evils and their aftermaths. Chapter 8 focuses on the powers of victims and their representatives, especially the aims and limitations of punishment and forgiveness. Concentration camp and rape survivors, like soldiers, suffer severe and lasting post-traumatic stress. They confront questions regarding how to live with a past that is never quite over—whom to tell and what to tell, what attitudes to take toward perpetrators and toward themselves. They may face choices about serving as witnesses in criminal trials. When is punishment appropriate, and what is its value? When is reparation worthwhile? When is reconciliation reasonable, and what sort of reconciliation? Are some evils unforgivable? Simon Wiesenthal's memoir *The Sunflower* offers a useful case study for approaching many questions regarding the ethical use of the power of forgiveness.[68]

Chapter 9 shifts the focus to the moral burdens and obligations of perpetrators, in particular, the obligations of gratitude (for forgiveness and mercy) and the burdens of guilt. It seems that the greater the atrocity, the greater the outcry against guilt, as there appears no way to finally be done with it. But when, if ever, ought culpable perpetrators to be done with guilt? In 1969, when Wiesenthal first published *The Sunflower* in Paris, there were popular demands in relation to the Holocaust for letting bygones be bygones, when little had yet been done in Europe in the way of public remembering. Chapter 9 defends guilt against critics who find it perverse. Guilt is not totally negative. It is tied to other practices besides punishment, such as apology and reparation. Guilt presupposes that we find ourselves capable of better and expect better of ourselves. It triggers conduct designed to repair damage to others and to relationships. We risk losing these important things by stifling guilt. Still, guilt carries a risk of excessive self-preoccupation, to the neglect of victims and their needs.

Finally, chapter 10 looks at the complex and difficult predicaments of some who are simultaneously victims and perpetrators. Drawing on Levi's chapter "The Gray Zone" in *The Drowned and the Saved*, it examines the positions of victims of evil under great stress, but not altogether without choice, who become implicated in perpetrating on others the evils that threaten themselves.[69] Levi reflects on the situations of prisoners who became kapos in the National Socialist death camps or served as ghetto police or on Jewish councils in the ghettos. Chapter 10 considers agents in gray areas other than those of the Holocaust. It uses the concept of the gray zone to present an alternative account of diabolical evil to that rejected by Kant and argues that the deliberate creation of a gray zone is a paradigm of diabolical evil. Outsiders are often in no position to hold those in a gray zone responsible for their choices. But evils may be prevented from perpetuating themselves in a potentially unending chain as long as victims who face grim alternatives continue to distinguish between bad and worse and refuse, insofar as possible, to abdicate responsibility to and for one another.

2

Nietzsche's Denial of Evil

Nietzsche's and Kant's are the two investigations of evil that I have found most interesting and insightful in the history of modern European philosophy. Yet it would be difficult to imagine two approaches more opposed to one another in spirit. Kant defines radical evil in the course of drawing distinctions regarding ways the human will can go bad. He reflects on the place of evil in human nature and how evil can be overcome. Nietzsche finds judgments of evil riddled with dishonesty and rooted in a hostile envy that he calls *ressentiment*. He rejects such judgments, along with their opposites, in favor of other, nonmoral judgments. This chapter defends the atrocity conception of evil against Nietzsche's critique. Chapter 3 criticizes utilitarian and stoic conceptions, as background to Kant's analysis, the subject of chapter 4.

Questioning the Concept of Evil

Nietzsche's characterization of modern European ethics as embodying a "slave mode of valuation" is ingenious. For the two outstanding qualities of good slaves are usefulness and obedience. And the two leading contenders in modern European philosophical ethics at the time of Nietzsche's writing are British utilitarianism and Kant's Categorical Imperative, which appear to exalt usefulness and obedience, respectively. Most philosophers perceive utilitarianism and Kant's ethics as rivals. Nietzsche appears to find their commonalities more interesting.

Nietzsche's thoughts on evil are most clearly stated in the first essay of his inquiry *On the Genealogy of Morality*.[1] The *Genealogy* consists of three essays, each broken into short sections with no transitions between essays, or even between sections, to help the reader. Interpreting Nietzsche is a challenge, and there is no consensus on many important issues. The *Genealogy* is a skeptical inquiry into morality generally, not just evil. Yet the concept of evil seems basic to what Nietzsche finds distinctive and troubling about morality. An important difference between my approach to evil and his is that his paradigms of evil are aggressive and predatory agents, whereas mine are atrocities, understood as culpably produced, foreseeable, and intolerable harms. Atrocity perpetrators need be neither aggressive nor predatory. Still, it seems fair to consider Nietzsche's rejection of evil as a challenge to the value of my project of developing a theory of evil. For I agree with him that judgments of evil are rooted in the perspectives of victims. And the rape, pillage, conquest, and enslavement that he presents as inflicted by aggressive and predatory conquerors, which elicit judgments of evil from their victims, surely are atrocities.

In the *Genealogy's* first essay Nietzsche calls into question the value of "good" when it is opposed to "evil." Distinguishing "good" in that sense from an earlier "good" that is opposed to "bad" rather than "evil," he calls for a rejection of the *negative valuation* of evil and for an appreciation of the positive value of what has been rejected by European culture for the past two thousand years as evil. Judging in terms of evil, he suggests, is ultimately bad for humanity.

The denial of evil has become an important strand of twentieth-century secular Western culture. Some critics find evil a chimera, like Santa Claus or the tooth fairy, but a dangerous one that calls forth disturbing emotions, such as hatred, and leads to such disturbing projects as revenge. The denial of evil is not peculiar to ethical relativists or value skeptics. Many reject the idea of evil because, like Nietzsche, they find it a *bad* idea, one that demonizes rather than humanizes "the enemy." Nietzsche's critique has helped engineer a shift from questions of what to do to prevent, reduce, or redress evils to skeptical psychological questions about what inclines people to make judgments of evil in the first place, what functions such judgments have served. I want to reverse that shift, not because I am enthusiastic about hatred and revenge but because evils, the worst wrongs people do, deserve to be taken seriously and to receive priority of attention over lesser wrongs, which are usually easier to talk about and easier to fix. On the atrocity theory, there should be less temptation to demonize "the enemy," since perpetrators are culpable in many ways.

Nietzsche finds the practice of making judgments of evil both dishonest and dangerous. Morality itself, he suggested, may be "the danger of dangers."[2] Hitherto, he wrote in the preface to the *Genealogy*, we have taken for granted the values of good and evil, ranking "the good" higher than "the evil." But what, he asks, if the reverse ranking were true?[3] To ask the question is not, of course, to answer it. It is not clear to me to what extent Nietzsche thought he had answered it satisfactorily in the *Genealogy*, and to what extent he was pursuing the implications of certain hypotheses without being absolutely committed to them.

The strategy of questioning honesty and motives can be turned back on Nietzsche. We can ask what functions or interests are served by his shift of focus from evils to those who judge. Addressing the critic's motives may be more manageable than confronting evils themselves. Treating haters as the problem deflects attention from what they hate. Perhaps eliminating hatred is more feasible than eliminating or redressing evils that evoke it. Antifeminists have long accused feminists (platitudinously described as "militant") of stirring up hatred against men. They treat feminist anger as the problem, rather than taking seriously what makes feminists angry.

Ad hominem arguments can be fun, but they can go back and forth forever. It would be a mistake to leave Nietzsche's discussion of the concept of evil with only a reciprocation of his ad hominems, however credible they may be (and they may all be credible). For not all of his arguments against "evil" are ad hominem. Further, even his ad hominem arguments identify features of the concept of evil that are helpful for nonskeptics who wish to understand that concept better. One such feature is the root of that concept in the perspectives of victims.

Nietzsche's discussion of evil is worth studying for both its insights and its prejudices. I find at least two, maybe three, important insights about evil in his work. That judgments of evil come, basically, from a victim's perspective is one. That judgments of evil are often accompanied by a distorting hatred is a second. That hatred is often rooted in one's fear of impotence may be a third, although at times Nietzsche seems to think sheer envy of another's power produces hatred, or that actual impotence is enough to do so. These two or three insights can be acknowledged independently of three of Nietzsche's beliefs that tend to accompany them. They are the beliefs (1) that the perspectives of the weak are more distorted and yield more dishonest judgments than those of the powerful, (2) that powerful perpetrators are not likely to hate their victims, and (3) that hatred underlies judgments of evil. I question each of these beliefs. As indicated by the "magnitude gap" introduced in chapter 1, the perceptions of perpetrators and victims are liable to distortions of different kinds, both in principle correctable without necessarily removing the bases for judgments of evil. If victims tend to exaggerate the reprehensibility of perpetrators' motives, perpetrators tend to underestimate the harm they do. The distortions of perpetrators are neither less serious nor more innocent than those of victims, and distortion is, in each kind of case, compatible with also having access to truths. Powerful perpetrators often do hate their victims, but their hatred is triggered in different ways. And, finally, judgments of evil can often be plausibly invoked to explain hatred, a clue that the judgment underlies the hatred rather than the other way around. But whether hatred precedes or follows judgments of evil, if the two are commonly linked, it will be important also to consider whether hatred is the danger that Nietzsche apparently thought it was. The remaining sections of the present chapter explore and develop these issues further. What is fundamentally at stake is whether evil is a perverse concept, whether humanity would be better off without it (that is, without the concept, not without the evils).

As noted, not all of Nietzsche's arguments against "evil" are ad hominem. He is concerned about the harm to human potential done by those who punish and annihilate evildoers wherever they can. Questions regarding the value of punishment I postpone to chapter 8 (on the moral powers of victims). My objective in this chapter is to defend a concept of evil against Nietzsche's view that judgments of evil are basically slavish and ultimately perverse. I argue for a different, more plausible source of such judgments in the perspectives of those who regard themselves as wronged and entitled to better. First, I consider Nietzsche's genealogical method and perspectivism, elements of his approach that I value and enjoy. I then obtain different results in applying them—different, that is, from those Nietzsche obtained when he applied them himself.

Genealogies and Perspectives

Nietzsche's genealogical method is exemplified in his remarks about punishment in the second essay of the *Genealogy*. What he says about the meaning of punishment can be applied to the meaning of morality as well, the larger subject under investigation in that work. We should also be able to apply the genealogical method to the concept of evil.

Nietzsche observes that the origin of punishment is one thing and its purposes are something else: "[A]ll purposes, all utilities, are only *signs* that a will to power has become lord over something less powerful and has stamped its own functional meaning onto it."[4] He lists a variety of functional meanings that punishment has had and continues to have, in support of his hypothesis that "the concept 'punishment' in fact no longer represents a single meaning at all but rather an entire synthesis of 'meanings,'" that its history "finally crystallizes into a kind of unity that is difficult to dissolve, difficult to analyze and—one must emphasize—is completely and utterly *indefinable*," to which he adds in a parenthesis, "only that which has no history is definable."[5]

This approach to the meaning of "punishment" is very like Ludwig Wittgenstein's "family resemblance" approach to the meanings of concepts that have evolved historically. In his *Philosophical Investigations*, pt. 1, par. 67, in regard to the similarities among various things called "games," Wittgenstein says, "I can think of no better expression to characterize these similarities than 'family resemblances,'" and, with respect to the kinds of things we call "number," he continues, "we extend our concept of number as in spinning a thread we twist fibre on fibre. And the strength of the thread does not reside in the fact that some one fibre runs through its whole length, but in the overlapping of many fibres."[6] Instead of a neat definition in the form of a set of necessary and sufficient conditions for something's being a game, or a number, we find clusters of overlapping similarities, overlapping and interwoven strands of meaning, based on what people have done with what they called games, or numbers. If we extend Wittgenstein's thread of fibers back through time rather than simply across space, family resemblance becomes shared genealogy, heritage. Combining Nietzsche's genealogy with Wittgenstein's family and fiber metaphors yields intersecting lines of history (like the fibers of a cable) that produce the present "family" of meanings of "punishment"—or of "morality," or of "evil."

I looked in Ray Monk's biography of Wittgenstein to try to learn whether Wittgenstein had read Nietzsche and found only that he had read *The Anti-Christ*.[7] I was unable to determine whether Wittgenstein's family resemblance idea or his cable metaphor was influenced by Nietzsche. Apparently, I am not alone in wondering about such questions of influence. The North American Nietzsche Society newsletter from 1996 includes a query from a reader who raises the possibility that Wittgenstein's later works may have been indirectly influenced by Nietzsche by way of the work of Fritz Mauthner (1849–1923), whose views on language were influenced by Nietzsche and were earlier rejected by Wittgenstein in the *Tractatus*.[8] Nevertheless—whether there was a direct or indirect influence or merely a remarkable coincidence—we might think of Wittgenstein's family resemblance as a current time slice of Nietzsche's genealogy, and, likewise, regard Nietzsche's genealogy as what a "family" of meanings becomes when the dimension of its history is considered. Both ideas are helpful for investigating the concept of evil, which appears to be cross-cultural and transhistorical, if not entirely global. The concept of evil may not be entirely global because, for example, there appears nothing quite corresponding to it in Aristotle's ethics. Aristotle refers to "brutish" traits, some of which could be considered evil. But traits he counts as "brutish" also include many that are not evil at all, such as nail biting.[9]

Nietzsche's observation about the distinction between origins and purposes (or "functional meanings") is made in the context of his essay on guilt. Guilt, he speculates, was originally simply an economic debt, but its meaning has evolved and undergone profound changes.[10] The distinction between origins and meanings is less clear in his discussion of values belonging to the "noble" and "slave" modes of valuation taken up in the first essay of the *Genealogy*. These values became detached, he notes, from their original political contexts and are held now by people who are neither nobles nor slaves. Nobility, for example, became a set of spiritual qualities that were originally associated with the politically elite but might in fact be possessed by individuals regardless of their social origins and might be lacking in some of the privileged. Other than that, it is not clear what changes, if any, noble and slave values have undergone. The meanings of these values appear, in Nietzsche's account, more highly colored by their origins than the meanings of guilt and punishment as discussed in *Genealogy* 2, and this stamp of their origins is what enables Nietzsche to evaluate Christian, and in general modern European, values as basically slavish.

Perspectivism may be understood as the idea that perspectives furnish all the material we have for comprehending the world and for the concepts we use to do so. In its unraveling of the ancestral lines of a concept, genealogical investigation yields a variety of perspectives. Following Maudemarie Clark, I do not understand Nietzsche's perspectivism in the *Genealogy* as entailing a rejection of truth.[11] As she notes, he asked, after all, in the *Genealogy*'s preface whether a reverse ranking of "the good" and "the evil" might be true—"Wie? wenn das Umgekehrte die Wahrheit wäre?"[12] We may understand his perspectivism simply as the idea that all thinking, like all perception, is from some angle or other and that the only way to correct errors is also from some angle or other. Thinking from a perspective does not imply distortion but only a bias, a "slant," which has limitations but also may offer special vantage points. The thinking within the limits of a particular bias (slant) may be good or bad, distorted or true, or exhibit some combination of truth and distortion. Whether Nietzsche would have agreed with it or not, this interpretation of his perspectivism makes good sense of his own evaluations and revaluations.

Ambiguity in the concept of "bias" is illustrated by cutting a fabric on the bias. "Biased" is ambiguous between "slanted" and "distorted." My high school sewing teacher taught us to "stay-stitch" a fabric after cutting it on the bias, to avoid distortion.[13] A fabric cut on the bias is cut across the grain; the cut is slanted in relation to the grid of threads. To keep the threads true as you continue to work, you run a loose line of "stay-stitches" along the path of the cut. Stay-stitching keeps the threads in place so they do not bend every which way, distorting the fabric out of shape. Although stay-stitching is not foolproof (it can come undone), it generally helps keep the alignment of threads true. It is intended to be removed easily when the risk of distortion is past.

Cutting on the bias is a useful metaphor for those who wish to maintain that we have only angles or slants on things and yet also wish to avoid epistemological and ethical relativisms that ultimately abandon the ideas of truth and value as anything distinct from what is believed and what is treasured. "Biased" and "slanted," when applied to a perspective or point of view, embody all the ambiguity of an angled cut that may or may not produce distortion. When researchers confess to biases, typically they mean to alert others to limitations and *possible* distortions, the price of being able to offer close-up views of truths that it would be easy to miss without special angles. To accuse people in negative tones of being biased is, of course, to insinuate that their views are unbalanced, unfair to facts. Still, bias does not necessarily distort. And where there is distortion, one who attends carefully to the paths of the threads may be able to discern what has been distorted and infer the nature of the lost alignment. I take Nietzsche's perspectivism to be an appreciation of the fact that all knowledge comes from one or another slant (or combination of them), which means that all of its sources have limitations but implies neither that there is no truth of the matter nor that we are doomed to be denied it.

Each of us traces a path across the grid of space and time. These paths give us the special angles (biases) from which we perceive and also subject our perceptions to certain liabilities of distortion. Further, they give us choices of possible angles from which to view at any given point. If our histories limit the perspectives available to us, they do not narrowly determine which we will embrace. Our paths also cross each other, and we learn to take up each other's perspectives. A natural beginning to the process of checking distortion is to take up others' points of view, which offer clues and correctives. They also, of course, pose the danger—to which Nietzsche was sensitive—of being caught up in perspectives that distort even more than our original ones.

To correct for distortion, it is not enough to be able to enter into a variety of perspectives. Nor need we abandon space and time for Plato's heaven with its perspectiveless understandings (or Thomas Nagel's "view from nowhere"), even if we could.[14] As reflexive animals, we can take points of view on our own points of view (or those we once held), in a (theoretically) endless process of critical self-assessment. This activity does not presuppose a Cartesian core self that is unlimited by perspectives.[15] The reflexive viewer is as bound by history and location as the spontaneous viewer but is more aware of that very fact.

Nietzsche presents the judgment "bad" as coming, originally, from the perspectives of noble elites, aristocrats, who first of all joyously affirmed themselves as good (exceptional, fortunate, happy, beautiful, powerful, and so on) and then, and only by comparison, looked down on common folk as "bad," that is, inferior (ordinary, common, miserable, unfortunate, ugly, and so on). He presents judgments of evil (dangerous, destructive, harmful, hurtful) as coming, originally, from the perspectives of the impotent masses, slaves, common people, who regarded as evil those who conquered and enslaved them, and then, and only by comparison, found themselves to be "good" (not dangerous or harmful but helpful, "nice," accommodating, pleasant, and so on). Thus, he represents the noble mode of valuation ("good" vs. "bad") as originating in a powerful victor's perspective and the slave mode ("good" vs. "evil") in that of a relatively impotent victim.

Both victors and victims judge themselves favorably and others negatively. But Nietzsche's etymological investigations lead him to the conclusion
that nobles were first to create values. He finds the slave mode of valuation a
merely reactive inversion of the noble mode: what the slave finds evil is precisely what the noble values as good (power, for example). As evidence that
this reversal is profoundly dishonest, he offers excerpts from a tract by Tertullian, an early church father, whose vision of heavenly reward includes being
treated to the joys of watching the damned fry eternally in Hell.[16] This vision
betrays that followers of Jesus' Sermon on the Mount, who profess to love
meekness and so forth, really want their chance to be on top after all and to see
their oppressors brought low.[17] He concludes that the reactive reversal of
noble values is rooted in a deep-seated hostile envy, for which he uses the
French term *ressentiment*.

In his critique, Nietzsche appears to identify with the perspectives of conquerors in that he sees their victims as one might expect conquerors to see
them, referring, for example, to conquered peoples with the derogatory terms
"herd," "rabble," and "masses," rather than, say, "the folk" (which would be
more respectful). Even in his characterizations of the perspectives of the dominated, Nietzsche seems to be looking through the eyes of the powerful and
imagining from that vantage point what their subordinates must be seeing.
The result is an arrogant distortion of the character and experience of common
folk. My bias is the opposite. I begin from the perspectives of common folk
and those who are dominated and argue with Nietzsche's perceptions of them.
But I aim to do more than simply substitute one bias for another at the level of
uncritical perception.

One way to view Nietzsche's project in the *Genealogy* is as an attempt to
discern which perspectives give us more truth in valuing, to infer from various
distortions what a true or truer valuing might be, if not to develop a mode of
self-criticism that might serve as a kind of "stay-stitching." This is an important set of projects for anyone confronted with deciding which perspectives to
adopt, which perspectives to identify with (to own), and for anyone who tries
to guard against distortion. These are serious concerns for anyone engaged
with consciousness-raising around issues of oppression, for example.

Because of our ability to enter imaginatively into each other's perspectives, the spatio-temporal locations from which we think at a given time need
not narrowly determine our perceptions. We can take up a perspective, try it
on and learn from it, without being committed to it. Calling a perspective one's
own implies more than that it is a perspective that one is in fact taking. It implies an endorsement, a judgment that this perspective does not distort truth
worse than available alternatives. Questions about perspective ownership
come alive for me especially in thinking about the perspectives of dominated

women and about the concept of the woman-identified woman, a matter to which I return.

In feminist ethics, it is natural to explore the perspectives of dominant and subordinate in relation to values that Nietzsche associates with them in his hypotheses about the origins of "good," "bad," and "evil." Feminist philosophers have long realized that the history of Western philosophical ethics has always been more specific than it usually pretends to be with respect to the perspectives it exemplifies. If philosophers reflect on the data of everyday life, Western philosophers have reflected on the lives of mostly relatively privileged, mostly Christian men of white European descent. These lives have often been very public, marked by activity in markets and governments.[18] Modern philosophical ethics has also increasingly exemplified what I call "the administrative point of view," because it emphasizes decision-making from the perspectives of those who must adjudicate conflicts of interest in public arenas.[19] This body of philosophy also includes some reflection on women, usually from the perspectives of men whose views of women embody distortions and whose views of everything in the world to which women are related tend to inherit the distortion. This state of affairs presents a project for feminist philosophy: to articulate the world, critically, from the perspectives of women.[20] It suggests such critical questions as: what has been presented accurately or helpfully from men's perspectives, and what have they distorted? how does understanding their perspectives help to understand why they got it right or wrong in just the ways that they did? Likewise for women and feminist philosophy, which tends to be done self-consciously from the perspectives of women who also often identify explicitly with ethnic and class standpoints: what have been women's special vantage points, and what have women distorted or got wrong? How does understanding our perspectives help to clarify why we have the insights we do and why we make the mistakes that we make? And what are these characteristic insights and errors?

To those who read Nietzsche as rejecting the idea of truth, such questions will not seem Nietzschean. Yet Clark argues persuasively that in his last six books, Nietzsche rejects his earlier skepticism about truth and that in the *Genealogy* he is not content simply to record different perspectives but is eager above all to evaluate them and to make judgments about their honesty and their utility, judgments that seem pointless without the presupposition that some such judgments are true and others false.[21] He seems at least to find some judgments epistemically preferable to others. What look at first like simple ad hominem arguments may be part of Nietzsche's search for the perspectives from which various ideas make sense. Their making sense, however, does not settle for Nietzsche (nor for us) the question of their truth or their value.

Distortion and Power Imbalances

I wish to argue with Nietzsche about two kinds of issues regarding what plausibly originates in the perspectives of powerless victims and powerful victors: first, about whose values so-called slave values really are (that is, from what perspective they originate and whose interests they serve); and second, about the distortions and lies characteristic of those who have each perspective. I argue that alternative interpretations, more plausible than Nietzsche's, undermine his conjecture that the concept evil is rooted in the *ressentiment* (envious hatred) and dishonesty of the weak. I do not deny that impotence can lead to envious and annihilating hatreds, that hatred can distort, nor even that impotent haters often bring accusations of evil. I argue, rather, that it is not necessary to hypothesize dishonesty and envy in the genesis of judgments of evil and that a different account, one that draws on a sense of entitlement, is more plausible.

My way into assessing Nietzsche's genealogy of evil is to draw on my experience of women as examples of dominated valuers. As I think about what our positions as dominated beings have led us to value, I also think about how these positions have enabled and required us to become self-critical and critical of our dominators, to learn to hear what is never said explicitly, to discriminate between appearance and reality, and to become proficient actors. I have also examined American slave narratives with analogous concerns in mind.[22]

It is true that in his genealogy of morality Nietzsche offers a hypothesis about the origins, ancestors, of present-day moral values, which is certainly distinct from his beliefs about the values held by the politically powerful and the politically impotent of his own day. Although he speculates that judgments of evil originated in the perspectives of those conquered and enslaved, it is not his view that only the downtrodden of his day judge in terms of evil. On the contrary, he finds judgments of evil running through the lives of powerful and powerless alike, and a deeply troubling slavishness in attitude characteristic of what is, among his (and our) contemporaries, considered respectable. In *Beyond Good and Evil* he had characterized contemporary morality as combining both noble and slave perspectives:

> There are *master morality* and *slave morality*—I add immediately that in all the higher and more mixed cultures there also appear attempts at mediation between these two moralities, and yet more often the interpenetration and mutual misunderstanding of both, and at times they occur directly alongside each other—even in the same human being, within a *single soul*.[23]

The *Genealogy* finds the slave mode dominant in the mixture of values that constitutes modern European morality. Even though it was not Nietzsche's view that his politically powerful contemporaries were noble (if anything, he believed the opposite and found nobility rare in any stratum of modern society), nor that the oppressed of modern Europe are necessarily slavish, or more slavish than others, still, the plausibility of his hypotheses about origins derives at least in part from his understanding of the psychologies of domination and subordination, what the powerful and powerless lie about, how they perceive each other, how they perceive themselves.

Initially, Nietzsche's speculations about different voices—masters and slaves, victors and victims, or nobles and common folk—appear to be a useful tool for approaching recent feminist work on care ethics. "Women's voice" ethics as articulated in 1982 by Harvard educational psychologist Carol Gilligan sounds a lot like Nietzsche's slave morality, purporting to value care and connection, where "care" is a likely euphemism for service, the connections are with men and their children, and women have little or no choice about either.[24] Such an ethic seems to exemplify the adage: if you cannot get what you want, learn to want what you can get. The rejection of the idea of justice by American feminist philosophers Nel Noddings and Sarah Hoagland and its demotion to a less important status in Gilligan's care perspective are reminiscent of Nietzsche's association of justice with the perspectives of the dominant.[25] The care versus justice ethics debates sparked by Gilligan's work on women's voices reminds me of fundamentalist Christianity, posing itself as a religion of love against Old Testament Judaism (portrayed by many Christians as a religion of "mere" justice) and of the aspirations of that Christianity to go beyond "mere" justice, while being in fact often manifestly deficient in that area. This stance of the Bible Belt Christianity of my childhood lay behind an early essay I wrote on mercy, before I had read Nietzsche in more than a cursory way.[26] Since then, I have raised the question of whether some allegedly feminist care ethics is vulnerable to Nietzsche's criticisms of (so-called) "Christian love."[27] What is this "care" worth? What does it get us? What does it make of us?

Contrary, however, to Nietzsche's crediting of slaves with the origin of "slave values," those values ("caring," for example) sound like ones that masters would apply to slaves, valuing them straightforwardly in terms of their utility (capacity to serve) or capacity to please—as entertainers, concubines, caretakers, servants, maintenance workers, and so forth. This is, of course, a different mode of valuation, no doubt less fundamental, from that used to rank masters and slaves, to determine who is who (who is master) in the first place. But they are still the master's values. When slaves learn to see themselves as their masters see them (through the lens of utility), they have a powerful tool for manipulation and deception. In using this tool, slaves need not fool themselves, however. They may put on an act to keep those in power off their backs, pretending (to the master) to value care (of the master) and connection (to the master) and to abhor what would be dangerous, harmful, and destructive (to the master). At the same time they may find their masters arrogant fools for being taken in by the pretense. Naive slaves who, through attachment to their masters, internalize a utilitarian self-concept have not yet discovered a perspective of their own, in any sense deeper than one they happen to be taking. For those who have internalized a such a self-concept, consciousness-raising can work a revolution.

The notion of one's perspective is ambiguous between whatever perspective one is taking (which could be internalized from elsewhere) and a perspective that one truly owns as the result of critical assessment (even if it is also taken by others). Neither nobles' nor slaves' perspectives are presented by Nietzsche as their own in this critical sense. Yet, in his genealogy of morality, Nietzsche does not present the slave perspective simply as one that slaves happen to have, either. He makes a great point of presenting its values as originating with them. Paradoxically, he seems to blame slaves for slavishness.[28]

But why attribute the genesis of so-called slave values to slaves, as Nietzsche does in *Genealogy*, 1:10: "[T]he slave revolt in morality begins when *ressentiment* becomes creative and gives birth to values. . . . [F]rom the outset slave morality says 'no' to an 'outside,' . . . and *this* 'no' is its creative deed."[29] Although the master/slave relationship does become interactive, those who enslave are more responsible for the existence and quality of the interaction. On the origins of slavishness, Nietzsche seems either inconsistent or ambivalent. Perhaps there are good reasons for ambivalence. There may be truth on both sides, in the view that masters created slavish values (by expecting slaves to live up to them and penalizing them for failing) and in the view that (some) slaves created (some) modes of slavishness. The creation of slave values by masters is more interesting, however, because it points to a distinction for slaves between internalizing or taking up a perspective and owning it, which is helpful for understanding psychological liberation.

When slaves take pride in caring for oppressors, we may rightly wonder, with Nietzsche, whether a sour grapes mentality is at work, whether the believer is perversely engaged in a self-deception that perpetuates domination: "Keep your old justice; we have something better." Slaves who take up a care ethic, however, need not believe in it. They may profess (to the master) values they know they do not truly hold. Their valuing of survival need not be as an end in itself but can be, rather, as a means to such things as being able to leave a legacy of testimony to descendants and others who may care.

In the *Genealogy* Nietzsche seems to think slave values originate with common people. Some of his earlier writings, however, suggest a deeper, more perceptive view. Nietzsche had toyed with the idea in *The Gay Science* 2:68 that women are not the source of womanliness. In an aphorism titled "Will and Willingness," he has a sage say, "It is men that corrupt women. . . . [I]t is man who creates for himself the image of woman, and woman forms herself according to this image."[30] Feminists could agree, if he means by "womanliness" what many feminists in the United States today mean by "femininity," a social construction embodying traits designed to serve men's interests. It may not have been the most obviously slavish aspects of femininity of which Nietzsche was thinking. It may have been stereotypes of attractiveness, various turn-ons, even the "tiger's claw under the glove," roles and images women learn to cultivate because of men's expectations and fantasies (which eventually have their downside for men who become disillusioned when they marry and the fantasy crumbles). But the point can be extended. Man creates for himself the image not only of exciting women but also of useful women, women who do not make trouble but are always there to soothe, to nurse the baby, cook meals, clean the house. How different is this from the image of a good house slave?

Utilitarian values might naturally originate as values that masters apply to slaves when managing and addressing slaves. If the noble mode articulates values that aristocrats invoke among themselves, the slave mode articulates values they would naturally invoke in slave management, praising usefulness and condemning disobedience. The apparent inferiority of slaves (by noble standards) has been used by aristocrats to justify measuring slaves by different and lesser standards—utility and obedience rather than intrinsic worth. Aristocrats estimate their own value by what gives vitality to their lives but evaluate slaves only extrinsically, albeit forever finding slaves to fall short even of standards of utility and obedience. Slaves who became psychologically attached to their masters might, then, learn to live up to the master's image of a good slave, just as, according to Nietzsche's sage, women learn to live up to men's images of womanliness. On this hypothesis, both noble and slave values originate in the perspectives of aristocrats, which actually fits with Nietzsche's observations about who creates values in *Beyond Good and Evil*:

> In all somehow dependent social·strata the common man *was* only what he was *considered*: not at all used to positing values himself, he also attached no other value to himself than his masters attached to him (it is the characteristic *right of masters* to create values).[31]

Although it seems sheer aristocratic arrogance to think that common people, or slaves, in fact had no values of their own but were only what they were considered (even aside from the fact that in ancient times, slaves were sometimes aristocrats themselves before their reversal of fortune), here, as in *Gay Science*, Nietzsche does appear to acknowledge, at least by implication, that some so-called slave values do not originate with slaves.

And yet in the *Genealogy*, it is slaves (rather than those whom they must please) who are credited with creating slave values.[32] In what Nietzsche calls "the slave revolt in morality," which he describes as the "revenge of the powerless," he speculates that priests, leaders of the common people and rivals of the noble elite, finally succeed, by way of Christianity, in getting aristocrats to hold their very assets (epitomized by their power) against themselves, to take as their ideal a pacific rather than violent temper, dangerous to no one, harmless, helpful, "nice," and so forth. These values express not simply the priests' *ressentiment* but that of the powerless "mob." The revenge of the "slave revolt in morals" is not just priestly but mob revenge.

I have never found plausible Nietzsche's hypothesis that priests were responsible for such a "slave revolt in morals," because he offers no account of how they obtained such a hold over aristocrats as to be able to pull it off. Yet it is easy to see how the institution of slavery might be instrumental in the rise of utilitarian and Kantian values (that is, more democratic ones). Slaves outnumbered their owners. House slaves participated in raising the master's children and were thereby among their earliest teachers and, plausibly, often among their earliest objects of attachment. House slaves, who learned "slave values" from their masters, might well teach those values to the master's children.

Another route to insinuating slave values into the aristocracy is through erotic bonding of master to slave. When masters used slaves sexually, some, like Thomas Jefferson, fell in love.[33] Milton Melzer, in his world history of slavery, speculates that most people in the world today are descendants of either slaves or masters or people who were both at different times in their lives.[34] It is not difficult to conclude that more of us descend from slaves than from masters and that those of us who also descend from masters descend from those who learned slave values first. If the rise of slave values accompanied increasing political power in the descendants of slaves and other common folk (most of us), that is, the rise of democracy, what we may have is not so much revenge as a depressing poetic justice. The legacy of the powerful, who originally lacked respect for and appreciation of folk vitality, may be that slave values come to be applied by everyone to everyone, with a universal diminishment of vitality (or at least of the valuing of vitality).

With the correction about origins, Nietzsche's slave mode of valuation provides a sobering critique of Benthamite ideals. Nietzsche's slave values are somber, not playful. They exalt tameness as a virtue along with servility (perhaps called "respect"), service (perhaps called "love"), connection ("loyalty"), obedience (to authority), and so forth. Those who are "good" in the slavish sense do not make waves but are obedient, dutiful. They are not dangerous or harmful (fomenters of rebellion) but, rather, faithful, attached (to their oppressors' values). They are like good dogs—good for their owners. A good dog does not necessarily have or lead a good life. A good dog is well-trained. Likewise a good slave, good children, and a good woman.

Nietzsche's slave mode of valuation so far sounds like "good dog" morality, and we know that dogs did not invent that. No doubt slaves who were psychologically attached to their masters internalized it. The "Uncle Tom" or "Sambo" hypothesis, which rests on the supposition that many did, however, is controversial among African American scholars, and there is good reason today to believe that a great many slaves were not emotionally attached to their masters.[35] "Good dog morality" has certainly been acted out by many dominated individuals who knew just what they were about. Nietzsche, of course, acknowledges that today one can be powerless and yet have noble values. Still, it is controversial to what extent the so-called noble stance ever was exceptional among dominated people. Perhaps all that was truly exceptional was the *assertion* of that stance by the powerless in the presence of oppressors (which can be suicidal).

Here is an informative piece of humor and irony from someone whose recent heritage includes slavery. African American poet Nikki Giovanni writes in her autobiography:

> We told our tales to their children and they thought we loved them. Just listen to "Rockabye Baby" and picture a Black woman singing it to a white baby. . . . They didn't know we were laughing at them, and we unfortunately were late to awaken to the fact that we can die laughing.[36]

"Rockabye Baby, in the treetop; When the wind blows, the cradle will rock; When the bough breaks, the cradle will fall; And down will come baby, cradle and all." This American nursery song, with its soft and sweet melody, does not at first sound like revenge. But the words can produce a double take, and then it may. The fact that white women of my mother's and grandmother's generations all sang it to their babies might be perceived as something like revenge. But perceived by whom? The poet does not hear it as revenge. To do so would center white folk, making the song merely reactive. Revenge is what arrogant whites may hear if they catch onto the lyrics, as doing so keeps themselves at the center. But the "laughing at them" that the poet hears sounds more like playfulness than revenge—playfulness meant to keep up Black spirits, create amusement, even maintain one's own perspective as something other than a slave. Such playfulness does not, of course, exhibit what Nietzsche regarded as "slave values."

Nietzsche might not have accepted the idea that slaves often simply put on an act, pretending to value utility and obedience. In his eagerness to avoid mind-body dualism, he seems reluctant to distinguish the actor from the act. In *Gay Science* 5:361, where he connects artistry with acting, he notes that "an instinct" for acting "will have developed most easily in families of the lower classes who had to survive under changing pressures and coercions, in deep dependency, who had to cut their coats according to the cloth, always adapting themselves again to new circumstances, who always had to change their mien and posture, until they learned gradually to turn their coat with *every* wind and thus virtually to *become* a coat," and he applies these observations to women: "Reflect on the whole history of women: do they not *have* to be first of all and above all else actresses? . . . [L]et yourself be 'hypnotized by them'! What is always the end result? That they 'put on something' even when they take off everything."[37]

In a thoughtful reflection on self-respect and protest, Bernard Boxill, also, points out the danger of becoming what one is pretending to be in carrying out a deferential act, for survival or advantage, that can engulf one's entire life. If one is not prepared to protest mistreatment at some point or other, what evidence, he asks, is there that one has not in fact become servile? "Unless it is already known to be pretense, apparent servility is evidence of servility."[38]

But perhaps both parties to a power imbalance have one persona for interacting with peers and another for interacting across power strata, with correspondingly different values and standards. If so, it would appear that most people in such situations engage in what psychologist Robert J. Lifton calls "doubling."[39] Slaves might use the "slave mode" for interaction across power strata, for survival and to stave off abuse. But in peer relationships they might exhibit other values—humor and artistry, for example—much as strictly disciplined children learn (or pretend to learn) that to be good is to be deferential and obedient when the parents are around (the somber mode) but also know that it is okay to have fun when they are not (the playful mode).

Nietzsche does present common folk as having two modes of valuation, one superficial and dishonest (the slave mode), the other truer but deeper and more hidden (a mode endorsing power and revenge). He distinguishes between what common folk really value (betrayed in the quote from Tertullian about the joys of heaven, for example) and their "lies" (such as Jesus' Sermon on the Mount: "Blessed are the poor in spirit, for theirs is the kingdom of heaven," etc.).[40] Yet he seems not to notice that nobles would also naturally have two analogous modes of valuation—one for interacting with peers (Nietzsche's spontaneous "noble mode"), another for managing slaves (the "slave mode," calculated and dishonest). Perhaps he does not notice this because he has internalized the aristocrats' concept of themselves as honest and straightforward, by contrast with the notorious pretense and hypocrisy they find in slaves.

Yet aristocrats lie routinely, also. They tell lies about slaves and common folk, such as that those lives lack joy and vitality. Nietzsche no doubt has such "lies" in mind when he quickly excuses nobles for sometimes getting it wrong about common people through sheer ignorance, insufficient acquaintance.[41] But those who hold power also notoriously lie about how they acquired their power (what is history? lies told by victors—an exaggeration, but not a fairy tale).[42] They lie about how they treat those subject to their power, how benevolent they are to slaves, for example ("just like one of the family"). And they lie *to* slaves. These are not innocent fabrications due to insufficient acquaintance but politically self-serving fictions. Edward Ball in *Slaves in the Family* records conflicting stories told by white descendants of his slave-owning ancestors and darker skinned descendants of slaves they owned on the question whether slaves were ever sold off from the plantation with the consequence of breaking up families.[43] Conquerors' tales are at least as convoluted and riddled with face-saving hypocrisies as those of their victims, although, naturally, it is the conqueror's perception of the victim as liar that survives.

The picture of the dominated incorporating their dominators' perspectives fits with the feminist view that women who are overly eager to please and serve men are "male-identified," as that term was used in the 1970s. For a woman to be "male-identified" did not mean that she identified herself as male. Rather, a "male-identified woman" saw herself primarily through the eyes of heterosexist men, valuing herself as they had learned to value her, in terms of a patriarchal male-defined cultural ideal for women, such as that of Kant in the third chapter of his essay *On the Beautiful and the Sublime* or that of Rousseau in book 5 of *Emile*.[44] A "male-identified woman" was contrasted with a "woman-identified woman," who sees herself through the eyes of women who do not see themselves through the eyes of patriarchally enculturated men. This picture also suggests a vision of liberation as coming with the development of a perspective of one's own through critical reflection and evaluation, after having been forced to see the world as seen by others whose interests oppose one's own.

To be unwilling to risk one's life for anything more important is a paradigm of slavishness. Yet many women, some of them slaves, and other dominated people have not made survival their highest goal. Consider Harriet Jacobs, who in 1861 published her memoirs of slavery under the pseudonym Linda Brent. Describing thoughts that she had while still a slave, she wrote, "When I lay down beside my child, I felt how much easier it would be to see her die than to see her master beat her about, as I daily saw him beat other little ones."[45] Harriet Jacobs refused a Northern white woman's offer to purchase her from her master (in order to free her), on the ground that this would be too much like being passed from one master to another. (The white woman did it anyway.) Toni Morrison's novel *Beloved* tells the story of a mother who acted on the same values as Harriet Jacobs, choosing death for her children rather than allowing them to be recaptured.[46] The history of Masada in 73 C.E. is an instance in which a Jewish community is said to have chosen death by their own hands over enslavement by Romans.[47] These do not sound like the Jewish values of which Nietzsche complains in the *Genealogy*. From such perspectives, what contributes to one's survival, or to that of loved ones, may also rob one's life of vitality. It seems sheer aristocratic arrogance to suppose that only "in the higher and more mixed cultures" could the powerless come to live by such values.

There is indeed distortion and dishonesty embedded in slave values, stemming from aristocrats who measure a slave's worth solely by the standard of utility. The distortions and dishonesty, predictably internalized somewhat by emotionally attached slaves, come first from aristocratic arrogance, failure or refusal to perceive any value but utility in those they oppress and failure or refusal to appreciate the oppressiveness of reducing others' lives to little more than service and suffering. Slavery is an evil. But from where does that judgment come? Is "evil" really a slave value? Nietzsche thought so. The next section argues otherwise.

Evil and Entitlement, Hatred and Impotence

In presenting the historic rise of the slave mode of valuation as a revenge of the impotent, Nietzsche refers to slave *creativity* in reversing noble values. It is not the utilitarian element of slave values that interests him here but the negative element of condemnation, the focus on what is other and to be rejected. "This 'no' [to what is outside itself] is its creative deed."[48]

Nietzsche may be right that judging one's oppressor to be evil is a creative act on the part of the victim. The point of this creation, however, need not be to take revenge but to develop a perspective of one's own, to break free of the oppressor's view of oneself, rejecting the primarily utilitarian values by which the oppressor measures one's worth. The "No," so understood, is to a certain view of oneself and is made necessary by that view's having been imposed in the first place. The focus is not so much on the oppressor as on what the oppressor has done to oneself. Such a judgment makes best sense as coming from those who do not, or who no longer, regard themselves basically as slaves, not from those who take pride in what good slaves they are. "Evil" presupposes a sense of entitlement to better treatment. But it is aristocrats, not slaves, who would first have had a sense of entitlement. The creativity for slaves lies in applying it to themselves.

Nietzsche finds only contempt or condescension (sometimes mixed with benevolence), not hatred, in aristocratic attitudes toward what they judge bad. But he finds a smoldering, envious hatred in slaves' condemnations of oppressors as evil, which he credits with a distortion of the facts going beyond any distortions that contempt may produce:

Consider that the affect of contempt, of looking down on, of the superior glance—assuming that it does *falsify* the image of the one held in contempt—will in any case fall far short of the falsification with which the suppressed hate, the revenge of the powerless, lays a hand on its opponent. . . . Indeed there is too much carelessness in contempt . . . for it to be capable of transforming its object into a real caricature and monster.[49]

On the atrocity paradigm of evil, the judgment that slavery is an evil includes the judgment that at least some of its practitioners engage in culpable wrongdoing. There is, of course, room for distortion here regarding the form of that culpability and regarding where it is truly present. According to the "magnitude gap," victims are apt to exaggerate the reprehensibility of a perpetrator's motives, to attribute malice, for example, rather than greed, to perceive monsters instead of ordinary people. But these distortions are in principle correctable, and their correction does not necessarily remove the bases for a judgment of evil. The judgment that slavery is an evil also includes the judgment that it causes its victims intolerable harm, and about this, victims are less likely than perpetrators to be wrong.

Nietzsche's parable of the bird of prey and the little lambs in *Genealogy* 1:13 seems to support his view that although the powerful condescend and are contemptuous, they do not hate, because they do not have to. This parable is easily used to interpret the stance of men (birds of prey) toward women (little lambs) in a sexist society: "We don't hate women; we *love* women—tasty little morsels. Bring on the women!" My students identify with this instantly. There also seems something to the idea that women are more likely to hate men than men are to hate women. Women certainly have much to envy men in a sexist society, and women also have the reputation for a certain liability to reactive hatred ("a woman scorned . . ." etc.). In contrast, heterosexual men routinely insult each other with the label "feminine," although they also enjoy women as an indulgence.

But it is false that the powerful exhibit only contempt for and not hatred of inferiors. They are most apt to feel contempt for *obedient* inferiors (and hardly envy them). But they are not above hating insubordinates. If the predator attitude captures how heterosexist men feel about women they can use, it hardly captures their attitudes toward lesbians. How do the powerful feel toward rebels? Not condescendingly benevolent. As Mary Daly noted in *Beyond God the Father*, what made Eve evil was not her power (she had none) but her insubordination, her lack of deference, and she was judged evil from the point of view of the powerful.[50] The attitude of the dominant toward insubordinates is not admiration, a reconsideration of their status as subordinates, or any tendency to view them as peers after all. Here, at the point of insubordination, is where hatred of subordinates surfaces in the powerful. Recaptured runaway slaves experience the master's full hatred, and battered women just at the point of near escape are often killed by an enraged abuser.

Judgments of evil do not basically represent the perspective of the powerless. They basically represent the perspective of those who find themselves (or others with whom they identify) wronged, victims only in that sense. Both powerful and powerless can see themselves as wronged, although slaves are less likely to do so than aristocrats. Slaves born to slavery are more likely to see themselves as just unlucky. It is aristocrats who are raised with a sense of entitlement and who develop a readiness to see insubordination as a violation.

Nietzsche may be on better grounds in associating hatred with fear of impotence, with insecurity, than in connecting it with envy. Masters, of course, are not apt to envy their subordinates, but they are hardly free from insecurity when they become materially dependent on the labor of subordinates, as they eventually do. Those who live in intimate association with slaves can even grow to mind what slaves think and how they feel, which elude total control. The minding is there when slaves are expected to show respect, to care for the masters' children, or to be sexually available. Materially and emotionally dependent aristocrats lie to themselves regularly about how happy slaves are to serve them ("like one of the family"). When it becomes evident that slaves see through the lies and have their own points of view—hostile, mocking, or indifferent—aristocrats, too, can hate. Slaves who willfully assert their point of view can incur a wrath that knows no more bounds than that of the man of *ressentiment* so dramatically portrayed by Nietzsche. Neither actual impotence nor simple envy of power but the fear of impotence, fear of a loss of power, commonly produces hatred. The powerful may be more vulnerable to that fear than the powerless, who have less to lose.

Nietzsche may betray some awareness of this point in his claim that "priests are, as is well known, the *most evil of enemies*."[51] He calls priests "evil" because they are such haters that they become a genuine threat to "nobler" human beings. Nietzsche seems to think the priests' hatred grows out of their powerlessness, their relative lack of vitality. On the contrary, priests hate and become dangerous when they have power to lose.

The powerful also hate mockery by those who do not think them as wonderful as they think themselves and who have the audacity to let that opinion show. An aspect of folk culture is the mockery and ridicule that consists in poking fun at elites. Understanding themselves as benefactors of the weak, oppressors are apt to perceive such levity as insubordination, undeserved ingratitude, disloyalty, even treachery. These are highly moralistic judgments, commonly used to justify reprisals. The hostility of oppressors who perceive their benefactions to be unappreciated can be enormously destructive, at least as much as the hostilities of the oppressed.

Although it seems obvious that the powerful are not apt to envy inferiors, subordinates need not envy the powerful, either (although they may). They can have grounds for hatred independent of envy. Fear for one's life or for the security of loved ones is sufficient to ground hatred of an oppressor who is perceived to be responsible for the danger. Of course, the fear also presupposes a felt lack of power sufficient to protect, and the hater would wish for that power. Protection, however, does not require that potential oppressors be annihilated or rendered impotent, only that they be rendered unsuccessful in their evil designs. This can be compatible with their retaining enough power to protect their own lives and those of their own loved ones.

But often enough, the oppressed do not hate or even show much awareness of the fact that they are oppressed rather than simply unlucky. Again Nietzsche's identification with the powerful lands him in their arrogance over the issue of the hostility of common folk. If he underestimates ordinary people's good sense, good will, and playfulness, he appears also to overestimate their hostility and the extent of their preoccupation with those who hold power over them. People who lack power are often less politically aware than those with power can afford to be. The fantasy of a "slave revolt in morals" sounds like aristocratic narcissism in an elite unable to conceive that they might not be the focus of everyone else's attention, that the meaning of what everyone else does (or values) might not be some kind of reaction to themselves. Such a view naturally finds feminism simply a reaction against men, the object of which is to make men suffer and the daily practice of which consists in man-hating—which may explain Nietzsche's scorn for feminism. The thought that feminists might be focused on women, or on overcoming certain destructive or disrespectful images of themselves, is foreign to this mind-set, as it removes men from center stage and understands women as agents, not simply as actors and reactors.

My take on Nietzsche's likely misunderstanding of feminism is rooted in my experience of feminist consciousness-raising. But my skepticism regarding his portrayal of common folk has roots in my childhood in a village (Pardeeville, Wisconsin) of the American heartland. Pardeeville morality exhibits a mixture of values. Still, if Nietzsche's folk psychology is right, its attitudes toward those with power should betray some of the psychology of subordination on which Nietzsche draws in formulating his genealogy of evil. Do the villagers of my roots regard those in power as evil, as little lambs might regard birds of prey? On the contrary, when they do think about those in power (not a thought that dominates their lives), for the most part, they either identify with them and regard as dangerous whoever condemns the establishment, or they tend to mock those with social status. Many do both (which betrays an interesting ambivalence). It was not until I left Pardeeville for the state university that I heard people dare to criticize the establishment as downright evil. Such judgments appeared to be part of university students' struggle to develop a perspective of their own.

Because they can vent their hostilities, Nietzsche seems to think that hatred in the powerful would not smolder and grow to the fearful proportions that he finds in the case of impotent victims. Yet ingratitude, disloyalty, and mockery or ridicule by insubordinate subordinates are persistent sources of renewed and increasing hostility in their oppressors. However able oppressors are to vent hostility and impose their will on the conduct of others, they may be unable to stifle such insubordinate attitudes. Here, they too may discover limits to their own power.

In the first essay of the *Genealogy* Nietzsche seems to treat evil as though it were a basic moral concept and as though it were simply how the impotent perceive those who behave harmfully or destructively toward them. On the atrocity paradigm, evil is not a basic moral concept. In presupposing the ideas of culpability and wrongdoing, it is higher order. Persons may be judged evil not only for having certain motives or culpable intentions but also for lacking decent ones, for being unrestrained in their treatment of others by such values as respect and dignity, or by belief in the right of human beings to be free from torture, to love and associate with others, to inquire and to criticize, to develop human potentialities for culture and creativity. This presupposition of basic moral concepts is a major difference between the negative evaluative concepts of bad and evil. Many judgments of badness do not presuppose moral concepts.

For judgments of evil, it is also important *what* was harmed or destroyed, how essential it is to the possibility of a tolerable or decent life. This factor is another difference between bad and evil. Conduct that is harmful or destructive of property without thereby threatening people's lives or rendering them intolerable may be morally bad without being evil. Evils manifest a lack of respect for humanity and for basic freedoms. Not all destructiveness is rightly perceived as evil. The destruction of the plantation way of life in the Old South of the United States, for example, was not an evil, however regretted by those who lived it.

Because "evil" is a higher order moral concept, Nietzsche may have been at a disadvantage in taking as his paradigms persons who are judged evil rather than deeds. He begins with the paradigm of the predator who is perceived by victims as a monster, which is, of course, the distortion characteristic of victims. The atrocity paradigm does not suffer from this disadvantage. Its core concept is that of an evil, rather than that of an evildoer. An evil is both suffered and perpetrated. Understood as foreseeably intolerable harm that is brought about by culpable wrongdoing, the concept of an evil gets us to focus more on the suffering and the deed than on the perpetrator and makes room for the idea that perpetrators can have many kinds of motives or even, in some cases, no motives at all. The focus on suffering also brings to the fore facts that perpetrators are apt to distort, willfully overlook, or fail to appreciate adequately, namely, facts pertaining to the nature and extent of harm caused others.

Hatred, a basic concern in Nietzsche's resistance to the concept of evil, is probably directed oftener at persons than at deeds. Hatred appears to be what he found dangerous about judgments of evil. Although one can hate without moral judgments and judge morally without hatred, it may be that to judge something evil is to regard it as at least worthy of hatred, as deserving of hatred, if anything is. Nietzsche apparently wished to be free of the impulse to hate, however deserved the hatred. Although I am not persuaded by his genealogy that evil is a concept to be transcended, that is not because I am eager to justify hatred. I remain ambivalent about hatred, as I am uncertain how dangerous it is. Sometimes the danger seems to lie, rather, in the inability to hate where hatred is earned.

Some ink has been spilled by feminists over whether man-hating is always bad. One of the best essays is by science fiction writer Joanna Russ.[52] Male-identified women (who see women through men's eyes) do not hate men, or not for oppressing women, although some hate women. It can be a sign of progress to hate rather than worship an oppressor or to hate the oppressor rather than oneself. Castigating ourselves for hating men is one of the patterns of sexism.

How much mythology surrounding hatred in a society shaped by Christianity comes from those who have earned others' hatreds? Consider the myths that hatred consumes the hater, that it wastes energy (wishful thinking?), or that to hate is to indulge in tabloid thinking and demonizing. These things are not true of all hatreds. Hatred of rapists, for example, need not consume us. We need not dwell on it or wallow in it. But when we do think of rapists, far from a waste of energy, as Nietzsche saw, hatred can be energizing. Nor need we demonize or make oversimplified judgments of character. We can allow that Hitler loved his dog and perhaps Eva Braun, whom he married at the very end when there was nothing ulterior to be gained from it (nor, of course, anything to be lost, either). We can acknowledge that although everyone is a mixture of good and bad, only some develop and come to be dominated by hateful traits (such as cruelty) or knowingly and without coercion perpetrate unforgivable deeds (such as mass murder). Hatred distances us from what we hate. It asserts a profound rejection. To reject is not to annihilate. Rejection can be good, depending on what is rejected by whom and how. Ironically, in his horror of hatred, Nietzsche may have been more of a Christian than he wanted us (or himself) to believe.

3

Utilitarian Attack and Stoic Withdrawal: Two Extremes

In a secular age, those seeking direction and insight regarding good and evil may look to philosophical ethics, rather than to theology. They are apt to be disappointed, however, at how seldom the concept of evil is explicitly discussed. "Good" and "right" are oftener the subject of reflection than their opposites. And "good" has many opposites, some, such as "undesirable" and "blameworthy," easier to discuss and more often investigated than evil. Much that is undesirable or blameworthy is, of course, hardly evil. Still, ethical theories do have implications regarding evils. Some theories appear to have been initially motivated by desires to come to terms with evil or to eliminate it. Utilitarianism and stoicism are two such theories, highly influential, which offer opposed stances toward evils. Since the atrocity theory combines features of both, this chapter considers why neither utilitarianism nor stoicism by itself is adequate.

Revisiting Ethical Theories

To place the atrocity view of evil in the context of ethical theory, I took a fresh look at the theories I teach and highlighted features different from those I was taught to notice. The theories I teach most are consequentialist ("teleological"), deontological (duty-based), and character-based (virtue ethics) approaches to ethics, illustrated, respectively, by the works of classical utilitarians Jeremy Bentham (1748–1832) and John Stuart Mill (1806–73), Immanuel Kant (1724–1804), and Aristotle (384–322 B.C.E.).[1] These works together illuminate three pairs of basic ethical concepts: (1) right and wrong (applied to conduct), (2) good and bad as desirable and undesirable (applied primarily to things, experiences, and states of affairs—possible objects of desire), and (3) good and bad as worthiness and unworthiness of esteem or admiration (applied to persons, motives, and character traits). Aristotle and Kant also consider the ethics of interpersonal relationships, a relatively neglected topic in modern ethics, which feminist moral philosophers are working to resuscitate.[2] With respect to the three pairs of basic concepts, each kind of theory deals insightfully with at most two and tends to focus on one.

Classical utilitarianism is studied for its views on the right and the desirable, with a focus on the desirable. Kant's deontology is studied for its analyses of right and worthiness of esteem, with a focus on rightness as defined by his principle of duty, the Categorical Imperative. Aristotle's character, or virtue, ethics is studied for its treatment of both desirability and worthiness of esteem, but especially for its accounts of goodness as worthiness of esteem ("nobility") and such related concepts as worthiness of praise or blame.

It is not obvious where evil fits in relation to these concepts, and theorists have not treated it uniformly. Bentham defines "undesirable" as "painful" and identifies evil with pain.[3] Thus, he understands evil as something suffered. Kant finds evil in the will to subordinate morality to self-interest. Thus, he sees evil in what we do, or in what we are willing to do, rather than in what we suffer. Aristotle seems to have no conception of evil at all but only of various ways of going wrong and failing to live a good life, although he offers sensitive discussions of culpability.

According to utilitarianism, right conduct by definition produces good consequences and wrong conduct harmful ones, on the whole and in the long run. To put the point negatively and in Benthamite terms, right conduct does no more "evil" than necessary to yield a balance of good. What is meant, of course, is that it does no more *harm* than necessary. Because utilitarians do not distinguish evils from lesser harms, they do not find it paradoxical to advocate doing just the right amount of evil. Wrong conduct is, by definition, simply productive of *too much* evil.

The next section examines difficulties of utilitarian approaches to evil. It concludes that after utilitarianism is amended to remedy its defects, the resulting theory is a whole lot less utilitarian than it was, although it still emphasizes the importance of harm. A major difficulty in utilitarianism, for a theory of evil, is its failure to place independent value on agents and on willing (agency), that is, value independent of the suffering or harm one's choices may cause.

As an account of the wrongdoing component in a theory of evil, many difficulties of utilitarianism are avoided by Kant's Categorical Imperatives: "Act only in accordance with that maxim through which you can at the same time will that it become a universal law" and "So act that you use humanity, whether in your own person or in the person of any other, always at the same time as an end, never merely as a means."[4] But Kant's principles have their own difficulties if taken as definitive of evildoing. For they make no mention at all of harm or suffering. The good will, a major concept in Kant's most influential ethical works, *The Groundwork of the Metaphysic of Morals* (1785) and *The Doctrine of Virtue, Part II of the Metaphysic of Morals* (1797), is widely discussed. His only comparably thoughtful account of an *evil* will occurs in book 1 of *Religion within the Boundaries of Mere Reason* (1793), less widely known. There, distinguishing stages of the will's decline, he presents a conception of radical evil in human nature. Yet, paradoxically, radical evil in human nature, on Kant's view, need not cause anyone serious harm. Both the good will and the will in its decline are defined independently of consequences to others.

Nothing in Aristotle's ethics quite corresponds to the concept of evil. What he calls vice, "brutish vice," and incontinence (*akrasia*), elucidated in books 2, 4, and 7 of *The Nicomachean Ethics*, come the closest. Yet each of these concepts encompasses much that is not evil. Boorishness is one of Aristotle's examples of vice, for example, and nail biting, of brutish vice. Neither is evil. Incontinence—acting against one's better judgment—is epitomized by dietary foolishness—hardly immoral, let alone evil. Still, worth noting for future reference are some distinctions that Aristotle makes regarding ways of going wrong, in distinguishing between vice and incontinence. People who have vices, he says, have corrupt judgment and think that what they do is right. But they are wrong about that, and their ignorance does not excuse them. This view clashes with a popular modern stereotype of evildoing, which represents evildoers as doing wrong willfully. Yet, since Hannah Arendt published her account of the character of Adolph Eichmann, many contemporary scholars are coming to a view of ordinary evildoers that is closer to Aristotle's view of people who have vices.[5]

An aspect of Aristotle's conception of incontinence does, however, fit a popular modern stereotype of wickedness. Incontinent people, he says, know (or believe) that what they do is wrong, but they do it anyway just because they want to. This characterization can, of course, apply to trivial wrongs, not just serious ones. Aristotle held greater hope for those who are incontinent than for people who have full-blown vices, because, since the judgment of the merely incontinent is uncorrupted, it can be appealed to in order to motivate change.

The three-part classification of ethical theories into consequentialisms, deontologies, and virtue or character ethics replaced a simpler dichotomy of teleology and deontology, to which I was introduced as a student in the early 1960s, which centers the concept of right. In his theory of justice, John Rawls defined deontological and teleological ethics by how they relate the right to the good (by which is basic, which defined in terms of which). Teleological theories, he held, specify the good independently of the right or they define right as what maximizes good, whereas deontological theories (by definition nonteleological) do neither.[6] Another way he puts the contrast is that teleological theories take good as basic and define right by reference to good, whereas deontological theories take right as basic and understand good as limited by right. Either way, utilitarian theories are teleological, and Kant's ethics is deontological (as is Rawls's theory of justice). But it is unclear how to classify Aristotle, who has a teleological conception of human nature (he thinks we have natural ends). Aristotle's teleology is a theory of goodness, not a theory of right. He defines right action not by its consequences but as lying in a mean between extremes and as having many dimensions, including appropriate motivation. And he offers no formula for locating the mean but instead discusses a fascinating array of individual virtues and vices, the concepts of voluntariness and choice, and a version of the problem known today as weakness of will. Hence, the creation of a third category, virtue or character theory, to accommodate Aristotelian ethics, which says next to nothing about the concept of right.

Because of the ambiguity of "good," both classifications of ethical theory are less than satisfying. "Good" is ambiguous between "worthy of esteem" and "worthy of desire," and so there is a possible ambiguity in claims about the good's independence from what is right: is it desirability that is independent? or worthiness of esteem (a less plausible view)? Further, given Kant's attention to good and evil in the will, it seems misleading to contrast Kant's ethics with "character ethics." It may be fairer to acknowledge, with Marcia Baron, Barbara Herman, and Martha Nussbaum, that Kant makes significant contributions to character ethics.[7]

To highlight conceptions of evil, a slightly different way of looking at the traditionally studied ethical theories is more helpful. Suppose we were to focus on which conception of goodness a theory centers. Bentham, Kant, and Aristotle all pay significant attention to goodness. But it is natural to group Kant and Aristotle together insofar as both treat worthiness of esteem (goodness as applied to character) as basic and treat desirability (goodness applied to possible objects of desire) as derivative or secondary. For Aristotle, what is truly worthy of desire is what a good (noble) person would desire, under moderately favorable circumstances. For Kant, the good will (which makes one worthy of esteem) is a condition of desirability in objects. In contrast, for Bentham desirability is basic. He treats judgments of character (worthiness of esteem, admiration, praise, or blame) as secondary or derivative. What makes a person good (admirable), he finds, are character traits that issue in choices that have desirable consequences. The case of Mill is more complex. For he begins with Bentham's view but then modifies it substantially in the direction of Kant and Aristotle.

In prioritizing the value of character over that of experience, Aristotle and Kant elevate what is most within our control, namely, our choices (in

Kant's language, our will). In contrast, Bentham places supreme value on experience, what happens to us. Because of their emphasis on will and agency, the ethics of Aristotle and Kant have an important stoic strain, although neither philosopher is a thoroughgoing stoic. Aristotle and Kant give us, respectively, aristocratic and democratic versions of a (moderate) stoicism, whereas Bentham offers us a democratic consequentialism. During the past two centuries the democratic approaches of Kant and Bentham have been more influential in Western European and North American thought than Aristotle's ethics. Yet, because of their opposed and uncompromising conceptions of goodness, each is fairly extreme in its understanding of evil. In the remaining sections of this chapter, I turn first to utilitarianism, especially its "purer" form as articulated by Bentham, and then, as background to Kant's ethics, to ancient stoicism.

Utilitarianism's War on Evil

Utilitarianism initially appears to be the most promising type of ethical theory for yielding a conception of evil adequate to the atrocity paradigm, because its emphasis on harm appears to give prominence to the sufferer, as does the concept of an atrocity. Especially in its classically hedonistic form, utilitarianism seems to evaluate evil deeds as we would expect victims to do, with a focus on suffering.

Utilitarian ethics is defined, by its creators and by contemporary followers, as directing us to promote good, if not the greatest good, for humanity. But the guiding inspiration of its founders, Bentham and Mill, was the far more urgent hope of abolishing evils, ideally reducing evil in the world around us as much as we can. Their moral philosophy was animated by very concrete concerns to reduce and prevent the social evils of poverty, oppression, and violence. They were not armchair academics but politically active men. Mill wrote in *Utilitarianism*, "The present wretched education and wretched social arrangements are the only real hindrance to [happiness] being attainable by almost all."[8] Following their lead, contemporary utilitarians have aimed to reduce misery rather than directly to produce happiness, in the faith that once liberated from misery, people can best find their own routes to happiness.[9] This hope is not just a philosopher's dream but is echoed in popular interpretations of the sentiment that favors leaving the world a better place than one found it. Bentham himself set an impressive example in his own war on evils in the criminal law of England. To rid the world of evils—what an ambitious and exciting idea! Unless, of course, the war on evils—like so many wars—risks perpetrating other evils, comparably serious. And that, of course, has been the problem haunting utilitarian ethics.

If its goal is to eliminate evils, it is natural to try to build into utilitarianism a theory of evil responsive to its motivating concerns, at least responsive to concerns likely to motivate contemporary interest. What motivation could be more urgent than concern to eliminate or reduce the likelihood of atrocities? If atrocities are our paradigms, however, several modifications must be introduced into the utilitarian conception of evil. First, because much suffering has natural causes, such as earthquakes, that are not amenable to human influence, an account adequate to the atrocity paradigm must specify that evils are produced (maintained, tolerated, wrongfully ignored, etc.) by human beings. This emendation allows, of course, that to neglect earthquake survivors or fail to warn of impending quakes can be evils, although the quake itself is not (however catastrophic). Evils, then, need not be the most destructive harms people suffer. But they are importantly *unnecessary*—they could have been avoided if people had made different choices. This specification importantly amends the views of those who, like Bentham, regard all harms as evils, no matter how caused. But the amendment is friendly, if I have correctly identified the animating concern. For there is no point in trying to abolish harms that are unamenable to human influence.

Yet that amendment is not enough. For not all intolerable harms produced by human agency are evils, but only those perpetrated culpably. Atrocities imply culpable agents, not just harmful ones, and this fact about them explains much of the horror they produce. Whether an agent was culpable depends on what the agent knew and could reasonably have known (whether reasonable care was exercised, for example), how much freedom the agent had to do otherwise, what scruples the agent had or lacked, and what purposes and intentions, if any, the agent had in acting. In brief, it depends on whether the agent's choices were wrongful and how much control the agent had. Utilitarianism, however, runs into major difficulties in defining wrongness, and it does not offer a satisfying account of the importance of agent control.

To begin with the control factor, atrocities are shocking in part because we expect better of human agents. Restricting evils to harms that were within the perpetrator's control is not grounded simply in concern for suffering. It is grounded in a valuing of moral agency. What is within one's control bears no particular relation to the harms or benefits one may produce. Those who lack control, through no fault of their own, can do harm as bad as or worse than those whose control is unimpaired. But they do not deserve the same responsive moral attitudes as evildoers—resentment, blame, censure, and the like. It is not that blaming them is useless, however. Blaming can actually be expedient in producing heightened future attention, even though there was (by hypothesis) nothing faulty about the attention already paid in this instance. But blaming agents who lacked control does them an injustice. It fails to respect their will. This point applies to wrongdoing generally, not just to evildoing. Conduct is unfortunate, not immoral, if the agent (faultlessly) lacked relevant knowledge or other aspects of control requisite to avoiding harm. To build a conception of evil compatible with the atrocity paradigm into utilitarian ethics, then, it is necessary to specify also that the only wrongdoing that counts as a component of evils is culpable wrongdoing. But the reason for that restriction is not itself utilitarian. And so the theory is becoming less utilitarian.

An important mode of lacking control is ignorance, lacking relevant information. Pondering the implications of faultless ignorance can lead us from the control factor to the wrongdoing factor in culpability and raise questions regarding utilitarian definitions of wrongdoing. Some, for example, have wanted to distinguish between what is "subjectively right" (what one can justify, within the limits of one's knowledge and beliefs; what *appears* to be right) and what is "objectively right" (free from the limitations of subjective error; what is *really* right), since one can easily be in error about consequences.[10] This distinction may give rise to the paradoxical question of which one actually ought to do (what is objectively right? or what is subjectively right?), when what appears to be right isn't really, since acting against one's beliefs indicates a lack of integrity, even if the beliefs are false.[11] For consequentialists, the distinction between subjective and objective right or wrong is natural. If conduct that is harmful on the whole is by definition wrong, nothing excludes the possibility of faultless or inevitable wrongdoing, for we can often be innocently mistaken about consequences. If we restrict the wrongdoing component of evils, however, to culpable wrongdoing, out of respect for moral agency, we do not need to distinguish objective from subjective right. For the agent's point of view and abilities, and our judgments about whether the agent exercised reasonable reflection and care, are built into our assessments of conduct as culpable. To be quite clear that faultless or inevitable "wrongdoing" is not a component of evils, I often use the expression "culpable wrongdoing" instead of simply the term "wrongdoing." Although I find "culpable wrongdoing" redundant and regard disastrous choices made innocently in ignorance of consequences as unfortunate rather than immoral, the redundancy may be useful, given the history of distinctions recognized by consequentialists.

We must also depart in other ways from utilitarian definitions of wrong conduct. Philosophical difficulties with the principle of utility as an ultimate standard for right conduct, and responses to those difficulties, have been endlessly elaborated by others, usually from the point of view of justice.[12] I want to try to get a fresh take on a few of them here, in order to highlight how they become specifically problems for the utilitarian war on evil.

Harm is, of course, sometimes unavoidable, even by conscientious human agents whose control is unimpaired. Some of the most difficult ethical questions concern justifications for conduct that inflicts harm on those who do not deserve it. Utilitarian ethics recognizes basically two kinds of justifications for harm. They are (1) that the action also produces a benefit that equals or out-weighs the harm, so that it does not do more harm than good on the whole, and (2) that no alternative course of action open to the agent at that time would have been less harmful overall. The calculations that these justifications call for present well-known difficulties. But the ones most discussed are not neces-sarily the most serious, with respect to evils.

The first case, where benefit equals or outweighs harm, has been well crit-icized by Rawls and others for ignoring distributive justice.[13] Rawls argues that it yields the wrong explanation of what is wrong with slavery, namely, that the institution simply does more harm than good. This kind of rationale appears, in principle, to permit harms to some people to be outweighed by greater benefits to others, as it offers no basis for determining a distribution of harms and benefits other than the greatest good on the whole. To rule out sac-rificing the well-being of some people for the sake of that of others, some moral philosophers advocate restricting the pursuit of utility by principles of equal-ity, whereas others reinterpret the principle of utility itself as applying to rules rather than directly to particular acts. Either way, the theory becomes less utilitarian.

I postpone looking at rule utilitarianism, for the moment. For there is a far more urgent problem than mere distributive equity. The "greater good" justi-fication for harm sets no upper limit to the extremity of harm that any individ-ual might be made to suffer in order to produce benefits for others. This is why the slavery example is so powerful. The problem is not just that slave labor is stolen. People who are enslaved too often have no effective protection against such things as torture, murder, malnutrition, the breakup of their families through sale, and, of course, no freedom to determine the course of their own lives. The utilitarian rationale appealing simply to benefits that outweigh harms seems compatible with letting a few die (or killing them outright) to spare many others a significant but nonfatal hardship. Drug testers for phar-maceutical companies face this temptation, as do automobile manufacturers tempted to decide, by cost-benefit analysis, to pay the costs of lawsuits rather than to recall vehicles to correct an unsafe design. Yet such choices are not only morally outrageous. They are evil, even if done to try to fight or guard against other evils.[14] Genocide is an evil way to reduce population in order to relieve a hunger problem, even if those killed were already unhappy and the survivors would have a relatively high quality of life. Slavery was an evil way to produce and maintain the material foundation of a society, even if without it farmers would have had shorter and harder lives and there would have been no leisure class to produce or commission poetry, music, and painting.[15]

Contrary to initial appearances, Bentham's utilitarianism does not clearly give prominence to sufferers. Rather, it gives prominence to suffering, ab-stracted from the lives of sufferers. Both utilitarian justifications—the "greater good" argument and the "no better alternative" argument—invite us to treat harms and goods as fungible, like money, as though we could interchange their forms with no serious change in value simply by making appropriate adjustments in quantity. Bentham's calculus, directing one to sum up the harms and benefits done to everyone affected and see where the balance lies, does not distinguish atrocities from lesser harms. By the process he advocates for estimating overall harm, an enormous number of minor harms appear to add up to an atrocity. But often they do not. Robbing millions of people of five dollars each is not worse than conning a retired couple out of their modest life savings. The point is not that numbers don't matter for an atrocity. Murdering millions is worse than murdering a few. The point is that the concepts "beneficial on the whole" and "least harmful on the whole" are too ambiguous to enable us to identify or rule out atrocities.

Mill's version of utilitarianism appears less vulnerable to this difficulty. He argued that we should consider quality in benefits and harms, not just quantity, in determining where the greater good lies (U 330–35). It is not obvious that Mill would have thought that minor harms add up to an atrocity. His "criterion of the only competent judges" comes close to acknowledging that some deprivations are such that no one who has had adequate experience of them and the capacity to appreciate them would voluntarily choose to endure them for any quantity of some kinds of benefits.[16] Introducing this criterion is a gesture in the right direction. It suggests that there are at least some goods no quantity of which could balance some serious deprivations. But it is not very specific and does not go far enough. It does not clearly rule out the drug tester's trade-off between known risks of fatality and serious relief for many. Although Mill's quality criterion estimates the value of different kinds of experiences, it is not a new definition of right and wrong. It does not indicate how such judgments of quality are to weigh in the determination of what to do—how, for example, conflicts between quality and quantity of harms and benefits affecting different individuals are to be resolved.

A different difficulty with the utilitarian definition of wrong is that it grants no special weight to the sufferer's choice, that is, no weight independent of the utility of the choice. It gives no special weight to a sufferer's refusal to consent to indoctrination, mind-numbing drugs, compulsory lobotomy, or "euthanasia," which could reduce or eliminate severe suffering and would ordinarily be such that the subject would afterward surely not regret the treatment. Involuntary treatment violates the sufferer's autonomy, even when it reduces overall dissatisfaction. Straightforwardly hedonistic utilitarianism, such as Bentham's, cannot convincingly explain why "involuntary euthanasia" of the suffering terminally ill is an evil.[17]

Mill, of course, argued that it is more useful in the long run to grant people autonomy, to respect their choices (L 248–71). But the meaning of "utility" shifts in his arguments, as he appeals to what kind of person we esteem and not just to the satisfaction of desires we happen to have. "It really is of importance," he wrote, "not only what men do but also what manner of men they are that do it" (L 253). This shift transforms his thought from straightforward utilitarianism into something significantly more stoic, bringing it closer to the ethics of Kant and Aristotle.[18]

This shift is not the only way Mill's "utilitarianism" moves in the direction of stoic ethics. He has also been interpreted as offering a version of rule utilitarianism, which appears to some critics to respond to the objection that the principle of utility is compatible with unacceptable distributions of harm and benefits.[19] According to rule utilitarianism, individual acts are justifiable by appeal to rules, provided the rules have a utilitarian justification; they are not justified by direct appeal to the principle of utility, except when rules conflict.[20] It allows that an act can be wrong by violating a useful rule, even though the act is more beneficial than alternatives. This view appeals not to actual or even probable harm but to hypothetical harm, harm that would result if enough others engaged in relevantly similar acts (even if they do not). Because the appeal is to a hypothetical harm that may be extremely improbable, it is not clear that this theory should be regarded as a form of utilitarianism. Some regard it as a compromise theory, lying between utilitarianism and something more Kantian.[21] One might also find it stoic insofar as it respects one's ability to act on principle independently of the causal effectiveness of doing so.

Mill appears to articulate such an idea with approval in chapter 2 of *Utilitarianism* when he writes, "In the case of abstinences indeed—of things which people forbear to do from moral considerations, though the consequences in the particular case might be beneficial—it would be unworthy of an intelligent agent not to be consciously aware that the action is of a class, which, if practised generally, would be generally injurious, and that this is the ground of the obligation to abstain from it" (U 344). It is not clear that Mill intended this kind of argument to apply to all kinds of acts, since he specifies "in the case of abstinences." Although he thinks we usually rely on rules handed down from prior generations (U 350–52), he does not regard rules as sacred but argues that the principle of utility, which establishes them in the first place, can also justify exceptions to them. He shows no explicit awareness of differences between justifying exceptions to rules that are based on hypothetical collective harm and justifying exceptions to rules that are simply summaries of the likely harm of individual acts (what Rawls calls "rules of thumb").[22] When Mill acknowledges that we must apply the principle of utility directly to individual acts in cases where rules conflict (U 352), he does not appeal to the hypothetical consequences of everyone's resolving the conflict in the same way. This is a difficulty for those, such as J. O. Urmson, who wish to interpret Mill as a rule utilitarian.[23]

Bentham is also sometimes regarded as a rule utilitarian because his motivating concern was to reform criminal legislation, which consists of enacted rules. But Bentham acknowledges no special differences between acts of legislation and any other acts; the principle of utility, apparently, is to apply to all of them alike. Yet an act of legislation is higher order—an act that is about (governs) other acts (which it prohibits or requires). Higher order acts present a complexity for utilitarian thinking that Bentham does not address. His "principles of morals and legislation" appears to assume that the principle of utility offers both a theory of legislation and a general ethical theory, as though the only significant difference were in the numbers of people affected by legislation and by the lower order acts of individuals.

To avoid confusion regarding so-called act utilitarianism, given that legislative acts are acts, too, the difference between so-called act and rule utilitarianism is sometimes marked by contemporary theorists with the terms "direct" and "indirect" utilitarianism.[24] Indirect, or rule, utilitarianism offers a good response to the free rider problem and thereby, potentially, to serious evils to which free riding can lead (such as environmental poisoning). But it does not adequately address evils in the rules themselves. Free riders make themselves unfair (arbitrary) exceptions to a rule or practice, enjoying the benefits it makes possible without doing their part to produce or maintain those benefits. But such unfairness is not the problem with evil practices, such as enslavement of captured people or compulsory "euthanasia" of people with disabilities. These practices are evil no matter how fairly (evenly) their rules are applied. Here the distribution and severity problems reassert themselves, unless the principle of utility is restricted by independent principles of equality that embody a respect for human beings, both as agents and as sufferers.

Rawls's Theory of Justice: A Response to Utilitarianism

Valuing freedom from basic harms need not imply a valuing of agency. But valuing agency should imply caring about basic harms, as they tend to corrupt and destroy one's capacity for agency. To identify evil practices, we should look for basic harms to which they expose us or from which they fail to protect us. Rawls's theory of justice comes close to centering this concern, although he emphasizes opportunities and goods rather than protection or harms. His principles make a valuable contribution to the wrongdoing component of a theory of evil. They do not support evil practices, and they do identify an important area—social injustice—within which we can expect to find social evils. Rawls's theory does not itself, however, sort out evils from lesser injustices.

Rawls's principles of justice appear to have evolved specifically to meet objections to utilitarianism. Although he does not present the theory as a new form of utilitarianism, he has characterized it as a compromise between utilitarianism and Kant's ethics. Rawls's principles are designed specifically to rule out the possibility of justifying hardships to some people simply by appeal to the benefits thereby made available for others. His two basic principles for institutions that define the basic structure of a society are presented as issuing from a point of view that takes seriously the well-being of each person. They are, first, "the liberty principle," which directs that institutions be so designed that everyone has the greatest basic liberty compatible with a like liberty for all (later, "an equal right to a fully adequate scheme of basic liberties"), and, second, "the difference principle," which specifies that social and economic inequalities are justifiable when (a) the positions to which they attach are open to all under conditions of fair equality of opportunity and (b) no one is made worse off with the inequality than under an equal distribution.[25] "Better off" and "worse off" are to be judged, from the point of view of the representative person affected, in terms of six or seven "primary goods," which he initially thought of as what everyone can be presumed to want, whatever else they may want.[26] The first several—rights and liberties, powers and opportunities, income and wealth—are instrumental goods. The last, self-respect, is an intrinsic good, although it is instrumentally valuable as well. In *Political Liberalism* and the revised edition of *A Theory of Justice*, Rawls defines primary goods as those necessary for the development of two basic moral capacities, the capacity for a conception of the good and the capacity for a sense of justice, emphasizing one's needs as a citizen, rather than one's preferences and desires.[27]

If we classify ethical theories as stoic or utilitarian in their values, Rawls's theory seems almost as utilitarian as it is stoic. Of the seven primary goods, self-respect is the most clearly stoic value, whereas income and wealth are the most clearly utilitarian. The other primary goods—rights and liberties, powers and opportunities—might be either or both, as they facilitate both character development and external security. But it is the stoic values that underlie the defense of his first principle, the greatest equal liberty principle, which allows liberty to be restricted only for the sake of liberty and does not permit trade-offs between basic liberties and income or wealth. The importance of basic liberties lies in what they do for self-respect. Thus, Rawls's theory appears to illustrate even more clearly than Mill's how, in responding to the difficulties of utilitarianism, one can gravitate toward stoicism.

The concept of evil does not explicitly play a role in Rawls's presentation of his theory of justice. Yet examples of gross injustice, such as slavery, prominent in his exposition are evidence that concerns about evils are a significant motivating factor. His published reflections on the bombing of Hiroshima and on the idea of justice among peoples are further evidence.[28] It may be Rawls's intent to distinguish evils from lesser injustices when he specifies that his principles are to govern the basic structure of society, where we have little or no choice and which profoundly affects our lives. However, even that restriction is not sufficient to pick out evils because, if a society is wealthy enough, its basic social institutions can be somewhat unjust without individuals suffering basic harms, without anyone's life being rendered impossible or intolerable. The principles only specify appropriate distributions of whatever wealth the society produces. They do not identify in absolute terms any harms that a just society should protect everyone against.

Avishai Margalit argues persuasively that a *decent* society—one the institutions of which do not humiliate people—need not be a just society, on Rawls's understanding of justice. In *The Law of Peoples* Rawls accepts a distinction between a decent society, which meets certain minimal conditions of right and justice, and a liberal society.[29] But it is not the same as Margalit's distinction. Rawls's conception of a decent society emphasizes citizens' roles in political decision making, whereas Margalit's emphasizes social welfare. A decent society, according to Margalit, avoids the evils of humiliation, even if in other respects it is less than just or positively unjust. His account of the decent society attempts to identify and prioritize some of the worst social wrongs against persons better than a general theory of distributive justice does. He is not concerned with distribution so much as with things that no one should be forced to suffer.

It may seem that Rawls's distinction between injustice and less-than-perfect justice could distinguish between evils and other, less serious departures from justice. A society is less than perfectly just when everyone might be even better off than they already are if additional justifiable inequalities were permitted. It is positively unjust if some groups are allowed to benefit from inequalities at the expense of others' being made even worse off than they would have been under an equal distribution. Although an unjust society is worse than one that is only imperfectly just, even an unjust society does not necessarily tolerate evils. If the society is very well off, even its unjust inequalities need not be such as to make anyone's life intolerable.

Rawls's idea of a social minimum below which no one is permitted to fall also seems like a step in the right direction. He proposes, however, that the social minimum be defined simply as maximizing the prospects of the least advantaged class.[30] But failure to meet a social minimum so defined would not necessarily subject anyone to evils. For the social minimum in a wealthy society may offer far more than is required to make life possible and tolerable or decent for all, so that falling below it could still leave one with a good life.

These difficulties do not, of course, count against the soundness of Rawls's principles as general ethical norms. I find no reason to think his principles would lend support to evils. There is no barrier to their serving as part of a background definition of right for a theory of evil based on the atrocity paradigm. There would be a problem only in treating Rawls's theory of justice as though it were itself also a theory of evil or included a theory of evil. For within Rawls's theory both evils and lesser injustices are wrong (unjust) for exactly the same reasons.

To determine which injustices are evils, we need a conception of basic harms, not simply a theory of primary goods. Basic harms are not just deprivations of primary goods, even on Rawls's revised understanding of them.[31] Not all such deprivations would render anyone's life, or a significant portion of it, impossible or intolerable (or seriously threaten to do so). Both the magnitude and the nature of the deprivation matter, as well as its reversibility and the possibility of compensation. Unlike Rawls's primary goods, which are mainly instrumentally valuable, basic harms need not be regarded mainly as instrumentally harmful (although they are that, too). To review briefly, basic harms include such things as severe and unremitting pain; lacking access to unpolluted water, food, and air; severe and prolonged restrictions on motility (as in being confined to a box that allows one room neither to stand, sit, nor lie down); extreme and prolonged isolation; extreme and prolonged impotence or insecurity; and deprivation of the bases of self-respect and human dignity (including death with dignity). Just as primary goods, as Rawls initially presented them, are what everyone can be presumed to want, whatever else they want, basic harms are the things that everyone can be presumed to want to avoid, whatever else they may want. Ascetics and those severely depressed may subject or expose themselves to such hardships because they have ceased to care, or think they deserve no better, or perhaps to prove they can do it. But, aside from building endurance, it is difficult to imagine anyone else voluntarily undergoing any such hardships for the sake of something else that they wanted.

Death is not on my list of basic harms. Although murder is an evil, that is not because death is an intolerable harm. Death itself is neither a harm nor a benefit but a natural fact of life. Death can be wrongfully caused, however, and the manner of death can be extremely harmful. Loss of the opportunity to live out a meaningful life can be a major harm. Whether the death penalty inflicts that harm, especially on young offenders, is controversial. Some would argue that the capital offender already threw away that opportunity in committing the offense.

Too often, however, criminal punishments have subjected convicted offenders to basic harms. That fact should make the justification of criminal punishment more difficult than philosophers have usually found it. It should not be necessary, even in inflicting the death penalty, to subject the convicted offender to basic harms. Ironically, during the past two centuries, when imprisonment was substituted for allegedly more inhumane corporal punishments, corporal cruelties have reappeared behind prison walls in the interests of maintaining discipline, where lack of public access makes exposure of the evils more difficult and less likely.

If utilitarianism, with its war on evil, seemed initially the most promising theory, stoic ethics seems initially the least promising for an adequate conception of evil. The problems of stoicism are opposite to those of utilitarianism. Stoicism discounts suffering, defines wrong in abstraction from it, and emphasizes how sufferers can still make life worth living. Critics have long objected to stoicism's tendency to discourage active resistance to social injustice. Insofar as active resistance can bring constructive change, this objection is serious. Even more troubling, however, may be the stoic's refusal to acknowledge the reality of social evils to be opposed.

But it is also true that a good theory of evil needs a stoic component in that it must give attention to the value of the will, independently of the value of the satisfaction of needs and desires. Further, given the comfort stoicism offers those whose prospects are truly hopeless, this kind of theory is worth a closer look.

The Stoic Defense Against Evil

A good contemporary source of the views of ancient stoic philosophers is A. A. Long and D. N. Sedley, *The Hellenistic Philosophers*, vol. 1, which includes a substantial section on stoic ethics, offering translations from Diogenes Laertius, Seneca, Epictetus, Hierocles, Plutarch, Cicero, Stobaeus, Sextus Empiricus, and, occasionally, anonymous authors.[32] I rely on this work and on Epictetus's *Discourses* and *Manual*, as translated by Whitney Oates for the Modern Library in *The Stoic and Epicurean Philosophers*.[33]

Stoic ethics begins by noting that some things are within our control whereas others are not and that ethics is concerned only with the former. Classical stoics had a fairly extreme view about the extent to which outward things elude our control, which led them to the conclusion that good and evil concern only uses of the will, the one area that remains within our control. This conclusion and its implications have come under critical scrutiny by Martha Nussbaum.

Nussbaum has not been so concerned to argue that stoics exaggerate our powerlessness as to question the premise that ethics is concerned only with what is within our control. The importance of contingencies for both the value of our lives and the quality of our character is a theme in many of her essays and in her book *The Fragility of Goodness: Luck and Ethics in Greek Tragedy and Philosophy*. Resisting the views that it is a mistake to attach great significance to contingencies, that we are wrong to place high value on what eludes our control, and that we can assure our own goodness by having the right values, she writes, with simple elegance:

> That I am an agent, but also a plant; that much that I did not make goes towards making me whatever I shall be praised or blamed for being; that I must constantly choose among competing and apparently incommensurable goods and that circumstances may force me to a position in which I cannot help being false to something or doing some wrong; that an event that simply happens to me may, without my consent, alter my life; that it is equally problematic to entrust one's good to friends, lovers, or country and to try to have a good life without them—all these I take to be not just the material of tragedy, but everyday facts of lived practical reason.[34]

Her later work on emotion suggests that it is *more* problematic to try to have a good life without entrusting one's good to friends, lovers, country, or something else that eludes one's control.[35] For without such commitments and risks, she argues, emotions would have no proper place in our lives. Our lives would not be fully human.

To continue this thought, without emotions, we would not mind anything others did to us. We would find intolerable no harms resulting from their wrongdoing. They could do us no evil. All we should find intolerable would be to do wrong ourselves—although even that suggests that we would not be entirely devoid of emotional response.

The ancient stoics did not agree that emotions have no proper place in a virtuous life. Epictetus (ca. 60–110 C.E.), a freed slave, advised adopting attitudes of caution regarding what is up to us and confidence regarding what is not (Oates 281). Caution and confidence are fairly general emotional attitudes. It is unclear what beliefs they embody about the values of things. But Diogenes Laertius reports more specific good feelings also endorsed by the stoics:

> (1) They [the Stoics] say that there are three good feelings: joy, watchfulness, wishing. (2) Joy, they say, is the opposite of pleasure, consisting in well-reasoned swelling [elation]; and watchfulness is the opposite of fear, consisting in well-reasoned shrinking. For the wise man will not be afraid at all, but he will be watchful. (3) They say that wishing is the opposite of appetite, consisting in well-reasoned stretching [desire]. (4) Just as certain passions fall under the primary ones, so too with the primary good feelings. Under wishing: kindness, generosity, warmth, affection. Under watchfulness: respect, cleanliness. Under joy: delight, sociability, cheerfulness. (Diogenes Laertius 412)

The emotions Nussbaum has in mind—fear, anger, grief—more clearly embody judgments that acknowledge our neediness and dependence (our plant side). Her point should not be misunderstood as one about intensity of feeling; it is not that stoic emotions (if we grant them) are comparatively pale. The point is, rather, about the kinds of emotions stoicism cannot support, because of what they reveal about the nature of our attachments.

Following Nussbaum, I understand stoicism as fundamentally the idea that good character, good willing, or good agency, is the most important value (for extreme stoics, the only thing that is truly good), along with the corollary that it is a mistake to place great value on contingencies, on what eludes or exceeds our control (for extreme stoics, that such things have no true value at all but are "indifferent"). This understanding of stoicism survives in the popular paradigm of a stoic attitude, the ability to bear pain or suffering calmly and without flinching, insofar as what underlies that attitude is the sufferer's assignment of an insignificant value to pain or suffering. A stoic outlook on life suggests not cultivating unnecessary tastes (fine wines) or desires (for the pleasures of skiing), to avoid the quest for ever more refined or exciting experiences and being overwhelmed by disappointment or no longer able to appreciate simple things in hard times. A stoic might not have animal companions, to avoid grieving at their deaths, or might resist falling in love to avoid its nonrequital. Those who cultivate such tastes or attachments would be careful what weight they placed on them and would maintain a certain reserve. Cultivating detachment, stoics resist being seduced by life. Nussbaum mentions Cicero's story of the father who said, upon being informed of his son's death, "I was already aware that I had begotten a mortal."[36]

She also notes, however, that, paradoxically, no major thinker in the stoic tradition has been willing to conclude that benevolence does not matter at all.[37] Ancient stoic ethics emphasized not only the importance of what we control but also the concept of living according to nature. Living according to nature meant acknowledging that for the kind of beings we are, it is natural to prefer some things (such as nourishing food and other "externals" that meet our physical needs) and likewise natural to acknowledge such preferences in others. But such "preferables," he maintained, are not genuinely good. Apparently, it is just that in a virtuous life, it is preferable to have them (rather than not to). Epictetus says they are in themselves neither good nor bad but indifferent. Responding to the question which things are "indifferent," he wrote, "things which lie outside the will's control," that "things indifferent concern me not at all" but good things are "a right will and a faculty of dealing rightly with impressions" (Oates 280). Benevolent concern for others' needs, then, seems grounded both in the acknowledgment of our common nature and in the feelings of generosity and kindness subsumed in Diogenes Laertius' report under the "good emotion" of joy. But, then, what does it mean to say of externals that they are indifferent?

In modern terms, Epictetus apparently wished to acknowledge as good only what is worthy of esteem and not what is merely worthy of desire. The modern concept of goodness as desirability seems to have no place in classical stoic philosophy. Yet Epictetus also appears to recommend, under the heading of "living according to nature," pursuing what is worthy of desire, as long as it does not interfere with the pursuit of what is noble.

To modern ears, there is a self-contradiction in the claim that what is indifferent is nevertheless worthy of pursuit. We hear indifference as a lacking of worthiness, leaving us unmoved. To find something worthy of pursuit is not to be totally indifferent toward it. And yet to live in accord with nature, one needs to be moved somewhat by the so-called "indifferents." According to the stoics, it is apparently natural to be so moved.

Lawrence Becker's "new stoicism" emphasizes primarily the theme of living according to nature. He presents an account of virtue as the capstone of such a life.[38] Virtue, on his account, is the perfection of agency. It is the ability to act, rather than the ability to control, that becomes the important thing. He finds unjustified the image of stoics as cold and unfeeling, although he does support their "hard doctrines" that virtue is unified, that it is the proper end of all activity, that it is "sufficient for happiness even on the rack," and that it does not admit of degrees.[39] He does not support the view that virtue is the *only* good, however, and he acknowledges that extreme suffering can undermine agency. But "the damage torture does to happiness," he says, "comes from the malice of the torturer and her defeat of the victim's agency, not from the pain she causes."[40] If this claim also gives an account of what is wrong with torture, it is very like the Kantian argument against murder and mayhem that Barbara Herman offers in her reading of Kant's ethics, which I take up in the next chapter.

What epitomizes stoicism for me, as for Nussbaum, is not the idea of living according to nature but the idea that true value (or the most important kind of value) is to be found only in one's will or inner self, that this is ultimately who one is, because this is what is most up to oneself. This element of stoicism in Kant's ethics has troubled Bernard Williams in his explorations of the idea of moral luck.[41] A major difference between the ancient stoics and Kant is, of course, that the stoics did not regard the inner self as nonmaterial. But the point concerns what is within our control, not what is or is not material.

Lest my presentation of stoicism sound too unattractive, I freely acknowledge that stoicism can protect us against being overwhelmed by misfortune that is genuinely beyond our power to mitigate in any other way. It can help us maintain dignity and self-respect under otherwise intolerable circumstances. It may offer a kind of salvation to slaves, for example. I also grant that if an emotionally impoverished life is less than human, a life reduced to misery by misfortune is not fully human, either. For consider to what fortune can expose us. Our friends and family can be murdered, our money and property stolen, our houses destroyed, our bodies maimed; we can be raped, tortured, starved, deprived of water and sleep, and finally infected with the diseases that follow lack of sanitation. That these are extremes is no reason to discount them, for they are common enough. Civilians suffer them in war globally, and individual victims can do little about them. Perhaps this is why Nussbaum often does not so much argue against stoicism as explore its implications, leaving readers to draw their own conclusions, appropriate to their circumstances.

But, as she also sees, the difficulties with stoicism run deep. For if control is what is at issue, it is not as though we have complete control over who we are or who we become, either. We have no control over what Rawls calls our "starting places" in life, the circumstances of our birth and early childhood, not only the social and economic positions of our parents but also their parenting skills and their choices about how to treat us, even whether we have parents who survive to care for us and choose to care for us.[42] With moderate luck and hard work, we can overcome some early disadvantages. And yet our wills are not invulnerable to fortune, and we cannot make them so simply by what we choose to value.[43] Even to develop our capacities for activity and control, we may need to embrace life through passionate attachments to others, and these attachments can be disastrous when they go bad.

Passionate attachments render our wills vulnerable at the same time that they offer potentialities for positive growth. If those for whom we care are murdered, we may end by losing our own self-respect and dignity. We may become monstrous in seeking revenge. Nussbaum takes Euripides' *Hecuba* as an example of someone whose character deteriorates under horrendous reversals of fortune.[44] After she has been enslaved and her daughter Polyxena sacrificed, Hecuba learns of the murder of her youngest son by the man with whom he was left for safekeeping. This knowledge tips her over the edge and sets her on a plan of terrible revenge that leaves her son's murderer blind and his own two children dead.[45] Hecuba becomes monstrous, inhuman. The stoic might say of Hecuba that had she not been so attached to her children and to continued worldly existence and the potential future restorations of power that especially the boy symbolized, she might have preserved her dignity and integrity, even her humanity. Yet, without such attachments, it is unclear also what humanity would have remained to her to preserve.

We do not need so dramatic a case as Hecuba to see how any of us might deteriorate. We can find ourselves between that rock and a hard place where to save a friend or loved one we must commit a wrong we would not otherwise have dreamt of. As Nussbaum notes, circumstances can force us to choose to what we will be false or whom we will wrong. We wrong a friend or we wrong someone else, not necessarily in acting unjustifiably but in causing hardships that are undeserved. If psychologists are right that having once crossed the line of wronging others makes doing so again and doing worse easier—as we may feel that we have less to lose the next time in the way of preserving a good self image or our dignity or integrity—such conflicts can initiate character deterioration.[46] Cultivating and expanding our relationships with others increases the likelihood that we will confront such conflicts, hence the likelihood of some that are not satisfactorily resolvable. (At the same time, it may increase our resources to meet them.) The point is that to embrace fortune is to take risks with our peace of mind and integrity, not just with our material well-being. This fact offers yet another reason that one may find stoicism attractive.

Nussbaum argues, further, that we will be unable to develop certain virtues without acknowledging the value of what eludes our control. Compassion, which lies at the root of mercy, is unlikely to be forthcoming in those who find it problematic to acknowledge human neediness and dependence.[47] It is not just one's own suffering that the stoic devalues but suffering in general. If so, then virtues that invoke compassion, such as the sense of justice—if Rawls is right about its connections with love and trust—are also unlikely to develop.[48]

Stoics may not find this an objection. They may find compassion a weakness, as Nietzsche did, rather than a virtue. They may develop understandings of justice that do not presuppose it. Stoics may find that those who seek compassion make too much of their bad luck, have the wrong values, are not tough enough, that they are more vulnerable to fortune than one need be. Stoics may take offense at others' sympathy and find it an affront to their pride and dignity in bearing up under trying circumstances.

The implications of stoicism, so understood, are troubling specifically for a theory of evil. Nussbaum seems right, especially in addressing academics, to focus on what we lose if we opt for stoicism. Much philosophy, as she notes, is an exercise in intellectual self-control and discipline. Combining that observation with what she says about mercy and compassion might explain the cruelty of many philosophers and other intellectuals, which can otherwise be astonishing. The costs of stoicism that worry me most are its failures to perceive and appreciate the evils of cruelty and oppression. My fear is not that stoics would initiate such evils but that they would be unmoved to prevent or alleviate them. As has often been noted, all that is required for evil to prevail is that good people do nothing.[49]

In refusing to take seriously most of the basic harms in the atrocity theory of evil, stoicism is unable to make adequate sense of the concept of atrocity or even of cruelty. One might even wonder whether stoicism had any place at all for the concept of evil. Yet Epictetus writes, "The essence of good and of evil lies in an attitude of the will" (Oates 275). He makes the following puzzling distinction. In a chapter on how a careful life is compatible with a noble spirit, he writes that it is not that outward things (in themselves indifferent) are to be used without care. That, he finds, is an evil. "They must be used with care," he says, "for their use is not a matter of indifference" although "in themselves they are indifferent" (Oates 288). Again, he writes, "though life is indifferent, the way you deal with it is not indifferent" (Oates 290).

But why is the way one uses outward things not indifferent, if outward things themselves are? What defines how one uses a thing as a correct or incorrect use of the will? Stoics need to distinguish right from wrong uses of the will without appealing to the value of what exceeds our control. Yet I find in their writings no illuminating answer to the question of how to make that distinction. Kant does offer a principle for the right use of the will (his Categorical Imperative), which is intended not to appeal to the value of what eludes our control, and that will be examined in the next chapter.

Even though Epictetus did not count *suffering* cruelty an evil, he did not want to deny that *inflicting* cruelty (*being* cruel) is evil, although it remains mysterious why. Cruelty is, apparently, a misuse of the will. The important things, he finds, are to resist *becoming* evil and to resist being defeated by the evil that others do. What matters is not to oppose others' conduct but to maintain the right values oneself and resist any temptation to do wrong. But if cruelty to others does them no harm, why is it wrong? To say that it harms the perpetrator begs the question. For it harms the perpetrator only if it is wrong. It does not necessarily make the perpetrator feel bad or less able to perform basic functions.

If it is impossible to harm others who place no special value on what eludes their control, stoics could not be harmed by anything others did to them, even though their bodies could be maimed and their lives terminated. For the stoic, to inflict or suffer a loss merely of "what one reasonably prefers" is not to inflict or suffer true harm. One is harmed only by having the wrong attitudes, and the attitudes we have, according to the stoics, are up to us. We neither harm nor wrong others in embracing the wrong values, even if they suffer from it. For our embracing the values we embrace is beyond their control (so he appears to have thought), whereas what they make of their suffering is not.

On this view, the Czechoslovakian Jews from Terezin, in "the family camp" at Auschwitz, who walked into the gas chambers singing the Czech national anthem and the Hatikva arguably suffered no evil.[50] For they retained their spiritual dignity to the very end; their wills were not broken. If those who value what eludes their control are thereby responsible for their own misery when they suffer at the hands of others, stoic wrongdoers cannot truly harm others, let alone do them evil. If they harm anyone, it is only themselves (by holding the wrong values). For the stoic, all that evil can possibly consist in is wrongdoing itself. All evils are, apparently, self-inflicted.

Like utilitarianism, stoicism collapses distinctions among the concepts of evil, wrongdoing, and harm, but in the opposite direction. For the utilitarian evil consists simply in the infliction of harm, which also defines wrongdoing. For the stoic evil consists simply in wrongdoing, which is the only true harm there is. Each kind of theory fails to capture atrocities as paradigms of evil, but for different reasons. Despite the good intentions of the classical utilitarians, the principle of utility might actually be invoked to justify what most would regard as atrocities (such as genocidal "ethnic cleansing") when a net balance of satisfaction resulted. Stoics should have difficulty, however, regarding as an atrocity any deprivation of goods needed for survival and any infliction of bodily harm, regardless of how massive or even fatal. Although, paradoxically, stoics might find it virtuous to assist others in need of material support, it is not clear that they would find it wrong not to.

Stoicism carried to such conclusions becomes extreme self-reliance.[51] It leaves little or no room for ethics in interpersonal relationships and social interaction. How could we betray each other if we did not trust to begin with? (Others' trustworthiness is beyond our control). If trust goes, who is wronged by lying and deception? Would stealing wrong anyone, if no one should be so attached to worldly goods as to suffer greatly from their loss? Why regard even murder as a wrong, if the true self is invulnerable? If morality in particular, as distinct from ethics in general, is socially oriented, it appears that stoics should reject most of morality, or at least the importance most people attach to it today. Perhaps Nussbaum is right about Nietzsche's stoicism.[52] Perhaps it was a stoic strain that led Nietzsche in that direction.

Since stoics do not regard the will itself as indifferent, we might expect them to regard evil as consisting not simply in the wrong use of the will but in the damaging of someone's will. The classical stoics, however, seem not to have considered the possibility of damage to the will itself, as opposed to misuse of the will. Today we take very seriously the possibility of damaging a person's will, diminishing a person's capacity for agency. Wrongful tampering with the ability of others to choose for themselves is an evil that the twentieth century has seen in the form of involuntary brain surgery, torture, and "brainwashing." If nothing is truly invulnerable, not even the will, then, to be consistent, extreme stoics should either abandon the claim that what exceeds our control has no true value or else admit that nothing, not even the will, is a source of true value, thereby becoming value nihilists. On the latter option, evil of any sort would become impossible.

We might argue that the stoic rejection of life is mistaken because we truly are needy and dependent beings. The illusion of becoming invulnerable to fortune is just that, an illusion.[53] Even stoics must acknowledge the reasonableness of the desire to avoid mental deterioration, so as to remain in control of their attitudes. But then, one might ask (in a Nietzschean mood), so what's wrong with illusions? Sometimes they can offer just what we need in order to go on.

Yet morally, we are not free to adjust our values for peace of mind whenever fortune is unkind. The stoics saw rightly that evil includes wrongful willing and that wrongful willing is not just a matter of causing suffering but is also exhibited in our attitudes toward and the values we place on ourselves and others as agents. But they need a fuller account of what constitute wrongful uses of the will, how wrongful willing differs from right willing. And even with such an account, wrongful willing is only a necessary condition of evil, not by itself sufficient. The other condition is that of harm.

4

Kant's Theory of Radical Evil

Kant's Stoicism

Immanuel Kant's ethics, today's paradigm of deontology, is basically stoic in its values. Kant's stoicism presents problems for his theory of evil that are opposite to the problems presented by utilitarianism. For it implies that the sufferings of victims are just incidental, not part of what makes evil deeds evil. Kant's stoicism is also an obstacle even to his being able to recognize important distinctions regarding forms of principled immorality and hence, evil. But his analysis has the virtue of showing a variety of ways in which people can come to do evil and of considering some possible relationships among them.

The stoic ideal is present in Kant's reduction of moral character to the good will, which he understands not as benevolence but as the will to do one's duty. A sympathetic disposition is no part of moral character, on his view. We can base the maxims of our actions on regard for duty even if we are unable to act on them successfully, but it is sheer coincidence, he thinks, if emotional attitudes incline us to do what duty requires. There is stoicism in Kant's tendency to regard inclinations as stumbling blocks to virtue. They tempt us to put too much value on contingencies. Stoicism may explain Kant's early paradoxical advice concerning friendship, which he finds consists at its best in mutual trust (not mutual aid). He advises us to so conduct ourselves toward friends that no harm is done should they become our enemies. Do not tell them secrets, for example, that they could one day use against us. This attitude leaves little room for the defining ideal of trust. Perhaps a realization of this implication led him to conclude that "by friendship we cultivate virtue in little things" (LE 27:423–430; Heath 184–90).[1]

On several philosophical issues, Kant differs from the ancient stoics. They were metaphysical materialists and did not believe in the incorporeality or immortality of the soul. They did not find suicide wrong. They identified happiness with virtue, whereas for Kant, happiness and virtue are distinct and need not go together. Kant was a Protestant Christian who, apparently, believed in an afterlife (at least, he defended belief in it as a rational faith). His metaphysics of noumena (reality) and phenomena (appearances) confines physicality to phenomena. The immorality of suicide is one of four central examples he offers to illustrate the application of his Categorical Imperative (which he identifies with the moral law). Still, in the value Kant places on agency, rationality, the will, and what we can control, his ethics is very stoic.

With his Categorical Imperative Kant offers an answer to the question raised for stoicism in chapter 3 about what it means to misuse the will, and he does so without appealing to the value of things that elude our control. The will is misused when the maxim of one's action cannot be willed universally without contradiction. In doing evil, we make ourselves less worthy—less worthy of happiness and certainly unworthy of esteem. If that is a harm, we harm ourselves. But whereas for the classical stoics evil deeds cannot truly victimize others, for Kant, evil deeds do not necessarily do so, although they can. His stoicism is more moderate than that of Epictetus.

In his *Groundwork of the Metaphysics of Morals* Kant introduces the good will as the only thing unconditionally (absolutely) good and as furthermore the condition of the goodness of anything else (G 393–94; Gregor 49–50), such as intelligence or even happiness. Yet he makes clear in the *Critique of Practical Reason* that he does not regard even the good will as the highest or complete good. Better than the good will alone is the union of a good will with happiness (CPrR 5:122–25; Gregor 238–40). "Happiness," he says in the second Critique, "is the state of a rational being in the world in the whole of whose existence *everything goes according to his wish and will*, and rests, therefore, on the harmony of nature with his whole end as well as with the essential determining ground of his will" (emphasis in the original; CPrR 5:125; Gregor 240). Whereas ancient stoics identified happiness with virtue, for Kant, happiness is virtue's deserved reward. We determine our own virtue by our choices, and we can significantly affect others' happiness, by satisfying or frustrating their desires. But we are powerless to insure the combination in either ourselves or others of both good will (virtue) and happiness. Only a deity would have the power to do that. Kant offers this belief, along with a duty to promote the highest good, to support the rationality of theistic faith. Thus, unlike the ancient stoics, Kant does recognize value in outward things (things that bring happiness), although for him their value is conditional on the presence of a good will.

An ambivalence runs through Kant's writings on aid and such related topics as gratitude.[2] Yet he does not find concern for atrocity victims misplaced. He finds it a duty to help others in distress, and he discourages avoidance of the sick and the poor (MM 6:457; Gregor 575). He also finds gratitude owed for favors rendered. Still, his concern with evil remains primarily a concern for the moral purity of potential perpetrators rather than for the quality or decency of the lives of potential victims.[3]

Like the ancient stoics, Kant does not regard our desires as central to who we really are. Interests and inclinations belong to us as phenomenal beings, whereas the will is noumenal (real). In the *Groundwork*, Kant associates acting on empirical desires and inclinations with heteronomy: "I will therefore call this basic principle [the Categorical Imperative] the principle of the *autonomy* of the will in contrast with every other, which I accordingly count as *heteronomy*" (emphasis in the original; G 4:433; Gregor 83). He associates heteronomy with natural necessity: "Natural necessity was a heteronomy of efficient causes, since every effect was possible only in accordance with the law that something else determines the efficient cause to causality" (G 4:446–7; Gregor 94). One can easily form the impression (as some have) that Kant thinks that when we do wrong, acting on an interest or inclination that conflicts with the moral law, we are determined only (heteronomously) by things external to ourselves, whereas when we act from duty, we are determined only (autonomously) by a moral law that we give ourselves. On that view, we would be responsible only for our right choices, not also for our wrong ones.

But, of course, that cannot have been Kant's intention, as he maintains in that same work that all of our acts, right or wrong, are capable of being regarded as both free and determined—determined as phenomenal and free as noumenal:

> [A] rational being must regard himself *as intelligence* . . . as belonging not to the world of sense but to the world of understanding; hence he has two standpoints from which he can regard himself and cognize laws for the use of his powers and consequently for **all his actions**: *first*, insofar as he belongs to the world of sense, under laws of nature (heteronomy); *second*, as belonging to the intelligible world, under laws which, being independent of nature, are not empirical but grounded merely in reason." (italics in the original; boldface mine; G 4:452; Gregor 99)

Yet Kant does not explain in the *Groundwork* how in doing wrong we are also determined by our noumenal selves, that is, autonomously. In *Religion Within the Boundaries of Mere Reason* Kant offers a more complex account of human motivation, which enables him to clarify this point.

Radical Evil

Kant's *Religion* distinguishes two levels of the will's action. At the level of "intelligible action," one adopts (although not in the world of time and space) a supreme principle for oneself, such as the Categorical Imperative. At the level of empirical action (in time and space), one performs in accordance with the supreme principle that one has adopted (R 6:31; Wood and di Giovanni 79), for example, by telling the truth even when tempted not to. The first deed may be regarded, following John Silber, as legislative.[4] Apparently, it is *only* intelligible, whereas the second, which applies the legislation, has both an intelligible and an empirical aspect. Both deeds are products of a free will.

Radical evil, for Kant, consists in making self-interest (which he identifies with prudence) one's supreme practical principle, subordinating the moral law to it. The "legislation" adopting this ordering is an intelligible action. Evil does not consist fundamentally in temporal (empirical) violations of the moral law, such as telling lies, although one whose will is evil surely will perform such acts sooner or later. Because prudence and morality often do not conflict, we can be radically evil, according to Kant, even while our temporal actions happen not to violate the moral law. We do the outwardly right thing, but for the wrong reason. Radical evil consists in the preparedness, because of the principle one has made supreme for one's conduct, to violate the moral law when its requirements conflict with pursuing one's interests.

In the *Religion*, Kant distinguishes three stages of "the natural propensity to evil in human beings" (R 6:29–30; Wood and di Giovanni 77–78). In the first stage, weakness, we adopt the right supreme principle (the Categorical Imperative) but give in on occasion to a desire or inclination that conflicts with it. This possibility requires a modification of Kant's conception of empirical choices, as it implies that our will in space and time does not necessarily *apply* our intelligible legislation but can *violate* it. Such conduct reveals that we have not developed enough strength of character to abide by our own principles. Although we do wrong, we are, arguably, not *radically* evil because our will is still good in what it legislates, although insufficiently strong to abide by its own legislation. Observers, however, may know only that we do wrong, not whether we do it from weakness or on principle.

In Kant's second stage of evil we act from morally impure (mixed) motives. Here, duty is not the only motive on which we rely to do as duty requires. We rely partly on interests or inclinations. As long as we act in accord with duty, to observers there may appear nothing wrong. But we act partly for the wrong reasons. We are honest not only because duty requires it but also from fear of a bad reputation. Although impurity also, arguably, is not radically evil, Kant finds it more dangerous than mere weakness, even though weak agents actually do wrong, whereas those with impure motives may not. Impurity is more dangerous because it begins a process of corruption in the will. It sets one on a slippery slope at the bottom of which one does not rely on the motive of duty at all. For this reason, Kant rejects methods of purportedly moral education that cite the prudential advantages of doing what is right.

Kant's third stage is reached at the bottom of the slippery slope. Here we have finally reversed the order of our practical principles. We now subordinate the requirements of duty to the pursuit of self-interest, rather than limiting that pursuit by duty. Only at this point is it quite clear that a radically evil will has emerged. Evil is finally rooted unambiguously in the legislative will, not just expressed in particular choices or existing ambiguously in mixed motivations.

Although Kant's good will is the will to do one's duty for duty's sake, there is, on his view, no such thing as the will to do wrong *for its own sake*. A radically evil will is not analogous, in that way, to a good one. "Hence the difference, whether the human being is good or evil, must not lie in the difference between the incentives that he incorporates into his maxim (not in the material of the maxim) but in their *subordination* (in the form of the maxim): *which of the two he makes the condition of the other*. It follows that the human being (even the best) is evil only because he reverses the moral order of incentives. . . . [H]e makes the incentives of self-love and their inclinations the condition of compliance with the moral law" (emphases in the original; R 6:36; Wood and di Giovanni 83). We do wrong for the sake of an interest or inclination, not for wrongness' sake. Doing wrong for its own sake would be, according to Kant, diabolical, not human. Human beings, he maintained, are never diabolical.

We can now see Kant's explanation of how we are responsible for our own wrongdoing. Although we do not choose our desires or inclinations, we choose what importance to accord them. In acting wrongly, we accord our desires or inclinations more importance than duty. We are not simply determined by them. We choose to let them determine what we do, just as in acting from duty, we choose to let the moral law be the determiner. Thus, even our wrong choices to act on a principle of heteronomy are fundamentally autonomous.

With respect to the question of why one would ever subordinate the moral law (duty, the Categorical Imperative) to self-interest, Kant finds it a mystery, incomprehensible, inexplicable:

[T]his propensity to evil, remains inexplicable to us, for, since it must itself be imputed to us, this supreme ground of all maxims must in turn require the adoption of an evil maxim. Evil can have originated only from moral evil (not just from the limitations of our nature); yet the original predisposition (which none other than the human being himself could have corrupted, if this corruption is to be imputed to him) is a predisposition to the good; there is no conceivable ground for us, therefore, from which moral evil could first have come in us (R 6:43; Wood and di Giovanni 88)

Commenting on the scriptural narrative of Eve and the serpent (a "spirit"), he writes:

The absolutely *first* beginning of all evil is thereby represented as in-comprehensible to us (for whence the evil in that spirit?); the human being, however, is represented as having lapsed into it only *through temptation*, hence not as corrupted *fundamentally* (in his very first pre-disposition to the good) but, on the contrary, as still capable of improve-ment, by contrast to a tempting *spirit*, i.e. one whom the temptation of the flesh cannot be accounted as a mitigation of guilt. And so for the human being, who despite a corrupted heart yet always possesses a good will, there still remains hope of a return to the good from which he has strayed. (R 6:43–44; Wood and di Giovanni 88–89)

An explanation of human evil in terms of empirical causes would not satisfy the inquirer who seeks a rationale for the choice, as it would remove responsi-bility if it were the only account. But an account in terms of the will is, ac-cording to Kant, inaccessible to us. If the question really concerns what we have made our *supreme* principle of conduct, we cannot cite any more funda-mental principle to explain our adoption of it. We know that some people make the moral law supreme while others subordinate it to self-interest. We know that it is possible to change one's supreme principle, to become evil and also to overcome it. Kant does not express puzzlement about why anyone makes the moral law supreme, for he thinks rational autonomy requires it. But he finds that we do not, indeed cannot, know why anyone fails to do so.

Kant's treatment of the ultimate springs of moral and immoral motivation as finally a mystery is deeply unsatisfying. First, if it is a mystery why anyone does not prioritize the moral law over self-interest, it should be equally a mys-tery why others do. That some do not proves that the capacity for rational au-tonomy does not make the choice for morality inevitable. The mystery, then, should be expressed as why any of us makes supreme whatever principle we make supreme, whether the moral law, self-interest, or even something else.

Second, if a practical principle is truly supreme, then, by definition, there cannot be any rationale for adopting it other than its being the principle that it is. But then we lack explanation for why some people fail to make the moral law their supreme principle. The "explanation" that they are simply being ir-rational is unsatisfying if we want to know why they are being irrational. If there is an empirical explanation for their irrationality, then the legislative act that subordinates morality to self-interest is not "purely intelligible" but is also a temporal deed. How, in that case, are we to understand that the legisla-tor is nevertheless free?

I return to these questions in the penultimate section of this chapter. But first, we need to look at two difficulties with Kant's proposed analysis of evil. The first is a difficulty regarding what is wrong with seriously harmful assaults. The second is a difficulty regarding the values of our interests and the range of possible supreme practical principles that may be available to us.

Murder and Mayhem

The discussion of evil in Kant's *Religion* proceeds abstractly, without examples of evil deeds, because Kant finds that the most important stage, radical evil, lies in the will alone, which is not really revealed by worldly deeds. Worldly deeds do not unambiguously show us an agent's principles. And yet, Kant's moral principle ultimately does refer to the world of time and space, by way of the material (the act and its purpose) in the maxims of one's action, which the Categorical Imperative, in its first formulation, says we must be able to will to be a universal law. Many critics find it misleading to say that Kant's ethics ignores consequences, because contradiction in *willing* a maxim universally (as opposed to contradiction merely in *conceiving* universal action on it) appears to be due to the hypothetical consequences of everyone's acting on it.

Even if critics are right that the Categorical Imperative embodies a tacit appeal to hypothetical consequences, it is not the *undesirability* of those consequences that makes the maxim wrong. That point distinguishes Kant's ethics from even rule utilitarianism. What makes the maxim wrong is, rather, a conflict between willing the purpose in the maxim and being willing at the same time that people act in ways that would defeat that purpose. Thus, the Categorical Imperative is well-suited to show what is wrong with free riderism. Free riders make exceptions for themselves, with no rationale to justify doing so.

It is not clear, however, that the principle shows as well what is wrong with the evils of murder and mayhem. Here the test of universality is apt to seem redundant. One may think that prior to universalizing we should already be able to see in maxims of inflicting severe harm or death that something is very wrong with the intended deed, whereas it is not surprising if we fail to see that in many maxims of cheating, which appear to hurt no one. To determine whether Kant's understanding of evil takes adequate account of victims, we need to consider whether the Categorical Imperative directs us to think about relationships between our conduct and the satisfaction of basic human needs or the avoidance of harms that would make life intolerable.

In an insightful chapter on whether the Categorical Imperative can give a plausible account of what is wrong with murder and mayhem, Barbara Herman argues that these actions are wrong, by Kant's principle, because they fail to treat people's capacity for rational agency as a reason not to kill or injure them when killing or injuring them is necessary to further one's own interests.[5] She finds, to her surprise, no self-contradiction in the *conception* of everyone's acting on the maxim of killing whoever gets in their way. Yet she finds it irrational to will that everyone adopt the maxim, because such a will, she argues, would conflict with the possibility of willing anything at all. Murder is wrong, by this argument, not because death is bad (in itself, death is natural) but because such universal readiness to take life would render rational human agency impossible. Universal mayhem, she holds, would likewise interfere with the conditions of human agency.

By the same argument she finds self-defense against murder or mayhem justified not because life is a good but because (when) resistance to aggression is necessary to sustain the integrity of one's moral agency. I justifiably defend my life not as such but as a necessary condition of the integrity of my rational human agency. Harm to the body is wrong only insofar as the body is necessary to human agency and insofar as harm manifests lack of respect for that agency. Infliction of pain is relevant only instrumentally to the wrongness of the deed, that is, only insofar as it interferes with the integrity of rational human agency. This sounds a lot like Becker's view, in his "new stoicism" (discussed in chapter 3), that "the damage torture does to happiness comes from . . . [the torturer's] defeat of the victim's agency, not from the pain she causes."[6] Everything comes back to the will. There is, apparently, nothing wrong with harming the bodies of nonrational beings, unless doing so also interferes with the rational agency of other beings. Thus, Kant finds cruelty to animals wrong only insofar as it makes us less sensitive to human needs and vulnerabilities and therefore more likely to be cruel to people.

As Herman notes, it is important to the adequacy of the Categorical Imperative as a fundamental moral principle not only that it correctly identify which acts are wrong and which right but also that it give the right kinds of reasons for finding them wrong or right. The Categorical Imperative appeals to coherence and consistency in willing. Our maxims can be wrong either because they cannot consistently be conceived as universal laws or because, although conceivable, they cannot rationally be so willed. An interpretation I have long accepted is that they cannot rationally be so willed when everyone's acting on them would defeat the action's point, its purpose. Herman proposes that the maxim cannot be willed as a universal law when doing so is incompatible with respecting the conditions of human agency.

On neither understanding does evaluation of the purpose in the maxim as good or bad enter into our moral reasoning but at most whether those purposes would be achievable, were everyone to act as we propose. Thus, Kant's answer to the question raised in chapter 3 for stoic ethics of how to distinguish right uses of the will does not appeal to the value of contingencies. Right uses restrict us in the pursuit of our aims to maxims on which everyone could act without thwarting the achievement of those aims (or conflicting with the conditions of rational agency).

For a theory of evil based on the atrocity paradigm, a major question remaining is whether Kant's Categorical Imperative gives the right reasons for why wrongful violence is wrong. The reasons it gives on Herman's interpretation are interesting and plausible, as far as they go. They may do full justice (and more) to Kant's texts. But they are strikingly incomplete. For it is not the case that the only truly important thing about us is our capacity for rational agency, understood as a capacity for coherence and consistency in action. We do not all have this capacity to the same extent, nor does it remain constant throughout our lives. In some of us, this capacity is severely diminished or barely there. Other things that make respect for our lives appropriate include the fact that we each have a point of view on the world and are curious about and interested in the world around us; we are capable of responding to others emotionally and with sensitivity; we care about each other and other living beings, and we form durable relationships; we teach and learn from each other; we are vulnerable to severe and unnecessary pain (pain that does us no good); we are capable of playfulness and joy; we participate in intergenerational projects; and we are sometimes highly creative. Although many of these capacities involve the use of reason, they are not reducible to consistency and coherence in willing. Many of these capacities can be found in other animals, and they make respect for their lives appropriate as well. When any of us is injured or killed, conditions of the possibility of many of these capacities are interfered with or destroyed. That is not always a conclusive reason against inflicting harm. But it is *a* reason not to. Such capacities give those who have them a more than utilitarian value, a value that makes their welfare worth respectful attention for its own sake.

Kant rightly distinguishes value merely as a means to some end (utility, market value, or value as an object of enjoyment) from nonfungible, absolute value—independent of uses and interests—which a being has when nothing can be put in its place without loss. In the *Groundwork* he calls the latter value dignity (*Würde*) to contrast it with utilitarian value, which he calls price (*Preis*) (G 4:434–36, Gregor 84–85). The second formulation of his Categorical Imperative—"So act that you use humanity, whether in your own person or in the person of any other, always at the same time as an end, never merely as a means" (G 4:429, Gregor 80)—defines moral wrongdoing as failure to treat human beings as having dignity, as ends in themselves. Nothing in the concepts of absolute value, dignity, worthiness of respect, or end in itself, however, requires Kant to restrict such value to rational beings. Environmental philosophers Paul Taylor and Gary Francione, among others, disagree with Kant's claim that "Beings the existence of which rests not on our will but on nature, if they are beings without reason, still have only a relative worth, as means, and are therefore called *things*" (G 4:428, Gregor 79).[7] Taylor and Francione find it wrong not only to treat people as mere means but also to treat animals, plants, and entire ecosystems without respect, as though their only, or even their most important, value were utilitarian.

Kant's theory of evil draws helpful distinctions among perpetrators but is deeply deficient in its recognition of harms. Interfering with conditions of rational human agency, as Kant understands such agency, is certainly harmful. But it is not the only harm that can make a human life intolerable. On Kant's view, the same evil is present in all wrongs—serious and trivial ones alike—that are committed by anyone who subordinates morality to self interest. The deliberate choices of both murderer and subway free rider are wrong in exactly the same way. The fact that no one suffers in one case and someone dies in the other is, for Kant, morally irrelevant. It affects neither his judgment of the act nor his judgment of the agent. Yet, on any ordinary understanding of evil, one act (murder) is evil, and the other, although wrong, is not.

Kant may appear to acknowledge degrees of seriousness of wrongdoing in his distinction between perfect and imperfect duties (G 4:421, Gregor 73), or, in the terminology of the *Metaphysics of Morals*, between duties of narrow and wide obligation (MM 6:390–91, Gregor 521). Duties of wide obligation (imperfect), such as the duty to help others, are duties to adopt certain ends. They allow us some latitude regarding when, how much, toward whom, and so on, that is absent in duties of narrow obligation, such as the duty not to make lying promises. Not living up to a duty of wide obligation, he says, indicates only lack of virtue, not presence of vice (unless one does it on principle), whereas failure to fulfill a duty of narrow obligation is wrong. In the *Groundwork* (G 4:424, Gregor 75) Kant notes that when the maxim of an action violates a perfect duty, there is a contradiction in our attempt even to conceive it as a universal law, whereas in the case of imperfect duties, there is no contradiction in conception but only a contradiction in willing both the maxim and its universalization. But is violating a perfect duty *worse* than failing to meet an imperfect one, as the terms "strict" or "narrow" and "wide" or "imperfect" might suggest?

There is good reason to think not. Herman finds, to her surprise, that Kantian duties against murder and mayhem sort with Kant's imperfect duties to help others and develop one's talents. A Categorical Imperative argument against murder does not fit the argument of Kant's perfect duties, she argues, as there is no contradiction in the conception of everyone murdering to achieve their ends. Such a world would be a Hobbesian state of nature—dreadful but, unfortunately, not impossible. If she is right, the difference between perfect and imperfect duties seems not to imply a difference in seriousness of wrongdoing, even if in many cases one should prioritize the perfect duty because of the latitude in the imperfect one.

There is also intuitive support for the idea that failure to fulfill a perfect duty is not necessarily worse than failure to live up to an imperfect one. It can be worse to refuse aid than to make a lying promise, depending on the points of the aid and the promise. Holocaust rescuers who lied to Nazis in order to aid fugitives were not guilty of the wrong priorities. Significantly, however, Kant's ethics has no obvious way to acknowledge the validity of this judgment, since he does not appeal to the values of our purposes.[8]

The difficulties with Kant's Categorical Imperative for a theory of evil based on the atrocity paradigm are more like the difficulties with Rawls's theory of justice than like those of utilitarianism. The principles of neither Kant nor Rawls are apt to condone atrocities (at least, against human beings). But they do not distinguish evils from less serious wrongdoing. Rawls does not claim to offer a theory of evil, however, whereas Kant does. It is with respect to evils that a serious difficulty in the Categorical Imperative becomes manifest, namely, that it offers a highly inadequate account of why such conduct as murder and mayhem is wrong, because it neglects most of the harm that turns mere wrongdoing into something positively evil.

Evil Interests and Principles

Daniel Goldhagen's controversial book *Hitler's Willing Executioners* centers the facts of widespread cruelty against Jews by ordinary Germans. He argues that ordinary Germans were moved by eliminationist anti-Semitism in the form of an extreme racism.[9] He finds that even members of the *Einsatzgruppen* (mobile killing units) believed their murders justified. Thus, he absolves them of wrongdoing for its own sake. On that, his account agrees with Kant's analysis of evil, although Kant does not think evildoers always act under the illusion that they are right. Goldhagen also finds that many acted not under orders but on their own initiative. Those moved by racism apparently acted on principles to which *both* morality *and* prudence were subordinated, a possibility not recognized in Kant's moral psychology. If the principles by which they believed they were justified were racist principles, not moral ones, their priorities were racist, not moral.

Christopher Browning offers a multilayered description of killers' motives, in which racism figures as one of many, not always prominent. Like Goldhagen, he also finds that it was not fear for their own lives that moved many to kill. In July 1942 Major Wilhelm Trapp offered older members of Reserve Police Battalion 101 the opportunity to step out if they did not feel up to their assigned task of shooting women, children, and the elderly from the 1,800 Jews of Józefów, Poland. One man stepped forward, ten or twelve others followed, and the rest stayed.[10] One who asked in advance for an alternative assignment was granted it. Those who asked to be relieved after the action began were given other tasks. If the killings by even a minority of those who

remained were motivated by racism, their interests did not just *happen* to conflict with morality. The problem was not lack of constraint on the pursuit of
other interests. The motivating interests were evil.

Two difficulties in Kant's understanding of evil are that he appears not to
acknowledge the existence of evil desires, interests, or inclinations, and he
does not acknowledge immoral principles other than that of subordinating
morality to prudence. Nationalist principles may be neither prudential nor
moral but capable of conflicting with both. Racist principles condoning genocide are evil. A principle subordinating morality to prudence is not the worst
practical principle that one can imagine, if the person whose principle it is
does not have evil desires or interests. Interests and desires are evil when their
objects include an infliction of intolerable harm that is morally wrong. An interest in being the instrument of another's undeserved suffering or death is not
on a par with desires for such things as wealth or fame, which are capable of
being pursued within moral bounds. A principle is immoral, by Kant's own account, if it fails to respect humanity in anyone's person. Subordinating another's humanity to one's personal interests is surely immoral. But just how immoral depends on what one's interests are.

Kant finds some inclinations, or "predispositions," as he calls them in the
Religion, to be given, part of our animal and human nature, in themselves
good (R 6:26–27, Wood and di Giovanni 75). He regards others, compre-
hended under the rubric of "self love," as social, since they arise out of a comparison of ourselves with others (R 6:27, Wood and di Giovanni 75), and these
he finds to be the basis of culture. He acknowledges that upon the social inclinations are also formed the "vices of culture"—"envy, ingratitude, joy in others' misfortunes, etc.," which are called "diabolical vices." But he argues that
the vices grafted upon our social inclinations "do not really issue from nature
as their root but are rather inclinations, in the face of the anxious endeavor of
others to attain a hateful superiority over us, to procure it for ourselves over
them for the sake of security, as preventive measure" (R 6:27, Wood and di
Giovanni 75). Thus, he supposes that what at first appears to be an evil inclination (even diabolical) is at bottom a response from fear based on our felt
need for the goods of protection and security. He insists that evil lies only
in our choices to accord too much importance to our inclinations, not in the
inclinations themselves. Sadism, on this view, is simply overreaction in the interest of self-defense.

Yet often there is no discernible causal relationship between cruel behavior and increased security for its agents nor any reason to suppose the agent
even thinks so. Cruelty commonly backfires. Its imprudence is well known.
Cruelty remains a problem for Kant. Sometimes it appears to be a source of
pleasure in itself. Richard Henry Dana, Jr., reports, in his narrative *Two Years
Before the Mast*, that his ship captain said, as he administered the lash, "swing-

ing half round between each blow, to give it full effect," to the back of a crew member for having asked why another crew member was flogged, "If you want to know what I flog you for, I'll tell you. It's because I like to do it!—because I like to do it!—It suits me! That's what I do it for!"[11]

S. I. Benn argues persuasively that there is ultimately no logical or even psychological incoherence in the idea of choosing evil for its own sake, once we acknowledge the distinctions between desiring something and finding it desirable and between finding a position reasonable and holding it as one's own reason.[12] Trivially, the satisfaction of being cruel is one's own. But, substantively, it is often patently incompatible with one's own fundamental interests or overall happiness. As Bishop Joseph Butler put it in his critique of psychological egoism, understood as the theory that self-love is the ultimate motive of all human conduct:

> If, because every particular affection is a man's own, and the pleasure arising from its gratification his own pleasure . . . such particular affection must be called self-love, according to this way of speaking no creature whatever can possibly act but merely from self-love. . . . But then this is not the language of mankind; or if it were, we should want words to express the difference between the principle of an action proceeding from cool consideration that it will be to my own advantage, and an action, suppose of revenge or of friendship, by which a man runs upon certain ruin to do evil or good to another.[13]

Such an act of revenge is justified neither morally nor prudentially. But if one chooses to do something that is neither morally right nor prudent, there appears to be no way left in Kant's philosophical psychology for the act to make sense as issuing from one's character.

Solving Kant's Mystery

Suppose we grant that the desire to be cruel is immoral, that satisfying it would often be imprudent as well, and that the perpetrator is aware of both of these things. It may still be that the basis of one's cruelty is not simply an attraction to immorality as such. What motivates the cruelty may be a certain normative self conception ("it suits me"), the desire to be a certain kind of person, one who would be worthy of the admiration or esteem of certain others whose admiration or esteem one values.

Self-interest is not reducible to prudence, although Kant equates these two concepts. Prudence is ordinarily understood as wisdom in the pursuit or protection of goods that we can obtain, secure for ourselves. But some of our interests are in being certain kinds of selves, that is, living up to certain self-conceptions, having a certain kind of character. As Christine Korsgaard puts it, they are about who we are, rather than about what we can get.[14] "Self-interest" in this sense is more fundamental than and presupposed by prudence. It shapes the more specific interests we come to have, fulfillment of which then becomes the business of prudence.

The desire to be the kind of person who is attractive to or worthy of certain parties' esteem (admiration, praise, approval) is a possible motive for adopting or rejecting morality as a limit on the pursuit of more specific interests. Sociologist Jack Katz's *Seductions of Crime* offers examples of criminal offenders who take pride in being "bad," where "bad" means simultaneously really bad and also worthy of (someone's) esteem.[15] Offenders he interviews, many youthful, really do very bad things (including murder), apparently to be worthy of colleagues' esteem. An analogous mechanism may have been at work among members of Reserve Police Battalion 101.

The conduct of one who does not reflectively endorse such a desire but acts on it unreflectively, or without awareness of its source, is not well characterized as wrongdoing simply for its own sake. An unreflective agent may know that certain choices are wrong but not understand or even wonder why they are so attractive. Such an agent has not yet *chosen* to grant the underlying desire importance. Rather, the underlying desire is potentially affirmable or rejectable by those who can reflect and become aware.

In his famous observation that "an impartial rational spectator can take no delight in seeing the uninterrupted prosperity of a being graced with no feature of a pure and good will, so that a good will seems to constitute the indispensable condition even of worthiness to be happy," Kant seems to imply that a good will is necessary to make one worthy of an impartial spectator's admiration or esteem (G 4:303, Gregor 49). He may have been thinking of God as the "impartial spectator." He argues in the second Critique that only God would have the power to bring it about that people of good will are rewarded (eventually) with happiness (CPrR 5:124–32; G 239–46), offering this belief as support for the rationality of theistic faith, in place of the traditional proofs (which, he argues in the first Critique, fail). Kant's observation regarding the impartial spectator appeals to a presumed desire (in the reader) to be worthy of the approval of such a (hypothetical) spectator or to a presumed tendency (in the reader) to identify with that spectator. The moral worth of an action in Kant's ethics, conferred by the motive of duty, makes one worthy of being rewarded with happiness by an omnipotent, omniscient, and perfectly just rational spectator. Actual reward is not the goal. (That goal would make the behavior prudent.) The goal is to be *worthy*—worthy of a reward that would symbolize the esteem of its bestower. (Even happiness thereby acquires a stoic value, for what it symbolizes about another's esteem for one's will.)

The idea that what underlies morally good character is one's desire to be worthy of the esteem of an all-powerful, omniscient, perfectly just being suggests a more general answer to Kant's mystery, namely, that our fundamental practical principles have roots in our wishes to be worthy or attractive persons, attractive to or worthy of the love or esteem of someone important. This someone could be, but need not be, the hypermoral God of Judaism or Christianity. If the persons whose esteem one seeks to deserve is are lesser beings than God, it should not be surprising that one's fundamental practical principles are frequently less than moral.

This solution to Kant's mystery concerning the roots of evil in human nature can be reached by application and synthesis of two mutually reinforcing but independent bodies of theory. One is Korsgaard's philosophical analysis of the sources of normativity, drawing on Kant's concepts to expand his moral psychology.[16] The other is Lorna Smith Benjamin's theory of social behavior, which combines interpersonal psychology in the traditions of Harry Stack Sullivan and George Herbert Mead with attachment theory in psychoanalysis.[17]

Korsgaard on Self-Conception as a Source of Normativity

Korsgaard develops a Kantian view of the sources of normativity that locates their roots in one's self-conception or "practical identity." She takes issue with the narrowness of Kant's own understanding of fundamental practical principles. Where he recognizes only one possible fundamental principle besides the Categorical Imperative, namely, the principle of prudence, she finds several.[18] Distinguishing, unlike Kant, between (a) "the categorical imperative" as "acting only on maxims you can will to be laws" and (b) the *moral* law as "the law of what Kant calls the Kingdom of Ends," which tells us "to act only on maxims that all rational beings could agree to act on together in a workable cooperative system," she finds that arguments establishing the Categorical Imperative as the law of a free will do not also establish that the Categorical Imperative is the *moral* law (Korsgaard 98–99). Whether the law that one wills categorically is the moral law or something else (the principle of prudence or even something else), she argues, will depend on one's self-conception, which is a jumble of conceptions of one's identity, in which some elements are more central than others.

By a conception of one's identity, she means something practical, "a description under which you value yourself, a description under which you find your life to be worth living and your actions to be worth undertaking" (Korsgaard 101). She mentions thinking of oneself as a citizen of Kant's realm of ends (as a member of humanity), "as someone's friend or lover, as a member of a family or an ethnic group or a nation," as "the steward of her own interests" (an egoist) or as "the slave of her passions" (a wanton). How she thinks of herself will determine whether it is the moral law ("the law of the Kingdom of Ends") or "the law of some smaller group, or the law of egoism, or the law of the wanton that will be the law that she is to herself" (Korsgaard 101).

Most of our identities, she notes, are contingent: "You are born into a certain family and community, perhaps even into a certain profession or craft. You find a vocation, or ally yourself with a movement. You fall in love and make friends. You are a mother of some particular children, a citizen of a particular country, an adherent of a particular religion. . ." (Korsgaard 120). What is not contingent is that we are governed by some conception or other of our practical identity. Without such governance, she maintains, "you will lose your grip on yourself as having any reason to do one thing rather than another" (Korsgaard 121). This reason to conform to our practical identities, she claims, springs from our identity as human beings, and to value ourselves simply as human beings puts us "in moral territory." Quoting Hume that to be virtuous is to think of yourself as a member of the "party of humankind," she notes that "the conception of *moral* wrongness as we now understand it belongs to the world *we* live in, the one brought about by the Enlightenment, where one's identity is one's relation to humanity itself" (Korsgaard 117).

With this framework, Korsgaard proposes something very like Kant's conception of radical evil, adding to Kant's principle of prudence the various principles associated with our contingent practical identities as possible supreme principles, to which morality might be subordinated (Korsgaard 243). She accepts Kant's view that an evil will has the wrong priorities. But she finds that what is given priority over morality need not be prudence but could be the good of some specific group, such as one's racial or ethnic group or one's gender (something with which one identifies). One could be as willing to give up one's own individual interests, or even to die, to promote that good as others are willing to do for the sake of moral ideals.

On her view, the unreflective tendency to treat our contingent practical identities as sources of reasons, unqualified by morality "may be condemned as insufficiently reflective," whereas the conscious and reflective decision to treat them that way is evil (Korsgaard 250). She concludes that self-conception is the root of both moral good and evil, that although "evil *may* take the form of ungoverned self-interest or selfishness . . . it takes many other forms as well," and that the selfish form, in which people "care only for what they get and not at all for who they are" is relatively uncommon (Korsgaard 250–51).

On caring for who one is, as opposed to caring for what one can get, she continues, "Self-conception is the source of some of our sweetest pleasures—knowing ourselves to be loved or to have done well; and our greatest (and often self-inflicted) torments—believing ourselves to be worthless, unlovely, or unlovable" (Korsgaard 251). Thus, she brings her understanding of self-conception close to the idea of being moved by the desire to be worthy of the love or esteem of important other people, people to whom one is attached and with whom one may identify. In view of Kant's observation regarding the approval of an impartial spectator, one could find her emendation of Kant's theory also very Kantian, a naturalization of Kant.

Korsgaard's view that both good and evil are rooted in the agent's self-conceptions is helpful for making sense of the behavior of those who appear to apply moral standards only to their treatment of people they regard as peers and at the same time are willing to treat others, such as members of a despised racial group, extremely immorally. Robert J. Lifton tries to make sense of this phenomenon, in accounting for the behavior of the Nazi doctors, with his concept of "doubling." In doubling, one develops "a second self" to avoid having to confront inconsistencies in one's own values and behavior.[19] Within ethical theory, especially virtue theory, it is puzzling to know what to say about the character of individuals who "double": is their good treatment of (kindness to, generosity toward, honesty with, etc.) those they respect really moral, or is it not? Who *does* the doubling? Is doubling itself a morally accountable choice? An irresponsible escape?

Korsgaard's analysis, which seems to presuppose a more unified self, can explain the inclination to say that such kindness and respect are not morally good. Kindness and respect are not morally good if they are based not on the humanity of their recipients but on the recipients' membership in a more limited group. Yet that behavior shares features with moral behavior that distinguish it from mere prudence: racist behavior can include self-sacrifice, for example. If the source of normativity is the conception of oneself as a member of a superior group who is free to treat outsiders in hostile ways, the resulting norms are neither moral nor prudential. There is currently no general category for such norms in ethical theory, although popular culture has a variety of descriptive epithets: "racist," "sexist," "anti-Semite," "homophobe," and the like.

Korsgaard's discussion seems to assume that we are, or can easily become, aware of our own self-concepts. Hence, her observation that our unreflective tendency to treat our contingent practical identities as sources of reasons unqualified by morality "may be condemned as insufficiently reflective." This judgment seem to presuppose that people can ordinarily be expected to become aware of the nature and influence of their self-conceptions. But that task can be difficult enough to require professional help. We are easily aware of self-concepts under such descriptions as "someone's friend or lover, or as a member of a family or an ethnic group or a nation." But if a self-concept is analyzed in terms of norms and values embodied in one's behavior (as a member of a particular family, for example), one may not be very aware of such specifics or their source. It can be hard work to learn to recognize some of the concepts we have constructed of ourselves, even to recognize some of those with whom we have identified, and hence to see that certain norms and values—some of which we would not endorse—in fact govern our behavior.

Interpersonal psychology lends support and amplification to Korsgaard's view that normativity is rooted in one's self-concept, but without assuming that we know in detail who we have become or that such knowledge is easily acquired. According to interpersonal psychology, one's self-concept, insofar as it is regulative of behavior, is greatly the product of interaction with other people who are important in one's life. Attachment theorists in psychoanalysis extend the exploration of interaction, its forms and consequences, to the intrapsychic domain.

Benjamin's "Important Persons and Their Internalized Representations" (IPIRs)

Using psychoanalytic concepts and building on John Bowlby's "attachment theory," Lorna Smith Benjamin argues that attachment to an internalized important other person can elucidate behavior that otherwise appears simply perverse, irrational, perhaps even diabolical.[20] She fleshes out the details with an elaborate coding system and tests based on it that can generate empirically testable predictions (and interesting "post"-dictions) of behavior. Internalization of an important other person, in her system, can take the form of imitation (of the person's treatment of others, such as oneself), recapitulation (of one's early responses to the person), or introjection (treating oneself as the person used to treat one).

Bowlby defines attachment behavior as "any form of behaviour that results in a person attaining or retaining proximity to some other differentiated and preferred individual, who is usually conceived as stronger and/or wiser." He finds that such behavior "characterizes human beings from the cradle to the grave" but that in adults it tends to be "especially evident when a person is distressed, ill, or afraid."[21] Adapting an idea from artificial intelligence pioneer Kenneth Craig, by way of the writings of neurobiologist J. Z. Young, that "organisms capable of forming complex 'internal working models' of their environment considerably improve their chances of survival," Bowlby held that children retain representations of their relationships with caregivers as internal working models, which they then use to evaluate potential interactions with others.[22]

Benjamin's hypothesis is that the quest for proximity also plays out intrapsychically in adults in relation to these internal working models, which she designates "important persons and their internalized representations" ("IPIRs"). Her idea is that imitation and introjection of the behavior of an important person (as we perceived the behavior, which may not do it justice), and recapitulation of our responses to that person, get us *psychic* proximity, "the mental equivalent of reunion with the mother after separation stress," providing "an 'intrapsychic hug,'" and that, likewise, "the need for psychic proximity to the IPIR increases under stress."[23]

Benjamin's approach to psychology and psychiatry is phenomenological and interpersonal. It takes us inside the agent's head to learn what sense behaviors make from the agent's point of view and then interprets that behavior in terms of patterns of either responses to or reenactments of the behavior of IPIRs. Treatment of personality disorders, in her system, includes helping the patient become aware of patterns of interaction and their meanings in terms of the patient's attachment to one or more IPIRs. Once aware, the patient can choose to endorse the attachment, try to disengage, or negotiate a different relationship with the IPIR. Disengaging requires giving up wishes for the IPIR's love, approval, and support and giving up fears of the IPIR's rejection, anger, and blame.[24] Having such choices offers the patient a freedom that did not exist before.

This idea has interesting implications for moral change (not only in psychiatric patients), if norms and values are implicit in behavior patterns that one imitates, recapitulates, or introjects. To the extent that attachment to an IPIR determines a self-concept that is a source of one's norms and values (Korsgaard's "normativity"), the freedom to disengage or renegotiate a relationship with an IPIR is also a freedom to remodel one's self-concept so that it is more (or less) supportive of moral norms and values. Such a freedom could be invaluable for anyone (personality disordered or not) who formed early unfortunate attachments or attachments that had unfortunate aspects. One who became aware of having a racist IPIR might wish to disengage or renegotiate, even though the IPIR is supportive in many ways and hostile only to other racial groups. What Lifton called "doubling" may reveal an ambivalence of attachments, attachments to different IPIRs whose (perceived) norms and values are mutually incompatible. If attachments are the sources of our fundamental norms and values, some selves may not be very unified; we may have conflicting self-conceptions. Perhaps nobody *does* the "doubling" (it may not be an action), even if somebody eventually chooses to bring about an integration.

If unfortunate attachments can be renegotiated or rejected, they can also be reflectively endorsed, leading in some cases to the willful perpetration of evils. Was Kant, then, wrong in his insistence that evil is never "diabolical" in human beings (that we never will to do wrong for its own sake)? It may seem that he was wrong, because reflectively choosing to be worthy of the admiration of an immoral IPIR looks like an endorsement of immorality as such. It is not, after all, just anyone's approval that is sought, but the approval of this particular IPIR, who is cruel. But one may value support from a cruel IPIR not *for the sake of* the cruelty but because the person internalized is or once was an important source of support, perhaps one's only source of support. Early attachment to cruel persons appears to be generated in spite of rather than because of their cruelty. Benjamin cites Harry Harlow's experiments with the unfortunate baby monkeys who tried to bond with extremely cruel "mothers" ("diabolical devices that included having a huggable cylinder that unpredictably projected sharp spikes, and another that sometimes would spring loose and violently throw the baby across the cage"), when that was all they had.[25] She notes that the baby monkeys clung even more tenaciously to the violent "mothers" than other baby monkeys did to their terry cloth "mothers," suggesting that this may be because "the tendency to cling to a protective 'parent' is enhanced when there is danger, irrespective of the source of the danger," since infants do not appreciate that the parent is the source of the danger.[26]

One's early "important persons" are a matter of luck, not choice; choice comes only later, if at all, in deciding whether to affirm or reject the fallout. An early important person may have had, or been perceived to have, values that are neither morally nor prudentially sound. Still, feeling affirmed in the eyes of important others may be a precondition of one's own eventual prudential motivation and perhaps of moral motivation as well.

Kant's general position that evil in human beings is not diabolical now seems partly right and partly wrong. What seems wrong is, first, his failure to recognize that people can knowingly choose to do evil without believing it even prudent. Second, one who becomes aware of an underlying attachment to an immoral IPIR as a source of attractions to wrongdoing can reaffirm the attachment rather than disengage. Perhaps a life of immorality can create habits that outlive such attachments. Perhaps one can become attached eventually to the behavior itself. In affirming an unfortunate attachment, however, one affirms not simply wrongdoing but a relationship that rewards one with a feeling of worthiness of love or esteem. Failure to disengage may indicate weakness rather than positive affirmation. What seems most right about the Kantian denial of diabolical evil, from the point of view of attachment theory, is that attachment even to an immoral IPIR is not initially diabolical, in Kant's sense of that term. It is not motivated initially by a prior proclivity for wrongdoing. It may have been necessary for the survival of a developing agent, too young to judge or appreciate.

Ever since Thomas Hobbes set the tone, modern Western philosophers have expended much energy either advocating egoism (the ethical theory that self-interest determines what is right or the psychological theory that it is the ultimate motive of human behavior, or both) or else defending morality against it.[27] Most of these philosophers have been men. (Ayn Rand is a notable exception.) They have treated egoism as a force to be reckoned with. Affiliation is what has been presumed to require explanation, not self-interest. In attachment theory, the presumption seems to be the reverse. Egoistic behavior is less fundamental than attachment. Attachment precedes self-interest, even any sense of self. So far from self-love being a given and the ultimate motive of all human conduct, perhaps even the most puzzling and bizarre human conduct is rooted in something like love for others, at any rate attachment to them and the need for something from them (or their internalized representations) that could make self-love possible. Thus, Benjamin has argued for years that "every psychopathology is a gift of love."[28]

If this psychoanalytic view is right, Kant's optimism about human freedom seems excessive (as does the pessimism of many determinists). Human beings are potentially free to accept or reject morality, and hence potentially free to reject or endorse evil. But the actualization of the potentiality depends not simply on the individual's will but on many factors that are beyond the individual's control. Some adults are freer from their early IPIRs than others, depending on such things as levels of stress in their lives, how early caregivers treated them, and whether those caregivers facilitated or hindered their letting go. Whether one's *initial* attachments are to people who have morally acceptable values is not within one's control. Coming to appreciate the nature and role of those early attachments also depends on a variety of contingencies. The possibility of becoming morally good appears, thus, greatly a matter of luck, although less mysterious than Kant thought. And likewise the possibility of becoming evil.

Conclusions

Contrary to Kant's view that principled evil in human beings is disanalogous to principled goodness but simply prioritizes one kind of goodness (prudence) over another (the moral law), attachment theory suggests an explanation of how the will to do evil for no apparent gain might find a place in human moral psychology. If people with no ulterior motives for their right conduct act on a self-conception that developed from early perceptions of childhood caregivers, people who have no ulterior motives for their cruelty may act on self-conceptions with the same kind of origin. Contrary to Kant's theory, evil wills may be analogous to good ones. Those who have either may aim to be worthy of the approval, esteem, or love of an important other, that is, to be the kind of person that the other could love or admire. It does not follow even that Kant was right that what we seek is basically good. Being worthy of love or esteem for one's cruelty is not good, even if it has instrumental value, although the impulse to seek love and approval is surely social.

If attachments to IPIRs are the sources of our principles of good and evil, we might still want to conclude, however, that Kant was right that human beings never do evil *simply for its own sake*. But if we do, we must also conclude that we never do good simply for its own sake, either. Conversely, if the origins of character in early attachments do not negate what we ordinarily mean by the idea that people of good will do what is right for its own sake, neither do they negate what we ordinarily mean by the idea that others choose evil for evil's sake.

Still, doing wrong for its own sake is a very simple and not the most interesting account of diabolical evil. Nor is it the only conception, if that term is intended to capture evil's most extreme forms. Kant locates evil entirely within the will. If we consider also the harm that evil does, another interpretation of diabolical evil suggests itself that is all too human and much more interesting. I find diabolical evil in the knowing or deliberate corruption of the character of others, especially if it is done not for prudential reasons, such as economic gain, but for the satisfaction of being able to look down on them or, at least, of not having to look up to them. The knowing or deliberate destruction of what is best in us, especially if Nussbaum is right about its fragility, is a very great evil, of which human beings have proved themselves all too capable. The last chapter of this book proposes that such an evil is found in the deliberate creation of gray zones, where victims of evil are used as instruments in the perpetration of evils on others.

Kant makes distinctions regarding motivation that are worth incorporating into a theory of evil based on the atrocity paradigm. He calls acting wrongly from weakness the first stage of evil. People who act wrongly from weakness, rather than on principle, may often be more justly considered evil-*doers* than evil people, even though they can do devastating harm.

From a utilitarian point of view, weakness can appear worse than principled evil. More, if not greater, evil appears to be done out of weakness. Yet the morally weak evildoer is not a worse person. Benjamin's theory of reconstructive therapy confirms Aristotle's belief (mentioned in chapter 1) that there is more hope for one who does wrong from weakness than for one who does it on principle, since the judgment of the merely weak remains uncorrupted and can be appealed to in order to motivate change (for example, to disengage or renegotiate a relationship with an IPIR). As long as one's judgment is corrupted, discovering behavior patterns rooted in early attachments may have no tendency to engage one's will in projects of change. Still, because both harm and willing are important to assessing evils, it is misleading to rate evil done out of weakness as either generally more or generally less serious than evil done on principle (it can be either). Kant implies not that it is less serious but that it is not radical, meaning that it is not rooted in the agent's legislative choices. It does not reflect the agent's principles.

The case of mixed motives, Kant's second stage of evil, requires clarification. Here I find Kant confused. It may be natural to think an act described simply as "morally required" best done from duty. But if the act is described as visiting a sick friend in the hospital, it seems more natural to prefer visiting from concern for the friend to visiting from a sense of duty.[29] Herman argues that what Kant says in the *Groundwork* should not commit him to the position that it is always better to fulfill duties from the motive of duty than from inclination, as long as it is no accident that one does what is right. It is no accident when one could have relied on a sense of duty if necessary (i.e., had no cooperating inclination been present).[30] That view seems correct, whether or not it was Kant's. But in the *Religion* Kant does appear to embrace the view that for acts required by duty, relying at all on motives other than duty is evil (in the second degree).

What seems right about his position is that there is such a thing as doing the right thing for the wrong reason (even partly). Visiting a friend in the hospital for the sake of appearances is doing it for the wrong reason. But it is dogmatic to think the only right reason is a sense of duty. The problem lies both in the narrowness of Kant's vision of practical principles and in his undue suspicion (in the *Religion*) that acting on a nonmoral motive makes it even partly accidental that one does the right thing (as though having relied on a motive meant that one had to). Moral principles often underlie what we are willing to do when we do not have to rely on them. Mostly we do not have to rely on them to avoid committing murder or mayhem. Contrary to Kant, I find nothing in any degree evil in the avoidance of murder from disinclination, although it would be misleading to say I acted *merely* from disinclination if my scruples would have prevented me from murdering, had I been so tempted.

On the atrocity paradigm, evil includes both a stoic and a utilitarian component. The stoic component defines wrongdoing partly independently of its effects on others' well-being, as having elements that lie within the perpetrator and are, at least potentially, within the perpetrator's control. The utilitarian component lies in basic hardships that people suffer from others' wrongs, harms that often exceed the doer's control, although triggered by the deed. According to Kant's basically stoic view, when we wrong others, we fail to treat them as equals in that we fail to place the same value on their rationality as on our own. I have argued that this view does not adequately explain the evils of murder and mayhem. The next chapter argues that the concept of social inequality is not adequate to the evil of oppression, either.

5

Prioritizing Evils over
Unjust Inequalities

Decency versus Relative Well-Being

Feminists and other political activists working for social justice or liberation should give priority to addressing evils over the goal of eliminating unjust inequalities. The value priorities in this judgment—decency over relative well-being—underlie many politically separatist movements, whose adherents have elected not to push for assimilation into mainstream American culture. One need not be a separatist, however, to share this basic belief about priorities and to be impatient with the emphasis often given to concepts of social equality by political activists, the media, law, and government. Equality as an ethical and political value abstracts from particular levels of welfare. Its concern is the distribution of benefits and burdens among persons or groups, not with the quality or even quantity of what is distributed. For that reason, implementing equality is not directly about eliminating evils. Unjust inequalities are defects in a practice and grounds for complaint. They can cause needless envy and resentment and should often be removed. But inequality, even when unjust, is not itself an intolerable harm. It is not an evil.

Moral concerns for equality are basically concerns to be fair in dealings with others or in the way a practice treats its participants. To be fair is to avoid arbitrariness, be consistent in administering policies, make sure the rules of a practice give each participant a fair share of its benefits and no more than a fair share of its burdens, and respect everyone as an equal, that is, not presume anyone generally more or less important as a human being than anyone else. Whether inconsistency or arbitrariness in policy administration results in evils depends on circumstances and the policies' content. In extreme scarcity, shorting someone on food rations in violation of the rules can hasten death, although in less harsh times, it might produce only resentment. Evenhandedness in administration does not, of course, address evils embedded within the policies administered. The rule that children born to slaves are also slaves perpetuates an evil, regardless of how evenly the rule is enforced. Yet rules that treat everyone as equals can still be inhumane, as in the village lottery of Shirley Jackson's famous short story.[1] Philip Hallie, who has written on both cruelty and rescue and whose views on evil appear to be in agreement with the atrocity theory of evil, argues in his posthumously published *Tales of Good and Evil, Help and Harm* that "evil does not happen only inside moral agents" but involves an "intimate linkage between the moral agents of evil and the sufferings and deaths those moral agents willingly perpetrate."[2] Citing Lewis Carroll's parable of the walrus and the carpenter, Hallie argues that Carroll was right to teach the importance of attending more to the harm done than to the feelings of its perpetrators.[3] He might have added "or the relationships between what some suffer and what others suffer."

More than a decade ago Harry Frankfurt wrote that "with respect to the distribution of economic assets, what *is* important from the point of view of morality is not that everyone should have *the same* but that each should have enough," a position he refers to as "the doctrine of sufficiency."[4] Whether or not he is right about morality, his observation seems just right from the point of view of evil. Even if equality does have moral value, inequalities are not evils. It is far more important that people have enough, when that is a feasible goal, than that they have the same. What is important from the standpoint of evil is that no one be wrongfully deprived of the basics that make life tolerable and decent. Joseph Raz, arguing against strict egalitarianism, distinguishes helpfully between equality as a social ideal and equality as merely a by-product of the generality of rules.[5] He notes that from the point of view of genuine principles of equality, the only intrinsic goods are relational ones.[6] The only reason they offer to avoid harming or hurting anyone is that others are unharmed or unhurt, which is absurd. Although neither Frankfurt nor Raz uses the language of evil, their worries about egalitarian ideals are important to the more specific idea that evils are of greater importance than mere inequalities and should receive priority of attention. That, at any rate, is the idea that this chapter develops.

Further, there are some things that no one should have a "share" of, such as torture and rape, or toxic air, water, and soil. Social justice requires not only fairness in distributing benefits of social cooperation and burdens necessary to produce or maintain them but also prevention of gratuitous, cruel, and inhumane burdens. Examples are the burdens of disrespect and humiliation that Avishai Margalit finds distinctive of societies that are less than decent.[7] Struggles for social justice should work to eliminate and redress the evils of such burdens.

One social justice movement that presents an instructive case is main-stream American feminism of the nineteenth and twentieth centuries. In the end, mainstream American feminism prioritized equal political and economic rights for women over ending such atrocities as domestic violence and the traffic in women and girls. Thanks to the efforts of Susan B. Anthony (1820–1906), Elizabeth Cady Stanton (1815–1902), and many others revered by mainstream feminists today, American women succeeded in securing the franchise, the right to own property while married, and access to higher education. Many entered the professions, the business world, and eventually government at many levels. But other feminists, such as anarchist socialist philosopher Emma Goldman (1869–1940), worked to expose the fundamental evils of intolerable, unsafe working conditions for paid laborers of both genders (often immigrants, like herself) and the international traffic in female flesh.[8] After distributing birth control literature and protesting the military draft, she was rewarded for her labors by being forcibly deported to Russia in 1919. Sexual harassment, sexual slavery, rape, battery, and intolerable working conditions for relatively unskilled laborers (many of them women, often immigrants) remain, despite the franchise, married women's property rights, and the access of those who can afford it to the professions, corporate business, and government office.[9] When feminism is dominated by the rhetoric of equality, it tends not even to discuss the worst evils.

Equality Feminism versus Feminist Opposition to Oppression

American feminism is commonly identified with the pursuit of women's equality, meaning rights for women equal to those of men. Not all men, however, have equal rights. In practice, equality feminism has meant rights for white middle-class women equal to those of white middle-class men, the generally unstated but implied comparison classes. The comparisons have not been women and men globally, white women and men of color, or middle class women and working class, jobless, or homeless men. Women who are not white or not middle class are often engaged less in the pursuit of gender equality than in struggles against other injustices.

Yet there is also a long, nonmainstream, less well-known history of feminist activism, including the efforts of Matilda Joselyn Gage (1826–1898) and Charlotte Perkins Gilman (1860–1935) as well as Goldman, that did not prioritize equality but sought to expose and end oppression. Media publicity of equality for women or gender equality (often focused on men rather than women) tends to draw attention away from the real evils of oppression. It risks trivializing feminism with its protracted protests of inequalities that, although unjust, are not oppressive ("glass ceilings" in corporate management) and convoluted defenses of inequalities arguably needed to redress or correct other injustices to women (preferential treatment in hiring or admissions). Legal scholars Catharine MacKinnon and Martha Minow, moving more in the direction of Goldman, have tried to put the pursuit of women's equality into perspective. MacKinnon contrasts inequality as difference with inequality as dominance, pointing out rightly that of these, domination (and the peculiar "differences" that it produces) has been feminism's appropriate target of criticism.[10] Minow points to "the dilemma of difference," noting that both treating women the same as men and offering special treatment on account of women's special needs can re-entrench "differences" oppressive to women.[11]

The concept of dominance, which MacKinnon highlights, does not make the ethically critical point as well as the concept of oppression. The reason is simply that unlike dominance, oppression, by definition, does harm. In the language of Marilyn Frye, it reduces, molds, and immobilizes the oppressed.[12] In contrast, dominance—a superior power position—may not actually do harm even when it is unjustified. Dominance can be benevolent and should be when parents are dominant over children. Dominance implies power inequality, however, which gives it a potential for oppression. When dominance becomes systematically harmful, we can subsume it under oppression as oppressive dominance. The point is that the practices most important to resist are those that do intolerable harm. Neither inequality nor dominance clearly identifies them.

The atrocity theory of evil lends support to the kinds of feminism and other social justice or liberation movements that target severe oppression. Severe oppression is a paradigm evil, although not all evils result from oppression. The oppressed—a people, a group, individuals—survive, but with seriously diminished potentialities. As Frye notes, they are caught between opposing social forces in such a way that they are in the wrong, and they lose, no matter what they do.[13] Iris Marion Young articulates the analysis of oppression further as a complex phenomenon manifested in the five characteristic "faces" of marginalization, powerlessness, violence, cultural imperialism, and exploitation.[14] Some faces are more salient in certain forms of oppression than in others.

Exploitation, for example, has been a historically salient face of slavery and of the abuse of women as wives. Despite differences in kinds and degrees of exploitation to which slaves and wives have been vulnerable, both have been stereotyped as simple-minded, even childlike, and have nonetheless been entrusted with such essential social tasks as cooking and childcare.[15] Oppressors count heavily on the loyalties of slaves and wives. Marginalization (with exclusion as its extreme), in contrast, is the face of oppression salient in anti-Semitism, in the abuse of women as prostitutes, and in "homophobia."[16] The oppressed here are regarded by oppressors (who do not count on their loyalties) as cunning, manipulative, untrustworthy, corrupt.

Slaves and to a lesser extent wives have been socially diminished, if not entirely "socially dead," in being cut off from kin, in both directions for slaves and in terms of identities of origin for wives. Both have been officially under their oppressors' "protection."[17] But lesbians, gay men, transgender people, and prostitutes tend to have outlaw status. "Passing" becomes an issue more frequently here. Jews, when not outlaws, have often been pariahs. These oppressed are neither officially nor unofficially under their oppressors' protection. All are common targets of hate crimes, and many have formed their own organizations for self-protection.

Both marginalization and exploitation exist to some degree in each pattern of oppression. But they play different roles, have different degrees of prominence, and to some extent exist in tension with each other. To exploit women as wives and mothers, patriarchal institutions long excluded them from careers and promotions that would compete for their time and energy with home management and childcare. Here, exclusion facilitated exploitation. Jewish men, excluded from the European mainstream, were exploited to perform social functions (moneylending) forbidden to Christians, which was then also held against them, morally, reinforcing their pariah status. Here, exploitation served exclusion. But when exploitation clashed strongly with exclusion in the racist anti-Semitism of the Third Reich, exclusion got priority. The Reich poured resources into killing Jews even while it needed workers and other resources for the war effort. In contrast, exploitation has been the more basic oppression of wives, who have been granted rights and limited forms of assimilation, reluctantly, by the argument that doing so would enable them to perform still better as mothers and homemakers. Arguably prostitutes get the worst of both forms of oppression: brutal exploitation and simultaneous outlaw status, many treated as "throwaway women" with no protection whatever.[18]

The ethically critical point that critics who target severe oppression can make with regard to the relative importance of equality can be articulated straightforwardly in the language of evil. Inequalities are not themselves evils, although they tend to accompany the evils of exploitation and oppression. For this reason it is a mistake to focus on inequality as the basic wrong to be addressed by feminism and other struggles against oppression. That inequalities should not be feminism's paramount concern is actually a modest claim, however startling it may sound in the context of American feminism. To clarify that, I turn to distinguishing within morality between evils and what is morally bad or wrong, undesirable, even unjust, but not evil.

Morally Bad versus Evil

Earlier chapters have asserted that not everything bad or wrong is an evil and that what distinguishes evils from ordinary wrongs is the element of intolerable harm. Many bad experiences are unpleasant but not really harmful, for example. But one may wonder whether a meaningful distinction can be drawn, from a *moral* point of view, between evil and bad or wrong. Many moral philosophers, including Kant, have treated evil as comprehending all forms of immorality. Nietzsche did not distinguish between evil and bad *within* morality. In his contrast of *schlecht* (bad) with *böse* (evil), *schlecht* appears not to be a moral judgment. It connotes inferiority in status, power, strength, vitality, and the like, but not moral inferiority. The implication seems to be that evil comprehends all forms of moral inferiority.

Yet common sense finds many motives and deeds morally deficient, bad, problematic, or wrong without finding them positively evil. Shoplifting, riding the subway without paying, and cheating on income tax are dishonest and in that respect morally bad, wrong. Anyone who makes a habit of such conduct has a morally bad habit. Calling it evil, however, is overkill; shoplifting is not evil. Saving someone's life solely in order to collect a debt is morally very bad (because of its motive, even though the act, abstracted from the motive, is actually right). Extorting money from the rich by threatening to "out" them as homosexuals is also very bad, but not necessarily evil—depending on whether outing makes the victim seriously vulnerable to major hate crimes. Accepting employment as a hired killer or torturer is evil. In Edith Wharton's novel *The House of Mirth*, Bertha Dorset's mendacious and exploitative public expulsion of Lily Bart, which foreseeably precipitated Lily's ultimately fatal downfall, was evil.[19]

Within morality, both from a common sense point of view and in the atrocity theory, bad is the more comprehensive concept. It applies to wrong acts, immoral motives, or both. Calling what is evil merely bad understates the case. It has been observed that "good" is a relatively tame term of commendation.[20] Within morality, "bad" is a relatively tame term of derogation. The child in William March's novel *The Bad Seed* is portrayed as evil, not merely bad.[21] Bad girls are naughty but not likely to be serial murderers. Mass rape in war is not just bad. It is also (that is, more specifically) evil. Because he distinguishes between two modes of valuation, Nietzsche finds it an open question whether those who are evil are also bad (in a nonmoral sense). He entertains seriously the proposition that many evil people were not bad but were actually superior. As examples he mentions Napoleon and the ancient Romans, both responsible for wanton destruction of human life and incalculable suffering. On the atrocity paradigm, it is not an open question whether evils are morally bad. Conduct is morally bad when it is culpable and wrong. It becomes evil when it also foreseeably deprives others of basics needed for their lives or deaths to be tolerable or decent. Inequalities can be bad (culpable and wrong, unjust), even though they are not evil (do not produce intolerable harm).

"Morally bad" does share in common with Nietzsche's *schlecht* that it is a less hostile judgment than evil. For that reason it is ordinarily easier to accuse oppressors of the unfairness of unequal treatment than to accuse them of downright evil. At times, Nietzsche seems not to consider *schlecht* a hostile judgment at all and even to suggest that it is relatively friendly, because it can be combined with a certain condescending benevolence. Still, even though it does not carry the hostility of judgments of evil, Nietzsche's *schlecht* is un-friendly in its distancing and in its implications that those so characterized are unworthy of admiration, esteem, or respect.

Unlike Nietzsche's *schlecht,* however, bad in the moral sense is more apt to express blame and disappointment than pity, although like *schlecht* it is often compatible with benevolent responses. Parents blame a misbehaving child for being bad (not evil), but also aim to correct, not reject, the child. "Bad girls" are not inferior children; they are bad in something closer to a moral sense. Still, morally bad is a less hostile, less aggressive, and less blaming judgment than evil. The atrocity paradigm suggests that the energy fueling the hostility in judgments of evil is better channeled into eliminating harms and abolishing evil institutions than into punishing evildoers. For it is the harm, rather than the culpable wrongdoing, that distinguishes evils from other wrongs.

On the atrocity paradigm, hostility against evildoers need not be total, all-out, or unforgiving. Because of the many forms that culpable wrongdoing takes, evildoers need not be perceived as sadistic monsters or as necessarily evil people. Nietzsche treats both bad and evil as applying basically to *people* who were perceived as either inferior (bad) or monstrous (evil). The judgment in both cases was totalizing; the whole person was judged, stereotyped, not just something the person *did*. This is far less true of judgments of *moral* bad-ness, and also less true of judgments of evil on the atrocity paradigm.

Applied to social practices or institutions, however, it is fair to say that "evil" really is a totalizing judgment, in the following sense. Even if not ab-solutely everything about an evil institution is unacceptable, evil institutions are rotten at the core. Practices that are bad but not evil tend to be unjust in limited, fixable, respects. Evil practices need to be abolished. Bad ones need repair. Genocide, slavery, torture, and rape are evil practices. "Glass ceil-ings"and arbitrary quotas are bad but often embedded within otherwise tol-erable institutions, to which they are inessential. Hence, those opposing op-pression tend to be revolutionaries and those opposing inequalities, reformists. It is, of course, possible to revolt against some practices while working to reform others.

Are Some Inequalities Evils?

It may be argued that some unjust inequalities, which would not be evils if they were merely sporadic or isolated incidents in a life otherwise flourishing, become evils when they are systematic and come to pervade one's life. Being excluded on the basis of one's race or gender from admission to any high school whatever, as was true of African Americans in Alabama in the 1930s, is an example, in contrast with being excluded from a particular high school. The systematic exclusions symbolize a social judgment of inferiority regarding one's humanity. If social confirmation is essential to maintaining one's sense of worth, that judgment assaults the human dignity of those suffering the injustice. Because one's social identity is partly constructed by social norms governing social interactions, such exclusions actually disfigure those who are excluded.[22] That disfigurement is at least an evil, whether or not it is an atrocity. It is indecent. Major historical examples come readily to mind: ghettos and expulsions of the Jews in late medieval Western Europe, South African apartheid, racial segregation in the United States.

Two factors can intensify the harm suffered when exclusions become systematic. One is the narrowing of opportunities. As opportunities narrow it becomes eventually impossible to acquire certain basics at all, an adequate education, for example. The other is negative symbolic meaning. Exclusions can take on a negative symbolic meaning, becoming an assault on the humanity of those excluded. Regarding the first factor, it is the increasing *lack* of opportunity, not inequality in opportunity, that turns rejections into evils. With regard to the second factor, it may be less clear. How do inequalities come to be an assault on human dignity? Can just any sort of unequal treatment do that, if it is systematic?

To what extent is it the unjust discrimination and to what extent the *quality*—that is, the *nature*—of the treatment, as distinct from the inequality of its distribution, that is responsible for the assault on dignity? "Unequal" grossly underdescribes the treatment of Blacks under South African apartheid and racial segregation in the United States. They were subject to unspeakable violence, terror, poverty, and degradation. What made their treatment indecent was not that Blacks were singled out for it. No one should have to endure that fate.

It may be that part of what is traumatic in some assaults, such as the sexual assault ("incest") of a child by a guardian, is that the victim is singled out to bear a special burden alone, or at least thinks so. It is true that no one should have to endure what the victim endures. But being singled out appears in some cases to aggravate the harm. Perhaps the same is true of apartheid and segregation, where whole groups are singled out.

In some cases, it is not obvious that the first factor, the harm created by such things as a lack of opportunity, is present as something distinct from the symbolic meaning of the maltreatment. Some forms of maltreatment humiliate by the very triviality or useless absurdity of what one is forced to do. A domestic abuser may insist that the towels in the bathroom be aligned just so and deliver severe punishment for violation of this and other similarly trivial requirements. Suppose punishment (admittedly harmful) is at least sometimes avoidable by compliance. It is not that aligning the towels is a harm. Rather, its imposition as a major requirement, violation of which is treated as a capital offense, is indecent. Still more extreme, Jews in Hitler's Vienna were made to scrub the pavement with toothbrushes, sometimes with their underwear. Here, disrespect, the absurdity of the task, the assault on privacy, and discrimination combine to humiliate. Yet it would be humiliating if people were randomly assigned such tasks and were ridiculed and maltreated while they performed them. The symbolic meaning of being made to perform such a task looms larger in such cases than the harmfulness of the task itself.

The basic point is that the symbolic meaning of a form of treatment can turn it into an assault on dignity that makes it an evil, somewhat independently of the nature of the treatment. That point holds regardless of whether the treatment is systematic or an isolated instance, and also regardless of whether those so treated are chosen randomly or not. Deprivations inflicted by Jim Crow laws (being denied access to a restroom or drinking fountain, being made to sit in the back of the bus), which might in other contexts have been annoying or inconvenient, became evils because they acquired the power to symbolize a social judgment of inferior humanity in those so restricted. They are most likely to have that power when the restriction is institutionalized, supported by the sanctions of law, and associated with a natural feature (such as skin color) or an imposed feature (such as badges or readily identifiable clothing). When one's life becomes permeated by such exclusions, they take on importance they would not otherwise have had. Thus, exclusions that look superficially like inconveniences may in fact contribute significantly to indignity in those who suffer them.

Still, there are distinctions to be made, even when an injury is to dignity rather than simply to the pursuit of one's interests. Not all indignities are equal; not all are evils. The above examples illustrate treating people as inferior with respect to their very humanity. Institutional support for such judgments is socially disfiguring to those so treated. Not every indignity communicates that harsh a judgment, however. The following case illustrates a certain indignity. Yet I would not go so far as to consider it an evil.

When I applied to Princeton to graduate school in 1961, I was rejected on the basis of my sex. But Harvard accepted me. In Harvard Yard, however, I was routinely denied access to the Lamont Library, the undergraduate men's library, on grounds of my sex. I tested the policy that excluded women by attempting more than once to enter that library. At the same time, male students were welcomed onto the first floor of the Radcliffe Library for undergraduate women, which enabled them to check out any books they wished. Women were not allowed even through the front door to Lamont. I was at first amazed and amused but eventually resented it. Some of my course assignments were in books obtainable only in Lamont. I could have asked a male friend to check them out for me. (The library did not provide men to offer this service to women.) But I generally did not, because it was embarrassing to have to make the request. This affront to my dignity, however, was compensated to no small extent by the privilege of being able to study at Harvard in the first place, in the same classrooms (not true for Radcliffe students of Helen Keller's era) and from the same teachers as male students. Being excluded from Lamont Library was not something that agitated me or even occupied my thoughts much, although the difference between the Lamont and Radcliffe Library policies did symbolize the judgment that female students were less important members of the university community than male students. Nor was this an isolated instance of discrimination against females on that campus, although it was remarkable for being so overt. Women received markedly less encouragement to participate in class discussions, although that was not (to my knowledge) an official policy. And undergraduate women were not supposed to appear on the streets in pants unless they also wore a long coat. Still, none of these discriminations was an evil, nor did they add up to an evil. They symbolized judgments that female students were less important to Harvard and were not to be confused with males (but were to be readily identifiable as female), but not that women were subhuman.

Not every affront to dignity is an evil, however wrong. There are degrees of seriousness even here, marked, for example, by the difference between an affront (or slight) and an assault (or attack). Not all injuries to dignity leave permanent or deeply disfiguring scars, even if they leave permanent memories and are just cause for resentment.

What Does It Mean to Prioritize?

I have said that evils deserve to be prioritized by social justice movements over unjust inequalities and that they deserve the first attention of those in a position to prevent or alleviate them. Feminism, for example, should in general prioritize ending domestic violence, rape (especially forcible "incest" perpetrated on children), severely hazardous working conditions, and involuntary homelessness over many, perhaps most, inequalities in wages, hiring, promotion, and admissions. Yet we hear relatively little about domestic violence, rape, hazardous working conditions, and homelessness, compared to debates regarding inequalities in wages, hiring, promotions, and admissions. College textbooks on contemporary moral issues seldom include selections on rape (almost never on homelessness or domestic violence) but almost always have something on affirmative action in hiring or admissions. But what does it mean to "prioritize" or give "first attention"?[23] Some interpretations of that idea make it sound absurd.

A natural objection, for example, is that since it appears unlikely that there will ever be a time when there are no more evils, prioritizing them threatens to absorb all of our attention, leaving no energy, time, or other resources for anything else. Maybe we should prioritize what is more manageable? Does prioritizing evils mean that we forgo everything less important, even addressing lesser injustices, some far more readily correctable than real evils? Should women who have jobs that pay a living wage ignore salary and promotion inequities as long as there are women who are sold, raped, and battered?

The answer to the general question is, I think, mostly no, but sometimes yes. Prioritizing evils does not have to mean not caring at all about lesser injustices, or not doing anything toward preventing or mitigating them. Giving first attention to evils is ordinarily compatible with also giving second attention to lesser injustices, about which we can frequently do more. Some people are better positioned to do something significant about inequality in hiring than to do anything significant about domestic violence. And yet the positions we occupy often result from prior choices and reflect our value priorities. We may have to get into position to do something significant about evils, by becoming informed, for example, in a society that does not disseminate the relevant information or permit it to be readily accessible. But even when we are in a good position to do something significant about evils, it is not necessary in order to prioritize them that we do nothing else. I have not suggested that addressing evils be prioritized over everything, but more specifically that social justice movements prioritize evils over unjust inequalities. Even that more limited idea does not imply that such movements should ignore unjust inequalities as long as there are evils to be addressed.

Where a political movement's first attention lies is revealed not only by how great a portion of its resources are devoted to it but also by its paradigms, to what examples it calls attention in exposing social injustice, what causes it publicizes first or most. The atrocity paradigm of evil prioritizes atrocities among evils. "Prioritizing" here does not imply a lexical ordering, like John Rawls's lexical ordering of principles of justice, according to which the first principle must be satisfied before the second one even comes into play.[24] We need not be satisfied that evils have been addressed as fully as *possible* before giving any attention to other matters. Prioritizing evils does mean, at least, making sure that significant attention is devoted to them, whatever else we do.

It may be helpful to consider some analogies. Giving priority to family, for example, is commonly done by making ourselves and our resources available to them rather than to others in times of crisis and also making sure that we spend time with them regularly (not just when they are in crisis), even if that means others get less of our time than we or they would like. Giving priority to family is not ordinarily understood to mean spending all of our time and resources on them. But family will get attention, even if that means that on some occasions work and friends get shorted or postponed.

Perhaps a difficulty with the family analogy is that not all family needs are urgent, whereas evils are, almost by definition, crises for their victims. When evils are ignored or postponed, people die and lives are ruined. Still, prioritizing family is not restricted to crises. Apart from crises, we can prioritize family without ordinarily neglecting others, by making sure that we reserve time for family, whatever else we also do. Likewise with evils, we can make sure that we give significant attention to evils, whatever else we also do.

Another kind of prioritizing is illustrated by setting the agenda for a meeting. The item listed first gets chronological priority. If there is a meeting, that item will be addressed even if nothing else is. But the idea is not necessarily to spend the entire meeting on it. Sometimes the hope is to get it out of the way quickly. Prioritizing in this sense is compatible with also limiting discussion time for the item, precisely in order that other things may also get done.

In the agenda analogy, prioritizing means giving our earliest and freshest attention. Prioritizing does not always have this sense. We can prioritize family, for example, even though we first go out to work and only later spend time at home, provided the time at home is a firm commitment, in that we would adjust the work schedule if need be. Even in the agenda analogy, the reason for placing a prioritized item chronologically first is often a judgment of its importance. The idea is to be sure that the meeting deals with this item, whatever else it does. The main sense of "prioritize" is "to grant importance to." Placing an item chronologically first is one way, but not the only way, to do this. Attending to evils need not be done chronologically prior to attending to anything else, although that is often a good way to make sure they receive attention.

Another example, familiar to college professors, is prioritizing one's research or one's teaching. Here the questions may be which activity will generally receive our freshest energies or which will on the whole receive the bulk of our efforts. When there is not enough time to give adequate attention to both, the question may be which will get the short shrift. An advantage of this analogy, like the family analogy, is that the prioritizing is done over rather long periods of time, not on each occasion where one has a choice to make, or even day by day.

The research and family analogies share the following important features. The risk is that unless research is given a certain priority, it will never get done. Teaching is in many ways easier, less overwhelming. But also there is room for endless improvement in teaching. Further, since its obligations are prescheduled, teaching will get done, whatever else does or does not. Research easily falls between the cracks. Yet without research, teaching eventually suffers. Similarly with family. Unless one gives it priority, family is easily neglected. It is easy to assume (wrongly) that family will always be there. Yet without family, much else loses its meaning. The problem with failing to prioritize evils is similar, the reverse of the initial objection to doing so, which was that prioritizing evils threatens to exclude everything else from attention. The danger is in fact much greater that if evils are not prioritized, they will never receive significant attention. They tend to be overwhelming, and we never run out of other tasks that are easier, on which we can make visible progress more rapidly. Yet it is more important to do something significant about evils.

By prioritizing evils I have in mind at least making sure that over time and in the design of social institutions, something very significant is done toward the prevention or alleviation of evils, whatever else may be done. "Something significant" is partly a relative concept, relative to what is done in other areas. But it is also partly not relative in that something significant is done when it makes a constructive difference to the lives of actual or potential victims of evil. If many people did something significant, and if major social institutions had this kind of objective, fewer people would need to devote entire lives to such projects in order to achieve anything significant.

Following the lead of Peter Singer in practical ethics, Peter Unger argues in *Living High and Letting Die* that we who are relatively privileged (e.g., college professors) should probably give away most of our income to alleviate poverty and prevent diseases that become unnecessarily fatal for so many children globally.[25] Although the language of evil is not prominent in his discussion, the causes with which he is concerned are fairly enough characterized as alleviating and preventing evils. That millions of children die each year "from easy to beat disease, from malnutrition, and from bad drinking water" is an atrocity (Unger, 3), or, rather, several atrocities. Judging from his examples, Unger's intention appears to be to argue against indulging in luxuries (fancy cars), rather than against devoting resources to lesser injustices. He easily gets the reader to ponder the question of whether we can ever be justified in spending any of our resources on ourselves as long as we are above the poverty line while others remain below. His answer appears to be that the best justification for spending on ourselves is simply instrumental, that is, that we are justified in doing so to the extent that it is necessary to maintain our ability to alleviate the evils suffered by others.

But Unger's reasoning may also lead one to raise the question why any resources should be devoted to lesser injustices as long as there are real evils to be resisted. There are many answers. One is that our commitments and interpersonal relationships rightly affect our priorities somewhat independently of the urgency of needs. But, presumably, we could sever many of those relationships and withdraw our commitments, and the question may be raised why not. One answer might appeal to the role of our relationships and commitments in a good life. Many of them have an intrinsic, not simply instrumental, value; they are partly constitutive of a good life.

Yet a different response, not relying on intrinsic value, might begin by pointing out that we cannot be sure of much success in most of our endeavors to resist injustice. Anything that one person does is apt to depend for its effectiveness on the cooperation of many others. Often that cooperation is highly uncertain, and we can be sure of more success both in our relationships and in less ambitious projects. Also, projects can be so interconnected that progress in one area, not urgent itself, may indirectly contribute to progress in others more urgent. Improving fairness in wages might alleviate poverty, depending on whose wages are improved and how much, and alleviating poverty might relieve domestic violence, for even though domestic violence crosses class lines, poverty may be one aggravating cause. Still, it would be a mistake to devote no substantial resources directly to preventing or alleviating evils. For however uncertain our success in that endeavor, the indirect contributions of other projects are usually less certain. Lesser projects themselves may be more certain of success. But their indirect impact on genuine evils tends to be far less certain.

Unger's examples of alleviating child hunger and illness (sending money for food and medicine) and increasing childhood resistance to disease (paying for vaccinations) illustrate one of many ways of attending to evils: sending money. Someone also needs to translate money into needed supplies, and someone needs to administer or deliver them, which can involve risks to themselves of infection, and someone needs to coordinate such activities. Some should do research on the sources of poverty, illness, and hunger, and some should work to eliminate those sources, as opposed simply to increasing resistance to the evils they produce. If everyone able were to devote some resources to alleviating evils in these and other ways, it should be unnecessary that anyone presently above the poverty line be reduced to near poverty by their own efforts to help. Admittedly, there appears to be in this argument an appeal to something like equality in bearing the burdens of addressing evils. Equal sharing of this task among those who are able might be ideal. But the main point is actually more modest. People should coordinate a variety of efforts, if they intend to make a serious, long-term dent in long-standing social evils. An important contribution is political or social organizing, including major fundraising. This is why I take up the relative importance of evils and inequalities in the context of social justice movements, rather than simply individual choice.

To make real headway with problems of widespread child malnutrition and lack of sanitation, it is necessary to think over long stretches of time and over social groups and movements, not just about individuals choosing whether to do something or nothing on a particular occasion. Unger's dramatic examples illustrate individual choices on particular occasions. Importantly, in both cases, others have already made significant higher order contributions, not simply monetary, in creating such things as hospitals and organizations like OXFAM and UNICEF, without which the options of the particular occasions Unger invites us to think about would not even exist. Unger invites us to reflect on how we would evaluate (1) throwing away the solicitation envelope rather than sending money to OXFAM or UNICEF relative to how we would evaluate (2) ignoring a plea for help from a man with a seriously injured leg, to save ourselves the cost of repairing the bloodied seats of our luxury car, rather than driving the injured man to the hospital in time to save his leg, but at the cost of his badly bloodying the car seats.[26] Finding that most people he asked seemed to find it much worse to fail the injured man than to fail OXFAM or UNICEF, he then argues vigorously for the irrationality of that comparative judgment. But these options confront individuals on particular occasions only because there are already hospitals, OXFAM, and UNICEF. The prioritizing I have in mind requires thinking over long stretches of time to create organizations like OXFAM or UNICEF, with wide bases of support, in the first place. With such organizations in place, it is not necessary for individuals to prioritize their special causes moment by moment. It is necessary that people support the organizations, but not that they reduce themselves to near poverty in so doing.

By "giving priority" to evils over inequalities I mean something analogous to what I think John Stuart Mill meant in the second chapter of "Utilitarianism" when he claimed that intellectual pleasures were "higher" (more important) than sensual ones. The most interesting way to interpret Mill's claim is to suppose he meant that intellectual pleasures deserve a certain priority over sensual ones. Unfortunately, Mill left himself open to the interpretation that it is always better to choose an intellectual over a sensual pleasure, whenever confronted with such a choice. This is an implausible position, if only because the starving are less capable of appreciating intellectual pleasures. Yet what he appears to have had in mind was a comparison between two ways of life, not two individual pleasures. In his best statement, he implies that a life that includes some intellectual pleasures is preferable to one that does not, even if the one that does not contains endless sensual pleasures. After defining "higher pleasures" as those that would be chosen by competent judges and defining "competent judge" as one who is acquainted with and capable of appreciating both pleasures to be compared, he writes:

Few human creatures would consent to be changed into any of the lower animals, for a promise of the fullest allowance of a beast's pleasures; no intelligent human being would consent to be a fool . . . even though they should be persuaded that the fool...is better satisfied with his lot than they are with theirs. They would not resign what they possess more than he for the most complete satisfaction of all the desires which they have in common with him.[27]

The alternatives here are not particular pleasures but whole ways of life. The choice between sensual and intellectual pleasures thus appears to be, for Mill, a higher order choice, a choice regarding what (more specific) choices one will be able to confront in one's life. He does not try to specify what proportion of one's pleasures will or should be intellectual rather than sensual in the life of someone capable of both. The idea seems to be that those capable of both often (rightly) prefer intellectual pleasures to a larger quantity of sensual ones. It may not be possible to be more specific than that.

Likewise, a social justice movement's prioritizing of evils may is best regarded as a higher order choice. It is the choice to get into positions from which it is possible to recognize and do something significant about evils, rather than resting content with even very great progress in areas of lesser concern, such as equal pay for equal work. The general idea is that those who appreciate real evils will often choose to do something significant to alleviate or prevent them, rather than make relatively greater progress with lesser projects. They would no more consent to be changed into someone ignorant of, oblivious to, or unable to do anything significant about evils than Mill's intellectuals would consent to be changed into contented ignoramuses. It may not be possible to be much more specific than that.

Application and Implications

Evils giving rise to feminism include domestic battery and other intimate partner abuse, sexual slavery, and "incest," when that term refers to prolonged child rape by a trusted adult or an adult with authority over the child, or to rape of a young child, regardless of frequency. These are the more obvious sexual evils suffered primarily by women and girls. Other evils to which women are especially vulnerable include forced homelessness and forcible imprisonment in insane asylums or nursing homes. Imprisonment can be an evil in itself. It also renders inmates vulnerable to further evils, such as the politically expedient lobotomies to which women like Frances Farmer were subjected in the United States a few decades ago, punitive electroshock treatments, and elder abuse, even murder, by poorly monitored employees.[28] The homeless are exposed to poor sanitation and increased risk of disease. Men, too, suffer homelessness and imprisonment in asylums and nursing homes, but less frequently. Rebellious women in patriarchy are more often judged insane by men in power. The elderly include more widows and spinsters than widowers or bachelors. Many widows, divorcees, and escapees from domestic violence are left without health insurance, Social Security, or the means to earn a livelihood. Historically, men in power have been less concerned to remedy inhumane conditions suffered primarily by women.

Many wrongs suffered by the relatively powerless, which are identified publically as inequalities are, more importantly, evils. Perhaps they are commonly identified as inequalities because it is easier to accuse those in power of discrimination than to accuse them of evildoing. "Unfair" is a less harsh judgment than "evil." The harsher the judgment against those with power to make a difference, the more likely they will use their power to try to defend and justify themselves rather than to make significant constructive differences in the lives of others.

The shift of focus suggested by the atrocity paradigm of evil, from the perpetrator's psychology to the intolerable harm done the victim, has potential to reduce that impact of accusations of evildoing, thereby making defensiveness a less natural response. This shift of focus with its retention of the seriousness of the judgment is preferable to downplaying the seriousness of what was done by calling it simply unfair or unequal treatment. For there is the risk, in thus tempering the judgment, of trivializing the object of concern. Arbitrary inequalities are less serious than evils. Historically, for example, female prison inmates had to do the laundry for both women's and men's prisons. However unfair, that assignment was not an evil. The rape of female inmates by prison guards is an evil. That assault is not simply discrimination or unfairness. One could point out that, in fact, male inmates are raped, too (by other inmates). That fact does not mitigate the evil of the rape of female inmates. The rapes of both sexes are evils.

A similar point can be made in regard to a television advertisement sponsored by a famous maker of athletic gear and aired frequently during women's basketball games on the ESPN channel a few years ago. The ad began, "If you let me play sports . . . ," and then girls, from preschool to puberty, told, one after another, of hardships and evils they would be better equipped to avoid or resist if they had the opportunity for sustained athletic development in their youth. ("I will be less likely to be depressed," "I will be more likely to leave a man who beats me," "I will be less likely to have breast cancer," etc.). At first, I cringed at "let me" and wanted to change it to "encourage me to play sports." "Let me" seemed to endorse patriarchal authority to give females permission. But then, listening to myself say it, I heard a less powerful message in "encourage me" than in "let me." "Encourage me" conveys that girls lack a natural desire to play sports. "Let me" conveys that only sexist prohibition and deprivation hold girls back. It means both "don't stop me" and "let me have the opportunity"—"leave me to" and "let me have a chance," rather than "permit me to." The ad was just right, one of the best I have seen.

What made this advertisement powerful was not that it was a plug for Title IX, that is, not its appeal to *equality* in government-supported educational programs. Title IX of the Education Amendments Act passed by Congress in 1972 states that "No person in the United States shall, on the basis of sex, be excluded from participation in, be denied the benefits of, or be subjected to discrimination under any education program or activity receiving federal financial assistance."[29] Yet nothing in the ad compares girls' athletics with boys'. Rather, the power of the ad came from its identification of evils women suffer in a misogynist environment as in part a result of girls' deprivation of opportunities for sustained athletic development. What is at stake here is a basic health issue, mental and physical. If we press the question of how much opportunity girls should have, the answer "as much as boys" does not get at the basic issue. Some boys have too much, others too little. The right kind of answer relates the opportunities for athletics to health and well-being, at least to the evils that such opportunities can prevent or mitigate.

Feminism's priorities should be to address the evils to which a misogynist environment exposes people and other living beings and to address the evils of oppression generally. In a society where men do not prioritize the evils of misogyny and other evils to which women are especially vulnerable, women are justified in giving them special attention. The reasons I have been drawn to radical feminism are that it has long had the right priorities (including concern for evils done to nonhuman animals and to entire ecosystems) and that it attends to evils others have either ignored or subordinated. Socialist feminists would no doubt say the same about why they are drawn to socialist feminism, although my concern regarding socialism has been that it may neglect or not readily perceive evils that are not reducible to matters of economics. Radical feminists have prioritized violence against women and girls and against other oppressed groups (often popularly derogated by being portrayed as feminine), which cut across social classes. The work of Mary Daly in *Gyn/Ecology*, of Susan Griffin in *Woman and Nature*, of Audre Lorde, Andrea Dworkin, María Lugones, Catharine MacKinnon, Adrienne Rich, and many others exemplifies this concern.[30] In contrast, it was impossible for me to develop anything like the same enthusiasm for the Equal Rights Amendment during the 1980s (not to deny that its defeat was a profound, if predictable, insult), although some may have seen that amendment as instrumentally important to addressing the evils that have concerned me.

What makes sense of many women of color in the United States not being enthusiastic to join forces with white feminists is the fear that white feminists will prioritize lesser injustices to white women over genuine evils suffered by people of color. Such fears are not without justification. There seems something timid about equality feminism. It suggests that the way to begin is by trying to right a wrong the pointing out of which will not (perhaps should not) cause very much offense or disturbance in those responsible for the wrong, in the faith that success is more likely with modest beginnings and in hopes that such beginnings will lay the foundation for more important social changes down the road. Yet the net result of that strategy is to prioritize what is least important and delay into the never-to-be-concluded future what is most important.

Does Respect for Humanity Imply Basic Equality?

One might object to the implied opposition between evils and inequalities, in the idea of prioritizing evils over inequalities, on the ground that it presupposes that evils do not essentially already involve a significant inequality. Suppose one were to maintain that an important sort of inequality is always at the root of evil, namely, the failure to treat someone with the basic respect that everyone deserves. I have myself characterized evils in terms of what anyone can be presumed to want to avoid and what no one should have to suffer. Do these terms "anyone" and "no one" import a significant ideal of equality into the very concept of evil?

If they do, it is not a kind of equality that I find it objectionable to prioritize over other inequalities. It seems, however, to be the kind of equality that Joseph Raz called simply a by-product of universality, rather than an aim itself.[31] It is not helpful to say that what is basically wrong here is a fundamental sort of inequality. What is genuinely helpful is to identify the kind of treatment that no one should have to endure. Further, there is the danger that emphasizing equality can lead to tolerating evils that should not be tolerated. For consider the following.

When evils are distributed unequally, it is no improvement to inflict them on those who have escaped thus far, so as to even things out, when doing so would not significantly lessen the burden on everyone who suffers over what is presently suffered by those who did not escape. When it is not possible to give relief to all who equally deserve it, or even to make sure that all who are equally deserving have an equal *opportunity* to obtain it, the best course is not to withhold relief from everyone alike so as to avoid unfairness. Better to help some arbitrarily, if that can be done without subjecting others to comparably serious evils, than to use the impossibility of fairness as an excuse to do nothing. At least, when it is a question of relieving evils, rather than distributing a luxury, it is better to help some arbitrarily. There is something to be said for withholding from everyone a luxury rather than bestowing it arbitrarily. Avoiding envy may be more important in that case. But envious resentment of all arbitrariness in alleviating genuine evils is mean.

It may be objected that equality does become important when resources are limited, although not so limited that it is impossible to do at least something for everyone. If there are not enough resources to make everyone safe from domestic battery, then the question arises of how much protection anyone should have a right to expect. Thus, when resources are limited, the question of how to distribute them is a fair one. "Equally" is one answer. But suppose we were then to conclude that women's safety in the home should receive as much resource allocation as men's safety in the home: an equal number of shelters, for example, for women as for men. If what is necessary to men's safety is taken as the defining standard, women will not be helped much. If what women need is taken as the defining standard, it is absurd to spend comparable resources on unnecessary shelters for men when there are genuine needs to be met elsewhere. But men may then resent the "extra" resource allocation for women and allow that resentment to reinforce existing condescension toward women. That will not help women much, either. We seem to have an example of what Martha Minow calls "the dilemma of difference." The way out, she rightly perceives, is to not take inequality of needs and the existing social values associated with them as givens but to consider what gives rise to differential needs, what they mean, and what gives rise to such things as the values underlying condescension toward women.

Equal resource allocation is also how the University of Wisconsin has been forced to deal with free emergency evening transit programs in regard to women's safety on campus at night: such transit must be equally available to men and to women. Equal resource allocation is how Title IX addresses female development in government supported educational institutions. It prohibits discrimination. It does not otherwise mandate programs.

As in the case of domestic battery, such policies risk offering women no significant relief. Sports equality can be attained by abolishing sports, rather than adding opportunities for women. In a misogynist environment women need *more* protection than men to be equally safe. Because female students are more likely to be assaulted by male students, an emergency transit system that pays no attention to the sexes of drivers, escorts, or co-riders puts females at greater risk. And still, the focus should not be on equal safety (which is compatible in principle with everyone in fact being quite unsafe) but, rather, on achieving certain minimum standards of safety.

The defender of equality as a basic value might then try to clarify that position as supporting a special kind of equality, namely, a guaranteed minimum standard of well-being for all. This returns to a focus on what everyone should have or what no one should have to suffer. Depending on how we understand the implementation of this utopian ideal, it may be compatible with my concern to prioritize evil. But I am not certain. Here is a lingering concern:

How important is the "equality" (or "for all") when it is possible to rescue only some, and there is no uncontroversially fair way to determine whom to save? It may be that if time is taken to try to be fair in choosing whom to rescue, the rescue will come too late, as in the case of refugees seeking asylum from oppression. In individual decision making of everyday life, this kind of situation seldom becomes much of a problem. If I can help one person who is suffering by spending time and energy doing things that make it impossible for me to help someone else who is suffering similarly, I ordinarily think it a good thing to help the one who confronts me now, even though which person confronts me now may be totally arbitrary. If I have no special prior relationship to either, I would hardly pause to draw straws or debate the merits of helping this one rather than that one, although I might easily engage in such reflection (as Virginia Woolf did in *Three Guineas*) with respect to sending money to OXFAM, UNICEF, Amnesty International, or the Southern Poverty Law Center.[32] When confronted directly with an individual facing an evil that I can alleviate here and now, it is less natural to raise the question of whether someone else might need my help even more. Something like this response seems appropriate also at the level of social policy in emergencies. It is good to relieve those who confront us now, even though others are equally in need, and even though it is arbitrary whom fate places in our paths.

This issue brings to mind the Mishnah declaration that in saving a single life, it is as if one had preserved an entire world (and that in destroying a single life, it is as if one had destroyed a whole world).[33] Although the Mishnah makes this point in the context of a discussion of capital punishment and begins with the part about destroying a life, there appear to be interesting implications for the morality of rescue. The idea appears not to be to sanction potential rescuers in saving fewer lives than they might, on the ground that one is enough. Rather, the idea seems to be to endorse potential rescuers' saving whomever they can, even though others are equally in need and there may be something arbitrary about the choice of those rescued. It can be good to save even one, perhaps any one, when one cannot save all, just as it can be evil to destroy even one, regardless how many others one did not destroy.

A Final Qualification

There is a way in which less serious inequalities may be justifiably given a political priority that would not otherwise be justified. Substantial concern for equality in resource distribution may become instrumentally important to securing the cooperation of those whose labors are needed to create further resources required to address genuine evils. Thus, even though the evils ultimately to be addressed are more important, perhaps political decision-makers should take very seriously equality in resource distribution so as to be able effectively to elicit the requisite cooperative efforts. Although it may appear that equality is given priority here, the priority is only chronological. It does not cease thereby to be the case that, ethically, the more important concern is to address the evils.

6

Rape in War

Invisible Atrocities

Rape in war includes many long-standing practices that are global in scope, devastating in the harms done to victims, and yet, until the 1990s, not generally known, publicly denounced, or prosecuted as war crimes. What accounts for the relative invisibility of these atrocities, which are often inflicted openly and shamelessly? What should be done about them? Answers to the invisibility question emerge in applying concepts arising from the atrocity paradigm. Some fantasies I then offer regarding responses do not so much provide answers as help to expose the limits of punishment for atrocities. I focus on two practices of rape in war. One is the enslavement of women and girls for recreational sexual service to soldiers and officers, "forced prostitution." The other is the mass rape of female civilians by soldiers and militias as a weapon of war.

Women and girls have been enslaved for sexual service in brothels for soldiers and in forced "marriages" (usually to officers who may select a woman or girl from one of the brothels or from a group of women or girls targeted for mass rape). The purpose is recreation for soldiers and officers. It is not part of the purpose to intimidate an enemy population, although that is sometimes an effect. Women and girls enslaved are not always selected from enemy populations. Some are kidnapped from homes or villages. Others have been lured by false promises of honorable employment. They are mostly very young (in the HIV era, ever younger), healthy, and good-looking, and range from adolescents to women in their mid-thirties. Women who tried to resist have reported that captors initiated them with beatings and rape (often gang rape) to break their spirit. Some resisters were publicly executed as an example to others. The women do not always receive protection against beatings by dissatisfied customers or time off to heal from injuries. Their medical care is determined by consumers' needs, not their own. Many survivors are sterile from surgeries performed to terminate or prevent pregnancies.

The best documented, most publicized case of wartime sexual slavery is that of the "comfort women" enslaved by the Japanese military during World War II. Women and girls, mostly Korean but also Filipino, Malayasian, Indonesian, and Chinese, were kidnapped or lured through deception to become comfort women. They were forced to service Japanese soldiers sexually in "comfort stations" for years, some as many as thirty a day, sometimes with a day or two off monthly for menstruation.[1] In the early years of the war Japanese women were also kidnapped for this purpose. That practice was terminated because it proved demoralizing to the home front, especially to Japanese families who had contributed soldiers to the war effort. Demoralizing families was a cost the Japanese military was willing to inflict on enemy peoples, but it was not the primary purpose of comfort women. Their rapes were not intended as a weapon of war. After the infamous Rape of Nanking, comfort stations were defended by the argument that they protected local females in enemy country from uncontrolled war rape by soldiers. This argument did not stem from concern for local women (who would not obviously have been treated worse than comfort women). It stemmed, rather, from fear that local populations would otherwise sympathize with and give aid to guerilla efforts. At the war's end, when many Japanese soldiers committed suicide to avoid capture, some of them first machine-gunned to death houses full of comfort women to keep them from falling into enemy hands.[2] Others were left to make their way in a strange land. Some survived. A very few survivors have come forward and pressed claims for compensation. Many, however, have refused to pursue monetary compensation on the ground that accepting "payment" would really turn them into prostitutes.

The war rapes publicized during the 1990s wars in Rwanda and the former Yugoslavia are mostly not of this sort, although there was more random, not formally organized, sexual slavery in these wars, too. Most of the rapes, however, were mass sexual assaults, performed in a variety of locations, by soldiers or militias on civilian females of an enemy population. Rape here was used as a weapon of war. Its purposes include intimidating and demoralizing the enemy, forced impregnation, tampering with the identity of the next generation, splintering families, and dispersing entire populations. When rape is used as a weapon, there is no pretense that the victim enjoys it. The primary purpose of policies that tolerate and encourage it is not to provide recreation for soldiers and officers, even if the activity happens to be sport for many of the perpetrators and the sporting element explains their willingness to do it. Victims range from infants to the very elderly and include women who are already pregnant. Among rapists are former neighbors and acquaintances of the victims. Rapes of a single victim are often multiple and public. Some rapists use physical instruments. Victims are commonly beaten, wounded with weapons, and often severely mutilated in the genital area. Many rapists kill their victims. Some first kill the women's children before their eyes. Survivors are often permanently disabled, physically and psychologically. Many are rejected by their families and communities. Some of the women become pregnant. Many of them have abortions, or they have stillbirths, or they abandon the infants. Some victims end in suicide and many in fatal illness, commonly HIV-related.

The Geneva Conventions of 12 August 1949 and the Protocols Additional to them prohibit rape in international and internal conflicts.[3] The second Protocol prohibits "violence to the life, health and physical or mental well-being of persons, in particular murder as well as cruel treatment such as torture, mutilation" and "outrages upon personal dignity, in particular humiliating and degrading treatment, rape, enforced prostitution and any form of indecent assault," as well as "slavery and the slave trade in all their forms."[4] According to Human Rights Watch, "under international law, perpetrators of sexual violence can be held accountable for rape as a war crime, as a crime against humanity, or as an act of genocide, if their actions meet the definitional elements of each."[5] In the second set of Nuremberg trials, rape is specifically listed as a crime against humanity, but it was not prosecuted at any of these trials.[6] In 1975 Susan Brownmiller included a powerful chapter on war rape in her groundbreaking book *Against Our Will*.[7] Yet war rape has rarely been punished or, until the 1990s, even denounced.

Human Rights Watch notes that, historically, military leaders have regarded the rape of civilian women of an enemy population as a private crime committed by individual soldiers and have actually tolerated it on the ground that it was so common. In 1995, however, Justice Richard Goldstone, Prosecutor for the International Criminal Tribunals for the Former Yugoslavia and Rwanda, wrote that "sexual assaults, committed particularly against women, can constitute torture under the Statute of the tribunal, and will be prosecuted as transgressions of international humanitarian law by my office" and that this legal position is "consistent with the evolving norm of torture"; he cites the statement of the Inter-American Commission of Human Rights' Report on Haiti that "the infliction of rapes on the female civilian population, was torture."[8] The problem, according to Human Rights Watch, has not been lack of appropriate legislation but the international community's reluctance to support the prosecution of sex crimes against women.

That reluctance requires explanation. How could these flagrant and widespread atrocities be tolerated, especially in a world that prosecutes some war crimes? The atrocity paradigm suggests searching for possible explanations in the magnitude gap, in the nature of the harm, in what happens to victims, and, finally, in the forms of culpability in various perpetrators. According to the magnitude gap discussed in chapter 1, perpetrators are apt to underestimate the magnitude and seriousness of the harm they do, whereas victims are apt to exaggerate the reprehensibility of the perpetrators' motives. In correcting for these distortions, victims' testimonies are a major source of information regarding the harm. Yet victims are often killed or silenced and their testimony forever lost. When atrocity victims are a defeated enemy, the testimony of willing survivors is likely not to find its way into the public record. As the magnitude gap leads us to expect, the dominant public record, formulated by the victors, commonly omits accounts of atrocities inflicted by the victors, who routinely edit the facts to justify the war and its outcome. This omission applies to war crimes generally, not just rape. The international community's failure to denounce and prosecute war rape by victorious perpetrators makes a certain sense if it takes the victor's point of view and depends on the victor's versions of the facts.

Such silences, gaps, in the public record help to explain failures to prosecute many kinds of war crimes. They do not, however, explain a greater reluctance, by those who know, to prosecute war rape than to prosecute other crimes. Given global sexism, it may be thought that because rape victims are overwhelmingly female and perpetrators male, the problem is women's lack of adequate access to and representation in the courts. There is no doubt some truth here. Yet women have testified freely and sooner against men indicted for other war crimes than rape. It matters not just who the victim is and her relative power position but also what kinds of harm the victim suffers and risks.

Prior to the 1970s, there was little public identification with rape victims in the United States by either women or men but, instead, a widespread blaming of victims coupled with pity for rapists, who were thought to have "a problem" (for which other women—the rapist's mother, wife, or "girlfriend"—were commonly blamed). Until the last quarter of the twentieth century, the vast majority of rape survivors maintained silence out of shame and fear of meeting with disbelief, victim blaming, and ostracism. Many (perhaps most) still do. A famous feminist philosophy professor wrote me recently in correspondence that were she raped today, she probably would not reveal it because of what the publicity would do to her life. Some survivors of war rape have been willing to tell their stories only anonymously, even decades later. Some testified only after the death of a spouse, whom they never told.

Public consciousness was raised regarding civilian rape long before there was public appreciation of war rape, even though war rape is often more sadistic. Sexist military traditions that support war rape in the first place also contribute to suppression of the facts surrounding it. The military is an ancient brotherhood. Women who might take up victims' causes have been barred from combat units, where they might witness war rape firsthand. Yet surely there are male witnesses who do not participate. Apparently, either they did not find it important enough to protest, or their attempts to do so have been routinely suppressed.[9]

Apart from the gap between the perceptions of perpetrator and victim, the magnitude of what soldiers and officers learn to regard as ordinary, if not justified, in wartime may also be a factor. War is, after all, the deliberate infliction of intolerable harm. When bombs destroy entire cities, killing hundreds of thousands of civilians of all ages and permanently ruining the lives of survivors, it may be difficult for perpetrators to appreciate the magnitude of rape trauma, even though the self-defense arguments invoked to justify bombing have no plausibility for rape.

Bombing may not be good for comparison with rape, however, because of the distance between perpetrator and victim. Although the harm of war rape may seem to perpetrators to pale in comparison to that of bombs, bombing may be easier, just because the perpetrator does not come face to face with victims. Writing about the psychological costs of learning to kill in war, Lt. Col. Dave Grossman cites impressive statistics on soldiers in the U.S. Civil War and in the trenches of World War I, who, when it was still possible to see the enemies' faces, have pretended that their weapons would not fire or have aimed above or below to avoid actual killing.[10] Rape, like most forms of torture, requires the still greater proximity of bodily contact. As Robin Schott observes, "the distancing from seeing the actual results of evil that characterized Eichmann's crime is not present in the example of rape."[11] Stanley Milgram found, in his studies of obedience to authority, that his subjects were less likely to inflict on others what they were led to believe was intolerable pain when their proximity to those others was increased.[12] The proximity of perpetrator to victim no doubt also makes it more difficult for others to sympathize with rapists, which should, theoretically, increase the likelihood of their being held accountable. Yet, although rapists are not shielded from perceptual awareness of victims' suffering, officers who order or tolerate it often are. Distance from victims is often there with respect to those who could prevent the rape. And they are almost never held accountable, which is also true for other forms of torture.

Investigative journalist John Conroy argues, in his exploration of three episodes of torture in the last third of the twentieth century, that "torture is the perfect crime," that although there are exceptions, "in the vast majority of cases, only the victim pays."[13] Although the title of his book is *Unspeakable Acts, Ordinary People*, some of the torturers he interviewed appear to have been extraordinary people, previously rewarded for heroism. Many of his explanations of why torture is rarely punished seem to apply also to the case of mass rape in war. Conroy found that "torturers are often decorated soldiers . . . who have served their country in time of need," that the abuse tends to be minimized (not described as torture) and the victims disparaged, that the treatment is defended as effective under the circumstances, that those who take up the cause of the tortured are charged with "aiding the enemies of the state," that those who would punish it are charged with "raking up the past," that the blame is put on "a few bad apples," that it is routinely argued that "someone else does or has done much worse things," and that the torturing nation rationalizes that "the victims will get over it" (Conroy's own inquiries into torture victims' subsequent careers indicate otherwise).[14] He cites studies of the Kitty Genovese murder in 1964, when thirty-eight bystanders failed to help (even to call for help). The studies concluded that when many people are equally positioned to intervene, most will do nothing, because "responsibility is diffused."[15]

Rape as a weapon of war is a recognized form of torture. It is plausible that most of the factors Conroy cites help to explain why it was not prosecuted for so long. If his findings are sound, most torture is not prosecuted, and when it is, perpetrators seldom receive punishment commensurate with the crime. The case is somewhat different with respect to sexual slavery. Although sexual service is a torture to the enslaved, torture is not the aim and that element is commonly hidden from consumers. There is some analogy with the civilian consumption of sexual services and pornography. When rape is recreation or a sport, the perpetrator focuses on his pleasure and fantasies, including the fantasy that the woman likes it. Enslaved women are under duress to smile and pretend that they do, facilitating the illusion that no harm is done.

Yet even soldiers ignorant of the histories of kidnapping and beating of the comfort women could hardly fail to notice that many of the "women" were barely teenagers, some even younger. Of course, meat eaters ignorant of the histories of the animals whose bodies they consume must also know, on a moment's reflection, that the animals were killed in infancy, youth, or early maturity. Yet that does not stop, or even trouble, most consumers. Human consumption of animals is defended by the arguments that animals lack the awareness that people have; they are "only animals," and they are said to be killed instantaneously, painlessly or nearly so. In war, soldiers learn that it is okay to use enemy women, since they are "only women" and "only the enemy," and they will likely soon be killed anyway (and so not aware for long).

Thus, many reasons appear to explain why war rape has been relatively invisible to outsiders, engaged in shamelessly by perpetrators, and rarely prosecuted or even denounced throughout its history. Victims have been silenced by death, shame, and fear, and survivors have lacked the opportunity, freedom, and encouragement to publicize their experience. Consumers who encounter smiles and good service may fail to appreciate the wrongness or depth of the harm in sexual slavery. Those most responsible for this practice and that of mass rape as a weapon may be sufficiently distanced from them not to be disturbed by what they know. Others may have difficulty, especially in the context of war's general destructiveness, appreciating the trauma of war rape.

Or they may discount the suffering of women of an enemy population. Military women who might identify with female victims have been prevented from witnessing their rapes by being excluded from combat units. Some of these things are now changing.

War rape has arrived even in the movies. During the middle 1990s, films that featured or portrayed rape in war, or in warlike situations, included *Death and the Maiden* (based on the play of that title by Ariel Dorfman), featuring a woman who survived rape by a physician who was hired to oversee her political torture; *Rob Roy* (based on Sir Walter Scott's novel), which portrayed a strategic rape—intended to provoke a husband—by an English "nobleman" charged with putting down a Scottish rebellion; and *Immortal Beloved* (on the life of Beethoven), which showed briefly in the background the rape of a civilian stagecoach passenger by one of Napoleon's soldiers. Closely related was *Braveheart*, which presented imperial rape in the "rite of the first night," a rite that licensed English nobles to rape Scottish commoner brides on their wedding nights.[16] Although not performed in the context of war, imperial rape had some of the same goals as mass rape in war: genetic imperialism and a realignment of loyalties in future generations (goals actually made explicit in *Braveheart*). No filmmaker to my knowledge has yet attempted to portray *mass* rape in war.

Rape as Torture and Terrorism

Torture and terrorism tame their survivors by relying on the energy-consuming and debilitating effects of fear and, as Nietzsche noted, the ability to remember what hurts.[17] Taming, like training, is often for service—utilitarian, recreational, or both. This purpose sets limits to torture in that taming carried too far produces someone who is no longer either useful or entertaining. Purposes ultimately served by both civilian and war rape include utilitarian and recreational exploitation. But the immediate result in victims who survive is an overwhelming sense of helplessness. Rape, like other forms of torture, effectively reduces or eliminates resistance.

Torture becomes a form of terrorism when some are tortured to get others to submit. Carl Wellman notes that terrorism, unlike simple torture, characteristically has two targets: a primary target, namely, the object of coercion to whom a message is sent by way of threats or harm done to a more immediate but actually secondary target, who is used as the instrument of coercion.[18] In some instances, as in an armed holdup, Wellman finds that the same person is both primary and secondary target. This does not necessarily transform the case into one of torture, for in some cases the victim may be only threatened with harm, not actually suffer it. And we can still distinguish, even when there is only one victim, between the immediate harm (or threat) and the coercive message it sends. Wellman also gives the example of a rapist beating up his victim (immediate harm) to give her the message that she is to submit (ulterior objective). This case illustrates both torture and terrorism. Not all torture is terrorist, however, for not all torture has a coercive intent. Some torture is meant as punishment. (Israeli torturers told Conroy their purpose in breaking Arab men's bones was punishment.) Or it may simply have the goal of eliminating resistance by wearing victims down.[19]

Paradigmatically, the targets of terrorism are different people, as when a bomber kills some to intimidate others. The targets can be different even in the case of rape. The woman raped is often a throwaway or sacrificial victim, a secondary target used to send a message to the primary target, namely, other women ("this is what will happen to you if you are insufficiently deferential and obedient") or to men ("this is what we will do to your women"). In war and in peace, the role of women raped and murdered is often like that of bomb victims. They are used to manipulate others whose compliance the terrorist seeks.

Elsewhere I have written about rapes that are often "domestic" in two senses: they are rapes of other citizens (or residents) of the same state, and they are often committed against other members of the same household.[20] Civilian rape is an instrument of domestication (breaking for house service) and exploitation. It breaks a woman's spirit, humiliates and tames, produces a docile, deferential soul. It teaches her that she will have in her own body only the control she is granted by another. Rape as terrorism contains the implicit threat of more and worse unless the victim cooperates. Its long-range message is that reprieve comes only through service.

The comfort women (often sexually inexperienced adolescents) who reported that their captors initiated them with multiple rapes to break their spirit and teach them obedience experienced both torture and terrorism. They were at once primary and secondary targets. When civilian women are raped in their homes or communities by enemy soldiers, the primary target is men—husbands, fathers, brothers. These rapes are meant to demoralize the men, make them manipulable. The aims of expulsion and dispersion, unlike the hope of future exploitation, set no limits to the extent and degree of the torture. If there is one set of fundamental functions of rape, civilian or martial, it is to display, communicate, and produce or maintain dominance, which is both enjoyed for its own sake and used for such ulterior ends as exploitation, expulsion, dispersion, and murder. Rape is a cross-cultural symbol of male domination.

Civilian rape by an acquaintance, family member, partner, or spouse often issues in exploitation for service, even though some civilian rape—such as the college fraternity party gang rapes researched by Peggy Sanday—may be a training for war.[21] Although stranger rape may be for the sake of dominance as an end in itself, a common function served by its toleration is to secure female heterosexual dependency and service. The rapes of some women send the message to others that they need protection. The ever-present threat of rape from childhood through old age produces a society of women oriented toward serving men, women who are animated by hopes of securing protection as a reward and who eventually feel bound to the men through misplaced gratitude for "protection" that is mostly only a withholding of abuse.[22]

In contrast, mass rape in war splinters families and alliances. It binds not women to men but warriors to one another. Accounts from recently surviving victims and perpetrators indicate that functions served by the 1990s martial rapes in Bosnia-Herzegovina included expulsion, obedience, revenge and the destruction of culture, that its ultimate targets were entire peoples.[23] The same patterns may be discernible historically in the rapes of Vietnamese women by U.S. GI's and of Native American women by British soldiers.[24] As forcible impregnation, mass rape in war is also a tool of genetic imperialism. When the child's social identity is determined by that of the biological father, impregnation by rape in war undermines family solidarity. Even if no pregnancy results, knowledge of the rape has been sufficient for men in patriarchal cultures to reject wives, mothers, and daughters, as in the case of Bengali women raped by Pakistani soldiers in 1971.[25] Ultimately, mass rape in war can undermine national, political, and cultural solidarity, changing the next generation's identity, confusing the loyalties of survivors.

There is more than one way to eliminate a people. The most straightforward way is, of course, mass murder, the slaughter of individuals of a national, political, or cultural group. Such killing is what is ordinarily meant by "genocide." Another way, however, is to destroy a group's identity by decimating its cultural and social bonds. Some political theorists prefer to call this "ethnicide." If survivors become pregnant or are known to have been raped, cultural, political, and national unity may be thrown into chaos. These have been among the apparently intended purposes of the mass rapes of women in Bosnia-Herzegovina and in Rwanda.[26]

When cultural decimation is the principal aim, general slaughter of captives is unnecessary. The victor may enslave the vanquished or disperse them. In his history of slavery, Milton Meltzer notes that one primary source of slaves in the ancient world was the practice of taking war captives who, in a preagricultural age, would have been slaughtered.[27] John Rawls also observed in *A Theory of Justice*:

> There may be transition cases where enslavement is better than current practice. For example, suppose that city-states that previously have not taken prisoners of war but have always put captives to death agree by treaty to hold prisoners as slaves instead. Although we cannot allow the institution of slavery on the grounds that the greater gains of some out-

weigh the losses to others, it may be that under these conditions, since all run the risk of capture in war, this form of slavery is less unjust than present custom. . . . The arrangement seems an advance on established institutions, if slaves are not treated too severely. In time it will presumably be abandoned altogether, since the exchange of prisoners of war is a still more desirable arrangement, the return of the captured members of the community being preferable to the services of slaves.[28]

Rawls's proposed rationale for the change from killing to enslavement of war captives assumes economic interests as a guiding consideration. But what if the guiding consideration were domination rather than economics? When a people can be effectively dominated and their culture decimated through enslavement, slaughter is also unnecessary. The goal of an eventual exchange of prisoners, however, requires forgoing the ends of domination and cultural decimation.

Historically, women have been enslaved in war for sexual service to captors. Rawls's speculation does not address their situation. Even in a preagricultural age, the practice prior to the enslavement of enemy soldiers appears to have been to enslave captured females for sexual service. Impregnated females might be "persuaded" to alter their loyalties as well as used to expand the conquering population, whereas nothing comparable could be done with the loyalties of fathers, brothers, or husbands, and additional males are not needed to grow the population. Mary Renault's historical novels present captive women and adolescents of both sexes as enslaved for sexual service in the ancient world and sold on an international market, a practice that apparently existed long before any agreement to exchange prisoners was reached among men.[29] Such agreements would not have been likely to improve the lot of women and other sexual slaves.

For men, enslavement rather than slaughter of war captives has two apparent advantages. First, if any man might become a war captive, it could be to his advantage to survive (rather than be killed) even as a slave and hope for a reversal of fortune. Second, slavery instituted a class system, providing exploitable productive labor for conquerors. But what advantages could a woman anticipate upon being enslaved rather than slaughtered? What would she gain by a change of political fortune if she had been captured, impregnated, gave birth, and then survived to be exchanged? What would have become of her identity? If she were not a lesbian, who would be eager to have her returned in an exchange of war prisoners? The effects on women of sexual slavery are less readily reversible than the effects on men of economic slavery.

Under universal (bisexual) slavery for productive labor, enslaved women have been permitted to live temporarily in families with enslaved men. This was the case under American slavery. Yet that practice coexisted with enslaved women's continual vulnerability to rape and to being sold away or separated from a spouse or children who were sold away. In such a situation rape continues to send the message of dominance and to enforce dominance. It has the potential to wreak havoc with bonds among the enslaved, as rape victims are often portrayed by perpetrators as willing rather than raped.

When I refer to the purposes of mass rape in war, I have in mind its strategic purposes, those appreciable at the levels of authority and command. Individual rapists who carry out the strategy may not intend those purposes or be moved by them, just as they may be ignorant of larger purposes served by various military orders they receive. There is room in particular acts of rape for a variety of motives. Like civilian rape, war rape is an institution. As with other institutions, the purposes that it serves and that lead those with power to maintain it in existence need not move or even be appreciated by many of its participants. The purpose is more likely to move those who choose not to intervene when they could or who support the practice in various ways as outsiders. Thus, civilian rape serves a domestic protection racket whereby males secure the services of females in exchange for protection against other males.[30] But men who carry out particular rapes need not intend to terrorize other women into seeking male protection. The intention to support protectionism is more likely to be found in beneficiaries and other supporters of the practice who judge that a raped woman was "asking for it."

Like civilian rape, the practice of mass rape in war has been defined by largely unwritten rules or norms (although rules governing comfort stations were sometimes written down in detail)—for example, the rules that females are the main victims, that their age does not matter, that soldiers who rape "enemy women" are not to be reported, and that anonymous publicity of rapes may be desirable. Action in accord with these norms serves purposes identifiable independently of individual rapists' motives or intentions. A soldier may rape because he was ordered to or because he felt like it. Superior officers, on the other hand, may look the other way because of the martial purposes rape can serve.

Some women survivors in Bosnia-Herzegovina assumed, because those who raped them had previously been neighbors whom they could not imagine treating them with such brutality, that the soldiers must have been under orders (Stiglmayer, 120). Yet rape violates international rules of war. Soldiers need not always be given direct orders. They may be induced or pressured in other ways—for example, by being given reason to believe that if they do not rape, they will be raped themselves or beaten or ostracized. Some rapist captives who have been interviewed gave other explanations. Borislav Herek from Sarajevo, who admitted to raping and shooting three unarmed women, said that if he did not do it, his superiors would have sent him "to the worst front line" or to jail and that they would have taken away the Muslim's house that they had given him (Stiglmayer, 147–54). One is reminded, in reading such accounts, of how banal the motives of evildoing can be. When pressed on why he was willing to kill people with whom he had no past history of animosity, he indicated that he was told—apparently in an attempt to incite revenge—that Muslims had killed his father and burned his house down. Another motive emerged when Herek admitted that his superiors gave him women to rape along with wine and food as a reward for good behavior and to induce camaraderie with fellow soldiers given the same treats.

At the level of individual rapists' motives, it is difficult to see patterns. It is at the level of strategy—of order giving, hate mongering, rewarding and penalizing and, equally, refusing to investigate and penalize on the part of military authorities—that coherent strategic patterns emerge. Stiglmayer reports (160–63) that in the opinion of some, paramilitary groups were using rapes "to build up a kind of solidarity" among the rapists, to teach "who is 'good' and who is 'contemptible,'" and to destroy bonds of friendship that had existed between former neighbors. Herek's testimony supports that view.

Acquiring a sense of the purposes served by martial rape is a step toward developing strategies of resistance. But we must also ask why it is rape that is used to achieve these purposes. Many other forms of terrorism or torture might achieve the purposes of demoralizing the enemy, disrupting bonds among them, and creating bonds among perpetrators. So, why rape?

Many forms of terrorism and torture are, of course, employed in war for such ends: burning and looting of residences, villages, and cities and destruction of domestic industries, for example. Nietzsche described the phenomenon well, under the illusion that he was describing a prehistoric practice, in his characterization of the blonde beasts ("lions," according to Walter Kaufmann) who "perhaps walk away from a hideous succession of murder, arson, rape, torture with such high spirits and equanimity that it seems as if they have only played a student prank, convinced that for years to come the poets will again have something to sing and to praise."[31] Yet because of its sexual character, rape in a patriarchal culture has a special potential to drive a wedge between family members and to carry the expression of the perpetrator's dominance into future generations. And the act of rape itself is a multicultural symbol of domination.

Responding to War Rape

Responding to institutionalized evils presents the challenge of how to dismantle or terminate existing evil practices without substituting new evils for old. War rape illustrates the difficulties. The Japanese military rationale for having comfort women—that otherwise soldiers would indiscriminately rape local women—illustrates a response to one evil that just substitutes another, more controlled but no less atrocious.

Women's most usual constructive responses tend to remove or nullify some of the harmful consequences. Survivors today, for example, commonly obtain abortions. According to Stiglmayer (135), writing about women and girls raped in Bosnia-Herzegovina, "Women who become pregnant following a rape normally reject both the pregnancy and the children," and she presents a chart with impressive statistics on abortion. A front page account in the *New York Times* reports that of more than 15,700 women and girls between the ages of 13 and 65 who were raped in Rwanda between April 1994 and 10 April 1995, more than 1,100 gave birth but 5,200 had abortions, and many more pregnancies were untrackable.[32] Many raped Rwandan women reportedly abandoned their newborns. Because of the greater availability of abortion, genetic domination may be defeated more readily today than in previous eras. Why women are rape targets in war now has more to do with the cross-cultural symbolic meaning of rape as dominance—dominance primarily over men who are presumed to take pride in protecting "their" women—than with genetic imperialism.

It is also true that women in patriarchy are relatively easy victims. Women who lack military or martial arts training are an easy mark for those who would send the message of domination. Women in patriarchies are commonly unarmed and untrained in self-defense and are consequently ordinarily affiliated with male protectors. Once the male protector is disarmed or removed, perpetrators need fear little direct reprisal, and it is easy to eliminate the only remaining witness who might otherwise later be able to identify them. These observations suggest more effective strategies of resistance. First, as short-term goals, women could become armed and skilled in weapons use, and women might infiltrate the military at every level (or alternatively construct independent military organizations). Second, as a more long-range goal building on the short-term goals, both domestic and international protection rackets might be dismantled, thereby creating the potential to alter the symbolic meaning of rape.

Suppose the responses to war rape were not for men to reject wives, mothers, and daughters nor for women and girls to commit suicide, run away, or hide, but rather for those raped to get abortions, if pregnant, and, for women generally, to become militarily armed and trained, and fight back, as Stiglmayer reports (91–93, 98–99) that Hatiza and Razija did after they were raped in Bosnia-Herzegovina. Suppose women entered military institutions in large numbers and were to be found at every rank and in every department. There would be fewer civilian females to rape, although children, the old, the sick, and their caretakers would remain. But what is the likelihood that men would rape while they fought side by side with equally trained and armed women and under the command of women? Gang rape is an unlikely instrument of heterosexual peer bonding. Male armies might still treat female soldiers as Achilles is reputed to have done with the Amazon Penthesilia after killing her in battle during the Trojan War.[33] But female soldiers would not be *easy* targets. It is unlikely that rape would continue to symbolize dominance if women had as much capacity to enforce their wills as men currently have to enforce theirs.

Some will object that this strategy perpetuates values we should replace rather than instantiate, that it is yet another case of substituting one evil for another. The case against military thinking has been well developed by Sara Ruddick, who finds it ultimately self-defeating.[34] Yet perhaps women can participate in military institutions in the spirit of conscientious draftees without succumbing to martial values. We would have to be alert to the dangers of getting so caught up in supporting military practices as to lose sight of the goal of dismantling protection rackets and of coming instead to enjoy participating in the rites and rights of the masters.

And what, one may ask, counts as participation? It might be argued that most adult women in the U.S. paid labor force participate already by paying federal taxes. Yet one may feel ambivalent about that support, regarding it as questionably tolerable rather than something to be expanded. Since the 1970s, however, cities throughout the United States have been the sites of martial arts training of women by women for the purpose of both physical skill acquisition and attitudinal change regarding options of resistance that involve uses of violence. Such individual training for one-on-one encounters has been important in saving and transforming individual lives.[35] Still, it does not put a large dent in protection rackets in a world where the formally organized violence of war is an ever-present possibility. Women need to be able to rely on each other in a more organized way. If it makes good sense to defend ourselves as individuals, it also makes good sense to defend ourselves as communities. When wars of self-defense are fought not primarily by those who enjoy war but by those who do it only under duress, it is less likely that military values will dominate. This has been a classic reason to prefer a universal draft to reliance on mercenaries or only on voluntary enlistment.

Imagine how the Thermondontine Amazons, described by ancient Greek historians and geographers, may have employed their double axes in their war against the Athenians who had raped their queen. Why do you suppose male historians have been so adamant and nearly unanimous for centuries in denying the existence of these Amazons (illiterate nomads, leaving no writings to be discovered one day to refute the historians' denials)? What would many women be tempted to do with a double axe today to rapist war captives? If one way to bring about improvements in the direction of justice for women, analogous to those envisaged for men by Rawls, is to improve women's threat advantage, another way is to change the social symbolic meaning of rape. Reflection on this possibility gives rise to the following fantasies.

Bobbitizing and So Forth

If the double axe battle fantasy is repellent, a similarly dramatic penalty might be carried out in a more civilized manner with the objective of changing the symbolic meaning of rape from dominance to something else. Rape is currently a crime that is highly tolerated in civilian and military life even by men who do not do it, many of whom nevertheless regard it as natural. The tendency to regard rape as natural has roots in the symbolic significance of rape as dominance. Wars have been fought with the explicit goal of domination. In civilian life, those who find rape natural tend to find male dominance natural. The Japanese military rationale for comfort stations takes it for granted that men must have women for sexual release, even if it means kidnap and rape. This assumption makes no sense. "Masturbation stations" should suffice. What makes sense of the preference for rape over masturbation is the idea that rape is natural male dominance.

Consumers of the services of sexual slaves are not publicly regarded as rapists. The more guilty parties are, of course, those with power to institute or abolish the practice. But they are not publicly regarded as rapists, either, if they do not perform the sexual acts. Only rapes not already sanctioned by the military have been officially regarded as rapes. For such crimes the death penalty has been officially instituted by the Uniform Code of Military Justice.[36] Instituting the death penalty for rape is a sure way to guarantee that men will not enforce the prohibition unless there is an ulterior reason (such as racism). Even when the penalty is imprisonment, however, rapists are seldom convicted. It could be advantageous to have a less extreme penalty than death, one that communicated that rape is unnatural and its reward not power and that did this so dramatically that it would be effective even if inflicted in relatively few well-publicized cases.

I have fantasies of such penalties made possible by medical technology. Although the fantasies are not frivolous, I would oppose their legal realization, because of the medical precedent they would set—a moot point, as there is no likelihood that currently existing states would inflict them. The fantasies are serious, however, in that *being able to regret the inadvisability* of carrying them out, because of unintended oppressive consequences to the innocent, is a significant step forward attitudinally for women in regard to rape, and these fantasies may serve as catalysts for envisaging more practicable measures. The penalties might be imagined as inflicted by a nonsexist state in response to martial rape by its own or enemy soldiers or as a response to such orders by officers. Or one might think of them as inflicted on martial rapists by guerilla warriors. If expensive to administer, research could no doubt help to reduce the cost. The expense of imprisonment, however, does not keep states from expanding its use. (According to public radio, Wisconsin now spends more on its prisons than on its public universities.)

My first fantasy penalty, motivated by a vision of something like poetic justice in which the crime bounces back on the perpetrator, was *compulsory transsexual surgery*, that is, removal of the penis and testicles and construction of a vagina, accompanied by whatever treatments may be advisable for the sake only of bodily health and integrity. The poetic justice idea in this fantasy is that those who help make the world unsafe for females would become members of the class for whom the world has thus been made unsafe and would no longer be members of the class who profit from that state of affairs.

Castration is an old feminist fantasy penalty for rape. In that fantasy, castration is envisaged as a fairly dramatic piece of surgery (as in Freud's castration complex and in the case of the Amazons and their double axes). Castration for sterilization need remove only the testes. That is not enough for present purposes. Testicular removal would prevent impregnation, but domination is communicated more by the ability to penetrate forcibly. Removal of the penis would not prevent rape with penis-like instruments. But it would attack the symbol of dominance with which a rapist is most likely to identify intimately. What needs to go is the phallus.

Yet the result of transsexual surgery is not so simple. Because male bodies tend to differ from female bodies throughout (for example, in bone structures of hands, hips, and jaws), and the surgery leaves most body structures intact, many postoperative rapists would be identifiable as transsexuals. That means, however, that the penalty would be unjust to voluntary male-to-female transsexuals, who would risk being widely and wrongly identified as former rapists. To combat that error, special identifying measures might be tried.[37] Still, use of such surgery as a punishment, however poetically suited to a rapist's values, would inevitably add to the damaged identities that transsexuals already suffer, whether or not they were wrongly identified as individuals.[38] Punishing by transsexual surgery would reinforce oppressive attitudes toward transsexuals in general and very likely increase the risk of violence to transsexual and transgendered people.

An analogous objection to this fantasy is that the penalty would reinforce misogyny, which would also make it self-defeating insofar as misogyny is a major source of rape. The fantasy might be viewed as extending and reversing a strategy that men use on each other to *encourage* rape. Stiglmayer's interviews reveal how men are goaded into raping women by threats from other men of being treated like, or regarded as, women. It works. The military has long used this strategy without going all the way. Mary Daly quotes David Halberstam on former Unites States President Lyndon Baines Johnson as saying of a member of his administration who was becoming a dove on Vietnam, "Hell, he has to squat to piss."[39] The fantasy attaches the threat of being regarded as a woman and treated like a woman not to *failing* to rape but to *doing* it. And yet, to the extent that it succeeded, its self-defeating character would also make it fail. An analogue of this objection is raised against "outing" prominent closeted lesbians and gay men as punishment for bad behavior toward gays and lesbians: the penalty relies on and reinforces homophobia.

A natural response to these objections is to modify the fantasy to eliminate construction of the vagina and stop after removing the penis, producing more of an "it" than a transsexual. Let's call this penalty "Bobbitizing" (although Lorena Bobbitt had second thoughts and got help in time to restore her rapist's penis). The intention in the first fantasy was not to deter by appealing to fear of being female as such. The intent was to appeal more abstractly to fears of being a *victim*, of losing one's male sexual identity, of defeating the purposes of rape. But even Bobbitized males are "weaponless" and thereby potential victims. The basic goal is to combat rape's symbolism of dominance by removing the instrument of power as a consequence of its abuse. The hope would be to eliminate reliance on rape as a weapon at the level of strategic planning. Were the symbolic meaning of rape changed, there would be less to fear about being female.

I envisage the infliction of such a penalty primarily in wartime. But an extension to civilian rapists might be natural. Further, I imagine the penalty inflicted not necessarily on the soldier rapist, who may have been under duress or consuming services falsely represented as voluntarily offered, but on those responsible for the sexual abuse, directly or indirectly, and on those who tolerate it by choosing not to exercise their power to investigate reports and pursue complaints.

The officer offender highlights a problem, however, for the offender may be already female. Women helped operate comfort stations, and women participated in atrocities against other women in Rwanda.[40] Such cases indicate further limitations of these fantasy penalties. For women, there is no bodily instrument of power to remove. Neither female-to-male transsexual surgery nor clitoridectomy could address the dominance issue in a patriarchal society.

I envisage these penalties not as substitutes for but as supplements to such conventional penalties as court martial and imprisonment. It might be objected, however, that compulsory surgery violates principles prohibiting cruel, unusual, and inhumane punishments. Further, this penalty shares with the death penalty the problem of irreversibility in cases of wrongful conviction, although future technologies might change that. These objections are interesting against the background of a history in which the death penalty has been officially instituted for rape. Is castration a fate worse than death? The objection from cruelty and inhumanity deserves to be taken more seriously than it usually is with respect to penalties currently in common use in penal systems. Respect for humanity might suggest at least that the surgeries be carried out under appropriate anesthesia in sanitary conditions by appropriately qualified medical personnel and transform the offender into a reasonably healthy being, except for being unsexed.

As noted, however, I would not support the enactment of these fantasies in reality, because their humane administration would require the participation of health care professionals. Physicians are already too involved in the administration of lethal injections in states with capital punishment, using their skills to aid in killing rather than to promote health. The history of medical practice in Germany under the Third Reich and by the Japanese military Unit 731 in China during World War II have demonstrated too well the potential for new atrocities when medical training is used for the purpose of inflicting harms and injuries.[41]

Male Victims and Racism

The possibility of female perpetrators, irreversibility of the penalty in cases of wrongful conviction, and the perversion of medical science are not the only serious objections to the Bobbitizing fantasy, although all are major objections. The fact that there are also male victims of sexual abuse in war shows that these fantasies and the currently popular understanding of war rape suffer from too narrow a view of the nature and motivation of the crime.

Journalist Beverly Allen quotes a United Nations report as documenting that the rape and death camps in Bosnia-Herzegovina have also been sites of forced castrations, "through crude means such as forcing other internees to bite off a prisoner's testicles."[42] Rezak Hukanovi, a survivor of the death camps in Bosnia, mentions an incident in which "the guards had cut off the man's sexual organ and half of his behind" and another in which "two prisoners were taken out and with a knife at their throats, ordered to bite off the genitals of the two young men from Kozarac."[43] Libby Tata Arcel, who has worked with rape survivors in the former Yugoslavia, reports that martial sex crimes by men against men have a long history, but also that they have almost universally been identified by men not as sex crimes, or even as sexual torture, but simply as torture.[44] Asked whether they were victims of sex crimes, Arcel said, the men answered negatively. She noted that they attached a great stigma to the idea of being the victim of a sex crime. Asked whether they had been tortured by instruments applied to their genitalia, however, the same men answered affirmatively.

These reports are some evidence that sex crimes in war are often racist as well as misogynist, insofar as the assaults have or are meant to have the consequence of hindering the reproductive continuation of a people. Both castration and forced impregnation can have this consequence. Mass rape of women in war may reflect more racial than gender animus, or it may reflect both. The men may have been right, in a sense, that they were not victims of sex crimes, in that the reason they were being tortured genitally as they were may have been only incidentally because they were men and more essentially because they were of "the wrong people." Some sex crimes against men, such as rape, may also carry misogynist symbolism. But castration, like rape, appears to have its own history of symbolizing domination. Historically, castration has also been inflicted predominantly by men. Perhaps it is in the light of that history that many historians perceive the ancient Amazons' double axes as symbols of imperialism rather than as weapons of self-defense or instruments of summary punishment.

Rape's symbolizing domination is, of course, compatible with castration's symbolizing it also. But if castration, like rape, is an intercultural symbol of domination, the very penalties of compulsory transsexual surgery and Bobbitizing could be read as themselves symbols of domination, since both include castration. The intention of the penalties was, of course, to reject domination symbolism, not to instantiate it in a new form. But castration's history of symbolizing domination threatens to make even the Bobbitizing fantasy self-defeating.

Reports, such as Beverly Allen's and Rezak Hukanovi's, of forced castration in war should also raise questions about the idea that integrating women into the military might effectively eliminate, or substantially reduce, rape as a weapon of war and might lead us to take Ruddick's concerns about military thinking more seriously. If Bosnian male soldiers could bring themselves to force others to bite off the testicles of captive men, it appears that racism overcame any tendency they might have had to identify with their victims as men. What reason have we, then, to think that militarily trained women would not, out of similarly racist attitudes, order or tolerate war rape, overcoming whatever tendency they might otherwise have to identify with their victims as women? As noted above, according to survivors' testimony, women participated in the Rwandan genocide, inflicting mortal harm on other women, and women were involved in the operation of Japanese military comfort stations. Yet even if women were as capable as men of supporting the rape of other women, the general self-defense advantage of female military training would remain: militarily trained women would no longer be such easy targets as at present.

In June of 1996 the *New York Times* carried a front-page article titled "For First Time, Court Defines Rape as War Crime."[45] It said that the United Nations International Criminal Tribunal of The Hague had just "announced the indictment of eight Bosnian Serb military and police officers in connection with rapes of Muslim women during the Bosnian war, marking the first time sexual assault has been treated separately as a crime of war." Early in 2001, three former Bosnian Serb soldiers were found guilty by the U.N. war crimes tribunal in The Hague of raping and torturing Muslim women and girls.[46] The tribunal "also convicted two of the three men of enslaving their captives, the first time that an international tribunal has prosecuted and condemned sexual slavery" (Simons 2001, A-1). Previous postwar courts had treated rape as "secondary, tolerated as part of soldiers' abusive behavior." The 1996 indictment described the ordeal of fourteen Muslim women and girls, some only twelve years old, most detained in a camp, where they were subjected to "almost constant rape and sexual assaults, torture and other abuses." European investigators were reported to have calculated that "in 1992, twenty thousand Muslim women and girls were raped by Serbs" (Simons 1996, A-1).

Christian Chartier, speaking for the U.N. tribunal, is reported to have said of this decision, "It is of major legal significance because it illustrates the court's strategy to focus on gender-related crimes and give them their proper place in the prosecution of war crimes" (Simons 1996, A-1). Court officials are also reported to have said, "this indictment gave organized rape and other sexual offenses their due place in international law as crimes against humanity" (Simons 1996, A-1). These characterizations are not inaccurate. But they are incomplete, in that they do not explicitly acknowledge that war rape is also race related. Perhaps this fact seemed too obvious to note in the context of the war in the former Yugoslavia, because the entire conflicts there have been so racially motivated. Yet it is worth pointing out that martial sex crimes can be as racist as they often are sexist, and that racism and sexism appear often to intersect in the rape of women and girls.

Despite fatal objections, the Bobbitizing fantasy remains interesting insofar as it directs attention to the symbolic significance of war sex crimes and suggests a different strategy for responding than strategies that take rapist inclinations as given. The fantasy suggests a social reconstruction of desire by removing the rewards of the crime. Other fantasies might work on how to get rapists, and those with power to abolish rape practices, to disaffiliate from or renegotiate relationships to important people and their internal representations (IPIRs), whose norms and values underlie cruel behavior.[47] Yet others, given the limitations of punishment as a response to atrocities, might focus on publicizing certain facts: perpetrators' identities and the truths of victims, including those of victims who fight back effectively. The particular fantasies are less important than the general idea that the symbolic significance of rape and castration as dominance needs to change, to undermine their use as weapons. Hopefully, those who find surgical fantasies troubling will envision better ways to bring about that kind of change.

7

Terrorism in the Home

The social institutions of marriage and motherhood are controversial among lesbians, gay men, bisexuals, and transgender people (LGBTs). The currently most visible position of LGBT activists in the United States favors the pursuit of legal recognition of same-sex marriage, the right to adopt, and in general, the same rights as heterosexual married couples. But there is also a vigorous skepticism, especially in lesbian feminist communities, regarding the value of marriage and motherhood as institutions. This chapter supports that skepticism by showing how these hallowed institutions encourage, shelter, and facilitate terrorism in the home.

Many families based on marriage and motherhood are, of course, happy. My concern is with the price of that joy borne by others trapped in homes where they are deeply unlucky in the company they find there. Nothing I say, however, is intended to disparage the character of many partners and parents who struggle in and around these institutions to make the best of a trying set of options. There is sometimes something to be said for taking advantage of an objectionable institution even as one works at the same time to dismantle it. Individuals' circumstances vary and are complex. My concern here is with higher order evaluations of institutions that define options for individuals, rather than with the choices made by individuals who confront those options.

Spousal Battering and Child Abuse

Family violence takes many forms. According to sociologists Richard Gelles and Murray Straus, the commonest, least widely recognized form is sibling violence, and another common but not widely recognized form is the abuse of parents by their teenaged children.[1] Elder abuse is especially difficult to detect when perpetrated in family homes. This chapter does not address all family violence but is concerned with the terrorism of intimates in two of its worst forms: severe, ongoing spousal battering, often leading to murder or to killing in self-defense, and the sexual and other physical abuse of children, which when prolonged also often leads to murder or killing and leaves lifelong scars.[2] Whatever the root causes, the violence might be mitigated if targets of terrorism had viable exits from the relationships defined by marriage and motherhood or if the terrorism were detectable in early stages by parties who could hold perpetrators accountable and offer victims effective support. The relations defined by marriage and motherhood trap victims of terrorism in the home. They pose serious obstacles to escape by granting perpetrators enforceable intimate access to victims and extensive control over the knowledge and access of others.

Institutions are evil when it is reasonably foreseeable, by those with power to change or abolish them, that their normal or correct operation will lead to or facilitate intolerably harmful injustices. Abolitionists object to capital punishment on this ground. The intent is to execute only those guilty of capital offenses. Yet, the argument goes, the ordinary, normal, or correct observance of the practice foreseeably results in the execution of innocents who cannot afford the legal talent to counteract routinely tolerated police and prosecutor incompetence and corruption. Critics' worst fears are being borne out by DNA reinvestigations of many death-row cases.[3]

Rules of an institution may provide a cover for evils by making wrongdoing difficult or impossible to detect or prove, by placing obstacles in the way of accountability for harm, giving persons in certain positions unchecked license to treat certain others as they see fit. The institution of slavery provided a cover for brutalities that eventually mobilized the antislavery movement in the United States. The purpose of slavery was to provide cheap labor. Arguably, brutalities were not essential. Not all slaves were beaten. Yet brutalities were not just incidental, either. The norms of slavery failed to hold slaveholders effectively accountable for their "discipline" of slaves.

The norms of marriage and motherhood, which structure families in contemporary Western society, also provide a cover for, if not a license to, the evils of spousal and child abuse. It is not, of course, the purpose of either marriage or motherhood to brutalize spouses or children. Not all children are abused, nor are all marriages violent. Yet neither is it just incidental that women and children are terrorized in homes structured by these institutions. According to statistics published in the early 1990s, battering is the largest cause of injury to women in the United States (more than automobile accidents, rapes, and muggings combined), one quarter of violent crime in the United States is wife assault, there is a pattern of abuse in one out of six marriages, the FBI estimates that 90 percent of domestic violence is not reported to police, 12 percent of all murders in the United States are spousal killings, every 11 days a woman is murdered by her husband, boyfriend, or live-in lover, and at least 70 percent of men who batter their wives also abuse their children sexually or physically in other ways.[4]

In their research on domestic violence globally as a human rights issue, Michele E. Beasley and Dorothy Q. Thomas found that "domestic violence is not unusual or an exception to normal private family life; the vast majority of crimes against women occur in the home and are usually committed by a spouse or relative in the form of murder, battery, or rape; domestic violence is endemic to all societies," that "wife-murderers receive greatly reduced sentences, domestic battery is rarely investigated, and rape frequently goes unpunished," and that "these examples stand in contrast to the treatment of violent crimes against male victims."[5] Statistical documentation of the contrast to treatment of violent crimes with male victims, showing a pattern of discrimination that establishes a state's failure to provide equal protection, has provided a wedge for human rights organizations to denounce states for failing to prosecute acts committed by private individuals (as opposed to agents of the state) that violate human rights the state has agreed to enforce.[6] The human rights approach, however, is limited to responding after the fact (when victims are already injured or dead), and its responses are limited to attempts at publicly humiliating states into taking action against individual perpetrators.

Information on maternal abuse is less readily available and less clear. Statistics are difficult to interpret because neglect is commonly defined as abuse along with assault, and women are held responsible, through "neglect," for assaults perpetrated against their children by others.[7] David Gil, who conducted the first nationwide study of all reports of child abuse in the late 1960s defines child abuse as "intentional, nonaccidental use of physical force, or intentional nonaccidental acts of omission, on the part of a parent or care taker interacting with a child in his care, aimed at hurting, injuring, or destroying that child," a definition widely copied.[8] Marie Asch and Naomi R. Cahn were surprised to discover abusive mothers far less studied in social science literature than they had expected and not well defined.[9] Linda Gordon found, in studying the records of the Massachusetts Society for the Prevention of Cruelty to Children from 1880 to 1960, that women were reported as "assailants" in 46 percent of cases, fathers in 54 percent, but notes also that this meant that fathers were far more likely to abuse children in proportion to how much time they spent in childcare.[10] She also found that many female abusers were themselves victims and that child-abusing women were no milder than the men. Mildred Daley Pagelow learned that, according to the American Humane Association report of 1980, of 106,611 substantiated cases of child abuse and neglect in one year, fathers were the primary *abusers* in 55 percent of parental abuse cases and mothers or mother-substitutes in 45 percent, while mothers were the primary *neglectors* in 68 percent.[11] She finds that "women are the largest category *at risk* of perpetrating child abuse," because of "the isolation of the modern nuclear family, the much greater responsibility assigned to mothers for the care, nourishment, and behavior of children, and the greater percentage of time they spend with children."[12] She quotes Jessie Bernard as observing that "the way we institutionalize motherhood, giving mothers the exclusive responsibility for the care of children and making this care their exclusive activity, has destructive effects on women as well as on children."[13] It is not "we," however, but the law that continues to structure motherhood in that way. Women have had little say about the law, and many are trapped by it, although some have found better environments for rearing children, such as extended families.

Maternal violence is better appreciated in its variety by looking at cases than by contemplating statistics. In the final chapter of her treatise on motherhood "as experience and as institution," Adrienne Rich opens with a 1974 case of maternal child murder in a suburb of Chicago and then discusses at length the history of women who have killed the children they knew they could not rear adequately and would not have chosen to have.[14] In *The Basement* Kate Millett reflected on the sadistic murder of teenaged Sylvia Likens, left with her sister Jenny in the care of Gertrude Baniszewski in Indiana by parents who worked state fairs in the Midwest.[15] Jenny finally was able to alert police, but not in time to save Sylvia from death by sexual torture inflicted by Baniszewski and her own teenaged children. Christina Crawford has left us *Mommie Dearest*, testifying to years of abuse by film star Joan Crawford, who adopted her.[16] Dave Pelzer's *A Child Called "It"* became in the 1990s one of the most widely read testimonies to maternal assault. Pelzer writes of being singled out from his siblings at an early age for years of unimaginably cruel, life-endangering tortures by a mother who was, apparently, never penalized for any of it. After Pelzer was rescued by schoolteachers, who acted at some risk to themselves, his mother apparently turned her hostilities on at least one of his brothers.[17]

Because parents, guardians, and spouses are not effectively held accountable for their treatment of intimates and because their access to intimates is backed by the force of law, I am skeptical of marriage as the way to a better life for LGBT lovers or as a supportive environment for children of LGBT parents. I likewise view with skepticism the strand of feminist care ethics that uses motherhood as a source of paradigms for good human relationships. The problem is not simply the absence of voluntariness in the relationship, at least on the child's side. Nor is it the bare existence of a power differential between parent and child or even between spouses. The problem is more specifically norms of marriage and motherhood that enable a parent or spouse to have and to control access in ways that facilitate getting away with terrorism. A relationship in which one party knows it can terrorize the other with impunity is not a good model for human relationships. Whether marriage and motherhood can be reformed so as not to support terrorism is a partly empirical and partly philosophical issue. My view is that we would do better with more flexible forms of intimate partnership and more communal or at least distributed childrearing.[18]

Terrorism, Coercion, Involuntary Servitude

A paradigm of the terrorist is the fanatical bomber engaged in manipulation to try to right something perceived as a deep social wrong—to gain the release of political prisoners, for example—and in the process, endangering or killing innocent strangers. When less problematic means of addressing evils have been unsuccessful, the question arises whether terrorism is morally justifiable. As R. M. Hare notes, for many of us the question of justifiability is a live one at least in regard to terrorist activities of the Resistance during World War II.[19] Political assassinations raise a similar issue. If morally justifiable, they are not evils, as they lack one of evil's defining elements, culpable wrongdoing, even though they inflict harms that make the lives of innocent people impossible or intolerable and thus leave the agents who choose such actions with "dirty hands."

Terrorists, however, do not always act with a social conscience. Terrorism, more generally, is a form of coercion, a calculated or systematic appeal to heightened fear (terror) in others as a means to obtaining something else the terrorist wants (which need not be a selfish goal), something the terrorist fears is unobtainable or too costly if sought by more conventional means.[20] Governments become terrorist when they rely on secret police who torture and terrorize a populace to keep them submissive and compliant.

As in the bomber paradigm, government terrorism is impersonal. Terrorism in the home is highly personal. Here, terrorists know their victims intimately. Because the popular stereotypes involve governments, the term "domestic terrorism" suggests terrorism within a nation, as opposed to international terrorism. And so, to avoid ambiguity, I use the phrase "terrorism in the home," rather than "domestic terrorism," to refer to spousal battering and ongoing sexual and other physical abuse of children. Like other terrorists, abusive intimates use threats and heightened fear to manipulate and control. Spousal batterers use terror to obtain service and deference in everything from sex and money to petty details of household management. Physically and sexually abusive parents use terror to secure the silence and compliance of children, often compliance with wrongful demands.

In addition to Dave Pelzman's memoir of maternal violence, two articulate testimonies of paternal terrorism from the (now adult) child's point of view are

Tobias Wolff's *This Boy's Life* (also a film) and Sue William Silverman's *Because I Remember Terror, Father, I Remember You.*[21] All describe terrorism by a parent or guardian in a fairly traditional family setting. Silverman recounts years of sexual abuse, starting when she was less than five, by a father who was from 1933 to 1953 chief counsel to the U.S. Secretary of the Interior. Wolff recounts years of general physical and emotional abuse by his stepfather in a working-class environment. Of the many accounts of survivors of spousal battering, the best known may be Faith McNulty's telling of the story of Francine Hughes in *The Burning Bed.*[22] Others include the testimonies by Beth Sipe, *I Am Not Your Victim,* and Charlotte Fedders, *Shattered Dreams,* as well as many accounts reported in studies by Angela Browne, Ann Jones, and Donna Ferrato.[23]

Judith Lewis Herman argues that the post-traumatic stress disorders of survivors of domestic violence and rape are importantly similar to the "shell shock" of World War I combat survivors. Finding that "the most common post-traumatic disorders are those not of men in war but of women in civilian life," she argues that women and children subject to civilian rape and domestic violence actually are in a war: "[T]he subordinate condition of women is maintained and enforced by the hidden violence of men. There is war between the sexes. Rape victims, battered women, and sexually abused children are its casualties. Hysteria is the combat neurosis of the sex war."[24] Silverman's memoir supports Herman's comparison. She writes, "I was a domestic prisoner of war. . . . All I knew was inside my house in my own prison-bedroom, as if chained to my bed, to my father. . . . I believed my father was like every father, a father who taught his daughter that terror and rape were normal, were even, in fact, love.... I lived in a state of shock," and she points out that "no child can escape on her own. I could never have escaped on my own. I was an adult before I was able to recover from the terror of my childhood prison and find the help I needed."[25] Herman's analysis also fits children abused nonsexually. Pelzer describes himself as having been both a slave and a prisoner of war—even being forced to sit for hours in a POW position.

In *Next Time She'll Be Dead: Battering and How to Stop It,* Ann Jones notes the applicability to abusive relationships in the home of the Amnesty International (AI) "chart of coercion," from its 1973 *Report on Torture.* These methods capture very well the multitude of forms that terrorism in the home takes. It is not just a matter of hitting. In fact, hitting is not even on the chart, although items on the chart make it easier for an abuser to get away with hitting. As summarized by Jones, AI's chart of coercion includes (1) *isolation* (deprives victims of social support for resistance; makes victim dependent on interrogator), (2) *monopolization of perception* ("fixes attention upon immediate predicament"; eliminates competing stimuli), (3) *inducing of debility and exhaustion* ("weakens mental and physical ability to resist"), (4) *threats* ("cultivates anxiety and despair"), (5) *occasional indulgences* ("provides positive motivation for compliance"), (6) *demonstration of omnipotence* ("suggests futility of resistance"), (7) *degradation* ("makes cost of resistance appear more damaging to self esteem than capitulation," "reduces prisoner to animal level concerns"), and (8) *enforcing trivial demands* ("develops habit of compliance").[26]

As this list shows, what makes a relationship coercive is not necessarily just an individual, datable deed, such as a physical assault, or even a series of clearly datable individual deeds, but a pattern of ongoing behaviors that work together, like the bars of a cage, to produce coercive domination.[27] This pattern is what contemporary feminists tend to understand by "battering." Barbara Hart, for example, defines lesbian battering as

> that pattern of violent and coercive behaviors whereby a lesbian seeks to control the thoughts, beliefs or conduct of her intimate partner or to punish the intimate for resisting the perpetrator's control over her. Individual acts of physical violence, by this definition, do not constitute lesbian battering. Physical violence is not battering unless it results in the enhanced control of the batterer over the recipient.[28]

To distinguish abuser from abused, this definition should be amended slightly to note that it is not just *control*—self-defense aims also at control, checking one's assailant—but *oppressive dominance* that the pattern of violent and coercive behaviors create or aim to create. "Battering" is the term widely used in lesbian feminist communities for intimate partner abuse that takes many forms besides hitting. "Battering" can be psychological or economic as well as physical. It includes acts ranging from throwing one's partner against a wall, hitting with and without weapons, choking, burning, stabbing, confining physically, robbing a partner of sleep and necessary physical aids (such as eyeglasses), violent property damage, and threats with guns, to less clearly or less immediately physical abuse, such as threats to significant third parties (including animal companions), threats to reveal secrets to employers or family, creating unauthorized credit card debts, humiliation, violent accusation, and character assassination.[29] "Batterers" are also inventive in tailoring abuses to partners' specific vulnerabilities, such as forcing a diabetic partner to eat sugar or leaving a physically disabled partner in a dangerous situation, such as an isolated wooded area.[30]

Reflecting on coercion that can prevent one from leaving a relationship, Kathleen Barry argued in her work on prostitution that when pimps prevent a prostitute from leaving "the life," she has become a slave, regardless of how voluntarily she may have gotten started.[31] More cautiously, but along similar lines, attorney Joyce McConnell builds a persuasive case that when a battered partner is held to the services of a wife, although she is not literally enslaved (she cannot be legally sold, for example), she is being held to *involuntary*

servitude in the sense of the Thirteenth Amendment, regardless of how voluntarily she entered the relationship.[32]

Terrorism in the home is not entirely the product of misogyny, although
misogyny often contributes and can aggravate violence that has other sources.
Sexist socialization eroticizes the vulnerable and rewards men for violent
anger, at the same time encouraging female vulnerability and heterosexual dependency. But there is potential for terrorism as long as insecure people with
violent dispositions, weak scruples, and passionate desires have intimate access to others who are vulnerable or who have scruples against using violence.
Misogyny enters significantly in the reluctance to act seriously on victims'-
complaints. Although women and girls are the most usual victims, some
women abuse both children and husbands, who are reluctant to admit it and
who encounter disbelief when they do. Assault is not a function of bodily
strength or muscle power but of such things as resentment, lack of scruples,
and willingness to use weapons.

Empirical approaches to terrorism in the home study the formation of violent dispositions and develop biological, psychological, and sociological theories of human nature and development. My philosophical approach inquires,
rather, into the ethics of access, questioning the wisdom of protecting opportunities for those with violent dispositions to act them out. The challenge in
this case is to design social practices so as to enable victims to protect themselves (or, if necessary, be protected) and defend themselves (or, if necessary,
be defended) adequately.

Some Alternatives, Past and Present

The institution of motherhood is not the only vehicle of childrearing, apart
from orphanages and boarding schools, even today. From age six to age seventeen, my childhood in a small village of the heartland was partially guided by
something close to what bell hooks calls "revolutionary parenting," although
social workers and psychiatrists are inclined to call it "neglect."[33] Hooks writes:

> Childrearing is a responsibility that can be shared with other childrear-
> ers, with people who do not live with children. This form of parenting is
> revolutionary in this society because it takes place in opposition to the
> idea that parents, especially mothers, should be the only childrearers.
> Many people raised in black communities experienced this type of com-
> munity-based child care.[34]

This practice may be more common in the United States than is generally acknowledged. It is only "neglect" in terms of the rules of an institution that

concentrates responsibility for childcare in one or two guardians. If guardians pay others to do childcare, or send the children to boarding school, the resulting distributed childcare is no longer considered neglect. Although hooks uses the language of "mothering" in describing "revolutionary parenting," her revolutionary practice of communal childrearing is better viewed as an alternative to mothering. Many, perhaps most, of the "parents" of whom hooks writes have neither the rights nor the responsibilities of legal guardians in relation to most of the children for whom they care. Nor are they paid caretakers, although perhaps some of them should be.[35]

In *Black Feminist Thought* Patricia Hill Collins writes of "a more generalized ethic of caring and personal accountability among African-American women who often feel accountable to all the Black community's children."[36] Collins's models for an "ethic of caring and personal accountability" involve a wider community that includes "othermothers" as well as "bloodmothers." These models fit hooks's revolutionary parenting.[37] Communal parenting has much to recommend it. But it is not the model currently enshrined in law, not the model guiding LGBT activists who seek equal rights, and not the model that has served as an inspiration in most feminist care ethics.

Audre Lorde wrote of her relationship with her son, leaving us reflections on yet another model of parenting, that of a lesbian relationship struggling against the models of heterosexual marriage and patriarchal motherhood.[38] She did not, however, generalize from her experience or treat it as a source of inspiration for ethical theory.

Confronted with my negative assessments of marriage and motherhood, some recoil as though I were proposing that we learn to do without water, food, and oxygen on the ground that they are polluted (even killing us). This reaction tends to come from certain misunderstandings, which I note here in order to set them aside.

First, my skepticism regarding marriage is not a skepticism regarding durable intimate partnerships.[39] It is directed at marriage as a relationship to which the state (or, in times past, a powerful religious institution, such as the church) is an essential third party. Legal marriage is not merely a private contract of limited duration and for a well-defined purpose. Nor is it merely personal exchange of vows. Like foot binding and sati, which, according to the research of Mary Daly, originated among the powerful classes, marriage in Europe was once available only to those with social power.[40] Apparently, the intent was to prevent a spouse from unilaterally dissolving the relationship, abandoning the other spouse and often children as well. Many women could expect to benefit from the practice when they lacked the means for economic independence. If originally only for the propertied classes, marriage is now available in Northern democracies to any adult heterosexual couple free of certain communicable diseases and not already related as close kin, if neither is already married to someone else. This is the legal right that LGBT activists seek, the right to a relationship enforced by the state, which neither party can terminate unilaterally and which the state will not terminate simply at the request of either party without demonstrable cause. This is the right that is the subject of my skepticism.

Second, my skepticism regarding motherhood is not a skepticism regarding children's need for guidance, education, and caretaking, nor regarding the formation of special, durable bonds between children and adults. I do not advocate the equal legal rights for children rejected by Laura Purdy, who has soundly criticized those who advocate that children have the same legal rights as adults, including the right not to attend school.[41] My skepticism about motherhood is about a legally defined status that concentrates powers and responsibilities regarding children in a certain way, thereby making child abuse difficult to detect, prevent, or terminate in early stages.

Nor am I skeptical about homes as places of long-term residence with others of a variety of ages with whom one has deeply committed relationships. When the family is credited with being a bulwark against a hostile world, as it has been for families in African and Jewish disaporas, the bulwark consists of deeply committed personal (as opposed to legal) relationships and the stability of caring they represent, or home as a site of these things. The bulwark is not the legitimation (often precarious or nonexistent) of such relationships through state institutions. The state was one of the things such relationships formed a bulwark against.

"Family" is itself a family resemblance concept. Many contemporary LGBT partnerships, households, and friendship networks fit no patriarchal stereotypes and are not sanctified by law, although their members regard themselves as "family."[42] But should they? Social institutions such as insurance companies do not honor such conceptions of "family." Family in contexts where material benefits are at stake are not recognized if constituted totally by noncontractual relationships. At the core of every family is at least one marriage contract. Enlarging the meaning of "family" to include totally noncontractual groupings contains the danger that retaining patriarchal vocabulary imports patriarchal ideals, inviting treatment as deviant or "second class."

"Family," our students learn in Women's Studies 101, comes from the Latin "familia," meaning "household," which came from "famulus," meaning "servant," according to the Oxford English Dictionary. The ancient Roman paterfamilias headed a household of servants and slaves, including his wife or wives, concubines, and children, over whom he had the power of life and death. The ability of contemporary heads of households to get away with battering, incest, and murder reveals that contemporary families bear the marks of their genealogies. The postpatriarchal "family" relationships envisioned by many feminist theorists and LGBTs should probably be called something else, to mark the intended radical departure from family history. But it is not just a matter of a word. It is a challenge to imagine how such relationships should be structured.

Similar observations apply to marriage reforms. Were intimate partnerships adequately restructured in the interests of justice, some might still want to call the resulting relationships "marriages," to emphasize continuities with more positive historical traditions in marriage, such as the idea of a public and lifetime (or long-term) commitment. Analogously, many social critics speak of "wage slaves"—who are not so vulnerable to beatings and murder as chattel slaves—when they wish to emphasize, morally and politically, certain continuities between wage workers and slaves. To mark discontinuities, however, a different term is better. I would not wish to call acceptably restructured relationships "marriages," however public and long term.

Surrounded by married couples, many of us raised by at least one, most of us think we know what "marriage" means, although laws vary from one jurisdiction to another and the dictionary, as Richard Mohr notes, sends us around in a circle, referring us to "husband" and "wife," in turn defined by "marriage."[43] Mohr argues convincingly that marriage need not presuppose the gendered concepts of husband and wife. History seems to support him. A reading of John Boswell's fascinating *Same-Sex Unions in Premodern Europe*, however, left me less than confidant of knowing when a "union" should count as a "marriage."[44] Boswell refrains from using the term "marriage" to describe the same-sex unions he researched, even when they were sanctified with religious ceremonies. Some such unions were compatible with the partners being at the same time married to someone of the other sex.

My approach to same-sex marriage is something like my approach to prostitution. Let us, by all means, *decriminalize* prostitution and sodomy. But for that, it is not necessary for the state to regulate those activities. Same-sex marriage rights would decriminalize sodomy for those who married. But lovers should not be forced to marry to avoid being outlaws or criminals. In removing barriers to LGBTs enjoying privileges currently available only to heterosexual married couples, let us not discriminate against those who choose not to marry. It would be better to *de*regulate heterosexual marriage than to regulate same-sex unions.

When marriage is both available and necessary to avoid outlaw status or for basic social protections, there is enormous pressure on lovers to marry. Consider the loss of freedom that the option of marriage can bring. My partner of more than a decade was not a domestic partner. She and I formed some kind of fairly common social unit that, so far as I know, remains nameless. Along with such namelessness goes a certain invisibility, a mixed blessing. We did not share a domicile. (She had her house; I had mine.) Nor did we form an economic unit. (She paid her bills; I paid mine.) Although we certainly had fun together, our relationship was not based simply on fun. We shared the sorts of mundane details of daily living that Mohr finds constitutive of marriage (often in her house, often in mine). We know a lot about each other's lives that the neighbors and our other friends will never know. In times of trouble, we were each other's first line of defense and in need, each other's main support. Still, we were not married. Nor did we yearn to marry. Yet had marrying become an option that would not only save us from becoming criminals but also make available to us social securities that become more important as we age, we, and many like us, might have been pushed into it. Marrying under such conditions is not a totally free choice.

To remedy injustices of discrimination in benefits, many municipalities are experimenting with domestic partnership legislation. This is a step in the right direction for the abuse problem, also, insofar as domestic partnerships are more voluntary, more specific, and more easily dissolved, even unilaterally. Yet, domestic partnership policies have their own flaws and retain some of the flaws of marriage. Married spouses need not cohabit for benefits. In this respect, domestic partnership can be more restrictive.[45]

The Same-Sex Marriage Dilemma

Special vantage points on marriage are offered by the now widely documented experience of lesbians and gay men, among whom there is no consensus (although much strong feeling on both sides) on whether to pursue the legal right to marry a same-sex lover. A range of positions and arguments can be found in articles by Christine Pierce, Victoria Brownworth, Ralph Wedgwood, Evan Wolfson, and Warren Blumenfeld and in books by William Eskridge and Mark Strasser.[46] When heterosexual partners consider marriage, they consider whether they (as individuals) should marry (each other), because the state gives them this option. Lesbians, gay men, and in some cases bisexuals and transgender people, consider the different question of whether to fight for that option. We all have marriage options, of course, in relation to the other sex. Many gays and lesbians exercise it as a cover, as insurance, for resident alien status, and so forth. If it is because we already have rights to marry heterosexually that right wing critics complain of gay activists pushing for "special rights," the reply is, of course, that it was never the intention to deny the right of same-sex marriage to heterosexuals. If the response to that reply is that such a "right" is meaningless, then the "right" of homosexuals to marry heterosexually is equally meaningless, and what is sought by activists who want same-sex marriage rights is equality in meaningful relationships, not "special rights."

The question of whether to pursue the right to marry someone of the same sex is not settled by whether the law is wrong in its current exclusions. Mohr,

Wedgwood, Eskridge, Strasser, and others have carefully exposed wrongs in the law.[47] Wedgwood also briefly considers polygamous marriage, but as a profeminist remains skeptical of it. Wolfson develops powerfully an analogy between the denial of marriage to same-sex couples and the antimiscegenation laws overturned in the United States in the 1960s. My concerns apply to racially mixed as well as to same-sex lovers and parents.

It is wrong to exclude same-sex lovers or racially mixed lovers from the rights of marriage. But if those rights define an evil institution, we should not fight to have them, even if we do not intend to exercise them. Suppose that slave owning in some mythical society were denied to otherwise free women, on the ground that female owners would pervert the institution of slavery. (Unfortunately, we could document empirically the falsity of that belief.) It would not follow that women should fight for the right to own slaves. Likewise, if marriage is an evil institution, it would not advance the cause of justice on the whole to remove that special injustice of discrimination, even though it is a special injustice to exclude same-sex unions.

Wedgwood finds that marriage, unlike slavery, is not essentially unjust. However, he does not address the issue of vulnerability to spousal battery and other physical abuse. Both are evils the existence of which in particular cases is extremely difficult to prove. This difficulty becomes critical when one spouse seeks a divorce or injunction against the other. The legal institution of marriage facilitates and provides a cover for such evils in ways that are probably not removable without radically changing that institution into something else. Marriage grants spouses virtually unlimited rights of access to each other, and it grants them the right to deny outsiders access, much as the institution of property grants owners access to a piece of property and the right to deny others access to it. And it is difficult for an abused spouse to terminate a marriage. Whether marriage is essentially unjust is less important than whether it can plausibly be restructured so that spouses can escape life-threatening abuse or defend themselves and their children adequately.

Because the attached social benefits make marriage not an entirely free choice for many, there are several interconnected problems with marriage. Not all are evils considered in themselves. Yet many lead to evils. Problems basically economic are most discussed in the literature. Remediable in principle and in practice, were they remedied, many who now marry might no longer have strong motives to do so. The problem of sheltering spousal battering and child abuse is least discussed in the literature. Yet it is the most serious and least fixable.

The problem easiest in principle to remedy is spousal benefits. Employers, local ordinances, and institutional rules routinely make available only to legally married couples benefits anyone can be presumed to want, married or not, such as affordable health and dental insurance, the right to live in attractive residential areas, visitation rights in relation to important others, and so forth. When spousal benefits are a significant portion of worker compensation, married workers are paid more for the same labor than unmarried workers.[48] People lacking independent income can be economically pressured into marrying. Historically, women have been in this position, including most pre-twentieth-century lesbians. Many married men for economic security.

The practice of making such benefits available only to spouses discriminates against those who choose not to marry. Because of the insurance issue, many heterosexuals who basically disapprove of legal marriage give in and marry anyway. Because of discrimination against same-sex unions and against people who choose not to marry, however, some heterosexuals reject legal marriage, although the state treats some of their relationships as common-law marriages. When spousal benefits are major, they offer an ulterior motive to turn a love relationship into a marriage, even to pretend to care for someone, deceiving oneself as well as others. As Emma Goldman argued in the early twentieth century, when marriage becomes an insurance policy, it may no longer be compatible with love.[49] With greater economic opportunities for women and more experimentation with domestic partnership legislation, progress is being made in this area. But there is a long way to go.

A second problem for some is monogamy. Mohr, in his suggestions for improving marriage law by attending to the experience of gay men, proposes that sexual fidelity not be a requirement.[50] By "non-monogamy" he means not multiple *spouses* but monogamous marriage in which neither partner expects sexual exclusiveness. Yet spousal benefits would not apply to additional partners, although the same reasons that led one to seek those benefits for a spouse might lead one to seek them for additional partners. In the same-sex unions Boswell researched, which did not preclude heterosexual marriages, the parties were not permitted to formalize unions with more than one person at a time of the *same* sex, nor were they permitted to have children with a person of the other sex to whom they were not married.[51] Thus, in a certain restricted sense, each formal union was monogamous, even though one could have both kinds at once. If same-sex marriages were acknowledged in Northern democracies today, they would be legally as monogamous as heterosexual marriage, regardless of the number of one's sexual partners.

A third problem, far more serious in my view, is the difficulty of nonamicable divorce. Divorce by mutual consent is now generally permitted in the United States, despite recent agitation to revoke it. But its economic and custodial consequences (shared property, alimony, child-support payments, difficulties regarding access to children, and so on) can be so difficult that many who should divorce do not. If partners can sue for support or receive a share of the other's assets to which they would not otherwise have been entitled, there are economic motives to preserve emotionally disastrous unions. Intimate partnerships based simply on erotic attraction tend to be of limited viability, even under favorable circumstances. About half of all married couples get divorced, and probably most of the other half should. But the foreseeable consequences of divorce provide motives for many spouses who no longer love each other and have even grown to hate each other to stay married. When spouses hate each other, the access that was a joy as lovers becomes dangerous. This danger moves us closer to real evil.

The fourth, probably least fixable and most serious problem, is the access problem. Legal rights of access that married partners have to each other's persons, property, and histories make it all but impossible for a spouse to defend herself (or himself), or be protected against rape, battery, stalking, mayhem, or murder by the other spouse. The danger of spousal murder is aggravated by economic entanglements and by the difficulties of divorce that lead many alienated spouses to stay married or trap partners with spouses unwilling to divorce. This trap can provide motives to violence in those who have violent tendencies or in those whose work requires them to engage in or be prepared to engage in violent behavior (police work, some forms of athletics, some forms of military employment). Since marriage licenses are granted without screening even for histories of criminally violent behavior, legal marriage enlists state support for conditions conducive to murder and mayhem. This support is genuinely evil.

Stalking, battering, rape, incest, and murder by a spouse or parent are extraordinarily difficult to prove in particular cases. The burden of proof is always on the accuser, frequently a surviving victim, who was the only witness, or a member of the victim's family who was not a witness at all. Even when there are visible bruises, cuts, broken bones, and hospital records to document injuries, causality is difficult to prove without outside witnesses. Many forms of abuse leave no visible evidence, although they facilitate severe injury and murder. None of AI's eight strategies of coercion specifically mentions physical hitting or sexual assault. Yet all can facilitate assaults, and even without hitting, these strategies render the victim a prisoner and make her life intolerable. Yet it is even more difficult to prove such things as monopolization of perception, the inducing of debility and exhaustion, threats, degradations, and the enforcement of trivial demands than to prove outright hitting and sexual assault. Without clear and convincing evidence of abuse, one whose spouse will not agree to divorce may be trapped in a relationship from which, eventually, the only avenue of exit appears to be murder.

The point is not that all marriages are violent. It is not about the frequency of violence, although the frequency is not negligible. The point is that the rules of marriage predictably give rise to stress that will often contribute to violence, and they then place obstacles in the way of escape, self-defense, protection, or rescue for spouses in crisis.

Married spouses and their children are not the only victims. As Barbara Hart's definition indicates, same-sex intimate partner battery is very real.[52] Abolishing marriage is not sufficient to address the problem. Yet it is a major step, because without marriage, it is possible to take one's life back without encountering the law as an obstacle. One may be able more easily to enlist legal help in getting it back. In this regard, uncloseted LGBTs currently have a certain advantage—which, by the way, "palimony" suits threaten to undermine by applying the idea of common-law marriage to same-sex couples.[53]

But what about closeted partners? It is sometimes argued that a battered same-sex partner would have more recourse if same-sex unions could be legalized as marriages than such a partner has currently when the relationship is closeted. Because seeking protection inevitably requires the partner who does it to "out" the relationship, closeted abuse victims are often deterred from seeking protection. This argument overlooks the dismal history of law enforcement's response to family violence for those who have no such closets to worry about. Rejecting the closet is a better solution than marriage. Without a marriage contract, it is easier to escape, because the state does not enforce accessibility by the abusive partner. One can sometimes enlist the law's cooperation in defending oneself against an abuser who is guilty of legal trespass. Trespass is easier to prove than assault, if only because there are more apt to be witnesses. Because there is no general presumption, as with married partners, that the perpetrator must have the victim's interests at heart, unmarried victims do not have the same burdens of justification as victimized spouses. Because it is enough that they choose to deny access, it matters less that they probably cannot prove abuse (although it continues to matter for those seeking injunctions).

Why, then, with all these problems, would anyone marry? Because it is a tradition, religiously sanctioned, glorified, and romanticized. It grants status. For men it is a social symbol of stability and reliability and for women in patriarchal societies, a significant social mark of adulthood. It is a way to avoid hassles from one's family of origin and from society at large. We need better traditions. And women have long needed other social marks of adulthood and ways to escape families of origin.

Under our present exclusion from the glories of legal matrimony, the usual reason why lesbians or gay men form partnerships and stay together is that we care for each other. We sometimes break up for reasons extraneous to our feelings (employment in different parts of the country). But when we stay together, it is usually because of our feelings for each other and our life together. Consider how this basic taken-for-granted fact might change if we could marry. There are many social benefits to tempt (and pressure) those who can into marrying, such as the improvement in one's reputation as a reliable citizen (and for those of us who are not reliable citizens, protection against having a spouse forced to testify against us in court). Christine Pierce argues, in support of the option to legalize same-sex marriages, that lesbian and gay images have been cast too much in terms of individuals—recall *The Well of Loneliness*—and not enough in terms of relationships, especially serious relationships involving long-term commitments.[54] Marriage, she notes, gives visibility to people "as couples, partners, family, and kin," a visibility lesbians and gay men have lacked. This visibility could be important to dispelling negative stereotypes and assumptions that our relationships fail to embody many of the same ideals as those of heterosexual couples, partners, family, and kin.

It is true that LGBT images have been cast too much in terms of individuals. It is probably also true that same-sex marriage would go some way toward undoing negative stereotypes. It is less clear, however, that marriage would offer visibility to our relationships as they presently exist. It might instead change our relationships so that they became more like heterosexual marriages, loveless after the first few years but hopelessly bogged down with financial entanglements or children (adopted or products of turkey-baster insemination or previous marriages), making separation or divorce too difficult to contemplate, giving rise to new motives for mayhem and murder. Those who never previously felt pressure to marry a lover would confront not just new options but new pressures and traps.

Some of the most moving stories in discussions of gay marriage point out that the care rendered the ill by families is a great service to society and that the chosen families of gay AIDS patients deserve to be honored the same as any family based on a heterosexual union. The same, of course, applies to those who care for lesbian or gay cancer patients or for those with long-term disabilities or other illnesses. But is this a service to society? Or to the state? The state has a history of depending on families to provide care that no human being should be without in infancy, illness, and old age. Lesbians and gay men certainly have demonstrated our ability to serve the state in this capacity as well as heterosexuals. From the point of view of economic justice, one might ask where this practice leaves those who have no families? Or those who object on principle to depending on families? Equally, if not more importantly, what protection have the ill, the disabled, and the aged against abuse by family members who are also their caretakers?

Contracts, Licenses, and Cohabitation Rights

Marriage is a "contract" the obligations of which tend to be, in a certain respect, highly informal. The "contract" is abstractly defined, unspecific and inexplicit about what spouses must do and the consequences of failing. In this regard, marital obligations differ from those created by a bank loan. In a loan contract, obligations are highly formalized. One knows exactly what must be done to discharge them. In discharging the obligations of a loan, one dissolves the relationship created by the contract. In living up to marital obligations, however, one does not dissolve the marriage or its obligations; if anything, one strengthens them. Elsewhere I have argued that the obligations of marriage and those of loan contracts exhibit different paradigms.[55] The debtor paradigm is highly formal, whereas the obligations of spouses tend to be relatively informal and fit better what I call the trustee paradigm. The obligations of a trustee, or guardian, are abstractly defined. A trustee or guardian is expected to exercise judgment and discretion in carrying out obligations to care, protect, or maintain. The trustee *status* may be relatively formal—precisely defined regarding dates on which it takes effect, compensation for continuing in good standing, and the consequences of losing the status. But consequences of failing to do this or that specific thing while one holds that status may not be specified or specifiable, because what is required to fulfill duties of caring, safekeeping, protection, or maintenance can be expected to vary with circumstances, changes in which may not be readily foreseeable. A large element of discretion seems ineliminable. *This makes it difficult to hold a trustee accountable for abuses.* It means that it is difficult to prove that the status should be terminated. Yet the only significant sanction against a trustee may be withdrawal of that status. Spousal and parental status fit the trustee model rather than debtor model of obligation. This means that it is difficult to hold a spouse, or a parent, accountable for abuse.

My skepticism regarding marriage may surprise those familiar with my work on the military ban.[56] For I have argued against the ban and in favor of lesbian and gay access to military service. I argued that even those who disapprove of the military should object to wrongful exclusions of lesbians and gay men. In the world in which we live, military institutions—however in need of restraint—may be less dispensable than marriage. But should I be moved here by what moved me there: that it is one thing not to exercise an option and another to be denied the option, that excluding people from an option for no good reason conveys that there is something wrong with them, thereby contributing to their public disfigurement and defamation, and that these considerations give good reasons to protest being denied the option even if one never intends to exercise it? I am somewhat moved, but not greatly, by those arguments in this case. The case of marriage seems to me more like the case of slavery than like that of the military. And contracts with the military tend to be very specific and very limited.

Ordinarily, marriage (like slavery) is much worse than military service, if only because its impact on our lives is usually greater. Marriage is supposed to be a lifetime commitment. It is at least open-ended. When available, it is not simply an option but tends to be coercive, especially for women in a misogynist society. For those who choose it, it threatens to be a dangerous trap. Military service is ordinarily neither a lifetime nor open-ended commitment; one signs up for a certain number of years, commonly less than five. (When a government kidnaps young men for forced military service for as long as twenty-five years, however, as the Russian government did with Jewish men in the nineteenth century, military service becomes a form of slavery.) During war, one may be drafted (for a limited term) and, of course, killed. But the issue has not been whether to draft lesbians and gay men. Past experience shows that gay men will be drafted in war, even if barred from enlistment in peace. When enlistment is an option, it does not threaten to trap one in a relationship from which future exit will be extremely difficult. There is some analogy with the economically coercive aspect of the marriage option. Because those who have never served are ineligible for substantial government educational and health benefits, many from low- (or no-) income families enlist to obtain such things as college education and even health and dental insurance. However, the service given for such benefits as an enlistee is limited compared to spousal service. Being killed is a risk in either case.

The contrast of marriage with military service suggests an innovation that might radically transform both marriage and domestic partnership in a positive direction. Suppose that, instead of a lifetime or open-ended commitment, intimate partners committed for a specified length of time, to be determined and renewable only by mutual consent. This practice would shift the burden of justification from breaking up to continuing, and justification would address the other partner (or partners) rather than the state. It would offer hope to abused partners. Were this contract to replace marriage contracts, new policies and practices would have also to be worked out regarding child guardianship. But child guardianship need not be closely tied to lovers' partnerships. One can imagine a spouse, under such circumstances, "campaigning" (to the other spouse) for renewal, like holders of political office campaigning for re-election, as the expiration date approaches. This is such a drastic change from marriage that many would, rightly I think, refuse to call it marriage. Other jurisdictions might well refuse to recognize such unions as marriages, should the couple relocate. That refusal would not necessarily be a bad thing.

State-sanctioned unions tend to become state defined, however they originated. When marriages are recognized in other jurisdictions, one's spousal rights and privileges can change dramatically with one's residence. Betty Mahmoody discovered this fact when she went with her husband to Iran for what he promised would be a temporary visit.[57] She found after arriving in Iran that she had no legal right to leave without her husband's consent. He refused. Her only option for returning to the United States was to face the dangers of illegal escape (which she did, successfully). Betty Mahmoody's case is especially interesting because it involves her husband's right of access.

Spousal access rights do not have the same sort of contingency in relation to marriage as, say, a right to family rates for airline tickets. And rights of access facilitate terrorism.

Central to marriage, historically, has been intimate access to the persons, belongings, activities, even histories of one another. Even more important than sexual access, marriage gives spouses physical access to each other's residences and belongings, and it gives access to information about each other, including financial statuses, that other friends and certainly the neighbors do not have. For all that has been said about the privacy that marriage protects, what astonishes me is how much privacy one gives up in marrying. Enforcement of this intimate access makes battery and other physical abuse the danger that it is for those who are married. It is what makes these evils so difficult to detect, prove, and terminate.

Boswell argued that, historically, what has been important to marriage is consent, not sexual relations. But, consent to what? What is the point of marrying? To what do the partners commit, for however long they do so? Wedding ceremonies characteristically describe the commitment as one of love, not money (although, ironically, one cannot really promise to love but could promise to honor financial obligations). And yet, historically, for the propertied classes, as Boswell notes, the point of heterosexual marriage was either dynastic or property concerns or both. Dynastic concerns do not usually figure in arguments for lesbian or gay marriage. Although property concerns do, they are better detached from marriage. That leaves as a central point of marriage the legal right of cohabitation and the access to each other's lives that this entails.

It might still be marriage if sexual exclusivity, or even sex, were not part of it. But would it still be marriage if rights of cohabitation were not part of it? Even spouses who voluntarily live apart retain the *right* of cohabitation. Many rights and privileges available to spouses today might exist in a legal relationship that did not involve cohabitation rights—for example, insurance rights, access to loved ones in hospitals, rights to inherit, and many other rights presently possessed by kin who do not live with each other. If the right of cohabitation is central to the concept of legal marriage, it deserves more critical attention than philosophers have given it.

Among the trappings of marriage that have received attention and become controversial, ceremonies and rituals are much discussed. A far more important issue seems to me to be marriage *licenses*, which receive hardly any attention. Ceremonies affirming a relationship can be held at any point. But licenses are needed to enter into a marriage. To marry, one applies to the state for a license, and marriage, once entered into, licenses spouses to certain kinds of access to each other's persons and lives. It is a mistake to think of licenses as simply enhancing everyone's freedom. One person's license can be another's prison. Linda Marciano, who was forced as Linda Lovelace to star in the pornographic film *Deep Throat*, landed in such a prison when the pimp who kidnapped her forced her to marry him so she could not be compelled to testify against him.[58] Prerequisites for marriage licenses are astonishingly lax. Anyone of a certain age, not presently married to someone else, not already close kin, and free of certain communicable diseases automatically qualifies. A history of criminal violence or an unambiguous record of violence against intimates is, to my knowledge, no bar.

Contrast the marriage license with other licenses, such as a driver's license. In Wisconsin, to retain a driver's license, we submit periodically to eye exams. Some states have more stringent periodic retesting requirements. To obtain a driver's license, all drivers have to pass a written and a behind-the-wheel test to demonstrate knowledge and skill. In Madison, Wisconsin, even to adopt a cat from the humane society, we have to fill out a form demonstrating knowledge of relevant ordinances for pet guardians. Yet to marry, applicants need demonstrate no knowledge of laws pertaining to marriage, nor any relationship skills, nor even the modicum of self-control required to respect another human being. And once the marriage exists, the burden of proof is always on those who would dissolve it, never on those who would continue it in perpetuity.

Further disanalogies between driver's and marriage licenses confirm that in our society there is greater concern for victims of bad driving than for those of bad marriages. You cannot legally drive without a license, whereas it is now in many jurisdictions not illegal for unmarried adults of whatever sex to cohabit at will. One can acquire the status of spouse simply by cohabiting heterosexually for several years, whereas one does not acquire a driver's license simply by driving for years without one. Driving without the requisite skills and scruples is recognized as a great hazard and treated accordingly. No comparable recognition is given the hazards of legally sanctioning the access of one person to the person and life of another without evidence of the relevant knowledge and scruples of those so licensed. The consequence is that married victims of partner battering and rape have less protection than anyone except children, the very elderly, and the severely dependent. At stake are permanently disabling and life-threatening injuries, for those who survive. I do not, at present, see how this vulnerability can be acceptably removed as long as marriage remains an open-ended (if not lifetime) commitment not dissolvable unilaterally. Measures could be taken to render its disastrous consequences less likely than they are at present, but at the cost of considerable state intrusion into our lives. Although many states now recognize on paper the crimes of marital rape and stalking and are better educated than before about marital battering, the progress has been mostly on paper. Wives continue to die at a dizzying rate.

Thus, I conclude that legalizing same-sex marriage, turning a personal commitment into a license regulable and enforceable by the state, would extend an evil greater than any of the unjust inequalities that it would remedy. LGBTs are better off on the whole without that option and its consequent pressures. It would be better to agitate for the abolition of marriage altogether.

Yet many will object that marriage provides an important environment for motherhood. An appreciation of marriage's conduciveness to murder and mayhem challenges that assumption. But also, the argument that marriage provides a valuable context for motherhood seems to presuppose that motherhood is a good thing. So let us consider, briefly, whether it is.

Why Motherhood?

Calling motherhood an evil may be more unsettling for feminists than calling marriage an evil, especially when what is meant is that its victims are not just mothers but children. Feminist critiques of motherhood tend to focus on harm to mothers.[59] My concern here is with danger to children. And so I want to be very clear that it is not my view that mothers are in general evil, any more than that spouses are in general murderers. Mothers are not responsible for motherhood (although some abuse it). Mothers' options are fairly limited, and many do an astonishing job with limited resources. Motherhood can also be a gray zone for battered wives whose daughters are paternal incest victims. But that complication I postpone to the final chapter.

The motherhood I question is defined by social norms and values that are intertwined with and have evolved with those of marriage. To question motherhood is not to question the importance of special relationships between mothers and children. The question is, rather, about how those relationships have been socially structured, the norms to which mothers are commonly held. If Rich is right, mothers almost universally fail to meet the social norms defining a "good mother." Mothers are held responsible when children turn out badly, and the norms of motherhood give mothers considerable discretion regarding child discipline. Just as not all marriages are violent, not all mothers abuse that discretion. But motherhood shelters abuse. The difficulty of rescuing a child from repeated life-threatening abuse, even over a period of years and with highly visible effects, is documented in the first and second volumes of Pelzer's trilogy.

Children abused by parents are often profoundly attached to them. The importance of early attachments raises questions about the advisability of removing children from abusive parents. But the dependency that gives rise to the attachment is not just given by biology. It is also socially structured by norms of marriage and motherhood. With childrearing practices that did not concentrate power over and responsibility for a child for many years in one or two caregivers, different patterns of attachment might develop, and separation from an abusive caregiver might leave the child with equally important attachments to other caregivers.

"Mother" is ambiguous between a woman who gives birth and a female who rears a child—often but not necessarily the same woman. "Motherhood" is also ambiguous between the experience of mothers (usually in the second sense) and the social institution that structures childrearing. It is the social institution that shelters abuse. Just as some would stretch "family" to cover any committed partnership, household, or close and enduring network of friends, others would stretch "motherhood" to cover any mode of childrearing. So understood, motherhood seems almost inevitable, as children need to be reared. I reject that loose understanding because it discourages creative thinking about alternatives. Just as not every durable intimate partnership is a marriage, not every mode of childrearing exemplifies motherhood. In fact, children are reared by grandparents, single parents (male, female, heterosexual, lesbian, gay, asexual), and extended families, all in the midst of patriarchies.

Apart from marriage and historical ideals of the family, it is uncertain what characteristics mother-child relationships would have. Many alternatives are possible. In good ones, mothers would less commonly find their lives burdened with unwanted, involuntary, uncompensated responsibility for children. Even today, an ever increasing amount of caregiving is done contractually in daycare centers, with the result that many middle-class mothers' relationship to their children is often far less a caregiving relationship than that of their mothers was to them. Nor are paid daycare workers "mothers" (although they engage in some "mothering activities"), because they are free to walk away from their jobs. Their relationships with a child may be no more permanent or special to the child than those of a babysitter. Boswell's history *The Kindness of Strangers* examines centuries of children taken in by those at whose doorsteps they were deposited, often anonymously, as babies.[60] Children have been raised in convents, orphanages, and boarding schools rather than in households, not always with good results. Many raised in households are cared for by a series of hired domestic workers, rather than by anyone called "Mother." Many children today commute between separated or divorced parents, spending less time in a single household than children of lesbian parents, some of whom, like Leslea Newman's Heather, have two people to call "Mother."[61] Many children are raised by siblings in households in which someone else is called "Mother."

My point is not to glorify orphanages but to put in perspective rhetoric about children's needs and ideal motherhood. Much feminist ink has been spilt debunking what passes for "love" in marriage. It is time to consider how much of the "love" that children are said to need is no more love than spousal service has been. Children do need stable intimate bonds with adults. They also need guidance, discipline, toilet training, education, health care, clean clothes, baths, balanced meals, and relationships with peers. What the state tends to enforce in motherhood is a mother's answerability for her child's waywardness and the child's access to its mother, which meet none of those basic needs.

A mother's answerability for her child's waywardness does, however, give her a motive for constant supervision of the child. That supervision thereby removes certain burdens from others but can easily endanger the child when the mother is ill supplied with resources. Lacking adequate social or material resources, many mothers resort to violent discipline, which the state has been reluctant to prevent, discourage, or even acknowledge. This is what it has meant, legally, for a child to be a mother's "own": her own is the child who has legal rights of access to her and for whose waywardness she becomes answerable.

Children raised by same-sex parents and other couples whose unions lack social support currently are more likely to be in environments carefully chosen and affirmed by their caregivers.[62] Turning same-sex unions into marriages, however, would enable the state to define more thoroughly than it does already who has the status of "parent." The state grants that status to whoever is married to a woman at the time that she gives birth and grants the status of parent to at most two persons at a time per child, giving the child legal rights of access to just those two parties. Likewise, the state concentrates in those two parties accountability for the child's waywardness. Under the present system, many LGBT couples do their best to emulate heterosexual models, which usually means assuming the responsibilities without the privileges. Others, however, attempt to undermine the assumption that responsibility should be concentrated in one or two people who have the power of a child's happiness and unhappiness in their hands for nearly two decades. Children raised without such models of the concentration of power may be less likely to reproduce patriarchal and other oppressive social relationships.

The revolutionary parenting that hooks describes dilutes the power of individual parents, distributes caregiving, and opens up space for greater accountability and rescue. The idea of revolutionary parenting is not yet precisely defined even by hooks with respect to the size and nature of the community who parents and with respect to who has what responsibilities within that community. Much more concrete proposals can be found in Eva Feder Kittay's work on public policy and dependency.[63] Refinements and variations are worth exploring. Although children retain special affectional ties to "bloodmothers" in revolutionary parenting, accountability for children's waywardness is more widely distributed. With many caregivers (those Collins calls "othermothers"), there is no pressure on anyone to be constantly accessible. But there is a general expectation that everyone will be somewhat accessible.

With many caregivers, it is more difficult to hide abuse. It is less likely that anyone will get away with prolonged abuse or even be tempted to it. One might fear that despite a reduced likelihood of parental assault, children might be in greater danger of being neglected, because when responsibility is diluted, people are less apt to step forward in time of need. Studies that reached that conclusion, however, were motivated by the murder of Kitty Genovese and the thirty-eight witnesses who failed to respond. Those studies looked at relationships among strangers, not between children and adults with whom they have bonds. Yet if neglect is a danger, Kittay's proposals regarding compensation for caregiving might begin to address it.

Many adults looked out for the children of my village. As a child I had a combination of both kinds of worlds. My parents had the legal rights and responsibilities of patriarchal parents. Yet some of those responsibilities were in fact assumed by "othermothers," including women and men who never married. Because it could always be assumed that wherever I roamed in the village, I would never be among strangers, my parents did not think they needed always to supervise me. Yet they were also ambivalent about that, as they were legally answerable for any trouble I caused. I dreaded the thought of moving to a city, where my freedom would be severely curtailed, as it was when we lived in a large middle-class urban environment during World War II. In the village, children had great freedom to move about and form relationships with adults who were not necessarily chosen by or even friends of their blood-mothers. There we often escaped the intensity of physical discipline that I experienced alone with my mother amidst a far larger and less friendly urban population.

There are both worse and better environments that can be imagined for children than stereotypical patriarchal families. Orphanages with frequently changing personnel are probably worse, as are urban environments where parents work away from home but can neither bring children nor assume that their children are watched by anyone. Children who have never had effective caregivers do not make good caregivers of each other. Feminism today is in a bind regarding the so-called postpatriarchal family. If both women and men are to be actively involved in markets and governments and free to become active members of all occupations and professions, when, where, and how is childcare to be done? The solution of many feminists has been for two parents to take turns with the children. To facilitate that arrangement, Joan Williams argues for more flexible work schedules with the same benefits and opportunities available to part-time as to full-time workers in the paid labor force.[64] Failing such arrangements, there is an increasing tendency for parents who divide childcare responsibilities to pay others to do the childcare, if they can afford it, when their turn comes. To the extent that this works, it is evidence that prolonged "mothering" is unnecessary. Children who have had effective caregivers may be better at taking care of themselves and each other, with minimal supervision, than many suppose.

Charlotte Perkins Gilman's solution in *Women and Economics* and *Herland* was twofold.[65] On one hand, she, like Kittay, would turn childcare into a profession open to everyone with the requisite talents and motivations. At the same time, she would make the public safe even for children, by an ethic that incorporated aspects of good caregiving. Virginia Held's *Feminist Morality* endorses the latter strategy.[66] Its risk, of course, is instituting paternalism among adults, spelled with an *m* instead of a *p*. Still, the idea of improving public safety is compelling. Were it improved enough, there might be little need for specialized childcare beyond the age of ten.

Held maintains that the mother-child relationship is the fundamental social relationship, in the sense that so much else depends on one's relationships to primary caretakers.[67] This idea, also urged by Annette Baier, seems to me in certain ways incontrovertible and its general appreciation by philosophers long overdue. There are at least two ways in which this idea seems to me incontrovertible. First, no one would survive without caregiving. Doing it well is worth careful thought. Second, when one does in fact have a primary caretaker who has, if not the power of life and death, then the power of one's happiness and unhappiness in their hands for many years in the early stages of one's life, the influence of that experience on the rest of one's life is profound. It appears, for example, to affect one's ability to form good relationships with others in ways that are extremely difficult to change, if they are changeable at all. Yet, there is another way in which the observation that the mother-child relationship is fundamental is misleading. It is misleading if it suggests that the caregiving one needs to survive must be structured by the institution of motherhood. It is misleading if it suggests that everyone really needs a single primary caretaker, or even pair of primary caretakers, with the power of one's happiness and unhappiness in their hands for the first decade and a half or more of one's life. Children may need that only in a society that refuses to take and share responsibility collectively for its own consciously and thoughtfully affirmed reproduction and maintenance. In that case, conscientious mothers may be the best protection a child has. But if so, it is misleading to say that the mother-child relationship is a fundamental social relationship.

Because mothers in a society that generally refuses collective responsibility for reproduction are often the best or even the only protection that children have, in the short run it is worth fighting for the right to adopt and raise children within lesbian and gay households. This is emergency care for young people who are desperately in need. At the same time, it seems advisable to keep open the option of making parenting more revolutionary along the lines of communal practices as described by hooks or distributed caregiving as envisioned by Kittay. Legal marriage interferes with the revolution, rather than encouraging it, in a state that glorifies marriage and takes the marriage relationship to be the healthiest, if not the only healthy, context in which to raise children. Lesbian and gay unions have great potentiality to further the revolution, in part because we cannot marry.

Even if the institution of motherhood is transcended, the importance of attending to the experiences and environments of children remains. The "children" in society are all of us. Not each of us will rear children. But each has been a child, and each future adult will first have childhood to survive. Rich's treatise on motherhood is distinguished from most in being written in part from the perspective of a daughter and addressed to all women as daughters. Both her work and the works of Baier, Collins, Held, hooks, Kittay, and Sara Ruddick have the potential to direct our attention not just to mothers but to those who have been (or have not been) mother*ed*.

Everyone would benefit from a society more attentive to the evils done children and to the conditions under which children grow into adulthood. Moral philosophy might be transformed by greater attention to the fact that the evils that adults do and their ability to respond to the evils done them are significantly conditioned by their childhoods. In getting us to take seriously the child's experience of childhood, to take up the standpoint of the child in all of us, philosophical work exploring the significance of mother-child relationships does feminism and moral philosophy a great service.

8

The Moral Powers of Victims

Living with Evils

Lesbian, gay, and transgender people in the United States live surrounded by the hatred of people who would eliminate us if they could.[1] Girls learn early that the world is dangerous for unprotected females and that female competence is more often punished than rewarded. Racial minorities are grossly overrepresented in U.S. prisons. Jewish and Gypsy histories are to a great extent histories of the survival of evils that were fatal for many. The world's poor, its vast majority, suffer daily living conditions conducive to high infant mortality, lifelong poor health, and early death for survivors of childhood.[2] The United States, justly proud of its early history as a haven for refugees, was nevertheless founded on a bedrock of slavery and mass murder. As John Stuart Mill observed, with characteristic understatement, "Unquestionably it is possible to do without happiness; it is done involuntarily by nineteen-twentieths of mankind."[3] Whether to live with evils and their legacies is seldom a choice. The questions are about how to do it well, especially, how to interrupt cycles of hostility generated by past evils and replace mutual ill will with good.

In *Living with One's Past*, Norman Care reflects on issues presented by problematic aspects of one's own moral history, choices that implicated one in the genesis of potentially serious harms to others.[4] His work is exceptional in contemporary ethics in addressing how to live with profound regrets, how to respond to wrongs done, rather than simply how to prevent future ones. Similarly, the concerns of this chapter and the next two are about living with evils, ongoing and past, and their aftermaths. I approach them first from the positions of victims, then from those of perpetrators, and finally, from those of people who are at once victims and perpetrators.

I begin with a discussion of rectifications and remainders, core concepts for responding to evils, and briefly consider limits of punishment as rectification for atrocities. I then take up moral powers of victims, negative and positive, that tend toward rectification. The negative power is blame (and related attitudes of condemnation and resentment), which can evoke guilt and associated senses of obligation in those blamed. The positive power, treated at greater length, is forgiveness, which can relieve burdens that may not be morally relievable in other ways. The chapter following takes up the burdens and obligations of perpetrators, especially burdens of guilt but also those imposed by gratitude for such things as forgiveness and mercy from victims. When gratitude and guilt are experienced as unpayable debts, both might be regarded as what Bernard Williams has called "remainders."[5]

Legacies of evil are receiving international attention as nations address histories of apartheid, genocide, mass rape, disappearances, and torture. Martha Minow and Carlos Santiago Nino write thoughtfully and informatively about social, political, and legal responses to atrocities, exploring alternatives to the opposite extremes of vengeance and amnesty. They discuss truth commissions, monument building, barring former collaborators from positions of social responsibility, and payments, trials, apologies, and other reparations.[6] These measures are undertaken by states and nongovernmental organizations with the pragmatic aim of ending cycles of atrocity in such countries as South Africa, Chile, or the former Yugoslavia. My concerns here are more with responses by individuals who do not hold positions of political influence but must find ways to go on feeling, thinking, and acting in the face of histories and legacies of evil, both interpersonal and institutional. To the extent that Nino is right that at the level of governmental action, "silence and impunity have been the norm rather than the exception" and that "the few investigations that have been undertaken often targeted the wrong actions and the wrong people," ordinary citizens often cannot take satisfaction in state action but must make their own peace.[7]

John Kekes writes insightfully on how to live with the knowledge that evils continue to be a significant part of the human condition. He evaluates attitudes philosophers have advocated toward life and toward humanity in general in light of this appreciation.[8] My concerns here are with attitudes not toward life or humanity as such but toward individuals—victims, perpetrators, bystanders, and beneficiaries (ourselves included)—who are connected with particular evils.

Evils change moral relationships among those who become perpetrators, bystanders, beneficiaries, or victims. They create moral powers in survivors, obligations in perpetrators, beneficiaries, and bystanders, and new options for many. Like benefactors, who can call upon the gratitude or indebtedness of beneficiaries, victims have moral powers: to blame or resent, to forgive, and, if politically empowered, to punish or retaliate, exact reparations and apologies, and to pardon or show mercy. Like creditors and benefactors who can forgive or exact debts, voluntarily releasing others or holding them to obligation, victims have moral powers to release or hold perpetrators to obligation. Beneficiaries can do little to change their own ethical status in relation to benefactors. Regardless of whether they meet their obligations, they remain indebted unless benefactors release them. Similarly, perpetrators can do little to change their own ethical status in relation to victims but remain morally dependent on them (or their representatives) for release. Yet benefactors and victims can forfeit moral powers through misconduct. Just as unscrupulous or abusive benefactors can cease to deserve gratitude, thereby involuntarily releasing beneficiaries from obligation, unscrupulous or abusive victims can cease to deserve apologies or reparations, involuntarily releasing perpetrators from obligation.

How one exercises moral powers or responds to obligations created by evildoing is important to one's character and relationships with others, even apart from deterrent or preventive effects of one's responses. Often perpetrators cannot repair harm or adequately compensate victims. Yet perpetrators and victims can communicate how they feel about what was done in ways that matter to those involved. Apologies, forgiveness or pardon (or the choice not to), and such responses as guilt, shame, gratitude, and resentment indicate how perpetrators and victims value what was done and what was suffered. These responses reveal how the parties see themselves in relation to each other and to the deed, showing something of who they are and thereby something of their worthiness to associate with each other.

The shift from a focus on escape, avoidance, and prevention to a focus on living with and responding to evils is found in Schopenhauer's masterpiece *The World as Will and Representation* and his essay *On the Basis of Morality* as well as in many of Nietzsche's writings, from *The Birth of Tragedy* to *On the Genealogy of Morality*.[9] For Schopenhauer, salvation comes with a quieting of the will, the stoicism of ceasing to value what inevitably brings suffering. His solution is an escape after all, not from suffering or harm but from experiencing it as intolerable, an ingenious escape through a revaluation of suffering. For Schopenhauer, salvation lies not only beyond ethics but beyond the phenomenal world.

Nietzsche rejected Schopenhauer's nihilism regarding the world of sense but stole his ideas of revaluation and moving beyond evil. Like Schopenhauer he abandoned traditional Western religious hopes of an afterlife with its promised rewards and compensations. Although he also abandoned moral categories, especially that of evil, he departed from Schopenhauer by embracing finite embodiment, with its vulnerabilities. Retaining Schopenhauer's pessimism regarding the prevalence of pain and suffering, Nietzsche found that to sustain an optimistic attitude of affirming life, he had to reconceive and revalue pain and suffering as concomitants of the will to power and reconceive morality as rooted in a dangerous attempt at domination by those who were lacking in vitality.[10]

But what if life as such is not worthy of affirmation? A more moderate view than either Schopenhauer's or Nietzsche's is that some lives are worthy of affirmation, whereas others truly are not. Moral concepts may be necessary or at least helpful to ultimately sustainable affirmations of particular lives. If Schopenhauer and Nietzsche are right about the prevalence of suffering and harm, as compared with joy and happiness, then in order to find many of our lives worthy of affirmation, we may need or be greatly helped by moral rectifications. And we may want or need to be able to acknowledge moral remainders—imbalances, debts, or unexpiated wrongs that remain even after we have done what can be done to put things right.

Rectifications, Remainders, and Punishment

Punishment, mercy, forgiveness, and sometimes paying or acknowledging debts of gratitude are common attempts at rectification. Rectifications aim to correct imbalances, redress wrongs, settle scores, put things right between us. In addition to punishment, resentment, praise, and blame, on which there is a large literature, the rectifications most explored by philosophers are forgiveness, mercy, and gratitude.[11] Other rectifications, such as amnesty, apology, compensation, pardon, repentance, restitution, and reward, can be considered in terms of their relationships to these.

Certain emotional residues have been referred to as "moral remainders" ever since Bernard Williams observed that "moral conflicts are neither systematically avoidable, nor all soluble without remainder."[12] Remainders are rectificatory feelings regarding what otherwise proves unrectifiable by our actions. Guilt, shame, remorse, regret, and often gratitude are remainders. These emotional residues acknowledge an unexpiated wrong, an unrectified shortcoming, or an unpaid debt. Remainders offer us a limited redemption in that they reveal our appreciation that all has not been made right, or that not all is as it should be (or would be, ideally) between us.

My use of the term "remainder" extends that of Williams in two ways. First, for Williams remainders are negative, produced by wrongdoing. And yet moral transactions also leave positive remainders when not everything good can be reciprocated. We acknowledge positive remainders in unpayable debts of gratitude. Second, for Williams remainders are not our lingering emotional responses but unexpiated wrongs themselves, the things inevitably not made right. I find it natural, however, to think of emotional and attitudinal responses to such moral facts as also remainders. Thus, regret, remorse, and sometimes shame and guilt are moral remainders. Like the insoluble parts of moral conflicts, these responses remain, even after we have done what we can to set matters right. They are rectificatory responses of feeling rather than action. They reveal important values of an agent who has acted wrongly or is identified with a bad action or bad state of affairs, or those of a beneficiary unable to reciprocate benefits. Remainders can survive both rectificatory action and hard choices in complex situations where inevitably some are wronged or receive less than their due and the best one can do is seek the least undesirable outcome.

Aristotle said of shame, in explaining its status as a "quasi-virtue," that ideally occasions for it will not arise but that if they do, it is better to have shame than to be shameless.[13] He appears to have had no conception of guilt as distinct from shame. Today shame, remorse, and regret are most discussed in terms of their relationships to guilt, a paradigmatic emotional remainder. According to Nietzsche's genealogy of morality, guilt was not always a remainder but was originally an economic debt or, rather, a substitute for it in those who could not or would not pay the original debt.[14] Guilt today is ambiguous between a verdict (which can lead to imposition of a "debt" to be paid others in the form of punishment) and emotional self-devaluation or self-punishment. Self-devaluation or punishment can linger sometimes as long as the verdict, which is not canceled by paying the debt. This lingering guilt is a moral remainder.

Punishment is held by most theorists to presuppose, as a matter of definition, a finding of guilt (the verdict). It is also commonly thought to expiate guilt (the debt), to enable the offender to atone for the offense. As a response to evils, punishment is truly a mixed bag. Only partially rectificatory, it takes on the project of prevention as well. Commonly defended as retribution and ideally enabling offenders to pay their debts as well as enabling victims to let go of the past, punishment is also defended by appeal to deterrent effects. Contemporary philosophers endorse compromise theories of punishment that treat both retribution and deterrence as principles limiting the justifiable infliction and severity of penalties. According to compromise theories, providing a certain range of penalties for a kind of offense is not justifiable unless the penalties are neither more severe than needed for adequate deterrence nor more severe than would be proportionate to the harm of the offense or the offender's culpability or both.[15] Both preventive and rectificatory aims are compromised in attempts to reach a set of penalties acceptable from both points of view.

For domestic violence and atrocities involving mass murder, penalties satisfying the compromise theories tend to fall dramatically short of what offenders deserve. As I write, the federal government is getting ready to execute Timothy McVeigh for the 1996 Oklahoma City bombing and to show the execution to the families of survivors on closed-circuit television. How could viewing that execution possibly compare with having seen or heard the building blow up, without warning, with all the children in daycare and workers just settling in to begin their day? It is also unclear what, if any, deterrent effect punishment can have regarding these crimes, as the causes of such behavior are poorly understood. Domestic violence often appears motivated by rage; mass murder, by ideology. In neither case is a prudential appeal to self-interest likely to obtain much purchase. Yet in calculating deterrence, rational self-interest on the part of potential offenders is assumed. The upshot is a paradoxical state of affairs in which deeds seemingly deserving of the worst punishments are frequently not punished at all or are punished more lightly than other, less harmful crimes. It was noted in chapter 6 that torture, for example, is seldom punished and that when it is, the penalties tend not to be commensurate with the offense and are usually inflicted on lesser ranking perpetrators rather than on those responsible for the orders. Nino observes that the same is true of war crimes generally. He discusses at length the case of Argentina, which eventually pardoned or issued amnesties to perpetrators of its "dirty war," including those who dropped many "disappeared" victims into the ocean from airplanes.[16] Blanket amnesties and pardons unaccompanied by other measures designed to acknowledge injustices and prevent perpetrators from profiting leave victims' needs and resentments unaddressed.

If resentment is, as Rawls argues, a natural response to others' unjustly being enriched at one's expense, punishment goes some way toward neutralizing resentment by acknowledging the injustice and removing at least some of the offender's profit from it.[17] Yet punishment does not go the whole distance required to neutralize resentment. For in removing or counterbalancing the offender's profit, punishment need not do anything to alleviate harm suffered by victims of the offense. Victims are sometimes surprised at how unsatisfying it can be simply to see the offender brought low, especially if the crime was atrocious and its harm enduring.

Historically, shunning and ostracism were alternatives to punishment. In ancient times, ostracism was practically a death sentence. Unlike shunning, punishment permits wrongdoers to pay for what are judged to be their wrongs and renew relationships or be readmitted to society without having to agree that they did what they were accused of, that they were to blame for it, or that it was wrong. Acknowledging fallibility in trials and judges, the practice of punishment allows the wrongfully convicted to maintain a certain integrity. To be consistent, punishment ought not to include penalties, such as death, that are entirely irreversible in cases of wrongful convictions.

The practice of shunning, in contrast to punishment, requires repentance as the price of reacceptance. It has the disadvantage of insufficiently acknowledging fallibility in accusers and judges. But in theory at least, shunning has the advantage of acknowledging the moral powers of victims, their powers to blame and forgive, as well as some obligations of perpetrators, such as the obligation to apologize. Punishment, in contrast, offers little room for the exercise of the moral powers of victims and inadequately acknowledges the obligations of perpetrators, such as the obligation to repair damage.

Yet considering how imprisonment and parole have (often not) worked in practice, the difference in real life between shunning and punishment is far from sharp. Former prisoners are often not regarded as having paid adequately for their offenses, and paroles may be contingent on prisoners' contrition, which presupposes admission of guilt. Both shunning and punishment with possible parole thereby encourage dishonesty in the wrongly accused or convicted, and both practices founder on major atrocities. No payment is adequate to mass murder, and mere contrition should not be sufficient for reacceptance while reparable damage remains. As a response to atrocities, legal punishment is highly incomplete. Yet monetary payments to victims of war rape notoriously risk adding insult to injury.

Increasingly, many find punishment insufficient to enable victims and perpetrators to move on, even when the offense is not an atrocity and when moving on is the outcome ultimately desired by all. Prisons tend to make prisoners worse.[18] They do not fit felons well for readmission to society. Only a fraction of the guilty are apprehended and convicted. There is unjust arbitrariness in who that fraction is. Many innocents are convicted. The death penalty becomes an atrocity itself when the innocent poor are foreseeably more likely to suffer it than the guilty rich.[19]

Even if penalties could be devised more nearly commensurate with evil deeds than convention currently allows, as in the case of the fantasized penalties of chapter 6 for war rape, many scruples would argue against their infliction. Minow notes that the adversarial trial system prioritizes winning cases rather than getting at truth.[20] This fact makes it even more important that punishments be revocable in cases of wrongful conviction. But revocable penalties tend to be less commensurate with evil deeds, the harm of which is commonly irrevocable, and so they tend to leave aspects of the evil unaddressed.

But even when there is no question of adequate retribution, compensation, or restitution, trials can still be held to get at the truth. Past deeds can be verified and publicized by truth commissions. Offenders can publicly apologize and reveal what they know. Their labors or assets can provide surviving victims with benefits to relieve health care costs incurred as a result of injury or trauma. Victims and rescuers can be memorialized in monuments and museums. Perpetrators and collaborators can be barred from future positions of social trust and honor. But there remain questions of individual response. How are perpetrators and victims to think, feel, and act in relation to one another after an atrocity, even if such measures are taken?

When a punishment is neither death nor life imprisonment without parole, criminal offenders, some guilty of evil deeds, are eventually released into society. Critics who would lengthen sentences and abolish parole to avoid or postpone this event do well to recall that most criminal offenders are never caught and that of those caught, only a fraction are convicted or plea-bargained into penalties. Most perpetrators remain free, publicly unidentified. Many evils are not criminal. Some that are exist in law enforcement, hidden for decades, as revealed by Conroy's inquiries into the practice in Chicago of police torture of those suspected of killing police.[21] We live already in a society in which victims and perpetrators share common spaces. The problem of paroling convicted offenders is probably not the risk of increasing crime but, rather, what sorts of accountability should be expected of freed felons. If living with ordinary freed felons is a challenge, how are victims to live with war criminals who have escaped, received amnesty, served limited sentences, or even been elected or appointed to influential social or political positions?

These questions can be heard to ask whether or how to exercise the moral powers of victims, if victims include all whose security is endangered by evil deeds. When blame evokes guilt and a sense of obligation, it further empowers victims, morally, who can then draw on that sense of obligation in the interests of rectification. If Joel Feinberg is right, however, that punishment has the expressive function of condemnation (a form of blame), Nietzsche also seems right that punishment (alone) does not make those who suffer it "better," but, rather, tames them, makes them more prudent, calculating, secretive, dishonest.[22] Punishment is, fortunately, not the only vehicle for expressing blame. Blame can be expressed also or instead in demands or requests for such things as confessions, apologies, restitution, and reparations.

The reciprocal goodwill that can be initiated by forgiveness and mercy—when they are perceived as issuing from strength rather than weakness—and by seeking accountability in the form of confessions, apologies, and reparations, rather than in the form of punishment, appears a promising substitute for the cycles of hostility that punishment alone seems unable to terminate. There is good reason to explore these responses as supplements, if not alternatives, to punishment for atrocities. The rest of this chapter explores the ethics of forgiveness, treating forgiveness as a complex moral power of victims that can release perpetrators from troubling remainders. Mercy and the burdens and obligations of perpetrators are reserved for the chapter following.

Forgiving Evildoers

Forgiveness is a liberal response to wrongdoers, as mercy is a liberal response to those whom we have the power or authority to harm or make suffer. There is no consensus among philosophers regarding the value of forgiveness or even the conditions of its possibility. Questions asked include when, what, and whom we can forgive (can we forgive the dead?), who "we" are (who is in a position to forgive?), what forgiveness does (for the forgiven, for the forgiver), what it implies (must punishment be remitted? must the parties reconcile?), when one ought to forgive, when forgiveness is deserved, optional, or, if ever, wrong (is it wrong to forgive the unrepentant?). These questions become more difficult and more important when the wrong is an evil.

Paradigm forgiveness is interpersonal (forgiver and forgiven are different persons). It has several characteristic features, which may be broken down as follows. In ideal interpersonal forgiveness there is a change of heart in the offended party regarding the offender, which consists of (1) a renunciation of hostility out of (2) a charitable or compassionate concern for the (perceived) offender; (3) an acceptance of the offender's apology and contrition; (4) a remission of punishment, if any, over which the forgiver has authority or control; and (5) an offer to renew relationship (to "start over") or accept the other as a (possible) friend or associate. Offered as a gift, forgiveness may be accepted or rejected. If accepted, it may evoke gratitude and place the recipient under new obligations. Offenders who do not acknowledge wrongdoing, however, may perceive offers of forgiveness as arrogant and offensive.

For the offender who accepts it, forgiveness lifts or eases the burden of guilt, much as forgiving a debt relieves the debtor of an obligation to repay. This relief often seems to be its major point. Relief is apt to be especially valued by debtors who could never fully repay anyway and for offenses for which reparations are inevitably inadequate. Forgiveness is thus a way of addressing negative remainders that perpetrators are unable to address adequately themselves. For the forgiver, forgiveness involves a renunciation of feelings of injury and hostility, although not of the judgment of having been wronged. To blame is to hold the offense against the offender, to hold the offender still accountable. The forgiver ceases to hold it against the offender but does not cease to regard it as an offense (or there is nothing to forgive). Thus, forgiveness frees both parties to move on. It is, as Hannah Arendt put it, one of our remedies for the irreversibility of the past.[23]

Although forgiveness cannot be compelled, one can be at fault in failing to offer it to those who deserve it or refusing to grant it when asked by those who have done all they can to atone. But one can also be at fault in offering it too freely or quickly. Because it is a power, those who are in other ways disempowered may be tempted to exercise it too freely. Victims of exploitation may be further exploited by oppressors who take advantage of this vulnerability by encouraging feelings of virtue for the readiness to forgive. Women often find themselves in this position in sexist relationships, where there is often much to forgive and women are praised for being "understanding." It may be more difficult to imagine being tempted to accept forgiveness when one ought not, when, for example, one has done no wrong to be forgiven (or is not sorry).

Yet women also find themselves in this position, as when Helmer decides to forgive Nora in Ibsen's play "A Doll's House."[24] Inappropriately accepting forgiveness can appear to be (or be) the easiest way to move past conflicts in sexist relationships, although in Ibsen's play, Nora refuses Helmer's "forgiveness."

Some features of the paradigm case of forgiveness are not naturally or unproblematically present in less central instances of forgiveness. Nonparadigmatic cases include those in which the offender does not admit wrongdoing, or is no longer living, or in which the offender is living but not sorry, or is unwilling or unable to express contrition, or the offense is especially heinous, or the victim is no longer living, or both offender and forgiver are oneself, or both are groups (such as nations), rather than individual persons. Some evils, such as genocide, are perpetrated not just by individuals but by groups or corporate bodies—nations, governments, armies, political parties. Victims of genocide are also not just individuals but groups—national, religious, ethnic, or racial.[25] But what can it mean for a group to forgive a group?[26] A group does not literally have a heart to change, neither feelings of hostility toward nor the capacity for compassion for perpetrators. What can it mean for even an individual to forgive a group? Groups lack feelings of contrition, although they can apologize and make amends. Group forgiveness is not simply reducible to members of one group forgiving members of another. Often, members of the respective groups are strangers to one another. Often, those who apologize or accept an apology are not those who did or suffered the wrong but belong to a later generation.

Questions of the possibility and value of forgiving evildoers become more tractable when we return to the several features of the paradigm case and make the questions more specific. Some features of the paradigm are possible and appropriate in nonstandard cases when others are not. Regarding unrepentant offenders, for example, there comes a time when it is good for victims to let go of resentment, even if there is no basis for compassion for the offender. When the victim has no authority to punish, the victim's forgiveness may be irrelevant to the wisdom of punishment. When one or both parties are groups, one can apologize and the other accept the apology and reduce penalties or press for smaller reparations, even though groups lack feelings. Groups can be harmed, and they can act. They can hold (or cease to hold) a perpetrator accountable and in that way hold an injury against the perpetrator. This opens a space for the possibility of forgiveness between groups, although such forgiveness is not a paradigm case.

People can forgive at least what they can resent. We can resent agents and deeds, as well as the results of wrongful deeds, such as the unearned wealth of others or undeserved poverty. We can forgive agents for wrongful deeds or for unearned privileges. In an eighteenth century sermon on the topic, still widely cited, Bishop Joseph Butler presented the Christian duty to forgive as a duty simply to avoid excess resentment.[27] It is true that ordinary wrongs are resented by those wronged. But "resentful," "angry," and even "indignant" grossly underdescribe characteristic moral responses to atrocities. We resent insults, cheating, and unfairness. But evils leave us speechless, appalled, horrified, nauseated. When we do find speech, atrocities evoke rage and condemnation. Like resentment, condemnation is a form of blame. It holds perpetrators' deeds against them. Forgiveness is no antidote to speechlessness, horror, nausea, and the like. But it is a possible antidote to blame and thus to condemnation.

Arendt wrote that people "are unable to forgive what they cannot punish" and that "they are unable to punish what has turned out to be unforgivable."[28] It is plausible that one would not wish to punish what is unforgivable, if punishing allows the offender to pay for the crime and thereafter be done with it. But is it true that we cannot forgive what cannot be paid for? If, because atrocities are not adequately punishable, they are also unforgivable, then it appears that we can forgive only ordinary wrongs, not extraordinary ones. Yet it is for extraordinary wrongs that forgiveness seems most needed and valued. Here the burdens of guilt can weigh heaviest and threaten to spiral into future hostilities. Perhaps it is not that we *cannot* forgive extraordinary wrongs but that often we ought not, that forgiveness should be granted only slowly and with caution, depending on what else the perpetrator does (by way of confession, apology, reparation, regeneration), that conditions that make it morally an option are difficult to satisfy, often unlikely. Even if atrocity victims eventually forgive evildoers, perhaps perpetrators should be slow to forgive themselves. But this thought supposes that forgiving oneself makes sense.

Arendt said we are unable to forgive ourselves, that only others can forgive us.[29] Butler's view of forgiveness as a renunciation of resentment explains Arendt's observations. For we resent only others, not ourselves. Yet we blame, even condemn, ourselves. Self-forgiveness makes sense as a renunciation of self-condemnation or self-blame. Self-forgiveness may be hasty when others who could forgive us have not done so or have not had the opportunity. Still, when others' forgiveness is not enough, or if they are unable or unlikely to forgive us, perhaps we should sometimes forgive ourselves. Based on our having owned up, apologized, undertaken reparations, and so forth, we might cease to regard ourselves negatively. Conversely, some willingness to forgive oneself, even for evil deeds, may be needed to sustain motivation to fulfill our obligations and avoid repeating wrongs. Perpetrators need the sense that they are worth the effort that self-improvement will require. Some self-forgiveness may be requisite to that sense of self-worth.

Perhaps the truth behind Arendt's claim that we are unable to forgive ourselves is that forgiving oneself and being forgiven by another have different aims and accomplish different things. Another's forgiveness is a gift, which we can accept or reject. Self-forgiveness is an achievement (as is forgiving another). One has to overcome hostility toward and develop a certain compassion for oneself. Forgiveness by another may be requisite to a renewal of relationship. But some measure of self-forgiveness may be requisite to one's own self-respect.

Although, like Butler, Arendt emphasizes the liberality of forgiveness, presenting it as letting go of the deed, she also presents it as charitable, claiming that we forgive the offense for the sake of the offender.[30] That idea suggests an explanation for why some evil organizations, such as the National Socialist Party or the Ku Klux Klan, are unforgivable. Unlike people who create and belong to them, organizations as such need have no dignity or inherent worth. The worth of an organization is a function of the principles and procedures that define it. If it is defined by evil principles and inadequate procedures for change and evolves no better ones, there is nothing to redeem it. (Nations often do evolve. The principles and values at their core change as generations and regimes succeed one another.) Unlike the worth of organizations, that of individuals is not determined simply by principles they happen to espouse but is a function also of traits and capacities that preexist and outlast particular endorsements. These traits and capacities can form a basis for a charitable response, even toward those who espouse evil principles.

Forgiveness, as a move from defensive hostility to a more compassionate, pacific attitude, is a natural response to an offender's apology. And yet, when former perpetrators are rendered powerless or at least no longer dangerous, the victim's need for hostile defensiveness can disappear even without any apology or amends. A more limited change of heart or attitude in the victim may then be possible and desirable, based not on charity for the offender but on the victim's own needs or desires to move on. This limited change of heart may be better regarded as forgiveness of the offense than as forgiveness of the offender. It consists of renouncing the sense of injury and concomitant hostilities and redirecting one's emotional energies in other, more constructive ways that need have nothing to do with the offender. Thus, Howard McGary argues that rational self-interest offers African Americans powerful reason to move beyond resentment regarding histories of slavery. He advocates such forgiveness (letting go) for the sake of the forgiver rather than for the sake of the forgiven.[31] A reason to agree with him in considering this letting go to be genuinely forgiveness is that it truly is a change of heart, not just (or even) forgetting. It includes a renunciation of something that underlies blaming, namely, the sense of injury and the hostilities that go with it. Unlike paradigm forgiveness, it need not be offered or granted to the offender, and it is not undertaken for the offender's sake. But forgiveness need not be "all or nothing" with respect to the five features of the paradigm case. Renouncing hostilities and feelings of injury can leave open the question of whether reparations should be sought. For the harm remains, even if one ceases to resent it.[32]

Ought one to forgive an unrepentant evildoer?[33] Ordinarily, a truly repentant offender deserves forgiveness. Paradigmatically, either a repentant offender apologizes and asks forgiveness, which is then granted, or else a victim offers forgiveness, which is accepted and then followed by repentance. Yet some find that they can forgive the dead who never asked for it when they were alive and never even admitted wrongdoing. Although here we can no longer offer forgiveness to the offender, we can cease to resent the dead and choose to remember them for their good qualities. In part 2 of *The Metaphysics of Morals*, Kant wrote that we ought to defend the ancients "from all attacks, accusations, and disdain, insofar as this is possible," out of gratitude to them as our teachers, although he also cautioned against romantically attributing to them superiority of goodwill over that of our contemporaries.[34] One might also think a charitable attitude warranted toward the dead on the ground that they can no longer defend themselves. It might be replied that if the dead cannot defend themselves, they cannot be further hurt, either. Their reputations, however, can suffer. But unrepentant perpetrators' inability to defend themselves or their reputations may not be a sufficiently good reason to forgive them, if their deeds were atrocious and they subsequently took no responsibility when they could have. Forgiving the unrepentant, dead or alive, is probably best decided by the interests of the forgiver.

Yet the question is often raised how we can forgive the unrepentant without condoning their offenses, tacitly approving them, and thereby tacitly encouraging their emulation. The question is also raised what remains to be forgiven when an offender does repent and regenerate? Aurel Kolnai presented these two questions as a paradox of forgiveness.[35] Together they suggest that forgiveness is either inappropriate or else redundant. Without repentance, it seems inappropriate. With repentance, it seems redundant.

For criminal evils, condonation can be avoided by combining the change of heart with such other measures as supporting punishment, or punishment together with responses that Minow presents as lying "between vengeance and forgiveness": reparations, commemorative monuments to victims and rescuers or resistors, investigations into the truth, publicity of facts, support services for victims, and refusals to place offenders in positions of honor or social trust.[36] Insofar as these activities do not imply emotional hostility toward offenders, they are compatible with some measure of forgiveness of even the unregenerate. They offer public evidence that the offender is held responsible and the offense not condoned. As to Kolnai's second question, what remains to be forgiven even in a transformed offender is the offense, for which the offender, however changed, remains responsible. A transformed offender does not cease to be guilty of or accountable for past deeds. A transformed offender is apt to feel more guilty than before and be in greater need of forgiveness. Forgiving does not dissolve responsibility, even though it conveys a sympathetic response to the offender, which can alleviate guilt.

Does forgiveness imply a willingness to renew relations? Must forgiver and forgiven reconcile? Must friendship now be possible between them? The thought that willingness to reconcile is implied by forgiveness might explain some inclinations to find atrocities unforgivable. In their jointly authored collection of essays, *Mercy and Forgiveness*, Jean Hampton suggests that normally forgiveness does imply a willingness to renew relationship, whereas Jeffrie Murphy regards renewal as an open question that depends on many factors.[37] Hampton finds the strongest case for reconciliation in repentant offenders. But she admits that renewal may be a bad idea with offenders who remain dangerous, as in the case of battered intimates who rightly believe their abusers unregenerate. Her thought appears to be that reconciliation may simply provide the offender easy opportunities to repeat the offense. Yet there are more factors to consider. Did the forgiveness leave open questions of reparation? Sometimes it is wise to reconcile only conditionally on the offender's living up to obligations of reparation or restitution. If an offender who is capable of restitution is unwilling, that unwillingness provides a reason not to reconcile. Like a failure to repent, it evidences lack of goodwill.

The wisdom of reconciliation depends partly on the reliability of the offender, not simply on the renunciation of hostilities by the forgiver. Repentance by itself is often insufficient to indicate reliability. Hampton's view seems to imply that renewal of relationships would be a normal course of events even with perpetrators of atrocities, provided that they were repentant and rightly judged no longer dangerous. And yet, for mass murder, repentance is grossly insufficient in that it neither addresses the harm to survivors, who may require continuing medical and psychological care, nor by itself does it imply regeneration. Repentance is a first step toward regeneration. But character change requires not just good intentions but time for the development of new habits of thought, feeling, and action. The offender can develop those new habits by interacting with others, not necessarily former victims. It is not as though the offender is prevented from regenerating if the forgiver chooses not to be a part of that process. Further, some perpetrators are no longer dangerous only because their circumstances have changed, not because they have changed. Reestablishment of some relations may be prudent or politic independently of forgiveness, to keep lines of communication open for one's own protection or the protection of others. But one can renounce hostility without becoming open to renewal of relations or friendly association. Even if ordinarily forgiveness does enable a renewal of relationships, some elements of forgiveness still free us to move on when we choose not to reconcile.

When punishment is at issue, the question often arises of whether forgiveness implies pardon or a penalty reduction or remission. Arendt called forgiveness and punishment alternative ways of trying to put an end to what is past. But she also noted that they are not opposites.[38] Hastings Rashdall found forgiveness and punishment to be in tension, especially in the case of a divine punisher.[39] Others, including Murphy, take human forgiveness of criminal offenders as their paradigm and find no incompatibility between punishment and forgiveness, arguing that legal punishment need not manifest resentment but may be required out of social justice in the distribution of power or advantage and for deterrence to protect the innocent. In his famous 1939 essay "Punishment," J. D. Mabbott argued that legal punishment and forgiveness are tasks that fall to different parties and hence that there is no incompatibility.[40] Murphy's and Mabbott's arguments support the conclusion that forgiveness need not imply total absolution. It frees one only from the forgiver's resentment or blame, not from that of others or even from the guilt that justifies punishment. It is at most a limited redemption of the past's irreversibility.

Still, when we ought to support the punishment of forgiven evildoers, just as when we are wise not to reconcile with those we forgive, we may at the same time rightly regret the fact. Such regret is a "moral remainder." This example shows, incidentally, that regret does not presuppose that the regretter acted wrongly or was even responsible for what is regretted. Such regret is primarily a sense of loss. Here it is the loss of a permissible opportunity to engage in such otherwise natural manifestations of a forgiving attitude as remitting or not supporting punishment.

A difficult and interesting question is whether some deeds truly are unforgivably heinous, however deeply repented. This question seems multiply ambiguous. First, does "unforgivable" mean "*incapable* of being forgiven"? Or "*unworthy* of being forgiven"? If it means "incapable," the question of whether some deeds are unforgivably heinous is either the logical question of whether forgiveness is incoherent as a response to some offenses or else an empirical, psychological question about whether survivors of some evils are simply not able to renounce hostility or offer others release. Of course, some victims die and others are so badly injured that they are physically unable to communicate. The empirical question of interest is about an otherwise competent survivor's ability or inability to undergo the requisite change of heart.

I find no logical incoherence in the idea of forgiving extremely heinous offenses, although the wisdom of doing so is a further question. And perhaps the harms suffered by some victims do in fact render them incapable of renouncing hostility, or of taking a charitable attitude toward the perpetrator, and so on. The ethically interesting question is, of course, whether some offenses are so heinous that they are unforgivable in the sense that they ought not to be forgiven. Again, the question becomes more manageable if we look individually at the elements of forgiveness in a paradigm case and consider which, if any, are unwise in the case of especially heinous offenses.

Are some offenses so heinous that victims and their sympathizers should never renounce hostility? That they should not take a charitable or compassionate attitude toward the perpetrator? That they should reject the perpetrator's contrition, apologies, repentance, reparations? That they should support no mitigation of punishment? That they should refuse ever to renew relations? Some of these questions seem answerable independently of others. Even if the offender is unworthy of compassion and deserves to be regarded ever after with distrust, it may still be advisable for victims to let go, eventually, of hostility. And as Mabbott and Murphy saw, the advisability of victims' letting go does not imply the advisability of the state's remitting punishment. Nor, for reasons just given, does it imply the advisability of reconciliation.

Still, some elements of paradigmatic forgiveness are interconnected with others. Accepting reparations, for example, is a way of renewing relations. If a renewal of relations is permanently unacceptable, victims may be justified in refusing to accept perpetrators' attempts at reparation. Such a refusal, however, would not commit them to never renouncing hostilities or never taking a charitable or compassionate attitude toward the perpetrators. Thus, there may be no simple answer to whether some atrocities are unforgivably heinous. It may be that some breaches of trust or goodwill can never be mended, that nothing the offender could do would be sufficient to provide others with good evidence of adequate reliability. If so, some atrocities are so heinous that some elements of forgiveness are wisely withheld permanently from some of its perpetrators.

The atrocities of slavery and genocide are popular candidates for unforgivable evils. Yet both slavery and genocide are practices that involve many individual perpetrators, corporate bodies, and organizations acting in a variety of circumstances, playing different roles, doing things at different times, some things much more serious than others, some deeds far more pivotal than others. Neither slavery nor genocide is itself one deed. Neither is perpetrated by one agent or even by one body of agents. Not surprisingly, survivors and their descendants find the issues complex. Some, such as Simon Wiesenthal, have published their reflections on specific episodes.

Wiesenthal's Dilemmas

In his memoir *The Sunflower* Simon Wiesenthal reflects upon a dilemma of forgiveness that he confronted as a concentration camp prisoner during the Holocaust.[41] He was asked for forgiveness by a youthful dying Nazi soldier, who identified himself simply as Karl and who confessed to having taken part in a merciless mass slaughter of Jews. Karl explained that shortly after this atrocity, he incurred his current fatal wounds in battle when he flashed back to the deed and was unable to fire his rifle in self-defense. That was a year before. He was near the end.

Wiesenthal had been on work detail and had no idea what he was about to confront when a nurse (at Karl's request) had brought him, a randomly chosen Jew, to hear Karl's confession and receive his deathbed plea for forgiveness. It was dangerous to leave the work detail and follow the nurse, as she had no authority over him, and if he were caught, not only would his own life be jeopardized but the lives of his fellow prisoners could be jeopardized as well. Still, there was the possibility that she might be leading him to hidden food, which could save lives. So he followed.

The nurse led Wiesenthal to a room where Karl was lying on a table, bandaged head to foot, with holes for mouth and nostrils. As Karl began to speak, Wiesenthal listened. He retrieved a letter from Karl's mother when it fell to the floor and brushed a fly from Karl's head. He silently heard Karl's anguish and repentance but also asked himself why a Jew should have to listen to this, as he was reminded vividly of atrocities he had witnessed and of what his family had suffered. Yet he did not withdraw his hand when Karl took it at one point to stay him from leaving. But finally, when Karl had finished, Wiesenthal got up and left without having spoken a word.

Karl died the next day, and Wiesenthal refused the package of his belongings which the nurse said Karl left him. After the war, remembering the address on the fallen letter, he visited Karl's widowed mother and gained an audience with her by pretending to have been Karl's friend. Her reminiscences confirmed Karl's account of his early years, which was evidence of his truthfulness. Wiesenthal then decided not to reveal Karl's murderous deed. He thereby granted one of Karl's dying wishes—that his mother be spared disillusionment about her son's honor.

The decision not to disillusion Karl's mother, like Wiesenthal's demeanor during the confession, appears compassionate. It appears to reciprocate Karl's final efforts at good will. Yet this reciprocity was not offered to Karl but at most to his memory. It preserved Karl's good image with his mother. All that remained of Karl at that point was his image, the memories. Karl himself was forever unaware of Wiesenthal's feelings and of most of Wiesenthal's actions.

Did Wiesenthal's compassionate conduct really demonstrate forgiveness? Perhaps no simple yes or no answer quite does justice to the case. Drawing on elements of paradigm forgiveness, we might say that Wiesenthal's conduct both at the confession and over the years demonstrates at most a very limited forgiveness. It exhibits some elements: compassion, a willingness to listen to apology and contrition, a granting of one of Karl's dying wishes. Yet other elements are unclear or absent. It is not clear that Wiesenthal accepted the apology he heard, although he may have done so eventually, during the visit to Karl's mother. Nor is it clear that he sympathized with Karl's remorse during the confession, although he was compassionate, at least decent, about Karl's helplessness. Most readers take Wiesenthal's silence at Karl's bedside as a refusal of forgiveness. Wiesenthal himself seems to take it that way. By not speaking, he did not offer Karl the gift of forgiveness. But what complex feelings lay in Wiesenthal's heart? Would he have been wrong to forgive a deed done to others? Readers of the memoir raised these questions.

Wiesenthal circulated his memoir to philosophers, rabbis, priests, ministers, novelists, and other prominent thinkers, soliciting their reflections about what he did, what they might have done in his place, what it would or would not have been right to do. Two overlapping sets of responses have been published as symposia, in two editions, with Wiesenthal's memoir.[42] Together, the memoir and symposia touch on most of the ethical and philosophical questions that have been asked about forgiveness.

Many of Wiesenthal's symposiasts thought he would have been wrong to forgive. They argued that it would be presumptuous to forgive in the name of those murdered or to forgive an offense done an entire group to which one belongs, that doing so would usurp others' prerogatives, even though the others did not survive to exercise those prerogatives. A few thought he should have spoken some comforting words or even words of forgiveness in response to Karl's dying wish. A few others thought that if they had been in Wiesenthal's place, they would have strangled Karl in his bed. Some thought that although Wiesenthal would not have been wrong to forgive, neither was he wrong not to.

We can never know how Karl's character would have developed had he miraculously survived. Would he have publicly renounced or denounced Nazism? Joined a resistance movement? Continued to risk his life for what he thought was right? Would he have become more concerned about others' suffering and less absorbed in his own needs for absolution? Or would he have become hardened to atrocities? Would he have rationalized that he had no power to change things and eventually refused to continue reflecting on the moral questions? Answers to such questions are relevant to the moral value of offering him whatever forgiveness was possible. They become especially important given that he was only twenty-one and had fallen under the spell of Nazism as a child in the Hitler Youth. Deathbed confessions are a pale substitute for character change, which requires continuing activity and development, not just insight or right intentions. But, of course, all that Karl was able to offer, given his previous inexperienced and disastrous choices, was that pale substitute.

Returning to the analysis of paradigm forgiveness, we may be able to clarify what was possible and what was at stake in the dilemmas confronting Wiesenthal. That analysis suggests that he confronted not one question but several. To review, in paradigm forgiveness, there is a change of heart based on (1) a renunciation of hostility and (2) undertaken out of compassion for the offender, which involves (3) an acceptance of the offender's apology and contrition, (4) remission of punishment, if any, over which the forgiver has control, and (5) a willingness to reconcile or be open to establishing friendly relations. Wiesenthal's conduct suggests that he chose compassion over hostility. But that does not imply acceptance of the apology and contrition. Remission of punishment and reconciliation may at first seem inapplicable in this case. Yet the facts are not so simple.

Regarding the arrogance of forgiving offenses committed against others, three kinds of observations seem in order. The first is that one need not be a victim in order to blame or condemn. If one element of forgiveness is renunciation of not only resentment but also blame or condemnation, there seems no logical reason why that element should be available only to victims. Second, in renouncing one's own blaming or condemning attitudes, one need not presume to speak for or in the name of others. One person's forgiveness is compatible with others' refusals. Insofar as forgiveness releases the forgiven from obligations, it releases only from obligations to the forgiver, not from obligations to others. But third, and perhaps more important, it is not clear that Wiesenthal was not a victim. Atrocities done to Jews simply because they are Jews endanger all Jews. Karl had the nurse bring him specifically "a Jew," not any particular Jew—apparently any Jew would do. The atrocity in which Karl participated was inflicted on its victims simply because they were Jews, not because of anything they had done or even might do in the future. And so it seems inaccurate to regard the offense as having been done only to third parties. Karl himself appears not to have regarded it that way. Nor does Wiesenthal.

Officially no punishment was in question. And yet what Karl suffered from his mortal injuries, in consequence of his remorse, could be regarded as something like a substitute for punishment, a piece of poetic justice in which the crime backfires. Wiesenthal could offer no relief from the injuries, nor was he asked to do so. He might have offered Karl a certain peace of mind by speaking words of comfort, and that he refused to do. But that refusal was not tantamount to imposing punishment. It did nothing to worsen Karl's injuries. It was simply a refusal to alleviate completely Karl's burdens of guilt. Still, just by listening to Karl's confession and contrition, Wiesenthal did relieve some of that burden. He offered Karl some relief just by staying, even though he wanted to leave.

The reconciliation element of forgiveness may appear moot in this case, as Karl did not live. Yet in refusing the package of Karl's belongings, Wiesenthal does appear to have refused reconciliation, or to have come as close as one could come to doing so under the circumstances. That package would have been a connection to Karl, and he refused that connection. He did not permanently reject all connections, however, because he followed up later by visiting Karl's mother to check out Karl's history. That visit was a voluntarily renewed connection with what remained of Karl, namely the memories that his mother was able to share, although it was not obviously undertaken for Karl's sake.

Did Wiesenthal make wise choices? It seems to me that he was appropriately cautious and that he was respectful, even generous. He did not rush to judgment either for or against, and in his conduct toward Karl, his demeanor was and continues to be exemplary. The only real point at which I could wish he had chosen differently—as he himself also seemed to wish, by the conclusion of his memoir—is the point at which he decided not to tell the mother the truth about how he met Karl, including the atrocity confession. The most charitable reading of that decision is that it was undertaken out of respect for Karl's dying wish that his mother never know of his participation in an atrocity. Wiesenthal realized, from listening to the mother, that Karl had been honest with him, and he apparently concluded that Karl's remorse was genuine. He may have excused or forgiven Karl's preoccupation, as a result of youthful naivete, with his own moral neediness, which led him to inflict his conscience on a concentration camp victim and further risk the life of that prisoner as well as those of other prisoners in order to do so.

But Karl's mother said to Wiesenthal, upon realizing that her visitor was Jewish, that she and her non-Jewish neighbors were not responsible for what was done to the Jews during the war and that her son was such a good person that he would never have participated in such things. She deserved to be disillusioned about those beliefs, regardless of what Karl deserved. Since she was alive, whereas he was not, I would weight this point more heavily. If, as it appears, one element of Wiesenthal's decision not to tell was a compassionate desire to spare the mother the pain of a spoiled memory of her son, since the good memory of her son seemed the most precious thing she had left after the war, it is difficult not to regard that aspect of his choice as misguided generosity. Women can survive the pain of knowing what their children have done and can sometimes grow from it. Those who said "we were not responsible" because "we didn't know," when they ignored what was happening around them and did not try to find out, had some moral growing to do. Wiesenthal might have taken Karl's mother more seriously by challenging her image of her son, and thereby her image of what "good" people are capable of doing, rather than leaving her with her comforting illusions and self-deceptions.

The point is not that Karl's mother's moral growth was Wiesenthal's responsibility. He had no obligation to visit her in the first place. But, paradoxically, he seemed almost more ready to forgive the mother, who apparently had no remorse, than the son who had. For in the former case, keeping silent is what forgiveness seemed to require, whereas in the latter, it would have been speaking up. Yet Wiesenthal seems uneasy about the element of silence in both instances.

The Sunflower is not just about forgiveness. It is at the same time about silence and witnessing. The sunflowers of the title were planted each on a soldier's grave in a cemetery that Wiesenthal and other prisoners passed on their way to work. They struck him as like silent periscopes, continuing vital connections of the dead to the world of the living. There were no markers for Jews cremated or buried in mass graves. Wiesenthal's memoir itself is like a sunflower for Jews who did not survive, a vital connection between the dead and the living from one who miraculously survived to bear witness, to be a periscope for those who cannot bear witness themselves. But unlike the sunflowers, the memoir speaks.

During an early flashback in the memoir, Wiesenthal recalls the "day without Jews" at his high school, when hooligans physically assaulted Jewish students to prevent them from taking their examinations. Only about 20 percent of students, he estimated, actually participated in the violence. But they could not have gotten away with it so handily if the rest of the non-Jewish students had not been silent.

When *Die Sonnenblume* was first published in 1969 in France, there had already been popular calls for letting bygones be bygones, with respect to World War II, when not that much had yet been done in the way of public rememberings of atrocities. Wiesenthal's memoir helped to break silence regarding the Holocaust. The question of whether and when to speak, whether and when to say anything at all, is as much at issue as the question of forgiveness in Wiesenthal's concluding questions about what he should have done. Throughout his encounter with Karl, he spoke not a word, although readers might not catch that immediately, since he carried on a busy interior monologue the whole time. But he writes in conclusion:

> Well, I kept silent when a young Nazi on his deathbed begged me to be his confessor. And later when I met his mother I again kept silent rather than shatter her illusions about her dead son's inherent goodness. And how many bystanders kept silent as they watched Jewish men, women, and children being led to the slaughterhouses of Europe? There are many kinds of silence, Indeed it can be more eloquent than words. . . . Was my silence at the bedside of the dying Nazi right or wrong? This is a profound moral question.[43]

Forgiveness breaks silence when it is offered to another, as does the refusal of forgiveness when that is given voice. Unexpressed questioning or changes of heart, like unexpressed dissent from evil, risks nothing and achieves nothing. It allows others to do as they will. What is difficult but has the potential to bring change is reaching out, taking risks, making explicit the complexities in one's heart. Karl was one German citizen who finally broke silence, in however limited a way, regarding major atrocities of his day and his role in them. Karl must have had a sunflower on his German soldier's grave. But Wiesenthal's memoir bears witness to Karl's truth also. It is at the same time Wiesenthal's own personal confession, reaching out to many hearts by breaking silence about the complexities in his own.

9

The Moral Burdens and Obligations of Perpetrators

In taking up responses to evils, the previous chapter focused on victims. It gave special attention to the moral power of forgiveness to interrupt cycles of hostility and initiate a process of substituting reciprocal goodwill for ill will. This chapter turns the spotlight onto perpetrators with the same end in view. Two caveats are in order, however. First, the powers of victims and the burdens of perpetrators are so interrelated that neither can be discussed in depth without extensive reference to the other. The focus on victims or perpetrators can only be a matter of emphasis. Second, although I refer to victims and perpetrators, it should always be kept in mind that, especially in large-scale atrocities, many parties are both victims of some evils and perpetrators of others. One deeply troubling form of that predicament is the special focus of the final chapter.

Victims' moral powers of forgiveness and blame are concerned basically with the offender's culpable wrongdoing. In contrast, the burdens and obligations of perpetrators are concerned not only with acknowledging wrongdoing but more with repairing harms done. In responding to evils, each party tends to focus on a different central element: victims on the perpetrators' culpability, perpetrators on the harm to victims. Each may need to attend to the element that, given the magnitude gap, they are most likely to distort or fail to appreciate. Such attention, ideally, brings corrections in perception and paves the way to better future interaction.

Mercy, Gratitude, and Guilt

Perpetrators incur moral burdens and obligations not only from their own wrongdoing but also in response to victims' exercise of their moral and political powers of forgiveness and mercy. We tend to think of burdens as, naturally, burdensome, to be got rid of as soon as possible, as they are heavy and weigh upon us. But burdens need not just pull us down. Carrying a burden well builds strength, which can help to gain or regain others' respect and develop or recover self-esteem. Burdens and obligations need not produce or feed hostility when those who incur them are able and willing to take significant steps toward meeting them. Taking those steps provides opportunities to demonstrate goodwill and build trustworthiness.

The eventual focus of this chapter is the burdens of guilt. But I begin with background discussions of the ethics of mercy and gratitude, concepts that I have treated at greater length elsewhere.[1] Allowing perpetrators to undertake many of the burdens of guilt and carry out obligations they have incurred requires an element of mercy from victims, especially after atrocities. The receptivity of victims to apologies and attempts at restitution is a benefit to perpetrators, an occasion for gratitude, as it encourages processes of repair to begin. In the context of responding to evils, mercy is ordinarily thought of as a political power, not simply a moral power. Mercy is a power, for example, that former victims have when they are in a position to punish or exact major reparations, a power to relieve or lighten perpetrators' burdens. But mercy is, more abstractly, a compassionate response that also shows itself (in circumstances where doing so involves some risk) in letting others undertake responsibilities that develop trustworthiness. Mercy for evildoers can rescue them not only from the full measure of merited punishment or from the full burden of reparations owed but, more importantly, from being unable to negotiate repairs and thereby earn back lost respect.

Gratitude is a natural response to rescue. Because gratitude entails further obligations, mercy may appear to aggravate perpetrators' guilt by increasing what they owe. What interests me about gratitude in this context is the general obligation that it imposes not to give one's benefactor just cause to regret the benefaction. Accepting this obligation should lead former perpetrators to seek opportunities to demonstrate goodwill. Thus, mercy and its responsive gratitude have the potential to substitute a mutually reinforcing good will for past ill will, provided that mercy can be shown without injustice. Avoiding injustice has been a major ethical challenge regarding mercy. For when mercy exhibits arbitrary favoritism or ignores danger to potential victims, it can generate as much new hostility as the old hostility that it replaces.

Mercy and gratitude in general need no defense. But guilt is not widely regarded as such a good thing. I want to defend guilt, within limits, against detractors who focus on its punitiveness or obsessive forms. I want also to defend it against alternative responses, such as shame. Burdens of guilt, especially coupled with obligations of gratitude, can lead the guilty to try to rectify imbalances in relationships by paying their debts, which supports their self-esteem and demonstrates goodwill. Gratitude and guilt may strike us initially as opposed higher order responses (by former perpetrators) to the correspondingly opposed lower order responses (by former victims) of mercy and blame. Gratitude is a natural response to mercy, as guilt may be to blame. But blame and mercy are also compatible, not just opposed. For those who blame can also be receptive to perpetrators' attempts to put things right. That receptivity is apt to require some trust by former victims of those who have wronged them and require it in the absence of evidence of wrongdoers' trustworthiness. As gratitude is a natural response to such extensions of trust (mercy), gratitude can underlie and make welcome even the burdens of guilt. For guilt is not as thoroughly negative as it is often represented to be. It is not just masochism, self-torture, or the internalization of victims' hostilities. It is also manifested in such constructive responses as confession, contrition, apology, restitution, and reparation, which relieve negative self-judgment.

The Ethics of Mercy

Whether or not Wiesenthal's treatment of Karl should count as a limited forgiveness, much of Wiesenthal's conduct was clearly merciful. He had the power to increase Karl's suffering with harsh words, to leave without having heard the painful story to its bitter end (which he could predict), to ignore flies and fallen letters, even to terminate Karl's life (some symposiasts said they would have). Morally, he was free later to tell Karl's mother an ugly truth about her son. He was free, after the liberation, to stop thinking about Karl. Yet he did none of these things. Although he did not speak, his presence during the confession eased Karl's dying, and the memoir, which he did not have to write, made that confession available to a wider public.

Mercy is the compassionate withholding or mitigation of a hardship or penalty that one has the authority or power to inflict on another or the power to allow another to suffer. Mercy in reducing or remitting punishment is a natural manifestation of forgiveness, even though not all other elements of forgiveness require it. But mercy can be shown even without forgiveness. That fact is especially important for future goodwill if some atrocities prove to be unforgivable.

Leniency and clemency, unlike mercy, imply mere indulgence, softness, mildness. They need not be granted out of compassion or for the recipient's sake. They can be granted for reasons of political expediency alone. Pardons and amnesties often exhibit simple clemency or leniency, although they can exemplify mercy. After a change of political power, pardons or amnesties are commonly granted military officers and government officials suspected, accused, or convicted of atrocities. These decisions tend to be based on political concern for social stability.[2] Pardons, ordinarily issued after a finding of guilt, remit punishment or the portion of it remaining, whereas amnesties preclude guilt findings.[3] Both presuppose someone at least accused or suspected of an offense. Mercy is not so restricted. We can be merciful in administering requirements that impose hardships where no offense is in question. We can be merciful in releasing others from obligations voluntarily undertaken. There is room for mercy regarding reparations (both allowing them to be undertaken and relieving burdensome demands) as well as in administering penalties. Mercy, unlike mere leniency, manifests goodwill toward those to whom it is shown and thereby has greater potential to evoke responsive goodwill.

Just as the relatively impotent may be tempted to exercise the power of forgiveness when it would be better not to, one who has the power to show mercy may be tempted to do so in ways in which or in circumstances under which it would be better not to. For mercy demonstrates both power and control. When it is well placed, showing mercy feels better than imposing hardship. It reflects better on and does more for the self-esteem of the person who shows it. But mercy for some can conflict with justice to others and, in some circumstances, with self-respect. When it conflicts with justice, mercy risks evoking as much ill will in potential victims as the goodwill it seeks to elicit from beneficiaries. And so, to respond to evildoing in ways likely to minimize future ill will and maximize goodwill, it is important to appreciate the ethics of mercy.

Mercy for perpetrators presents itself as an option in two kinds of contexts. One is punishment. The other is in negotiating for and receiving such things as apologies, compensation, reparations, and restitution. In a helpful essay on the ethics of mercy, Peter Twambley distinguishes these kinds of situations as yielding as "the criminal court model" of mercy (where punishment is at stake) and "the civil court model" (where compensation or reparation is at stake).[4] Mercy is most controversial on the criminal court model, where the challenge is to define an appropriate desert basis for mercy that would distinguish some offenders from others, thereby eliminating arbitrariness. Twambley argues that to avoid injustice, mercy on the criminal court model must be deserved by the offender but that on the civil court model, there need be no injustice in mercy even for recipients who do not particularly deserve it. Two questions then present themselves. What is an appropriate desert basis for mercy on the criminal court model for perpetrators of evils? And, on what grounds might mercy (as distinct from mere leniency) be recommended on the civil court model for evildoers who do not particularly deserve it?

Regarding the first question, the criminal court model raises the question of how judges and juries can be merciful to one offender without at the same time being unjust to others who do not receive mercy and to potential future victims who depend on the protection of the law. "Tempering justice with mercy" may suggest being a little unjust in order to make room for a little mercy. But that cannot be right. If a criminal offender receives mercy, then, in fairness, every relevantly similar offender should receive it. But then the reduced penalty becomes an offender's right and is, by definition, no longer mercy. Showing mercy only to some on the basis of personal inclinations is unjust favoritism. Reducing penalties for all beyond what justice requires risks injustice to the innocent who depend on deterrence for protection. Thus, some philosophers, including Kant, hold that agents of the law should never show criminals clemency (and by implication, mercy), although heads of state may pardon personal offenses to themselves.[5] Others, such as Alwynne Smart, conclude that mercy for criminals is permissible only when contrary obligations, such as support of a criminal's family, require mitigation of the penalty anyhow.[6] Kant's position seems excessively severe, especially when we recall that the offenders who are most likely to be apprehended are often also victims themselves. What Smart's argument supports is a limited leniency that is not really mercy, because compassion for the offender does not enter into it. This limited leniency is also unsatisfying, as it ignores the offender's deserts.

To discriminate among offenders without arbitrariness or favoritism, a principle is needed to define desert bases of a case for mercy. The desert basis of mercy is not the same as that of forgiveness. We can deserve forgiveness on the basis of our conduct or attitudes subsequent to the offense. But, as I have argued elsewhere, we deserve mercy on the basis of what we have suffered, not what we have done, and the suffering need have no connection with the offense.[7] We deserve mercy because of extraordinarily severe undeserved misfortunes in our own lives, relative to the lives of our victims and the lives of those who depend for protection on enforcement of the rules or laws that we violated. When this condition is met, even an unrepentant offender who does not deserve forgiveness may deserve mercy. Although other considerations may outweigh the offender's desert in the decision on whether to reduce a justly deserved sentence, the objection from arbitrariness in showing mercy can be met by appeal to the offender's own suffering.

To meet the objection from those who depend for protection on the law, the suffering that grounds a case for mercy would have to be greater than that which threatens future potential victims of the offense. It is unlikely that the lives of principal perpetrators of atrocities would meet that condition. Mercy on the criminal court model is apt to be justified in relatively few instances where the offense is an atrocity. For it is difficult to imagine how perpetrators of mass rape or mass murder, for example, might have already suffered more than just punishment would impose. In cases such as the former Yugoslavia, atrocity perpetrators may identify with groups that have been comparably victimized in years past. Yet that seems relevant at most to mercy for groups, not for individual perpetrators. With respect to individual perpetrators, ordinarily punishment would impose *less* than they deserve, not more. In contrast, it is not difficult to imagine that some domestic batterers or parents guilty of child abuse or neglect have already suffered (in their own childhoods) more than just punishment could impose.[8]

That past suffering can ground a case for mercy is sometimes confused with a different view, which is ordinarily false. That is the view that having endured severe past abuse *excuses* one's later abuse of others. A certain body of criticism in the 1990s was directed against "the abuse excuse" for domestic batterers who were abused as children.[9] The so-called abuse excuse, however, is usually a straw target. What is plausible is not excusing but having compassion for offenders who have been as much "sinned against as sinning." For excuse, the offender's responsibility must be diminished. Extreme suffering can cloud judgment concurrent with it. But this suffering was years before the current offense. Also, as the next chapter discusses, the abused often identify with their abusers, which can increase their likelihood of survival during the period of their abuse. But the time span between childhood abuse and the current violence allows for opportunities for the development of capacities for moral judgment. Ordinarily that development makes early identification with an abuser inadequate as an explanation of current choices, even if it accounts for current temptations.[10] A history of childhood abuse explains how abusers learned that behavior but not why, as adults, they choose to embrace it rather than reject it (which many others do). More plausible is that some such offenders have already suffered more than just or humane punishment could impose. But this is the argument for mercy, not excuse.

As the bases of mercy are different from the bases of both excuse and justification, mercy does not always argue for a lightening of burdens. The bases of excuse and justification lie in facts about the commission of the offense. Excuses remove or reduce responsibility, whereas justifications nullify or soften judgments of wrongness.[11] In contrast, mercy for an offender presupposes both the responsibility and the wrongness. The case for mercy rests on what offenders have suffered, not on what they have done. It need not cite their offenses or even their repentance. An offender's undeserved misfortune might include such things as having been victimized by the even worse crimes of others or having suffered severe natural catastrophes that have nothing to do with abuse. Deserved mercy, so understood, moves in the direction of cosmic moral compensation for inequalities in undeserved misfortune.[12] It is a kind of equity and thus a point at which justice and charity come together. Deserved mercy offers its recipients a bit of compensating good fortune, which can take the form of opportunities to redeem themselves.

When laws are just, there appears no rightful place for mercy in criminal court unless the offender deserves it. There seems no way to be merciful to those who do not deserve it without being unjust to others who do not receive it and to the innocent who deserve protection. On the civil court model (as in Shakespeare's *The Merchant of Venice*), however, there appears to be no conflict with justice in showing mercy even to those who may not deserve it. Just as one had a choice whether to bring suit in the first place, the choice remains whether to call it off or settle. There is no issue of favoritism when the merciful party does not occupy an administrative position. Ordinarily, ethical questions on the civil court model are questions of when mercy is consistent with the self-respect of those who would show it and when it is tantamount to their condoning abuse. The ethical burden to be met when mercy is undeserved is showing how mercy for perpetrators who have not suffered more than just punishment would impose is compatible with respect for victims of the offense, who have suffered more than the perpetrators.

Cases in which these issues are clearest may be those in which negotiating reparations is actually undertaken by parties who do hold positions of administration (representatives of governments, for example), rather than by private parties (such as survivors who may sue private companies who profited from their forced labor during World War II). Here, the most difficult issue is whether to allow perpetrators to make reparations at all. For doing so involves a renewal of relations between victims and perpetrators, which victims may be understandably reluctant to do. The issue is especially difficult when a satisfying apology is not forthcoming or an unsatisfying one is offered. Without adequate apology, accepting reparations can convey that the harms can simply be paid for, that nothing irreparable has been lost. It is also compatible with there having been no real fault and therefore with regarding the wrong as not an evil. When the wrong was an evil, respect and self-respect are at stake for survivors. Respect and self-respect were major issues for Menahem Begin and others who were highly dissatisfied with apologies offered by Germany in the 1950s, upon which Israel decided to negotiate with Germany for Holocaust reparations.[13] To allow former perpetrators to do what they can in the way of reparations is generous, as doing so allows them to demonstrate goodwill and thereby reclaim lost respect. But it is important to preserve the respect of victims at the same time. As with forgiving the undeserving, issues of condonation and respect can sometimes be addressed by supplementary measures, such as truth commissions, monuments and memorials, educational programs, and the like, that explicitly acknowledge the evil and the moral concerns of survivors.

The Obligations of Gratitude

Gratitude is a natural response to rescue from evil, from deserved punishment or its full measure, and also from the status of irredeemability. These are rescues that mercy and forgiveness can effect. Beneficiaries manifest gratitude by reciprocity of goodwill and a sense of obligation to benefactors. Yet gratitude is not always welcome. It may be unwelcome when it carries a suggestion of bonding or friendship, as former victims may wish only to release perpetrators, not to become further connected or close to them. Gratitude may also be unwelcome if it carries the suggestion that a rescuer might have done less. For rescuers often view their actions as only what basic decency required. Still, gratitude is not misplaced when rescuers incur substantial costs or forgo significant benefits, when they were exposed to significant danger or took serious risks, or when the pressure to do nothing was great, even if the rescuer feels there was, morally, no choice. Unlike almsgivers, those who rescue, forgive, or grant mercy can seldom hide behind anonymity to avoid putting others in their debt. But what sort of debt do beneficiaries incur? What kinds of reciprocity are appropriate? The positions of a particular rescuer and rescued party may never be reversed in relation to each other. In such cases, what obligations does gratitude impose?

Clues are found in the nature of gratitude and what it achieves. Gratitude is at least an appreciative acknowledgment of another's goodwill. We may be grateful for gifts, favors, support and encouragement, recognition, sympathy, many things that others do for us or give us beyond what they owed us or were constrained to offer, including mercy and forgiveness. In an insightful paper Fred Berger argued that gratitude demonstrates that we do not value the beneficiary simply as useful for our own ends.[14] Gratitude is deserved when a beneficiary who was the intended recipient of the benefactor's freely bestowed goodwill freely accepts it. Two things gratitude achieves, then, are, first, communication of the beneficiary's appreciation of the benefactor's intention and, second, the beneficiary's acceptance of the intended benefit. Sometimes, this is enough. In other cases, as we will see, it is only the beginning.

In an extended (nonethical) sense, of course, we can be also grateful for things like the sunshine without being grateful to anyone. One might also simply be grateful for benefits bestowed but not to their bestowers. This is apt to be the case when a forgiven offender or one shown mercy does not acknowledge wrongdoing or when a rescued party fails to appreciate risks or costs incurred by the rescuer. Here, gratitude may exist without any sense of obligation.

If one can be grateful without any sense of obligation, it is also possible to be grateful with a sense of obligation to others who do not deserve it. Undeserved forgiveness and mercy are sometimes virtuous, even supererogatory. But undeserved gratitude to others is misplaced. It can indicate a deficiency of respect or self-respect. Gratitude is misplaced for "offers one cannot refuse," as the phrase is used in organized crime. Gratitude is misplaced when the "benefactor" was only refraining from abuse or was compelled to provide the benefit, when the recipient was forced by the donor to accept it, or when the benefit was made possible only by wrongdoing to others. It is not obvious that gratitude is appropriate for reparations or restitution. Recipients may simply be grateful *that* compensation is being made, grateful for not having to exercise coercion in order to collect and for underlying goodwill. Similarly, one may be grateful for a freely offered apology, especially if it is heartfelt and clearly demonstrates goodwill and acknowledgment of the offense. In these cases, gratitude seems not to impose any particular obligation beyond conveying appreciation and acceptance.

But desert of gratitude can also impose a debt that goes beyond acknowledging appreciation and indicating acceptance. In a thoughtful essay on the concepts of duty and obligation, Richard Brandt notes that we incur obligations in two ways, one in undertaking commitments (as in contracts and promises), the other in accepting benefactions.[15] Many questions arise regarding the special obligation incurred in accepting a benefit, which is commonly regarded as an obligation to reciprocate. What counts as reciprocity? How great must the benefit be to impose this special debt? Should the value of the benefit be measured by what it means to the recipient? or by what it cost the giver? What and how much should one do in return? Is one ever completely finished with it? When the benefit consists in saving a life, as it often does in rescues and in mercy or forgiveness for evildoers, these questions become difficult.

On how to measure the worth of the deed, Henry Sidgwick found "no clear accepted principle" but noted that if either effort or benefit are great, we tend to feel strong gratitude.[16] Aristotle said that if our relationship to the doer is based on utility, the value to the recipient is what counts, but that in true friendship, the purpose of the doer is what counts.[17] But the relationship between rescued and rescuer may be neither utilitarian nor one of friendship. The parties may be strangers or bare acquaintances.

What if the value of the effort is high but the benefit meager, or the donor well-off and the recipient poor? Sidgwick thought that for such discrepancies reciprocating "something between" is what "seems to suit our moral taste."[18] This response seems geared to gratitude for gifts and favors that consist of things and services with a relatively objective value. It is not helpful when what one is given is "a second chance," a reprieve from the death penalty, or a place to hide from would-be murderers. The form to be taken by reciprocity of goodwill may be very different in such cases from the form it would naturally take in response to gifts of things or services.

Like picking up hitchhikers and writing letters of recommendation, the cases of mercy, forgiveness, and rescue offer examples where reciprocity of goodwill is often more naturally shown toward others than directly to the benefactor. Such conduct fulfills a general obligation, first given philosophical articulation (to the best of my knowledge) by Thomas Hobbes: the obligation to avoid giving one's benefactor just cause to regret the benefaction.[19]

This obligation makes good sense of the otherwise paradoxical idea of a "debt of gratitude."[20]

Two puzzles regarding the idea of a "debt of gratitude" seem to put in jeopardy the special goodwill that gratitude otherwise promises. First, debts are burdensome, and paying them off a relief. Doesn't the sense of indebtedness, then, undermine the sense of gratitude? Second, how can one even owe for a benefit freely bestowed, with no strings attached? How can one repay without so transforming the transaction that there is nothing for which to be grateful?

The first puzzle may arise from the assumption that burdens are undesirable or that having to carry them is harmful. Many burdens, such as the burden of social stigma, are undesirable or harmful. But it is also true that being allowed to carry some burdens (to take out a loan, for example) can open up opportunities and enable one to do things that more than compensate for the weight of the burden. Children are unquestionably a burden to parents. They are expensive, for example. But many parents voluntarily incur these burdens and enjoy carrying them. Likewise, regarding debts of gratitude, we are often happy to be obliged. The connection is welcome.

The second puzzle is solved when we see such debts as underlying and more fundamental than a borrower's obligation to repay. Borrowers prove their reliability by paying off the loan, discharging that obligation. But they were also granted a measure of trust in being given the loan in the first place. Terminating the obligation to a particular creditor in a timely way allows them to create more fundamental ongoing relations with others as well, to whom one's trustworthiness matters. It earns the borrower a credit rating, definitely a benefit that extends beyond the benefits of the particular loan. The borrower repays the loan and pays interest for the privilege of using the money. But the opportunity to earn a credit rating is not paid for. Rather, the appropriate response for that benefit is to honor the obligation not to abuse the credit rating in the future.

Accepting forgiveness or mercy is like borrowing by someone whose credit rating has suffered. It offers the recipient the opportunity to build credit and imposes the general obligation of gratitude, as well as whatever specific obligations may be attached as conditions of the mercy or forgiveness. Hobbes captured the general obligation of gratitude in his "natural law" that "[you are to] suffer him not to be the worst for you, who out of the confidence he had in you, first did you a good turn," and that one should "endeavor, that the giver shall have no just occasion to repent him of his gift."[21] Ingratitude consists not fundamentally in failing to return favors but in failing to live up to this basic obligation, giving the benefactor reasonable cause for regret. Failing to return a favor is a possible cause for benefactor regret. But it is not the commonest or the worst. Clear ingratitude consists in using benefits to exploit unjustly or harm one's benefactor, or sometimes in failing to compensate a benefactor, when one could, for heavy losses or costs. Just cause for regret also depends on the nature of the benefit. If the benefit is forgiveness, just cause for regret might be repeating the offense. If it is mercy, just cause might be cruelty to others.

Thus, one repays a benefactor, without so transforming the transaction that there is nothing for which to be grateful, by never giving the benefactor just cause to regret the benefaction. Ideally, the offender who receives forgiveness or mercy will aim to be worthy of it by, first of all, apologizing and not repeating the offense; second, by making restitution or reparations to the extent possible; and third, by treating others in appropriately merciful or forgiving ways in the future. Those rescued ideally compensate rescuers for losses incurred and are willing themselves to incur costs or risks, if need be, to rescue others. There is ordinarily no reason to do anything else, other than verbally express appreciation and acceptance. Gratitude need not lead to personal relationships, such as friendship, although sometimes it does. As gratitude is itself among the things for which gratitude is felt, it is conducive to a cycle, or spiral, of goodwill.

There are no guarantees of ideal behavior from beneficiaries of mercy or forgiveness. One might speculate that evildoers are unlikely to respond well. Yet, on the atrocity paradigm, such a generalization would be unwarranted. For evildoers, on the atrocity paradigm, need not be evil people. Being implicated in the infliction of intolerable harm on others may be the result of gross inattentiveness, weakness, or fear.

Reciprocity, however, appears deeply ingrained in human nature. Political scientist Robert Axelrod argues powerfully that the impulse to reciprocate lies at the roots of cooperation in human society, citing evidence that people have often found their way out of "prisoner's dilemma" situations—which threaten to make everyone significantly worse off than is necessary—by following the principle "show goodwill and then reciprocate what others do in response."[22] When everyone follows that principle, goodwill prevails. By that principle, granting forgiveness and mercy, where one can do so in a way that provides recipients with a sound basis for gratitude, seems a promising way to terminate potentially interminable cycles of ill will.

Thus, a powerful pragmatic argument can be constructed for supporting such practices as amnesty and commissions on truth and reconciliation in countries with long-standing histories of atrocity involving masses of people, where revenge can (sometimes does) otherwise spiral out of control for centuries. It is one thing, however, for a people to support such practices voluntarily and another for representatives of the people to engage in them without popular support. There is no reason to expect cycles of mutual goodwill to issue from the latter practice.

When forgiveness and mercy are not forthcoming, former perpetrators lack opportunities to demonstrate goodwill through gratitude. Yet they may still be able to take good will initiatives in assuming some of the burdens of guilt and, in some cases, eventually come to deserve a measure of forgiveness. Even when mercy or forgiveness is forthcoming, it is likely that perpetrators will still carry many of these burdens.

The Burdens of Guilt

The value of guilt is controversial and rightly so. Yet neither a wholesale endorsement nor a wholesale rejection of it is wise. Guilt has both negative and positive aspects, each with special functions. But each of these aspects can also get out of hand. Guilt has both values and disvalues.

Guilt has had severe detractors ever since Nietzsche undertook its appraisal in the second essay of his *Genealogy of Morality*, tracing its origins to the economic relationship between debtor and creditor and its further development to religious ancestor worship. Noting that the German word *"Schuld"* means both "guilt" and "debt," he speculated that guilt began life as a substitute payment, namely, the pleasure of inflicting pain on a debtor who defaulted. He saw at least part of this idea in legal punishment as provided by a social contract, according to which legal offenders have defaulted on what they owe society (obedience to its laws) in return for its protection.[23] He speculated further that natural human aggression became internalized, directed against the self, when the human beast was enclosed in cities by conquerors. The moralization of guilt, he thought, was eventually bound up with this internalized aggression. Guilt became moralized by the religious idea of owing a debt to one's ancestors. When this debt eventually became unpayable (as generations accumulated), hostility to self turned into a kind of deserved self-punishment for being sinful and unworthy.[24] The "bad conscience" (*schlechtes Gewissen*) is an illness, according to Nietzsche, from which we have not yet recovered. On his view, guilt feelings are, ideally, to be transcended with revaluations that take us "beyond good and evil."

Norman O. Brown argued that Nietzsche had the connection between guilt and debt backwards, that economic debts were an expression of, rather than a source of, guilt. He maintained that "the ultimate problem is not guilt but the incapacity to live" and that "the illusion of guilt is necessary for an animal that cannot enjoy life, in order to organize a life of nonenjoyment."[25] On Brown's view, guilt is engaged in the service of truly perverse aims. Human beings could live more authentic lives without it.

Like Nietzsche, Freud treated guilt feelings as a redirection of aggression, taking it out on oneself rather than on others.[26] But Freud also thought of guilt as rooted in the infant's relationship of dependency on a loved protector, which seems more realistic and less irrational than Nietzsche's speculations about the consequences of ancestor worship. It is not clear, on Freud's view, that guilt is perverse. It may play a constructive role in maintaining relationships.

John Rawls, following Jean Piaget's work on the moral development of children and borrowing also from Freud, treats guilt as rooted in relationships of love and trust.[27] Rawls regards guilt as, initially, a natural response to breaking faith with someone who is loved and respected, and eventually later, also a response to one's own acknowledged injustices toward others in the context of a basically just society. He finds the liability to guilt for one's own transgressions a necessary part of having a sense of justice. Guilt feelings, on his view, tend to motivate behavior that would restore the relationship or correct a social injustice. Guilt is not fundamentally bad on this view. If Rawls is right, what appears unhealthy is not guilt but the incapacity for it, given how essential relationships and justice are to human thriving.

But if the value of guilt turns on its reparative tendencies or its leading to the correction of injustices, one may wonder whether guilt can play any constructive role with respect to atrocities, such as genocide, torture, or the saturation bombing of cities. For how is it possible to repair the harm of such evils? Can guilt do anything significant? To some extent, it can. Even when full compensation is impossible, steps can usually be taken to alleviate hardships caused survivors and their descendants. Medical bills, psychiatric bills, and elder care can be paid; children can be cared for and educated. Property restitution is often possible. Perpetrators might support or institute practices that aim to reduce the likelihood that others will perpetrate the same evils in the future. This kind of response normally brings some satisfaction to survivors.

What emerges from the views of philosophers and psychologists is that guilt has both a negative and a positive aspect, which appear to correspond to the culpability and harm elements of evils. The negative aspect is the pain of self-blame or self-condemnation, a hostility that is grounded in the sense of one's culpability for wrongdoing. Yet even this aspect of guilt is not totally negative. For it shows, or rather presupposes, that we care about what is right (or there would be no pain at doing wrong) and also that we can recognize and acknowledge our failure to do it. The pain of guilt reveals that we have standards and that they count for something. Like shame that we cannot totally live down, even inexpiable guilt reminds us that we still have worthy aspirations. In order to do better in the future, such values and recognitions are required, even if they are not sufficient.

We may also sometimes console ourselves with the knowledge that it is partly luck to have been morally tested as we were and that many others who were lucky enough to escape similar tests, including some who rightly blame us, would have responded no better. This may counteract the potentially self-destructive power of shame and guilt by alleviating the fear that we are not worthy of the association and companionship of other human beings. If so, we need not reject guilt in order to reject its potentially self-destructive power. Appreciating moral luck in general, as well as our own strengths and weaknesses in particular, may be one intermediate position between the refusal to feel guilt and obsessive self-torture.

Still, there must be antidotes to guilt, ways to relieve hostility to self, in order for the guilty to be able to act constructively. Feeling one's worth seriously diminished is depressing. Further, many who feel that they have little or nothing to lose become dangerous to others and themselves. Stalkers, domestic batterers, and workplace murderers often turn the gun on themselves after killing their victims.

The burdens of guilt can often be lifted in constructive ways by reparative and restitutive actions that they motivate. This is guilt's positive side. Feeling guilty includes appreciating that one now owes others something for the wrong. It can move one to try to compensate for the harm, or at least acknowledge the wrong and apologize. Insofar as such responses tend to mend relationship breaches or defuse hostilities, the guilt motivating them seems natural and healthy.

Guilt so far sounds simply psychological. "Guilt" is ambiguous, however, between internal feelings (emotional self-punishment for having wronged another, feelings of owing others for the wrong) and the relatively objective fact or finding of a transgression, a verdict. Guilt in the psychological sense (the internal feelings) is what has been controversial, especially the negative self-judgment. But the guilty, like borrowers, also owe as a matter of objective social fact or finding, irrespective of their feelings about the matter.

Guilt in the sense of the objective debt owed can sometimes be expiated by punishment, which uses the offender's suffering to buttress deterrence (not necessarily to give pleasure to victims). In a basically just society, criminal offenders who were punished fairly should be able to feel that they have paid their debt to society in general, although they may still owe special compensation to victims. But some guilt cannot be expiated even in part by punishment, such as guilt for failures to be forgiving, merciful or even grateful. These failures are unpunishable because forgiveness, mercy, and gratitude cannot rightly be compelled; others cannot claim them as their right, even when these responses are deserved. Internal guilt is a moral remainder when the offense is unpunishable or when nothing one can do or suffer will be enough to put things right. Guilt also remains for perpetrators of atrocities who are justly punished, because justice will not permit penalties truly commensurate with the harm. In practice, perpetrators are seldom punished even as severely as the law allows, as the case of war rape illustrates. In some cases, forgiveness of what is unpunishable may be able to restore a moral equilibrium.

"Blameless Guilt"

It is often assumed that one's guilt feelings are irrational when they are not based on the belief that one was truly morally at fault in having committed an offense. The ideas are widely held that "blameless guilt" is irrational and that it is not justifiable to blame a person unless that person was, or at least is believed to have been, at fault. Thus, those who blame citizens of another country for its war crimes are often thought irrational insofar as ordinary citizens were not at fault for and are thus not guilty of the acts of their country. Likewise, the "blood feud" is widely regarded as irrational, insofar as members of a family targeted for revenge were not at fault for wrongs committed by other members of their family and are themselves guilty of no wrongdoing. If there really has been no fault, guilt is irrational, and reparative action is not called for. Truly irrational guilt should be transcended, not expiated. Such cases are worth distinguishing carefully, however, from others, in which guilt actually does have a rational foundation. The examples just given may not be as irrational as they at first appear.

Some guilt is truly irrational. In one who no longer accepts the beliefs of a religion that prohibits dancing, card playing, or abortion and no longer finds such conduct wrong, feeling guilty for doing these things is irrational. These are instances of what Amelie Rorty calls "emotional *akrasia*," where one's emotional responses lag behind and conflict with one's current judgment.[28] Also, one can feel guilty simply upon being accused, however mistakenly. Here, not only need one who feels guilty have done nothing blameworthy but no one else need be at fault, either.

Yet there are other cases in which the assumption that it is irrational to feel guilty for what is not one's fault is not clearly valid. In some of these cases, there actually has been wrongdoing, but it is not one's own. Yet one bears a morally significant relation to either the wrongdoer or the deed. In another kind of case, there is something for which one might be at fault, but it is not an action. Thus, Herbert Morris, philosopher of jurisprudence, finds at least three kinds of "blameless guilt" that are not irrational. They are (1) survivor guilt, which may be a form of guilt over involuntary unjust enrichment, that is, involuntarily benefiting from injustices done to others by others, (2) guilt over acts of one's country or other groups to which one belongs (such as one's family) and to which one remains loyal, even though one had no effective say over those acts, and (3) guilt for feelings and desires that one did not act upon.[29] The first two are also taken up by Sandra Bartky in her recent defense of guilt against liberal feminist critics.[30] Atrocities give rise to "blameless guilt" of each of these three kinds. In such cases, unlike emotional *akrasia* or being wrongly accused, reparative actions or corrective measures may actually be in order. Simply trying to "get over" the guilt or dismiss it as irrational may be irresponsible.

Guilt over involuntary unjust enrichment is what we may feel instead of gratitude for benefits made possible by others' injustices or evils. Here guilt does not have exactly the same structure as when the evil or injustice is one's own. The negative element is different from that in guilt for one's own blameworthy conduct. It consists not in judging oneself negatively (self-blame) but in finding one's good fortune morally tainted, feeling that joy over it is inappropriate. Some Anglo-Americans today find their situations morally tainted in that way because of how the North American continent was colonized and developed by European ancestors who were responsible for the death and displacement of most of its indigenous peoples. Similarly, guilt feelings in atrocity survivors are sometimes grounded reasonably enough in the belief that their own survival was made possible by the wrongful deaths of others, which the survivors did not cause. In some cases, another person was literally made to take the survivor's place in a group of prisoners who were then shot. It can be difficult for such survivors to take joy in their own escape. Their own continued existence may come to feel morally tainted.

Although one may rightly find one's good fortune morally tainted, there need be no basis for negative self-judgment in such a case, depending on how one feels about and uses the benefits. When it is not possible to reject the benefits, one may feel a responsibility to use all or a portion of them to aid those whose unjust treatment made the benefits possible. When survivors of the particular atrocity cannot be benefited, it may be possible to enrich other survivors of similar atrocities or the descendants of victims. Or one may be able to fight against the kind of injustice or evil involved in producing the benefits. Some atrocity survivors devote a substantial portion of the remainder of their lives to such causes. Simon Wiesenthal, who narrowly escaped death in the camps on many occasions, not only pursues escaped war criminals but works to exonerate persons wrongly accused, and he has initiated major educational endeavors, such as the Wiesenthal Museum of Tolerance in Los Angeles, which exhibits materials on many atrocities in addition to the Holocaust.[31] I know at least one philosopher descended from slave owners who has devoted much of his career to work on the concept of social justice.

When rejection of tainted benefits is possible, however, as in the case of whether to make use of or even cite the data from the Nazi medical experiments, the question arises of whether it makes more sense to try to use the benefits wisely or whether the most humane response is to reject them on grounds of the moral indecency of how they were obtained.[32] Using them involves incurring the guilt of unjust enrichment, whereas rejecting them seems to maintain one's moral purity (relative to this particular matter). Yet such "purity" may not always be the highest value.

Whether to use or even cite the data is an issue on which survivors of Nazi medical experiments disagree. Some critics find the question moot, arguing that the data are useless because the "experiments" were conducted without adequate controls or record keeping.[33] Kristen Moe, who found that "at least forty-five research articles published since World War II draw upon data from the Nazi experiments," argues in a *Hastings Center Report* that "a decision to use the data should not be made without regret or without acknowledging the incomprehensible horrors that produced them" but that we should not "let the inhumanity of the experiments blind us to the possibility that some good may be salvaged from the ashes."[34] Although some survivors agree with her, others, such as Eva Mozes Kor, one of the twins who survived Mengele's "experiments," find all such uses disrespectful.[35] Many are concerned that the phoenix argument (salvaging good from ashes) is too easily turned into a retrospective "justification" of the atrocity on the basis of good consequences for others. Some think the data should be shredded and displayed in a glass case, as a memorial to those who died.

Other medical knowledge that has sources in atrocities is, of course, already integrated into medical practice. Examples are data from the twentieth-century Tuskegee syphilis experiments on black men who were not offered or even informed of the option of penicillin treatment when it was discovered and data from the nineteenth-century experiments of J. Marion Sims ("architect of the vagina") on unanesthetized black women, slaves, whom he purchased to use as guinea pigs for gynecological experiments conducted in his backyard.[36] The only effective way for consumers to reject the tainted benefits of medical practice in general may be to forgo medical services entirely, which for some would be suicidal. It may make better sense to assume the burdens of guilt for benefiting from atrocities and do what one can to prevent future atrocities. Avoiding the burdens of guilt is not necessarily the most humane option.

With respect to so-called "blameless guilt," the question also arises of whether one can ever be forgiven. Unless one has done wrong, it may seem that there is nothing to forgive. Yet even people who did nothing wrong understandably become the object of others' resentment in the kinds of guilt that Morris discusses. If resentment is a form of blame, "blameless" may not be the best way to think of these cases. What they have in common is that the guilty party has not committed a wrongful act. But atrocities often result in deeply resented unjust distributions or redistributions of wealth to parties who had no control over the decisions that led to the atrocities. The wealth owned by descendants of slave owners is an example, given the poverty of many descendants of slaves. Atrocities are often committed in the name of a nation by a government that was not under the control of even a majority of its citizens, as in the cases of Germany and Japan during World War II. Yet citizens of those countries have been powerfully resented by victims. Citizens of countries that perpetrate atrocities bear a heavy burden of guilt for what is done in their name, not because they are at fault in the commission of the atrocities but because of benefits they enjoy as a result or because of relationships of loyalty and support for those who were at fault. Such benefits and loyalties are often resented by atrocity survivors and their families. And where there is resentment, there seems also room for the possibility of forgiveness.

Morris's third kind of "blameless guilt" can be illustrated by concentration camp survivors who have also written of their own shame and guilt over being tempted to steal bread on which another's life depended, even when they did not yield to the temptation. Some have written of shame at being glad when another prisoner died, because of bread under the pillow or because the prisoner's illness or disability posed risks to those who were close to that prisoner. In *Night* Elie Wiesel writes with remorse of such feelings as a boy upon the death of his father when both were at Auschwitz.[37] Wiesel seems to have blamed himself, not for anything he did, but for how he felt. And where there is self-blame, there seems also room for the possibility of self-forgiveness.

Because resentment or blame by those who know the facts is possible in these cases, forgiveness also seems possible. Those who can resent or blame can certainly undergo the change of heart central to paradigm forgiveness. Descendants of slaves might understandably resent the greater advantages of the descendants of slaveholders and blame them for what they enjoy unless and until the beneficiaries of slavery apologize for the evils from which they have profited and take responsibility for working toward a more just use of those profits in the future. In July 2000, the *New York Times* ran an article on the apology by the *Hartford Courant*, Connecticut's largest newspaper, for having published advertisements for the sale of slaves in the eighteenth and nineteenth centuries. Those responsible for running the ads were, of course, no longer living, nor were the slaves whose sales were advertised. African Americans who were interviewed about their response to the article reacted positively. One said, "I think it makes a big difference. I appreciate it. It should be brought to the forefront."[38]

Thus, resentment of those who profit from others' injustice need not be irrational, depending on the attitude of those who profit and what they choose to do about it. Although blaming them for the injustice is unwarranted, blaming them for their attitudes toward it and toward their relationship to it need not be. Resentment is somewhat neutralized when beneficiaries use at least a part of their ill-gotten gains to fight the underlying injustice or compensate victims, or when they publicly appreciate and deplore the injustice or apologize for it, as in the case of the *Hartford Courant*. What is resented is the failure or outright refusal to acknowledge any debt or responsibility. Thus, feminists may resent men for the greater benefits made available to them by inegalitarian social and political practices established by prior generations, when the men who benefit simply take the attitude that since it was not their fault, they do not owe anybody anything. Likewise, others can resent us for acts of our country over which we had no control, because, for as long as we do not renounce our citizenship, we can be presumed to identify as its citizens, enjoy the protections and benefits that it offers, and offer it in return our loyalty. We have choices about what attitudes to take toward what our country does and how to respond to its perceived acts of injustice. Others can resent our inappropriate feelings and desires, even when we do not act on them, because, again, we can evaluate those feelings and desires, and we may have some explaining to do, as they seem to indicate something about our values.

Alternatives and Supplements to Guilt

As in paradigm guilt, there is in Morris's "blameless guilt" both a negative aspect (the feeling of taintedness in one's good fortune) and a positive aspect (the sense of responsibility to take constructive action and attitudes). One may wonder, however, whether the negative element of guilt is necessary, even in paradigm cases, to have the positive elements of the appreciation of wrongdoing and motivation to make the future better. Are there alternative emotional responses, such as shame, regret, or remorse, that might be equally good or better for these purposes?

Guilt may not be a universal human phenomenon. Neither guilt feelings nor the voice of conscience is mentioned explicitly in Aristotle's ethics, although he discussed the fault of *akrasia* (acting contrary to one's better judgment), which we might expect to be naturally accompanied by something like guilt feelings, perhaps, shame. The disposition to feel guilt as something distinct from shame may not be learned in all cultures. Ruth Benedict characterized Japanese culture as a shame culture by contrast with the guilt cultures of Europe and North America.[39]

A widely accepted view of the difference between shame and guilt is that shame is a response to falling short of aims or standards; whereas guilt responds to boundary transgressions.[40] Guilt includes the idea of owing, whereas shame includes that of dishonor or humiliation. In expiating guilt, we seek respect and reacceptance. In removing shame, we seek esteem or admiration. Guilt correlates with others' resentment or blame and can be neutralized when they forgive. Shame correlates with others' ridicule or contempt and is relieved when their feelings change to admiration or esteem (or when one has good reason to think they should).

Clearly, there is room for overlap. Shame is moral when the aim or standard we fail to reach is moral, and if failing to reach the standard involves transgressing a boundary, one incurs guilt as well. But guilt can be relieved by forgiveness, whereas shame cannot. The fact that shame cannot be relieved by forgiveness provides an argument against the use of shame penalties. Shame penalties are recent analogues of the scarlet letter. Examples are the penalty for drunk drivers or child abusers of being required to parade in front of their neighbors with signs labeling them drunk drivers or child abusers.[41] Such penalties are especially unwise when they interfere with the possibility of redemption by achievement.

Although guilt has an important positive (reparative) side, it can also degenerate. Just as others can be grateful for our gratitude, they can feel guilty about our guilt, and they can resent feeling guilty about our guilt. Or we may resent being resented because it makes us feel guilty, and our resentment may then evoke guilt in those who first resented us. They may, in turn, justifiably resent being made to feel guilty for resenting our wrongdoing in the first place. Obsessive or ostentatious guilt in perpetrators interferes with a just appreciation of who owes what to whom. If wrongdoers parade their guilt, they may manipulate victims into feeling responsible or taking responsibility for the pain of that guilt. Because victims have the moral power to offer relief through forgiveness, their not doing so may come to eclipse unjustly the original wrong. The potential for this kind of reversal existed in Karl's meeting with Wiesenthal.

There may be an analogous potential for reversal in shame. One can be ashamed of shaming others and can become an object of contempt for taking pleasure in doing it. But shame has a further disadvantage. Being shamed by others can evoke rage, a far more hostile response than the resentment of being made to feel guilty.

An advantage of guilt is that when it is not excessive or obsessive, the confessions, apologies, restitution, and reparations that it tends to motivate can remove cause for continued resentment. Achievements that overcome shame may offer grounds for admiration. But they need do nothing to remove causes for resentment of the wrong, nothing to compensate victims, for example. Thus, shame seems less complete than guilt as a moral response to participation in evil.

A disadvantage of both guilt and shame is the danger of misdirecting our attention. Each can lead to excessive self-absorption, centering one's own character, culpability, or defectiveness, one's own need to be redeemed or reinstated. Karl was so absorbed in his own moral neediness that he seems not to have given thought to how it would feel or what it would do to an atrocity victim to listen to a rehearsal of the details of atrocities. How others have been harmed is often more worthy of attention than one's own moral neediness. Also, excessive self-absorption can hinder moral regeneration, which requires us to act in the world and get involved in projects sensitive to others' needs— other than their need to know that we are aware of our faults.

Self-absorption is especially out of place when the harm done to others is egregious. How much better should we have thought of Adolph Eichmann, for example, if he had wallowed in guilt or shame, instead of trying to justify and excuse his role in the Holocaust at his trial in Jerusalem? Would he have been less morally absurd if he had focused on his own moral wretchedness instead of insisting that he was not all bad? Perhaps a little, although that appreciation would have come too late and at the wrong moment (in the face of a death sentence). Better would have been his genuine appreciation of the harm done to others by the evils he facilitated. His evident failure to appreciate the experience of victims may partly explain why the trial came to focus on survivor testimonies that did not always bear directly on the question of Eichmann's culpability, an aspect of the trial of which Hannah Arendt complains repeatedly in her coverage of that event.[42] What Eichmann deserved to feel is remorse. The only thing that could come close to being satisfying would have been his true and unending remorseful appreciation of what others suffered from what he did.

Remorse, regret, and repentance can also be alternatives to guilt, although like shame, they need not exclude it. Repentance is that change of heart whereby a transgressor becomes contrite or remorseful for major offenses. Like guilt, it can motivate constructive steps toward rebuilding relationships or correcting social injustices. In the case of repentance, however, the object is regeneration rather than repayment. Repentance is more self-absorbed than guilt. Yet it is often a first step in forgiveness seeking. Like shame, repentance involves humility, which is not always an asset for repairing wrongs.

Remorse is intense, often lasting, moral regret regarding one's own conduct. Regret, more generally, is sorrow over a fault, offense, mistake or loss, ranging in intensity from mild to deep. Regret in general does not presuppose one's responsibility for what is regretted, although remorse does. More painful than guilt, remorse is an emotional gnawing at oneself over one's wrongdoing. Etymologically, it means "to bite again," suggesting a continual reopening of wounds as one rehearses again and again a vivid appreciation of one's wrongdoing. In contrast, unrelieved internal guilt becomes a wallowing in self-deprecation that eventually dulls one's appreciation of the wrong itself. Remorse is often accompanied by shame, and forgiveness relieves neither.

For perpetrators of atrocities that cause irreparable harm, remorse may counteract some of the tendencies toward self-absorption of guilt. Remorse focuses the perpetrator's attention on the deed, rather than on what can be done about it, and on how the deed wronged and harmed others. Remorse is deep moral regret coupled with acute awareness of one's own wrongdoing, profoundly wishing we had not done a wrongful deed, not because of the stain on our own character but because of how it wronged others. The purpose of remorse is not self-punishment, even if that is an effect. Its point is to not let us forget or lose the appreciation of what we did.

Ordinary guilt feelings, in contrast, have as at least part of their point self-punishment. Self-punishment steals thunder from others' desires to punish us, making us feel more in control. Remorse can hurt as much as guilt or worse. But its focus is not our own status or unworthiness. Remorse seems to capture and magnify an element of guilt that is not utilitarian (not obviously retributive in intention, either). That element is the appreciation of the wrongness of what we did or the harm we caused. If guilt tends, as Rawls says, to motivate confession and forgiveness seeking, remorse is not so social. It may have no tendency to motivate confession. Insofar as one point of blaming wrongdoers is to get them to appreciate the wrongness of what they did, guilt and remorse relieve the need to blame.

Appreciating the wrongness has a certain value in itself, even when it does not help repair relationships and even if it is not accompanied by regeneration. It reveals something of the perpetrators' values and standards. Victims take some satisfaction just in knowing that perpetrators appreciate the wrongness of what they did and how it might feel to be in the victims' position. It aggravates moral dissatisfaction to know or believe that perpetrators do not adequately acknowledge or appreciate what they did. The problem is not merely frustration about how to change their future conduct. Don Juan is incorrigible, but he seems worse when he thinks he does nothing wrong. Even a guilty Juan who tries to buy off victims with irrelevant gifts, such as flowers, betrays that he knows he owes them something.

If the negative self-judgment in guilt and shame poses the danger of focusing perpetrators too much on themselves, the basically positive element of reaching out to victims can pose the opposite danger of identifying too much with victims whose attitudes toward perpetrators may be more hostile than would be warranted by a true appreciation of their position. Identifying with victims is not always the right way to be concerned about them. Perpetrators may not even know their victims well enough to know how to identify with them. They may need to guard against temptations to romanticize victims, to assume that they are innocent, for example. Identifying with romanticized victims may make former perpetrators feel better. But victims need not be innocent, even if they have not wronged their assailants. The less than saintly (or even cruel) character of victims does not negate the evils done to them. That Aztecs cut out the hearts of masses of live slaves in sacrifice to their gods does not imply that the conquest of the Aztecs by Hernan Cortès was not evil.[43]

If the excesses of self-absorption and identification with victims are avoided, the burdens of guilt need not be self-destructive or perverse, as some critics have thought. Nor are those burdens relievable only by others through their powers to forgive, as some theists have thought. The burdens of guilt can be carried with dignity and lead perpetrators to seek opportunities to manifest goodwill through some kinds of reparative activities, acknowledgments, and, in some cases, social activism. Those activities can go some way toward alleviating guilt, independently of their reception by victims. A certain measure of self-forgiveness may be both possible and required for continued self-respect, and such activities can provide a basis for it. Even if some breaches of trust cannot be healed by reparations and apologies, doing as much as one can may help to make possible constructive new relationships with others.

10

Gray Zones: Diabolical Evil Revisited

The Reality of Diabolical Evil

Immanuel Kant denied that evil in human beings was ever diabolical.[1] By diabolical evil he meant a commitment to wrongdoing just because it is wrong. We always, he thought, seek good. People of good will do what is right for its own sake. But no human being, he thought, does wrong for its own sake. Not even radical evil is diabolical. A radically evil will, for which evil has become a matter of principle, just prioritizes the wrong goods. It puts happiness ahead of virtue.

In chapter 4 I proposed an alternative, or rather expanded, conception of *radical* evil, based on the work of Christine Korsgaard and Lorna Smith Benjamin. In this chapter, I propose and illustrate a conception of *diabolical* evil alternative to the one that Kant finds inapplicable to humans. For Kant, radical evil is the worst of which human beings are capable. Yet Kant's conception of the worst is tame. It neglects complexities of human relationships. People have subordinated morality to far worse goals than that of their own happiness. My conception of diabolical evil is all too human. Like Kant's, it is not identical with radical evil. But it clarifies better than the concept of radical (principled) evil the worst that human beings do. And it is more in accord with traditional views of what the devil does than is Kant's own view of the diabolical.

Kant's focus is entirely on the will, on one's reasons for acting. He may be right that there is in human nature no initial predisposition to wrongdoing or harm, no basic hostility. But suppose we understand diabolical evil, instead, with a focus on the *harm* one is willing to inflict rather than on the reasons why. Suppose we regard diabolical evil as knowingly and culpably seeking others' moral corruption, putting them into situations where in order to survive they must, by their own choices, risk their own moral deterioration or moral death. This understanding of diabolical evil comes closer than Kant's does to the classic view of Satan as a corrupter, as one who tempts others to abandon morality or demote it to a low position on their scale of values. Not even all atrocities are diabolical. Whether diabolical evil is also radical (that is, rooted in the will as a matter of principle) is a further question in particular cases. Diabolical evil, on my understanding, is not defined by the nature of its motives, although, like all evils, it presupposes culpability.

The writings of Nietzsche have tempted many to demote moral values to a low ranking. Nietzsche billed himself as an "anti-Christ." Some of his philosophical opponents seem to regard him as diabolical. It is true that evil, even diabolical, crimes have been committed in the name of his philosophy.[2] But nothing in Nietzsche's writings is diabolical in the sense intended here. He hoped to salvage the best in humanity, rather than destroy it, although he had an amoral conception of excellence. Nietzsche is no devil, because he is not a "tempter" in the relevant sense. His appeals to emotion and intellect are not coercive. Diabolical evil, on my view, consists in placing others under the extreme stress, even severe duress, of having to choose between grave risks of horrible physical suffering or death (not necessarily their own) and equally grave risks of severe moral compromise, the loss of moral integrity, even moral death. This is stress geared to break the wills of decent people, to destroy what is best in us on any plausible conception of human excellence. For that reason, it deserves to be regarded as diabolical. The devil wants company and is a willing corrupter, plotting others' downfall. This is how evil extends its power. Nietzsche had no such ambitions.

But diabolical evil in human beings is very real. Some knowingly place others in stressful situations designed to corrupt their wills. They make "offers" intended to be unrefusable. Most notoriously, in the twentieth century, this was done in Adolph Hitler's death camps. In these special hells were areas that survivor Primo Levi called "the gray zone," where prisoners, already victims themselves, were selected for positions of authority over other prisoners.[3] (He notes that the Mafia has always practiced this method.) Prisoner kapos (captains) and other functionaries were rewarded, by a variety of temporary reductions in their own torture, for administering the evils of the camps to others. Many of these unfortunates bore, in addition to the harms and the suffering inflicted on them, the burdens of shame and guilt for what they did to others. Levi notes that one is stunned by "the paroxysm of perfidy and hatred" of those who designed this system in an "attempt to shift onto others—specifically, the victims—the burden of guilt" and show that "the Jews, the subrace, the submen, bow to any and all humiliation, even to destroying themselves."[4]

The deliberate creation of gray zones exemplifies diabolical evil, if anything does, regardless of why it is done. Agents' choices *within* gray zones are often morally problematic, not unqualifiedly evil. But gray zones jeopardize the character and self-respect of survivors. Although this chapter explores dilemmas within gray zones, my interest is ultimately more in the evil done *to* their inhabitants than in any evils they do. The evil done to them is one that neither perpetrators nor victims are eager to acknowledge publicly, as will become clear, each for their own reasons.

My interest in gray zones is twofold. First, I wish to make philosophical sense of the idea of diabolical evil by way of concrete examples that some gray zones offer. At the same time, I wish to understand better the moral positions and responsibilities of those who inhabit gray zones. The two concerns are related in that developing a capacity for perpetrating diabolical evil appears to be one potential outcome of failing to meet moral challenges within a gray zone.

The "Stockholm Syndrome"

Fighting oppression from within—where it must be fought to be lastingly effective—is difficult and unlikely because of psychological and moral damage to the oppressed. Some damage is unintended. It can interfere with the exploitability of the oppressed. But often enough oppressors knowingly break and mold victims. Joseph Stalin did it on a grand scale; J. Edgar Hoover and Roy Cohn on a more limited scale. With time and luck, some victims overcome the damage. Many do not. Some survivors find they cannot live with the knowledge of what they have done, or failed to do, and what they have seen become of decent human beings.

An early task in fighting oppression is to address undeserved negative judgments and unfriendly stereotypes of the oppressed. Thus, early feminism addressed undeserved negative stereotypes of women. The more difficult task for survivors is to identify and overcome the *real* damage that oppression works in its victims. Oppressive institutions, whether they favor or disfavor us, offer an inhospitable context for developing or maintaining moral integrity. Women confront the likelihood that many (perhaps most) of us have developed morally problematic habits of thought, feeling, and action under misogynous practices. The gray zones of this chapter are danger zones, where those who are already victims are at risk of moral character deterioration, of becoming complicit in deeds the memory of which will, or should, produce shame.

What has come to be known as "the hostage phenomenon" illustrates a kind of damage to which oppressed people may be susceptible in varying degrees. Also known as "Hostage Identification Syndrome" and the "Stockholm Syndrome," this phenomenon was so named after a hostage incident during a 1973 holdup of the Sveriges Kreditbank in Stockholm, when four employees were held captive by two robbers for almost six days. Contrary to what others expected, the victims feared the police more than they feared the robbers. Some hostages became sympathetic toward their captors. One hostage fell in love with and became engaged to one of the robbers and publicly berated the Swedish prime minister for his failure to understand the robber's point of view.[5] "In other instances," one analyst reports, "hostages have been known to visit their captors in jail up to two years after the incident."[6] I know of no evidence that these robbers aimed to create such an identification in their hostages or even anticipated it. But knowledge of such possibilities is a powerful tool for those with exploitative aims.

The next year (1974), nineteen-year-old Patricia Hearst, granddaughter of newspaper magnate William Randolph Hearst, was kidnapped in San Francisco by the Symbionese Liberation Army (SLA) and held for a ransom demand of $6 million for a food giveaway program for the poor of California. After fifty-seven days, during which she was kept tied and blindfolded in a closet, where she was also raped, she agreed to join the SLA, taking the name Tania, and later Pearl. Convicted and sentenced to prison for her part in the SLA's most infamous bank robbery (which was videotaped and aired on network television news), she later had her sentence commuted by President Carter, after psychiatrists determined that she had developed a pseudo-identity as a survival strategy.[7] She was finally pardoned by President Clinton, hours before he left office in January 2001. Her experience is frequently mentioned in discussions of the Stockholm Syndrome.

In 1979 Kathleen Barry wrote about a phenomenon similar to Stockholm Syndrome in *Female Sexual Slavery*, including a chapter on Patricia Hearst.[8] She found that young girls "seasoned" for prostitution through torture by pimps come to identify with the pimp's perspective to the point of being able to predict his wants before he knows them himself. The "seasoning" process—which includes isolation, severe deprivation, and gradual restoration of "privileges" in response to "good behavior"—is very deliberate. If identifying with the pimp is not likewise simply a deliberate and calculated act, the captive may take up that perspective not just as *though* it were her own but *as* her own, at least in the sense of its being the only operative perspective that she now has. Her choices may come to seem normal to her, no longer even morally problematic.

These examples are of episodes that range from a few days to several months or even a few years. Although some survivors, even after they are freed, continue to defend their captors, eventually they cease to identify with their captors' points of view. The basic idea of the Stockholm Syndrome has since been extended, however, to victims of domestic battery and to children abused by caretakers.[9] This abuse may last for many years, and the victim's identification with the abuser may never totally die.

Survivors of domestic battery or child abuse may be plausibly recognized as having been prisoners, if not hostages, for at least part of their lives. But many who are dominated and abused are not obviously prisoners or hostages. Still, the victim may identify strongly with the abuser. As with Patricia Hearst, that identification can enhance their chances of survival, making them useful to abusers and encouraging a reciprocal identification that makes it psychologically more difficult for abusers to depersonalize and destroy their victims.

In the early twentieth century, sociologist W. E. B. Du Bois wrote of his own experience of what he called "twoness," having two selves. He was not referring to any incident, long or short, of being held captive or subjected to obvious abuse. One self he called "American," and one he called "Negro." He also described "this double-consciousness" as a sense of "always looking at oneself through the eyes of others."[10] Du Bois was well aware of the conflict of ideals between the two perspectives, although he did not explicitly relate his experience to oppression, and he did not want to abandon either self completely. But it is possible to be less aware than he was and to discover eventually, through reflection, that one's true self has been smothered, rendered inoperative through a combination of fear and the hope of being able to deflect dangers by learning to perceive and think as one's oppressor does.

African Americans whom other African Americans call "oreos" (black outside, white inside)—not ordinarily an affectionate term—are perceived not as struggling, like Du Bois, with a double consciousness but as having resolved the struggle by opting to identify at heart with white culture. Larry Koger writes in *Black Slaveowners* of prosperous African Americans of lighter skin who, in the nineteenth century, bought family members and other slaves for humanitarian reasons. But some, he found, also acquired slaves for labor both because they had little access to other sources of labor and also to elevate themselves above the masses.[11] Such a concept of "elevation" suggests an identification with white slave-owners.

Feminist consciousness-raising (CR) swept the United States in the early 1970s. In local CR groups that met weekly in private homes, many of us who were professional and middle-class women found that we had internalized oppressive misogynist stereotypes. Like Du Bois, we were not prisoners in any straightforward sense. Nor were we all victims of rape or domestic battery. Yet the pattern of values we strove to overcome bears more than a passing resemblance to that of what Nietzsche called "the slave mode of valuation." We had learned to take pride in our ability to please and be of service to those who were glad they had not been born female.

Closeted lesbians and gay men, like Patricia Hearst in her closet, have been drawn into participating in their own oppression. Some have participated in so-called witch-hunts for homosexuals in military service, turning in lists of names in return for protection of their own secrets by those to whom they betray others.[12] Others have enforced rules and regulations hostile to same-sex intimacy in same-sex educational environments, often in an effort to create or reinforce a public impression of their own heterosexuality. The most infamous examples in the United States of gay identification with the oppressor are the homosexual-baiting activities before the House Un-American Activities Committee during the 1950s of former FBI Director J. Edgar Hoover and Roy Cohn, who was Senator Joseph McCarthy's gay aide.[13] Hoover and Cohn were sorry exemplars as well as victims of what George H. Weinberg, heterosexual psychologist and friend of the gay community, came to call, two decades later, "homophobia."[14]

The same psychological processes at work in the hostage cases, where prisoners identify with captors, appear to be found in many forms of abuse and oppression when victims come into close contact with abusers on whom they are deeply dependent. Ironically, abuse victims often become emotionally attached to their abusers, who can be important persons indeed, as the victim's very life may be in the abuser's hands. When the attachment persists, the abuser appears to have become for the victim what Lorna Smith Benjamin calls an IPIR, an Important Person with an Internalized Representation that serves as a model and source of esteem.[15] A priori, one might expect those who have been abused to be the last persons on earth to want to hurt others, because they know what it is like to be on the receiving end. And that is in fact true of many who survive abuse and then go on to dedicate much of the remainder of their lives to fighting the injustices they have suffered. Empirically, however, it also appears to be the case that instead of Kant's Categorical Imperative, the fundamental norms guiding many survivors are those of their abusers and former abusers. Perhaps some feel the pull of both kinds of norms.

Gray Zones

The medical model operative in the terms "Hostage Identification *Syndrome*" and "Stockholm *Syndrome*" suggests that the captive is overcome by something like an illness, that the identification process is not voluntary and the captive not morally responsible for her choices. Yet when we look at cases such as Hearst's, it is not clear that the captive acts involuntarily or is not morally responsible. Some of her choices seem justifiable as maximizing her chances of survival, even providing her only chance. There are also good reasons not to regard all her choices as simply calculated, either. Genuine sympathy for her captors' point of view—even mutual bonding—appeared to develop. Actions based on sympathy or bonding are not ordinarily considered involuntary. The medical model may not be useful here. We may have, rather, a morally gray area, where there is real danger of becoming complicit in evildoing and where the captive's responsibility is better described as problematic than as nonexistent.

In her autobiography Patricia Hearst wrote of her decision to join the SLA as a calculated pretense that would maximize her chances of survival. She did not accept SLA values and objectives but pretended, in order to gain her captors' trust and respect, that she did. It worked. And yet, months later, after she had been drilled in weapons use and emergency response, she found herself alone in the getaway car using her weapon to help two SLA comrades escape from a store where they were being apprehended for shoplifting, instead of taking that opportunity to use the weapon to try to escape herself. That is, she sided with her captors, the SLA, instead of with those who might rescue her from them. When she realized what she had done, she was puzzled. Explanations she offers are that her response was automatic because she had been drilled by the SLA to respond automatically and also that she felt by then as much of a criminal in the eyes of the law as the other members of the SLA, that in joining the SLA she had made a decision from which there was no turning back and no possible redemption. The second explanation, referring to her own decision, is ethically more interesting because in it she takes responsibility for her choices.

Perhaps the greatest danger threatening victims of oppression is that of becoming evil themselves. Knowingly to enlist others in their own severe oppression or murder and in the betrayal, oppression, or murder of those they love is as diabolical an evil as I can imagine. Not all of the oppressed actually do become complicit in the perpetration of evils. Some resist to the end. Many of them do not survive. Nor among those who become complicit is everyone equally so. Nor does morality totally die in all who compromise. But avoiding or ceasing complicity can require more alertness, habits of reflection, loss of innocence, sensitivity to risks—not to mention moral imagination, creativity, and courage—than most young people have. Women, gay people, and people of color in the United States today face to some degree the challenges of avoiding or ceasing complicity in oppressive practices. When the complicity is with real evildoing and the stress extreme, they face morally gray choices.

In the 1970s feminists identified women's complicity in misogyny in the "Athena" syndrome (being born again from Daddy's head) and in "harem politics" (a power hierarchy among female slaves, some charged to discipline others). In both cases, women appear to be drawn, by hope of favor and privilege, into being men's conspicuous instruments of oppression. "Favor and privilege" sound like superfluous goods. In reality they tend to be no more than temporary reprieves from abuse. To resist being "divided and conquered," some women who refuse such favors nevertheless stand in solidarity with those who do not, refraining from judging women who give in. Yet refusing to evaluate the *choices* made by those who give in exposes one to being manipulated and worse.

It is important to reflect on the involvement of the oppressed in the perpetration of evils, not just on coercion inflicted by others. Doing so does not presuppose that the oppressed lacked character to begin with or were already hostile toward those they finally betray. On the contrary, the oppressed have, as Margaret Walker puts it, "harder lives" but not necessarily lives that exhibit less integrity.[16] Many who struggle under oppressive situations resist its pitfalls. Still, oppression has degrees. Some with harder lives are relatively fortunate not to confront the worst. Many women's strongest bonds are with other women, despite the double binds of patriarchy that do so much to pit women against one another. Yet people who are attached to others can also abuse them. The realization of women's—or any victim's—capacity to compromise with evil is disillusioning. Yet its undeniable history requires us to reflect on its implications. Being a victim does not imply that one is innocent. If initially an appreciation of female involvement in evil poses a risk to feminist solidarity, ignoring that involvement produces a superficial feminism. Good reasons for women to take seriously women's capacity for evil are to move beyond myths of female innocence in our relationships with each other, to confront our responsibilities for past and potential damage to others, and to overcome the moral traps that oppression sets for us.

My interest is especially in the dangers of deterioration for victims who have already developed moral sensitivities and a basically decent character. Human goodness is, as Martha Nussbaum puts it, fragile.[17] Those who knowingly place others in gray zones jeopardize and destroy human goodness. Of course, some abusers prevent goodness from ever developing in their victims in the first place. One might also find this abuse diabolical when perpetrators can reasonably be expected to foresee the consequence. In an essay that reflects on Peter Strawson's well-known "Freedom and Resentment," Gary Watson presents the case of Robert Harris, one of the most sadistic of murderers on death row, whose twenty-nine years had been "dominated by incessant cruelty and profound suffering that he [had] both experienced and provoked."[18] The details are horrible. Yet Harris's sister could recall a time when Robert was a sweet, affectionate little boy. For one who has never known life without crushing abuse or who has been attached from childhood to abusers, the entire world may be gray. But it is a different kind of gray from that of Levi's gray zones. Goodness appears to have been extinguished in Harris's soul before it had much chance to grow. Harris's own experience of his murderous and sadistic choices does not appear to have had a phenomenologically moral character. It is more difficult to regard Harris, than Hearst, as a responsible agent.

For victims who, despite harder lives, do have well-developed moral sensitivities and a decent character, there is a special moral anguish in confronting gray zones. Harris appears not to have experienced that anguish. Gray zones carry a risk of even greater loss than Harris's own. Only someone who has moral sensitivities can carry the burdens of guilt and the obligations of perpetrators, as well as possess the moral powers of a victim. These are the capacities that hold the promise of disrupting cycles of evil. To destroy them is to destroy this promise as well as goodness in the soul of the individual.

Many cases of systematic oppression, extending over many years, fall somewhere between Levi's gray zones and Harris's sadistic amoralism. Misogyny is an evil that destroys goodness at many stages of development. It prevents some women from developing moral sensitivities but also undermines decent character in others. Although "misogyny" means "woman hating," feminists use the term to refer to practices, behaviors, and socially created environments that are deeply hostile to women and girls. Hostility in this context is not identical with (although it is compatible with) emotional hatred. It refers, basically, to the hindrance of female health and development. Misogynous environments are hostile to women as polluted ground and water are hostile to plants. To find misogynous environments evil, on the atrocity paradigm, is to find that they are also the product of culpable wrongdoing and that the hindrance they pose to female health and development deprives females of what is basic to a tolerable existence.

It has long been observed that misogynous environments are routinely maintained by women. There are many degrees of (in)voluntariness in this participation. Many who appear to participate voluntarily would only do so in an oppressive situation already created by others. Women run whorehouses, often with pride. Mothers socialize daughters into aspects of femininity that endanger their health and safety. Sometimes they ostracize lesbian daughters. Women who are victims of severely misogynous practices routinely pass them along to the next generation. The *Christian Science Monitor* ran a four-part series called "Arab Women: Out of the Shadows" during the summer of 2000, introduced by reporter Ilene R. Prusher with the following recollection of an "honor killing":

> Two years ago, I came across a story that will stay with me for a long time. A girl with a face as sweet as a summer plum sat with me in a shelter in this colorless desert suburb of Amman, Jordan and calmly told me how she killed her own mother. Salwa had set her mother's bed on fire, because her grandmother goaded her into it. She told 15-year-old Salwa that her divorced mother's dating habits had brought dishonor upon the family and would ruin Salwa's own marriage prospects.[19]

Women who do patriarchy's dirty work occupy positions of trust and responsibility, some not only accepted but actively sought. Their tasks draw on female initiative, energy, imagination, creativity, brilliance, and virtuosity. In other cases, such as Salwa's grandmother, women's oppressive behavior is not so much advantageous as cruel, sometimes neglectful, common results of the demoralization produced by oppression.

Consider Hedda Nussbaum, widely held to share blame in the 1987 death of six-year old Lisa Steinberg. Nussbaum was nearly as battered by Joel Steinberg, with whom she had lived since 1976, as was Lisa, his illegally adopted daughter, who died from his abuse. Nussbaum's sojourn with Steinberg was a living death. She did not deserve his abuse. But neither did she, apparently, seek help by dialing 911 for Lisa, who was even more vulnerable and had no one else to help her. Years of battering by Steinberg and years of her own compromises had thoroughly demoralized Nussbaum. Andrea Dworkin, herself a survivor of domestic battery, writes, "I don't think Hedda Nussbaum is 'innocent.' I don't know any innocent adult women. Life is harder than that for everyone. But adult women who have been battered are especially not innocent. Battery is a forced descent into hell and you don't get by in hell by moral goodness."[20] But she continues, "I am upset by the phony mourning for Lisa Steinberg—the hypocritical sentimentality of a society that would not really mind her being beaten to death once she was an adult," and she notes, "There was a little boy, too, Mitchell, seventeen months old, tied up and covered in feces. And the only way to have spared him was to rescue Hedda. Now he has been tortured and he did not die. What kind of man will he grow up to be?"[21]

Like the predicament of Patricia Hearst in relation to the SLA, the predicament of Hedda Nussbaum—who had every reason to fear what Steinberg might do if she crossed him—comes close to what Levi called a "gray zone, poorly defined, where the two camps of masters and servants both diverge and converge."[22] For Levi, the "gray zone" was the moral area occupied by kapos and other prisoners who held positions of responsibility and administration in the National Socialist death camps and ghettos.[23] Gray zones, Levi found, "confuse our need to judge."[24] They are inhabited by people who become implicated, through their choices, in perpetrating on others the evil that threatens or engulfs themselves.

Levi does not define the gray zone specifically. Rather, he conveys the idea by example, noting that gray zones are varied and ambiguous and that they have multiple roots. Among these roots are the oppressors' need for "external auxiliaries" and the oppressors' realization that the best way to bind those auxiliaries is "to burden them with guilt, cover them with blood, compromise them as much as possible, thus establishing a bond of complicity so that they can no longer turn back."[25] Only those with moral sensibilities can be burdened with guilt. Hearst felt there was no turning back (suggesting she would have if she had thought it an option). Harris appears to have had no desire to turn back, no memory of anything worth turning back to. I wonder what will become of Salwa, who is still younger and may not have been so unfortunate that future experience or reflection will fail to bring remorse.

"Gray zone" is a problematic term, if it presupposes that "dark" or "black" represents evil. That use of color terms may unwittingly reinforce racism, even if the metaphor of dark as evil originated historically in references to the night in a society where nights are dangerous or difficult (because it is hard for the visually dependent to make their way). For that reason I would welcome an alternative metaphor.[26] Meanwhile, I use Levi's term "gray zone," acknowledging, in case it instantiates what it names, that "gray zone" may be itself a gray term.

There is also risk in appropriating Levi's term "gray zone" of misappropriating the experience of Holocaust victims, although Levi is not the only writer to use the term "gray" to refer to what is morally unclear or problematic.[27] I do not wish to trade on the horrors of the camps and ghettos to get attention to other evils. From respect for the lives motivating Levi's discussion, I sometimes use the term "gray area," rather than "gray zone," for less desperate cases that share morally important features. I do wish to explore the significance of the concept that Levi has identified for more contexts than those that led him to articulate it. It complicates our understandings of choices people make in oppressive circumstances, our assessments of the moral positions of victims of oppression, and our view of the responsibilities victims may have to and for one another. The choices facing most victims of misogyny bear no comparison with choices that confronted camp or ghetto prisoners. Most women are not Hedda Nussbaum (although more are than is commonly acknowledged). My point, however, is not to compare degrees of suffering or even evil but to note patterns in the complexity of choices and judgments of responsibility under severe moral stress.

Levi wrote in his chapter on the gray zone about prisoners whose labors were used to carry out the National Socialist oppression and genocide. He also reflects on the ambiguous figure Chaim Rumkowski, Elder of the Łodz ghetto, who was called "king of the Jews."[28] Some prisoners were drafted; others offered their services. Some did clerical or domestic work for officers. Some became camp doctors. Prisoners also served on ghetto councils, such as that headed by Rumkowski, which were eventually charged with selection and deportation tasks.[29] Others became ghetto police and found themselves charged with rounding up prisoners for deportation.[30] In death camps, prisoners were routinely chosen for the *Sonderkommando* (Special Squad), which was charged with cremation detail. Almost all Sonderkommando prisoners were murdered within months or weeks.[31] Prisoners who became kapos in exchange for food and other privileges held power over other prisoners. Levi notes that although a minimum of harshness was expected of kapos, there was no upper limit to the cruelty they could inflict with impunity.

Prisoners who occupied such positions lost their innocence.[32] Loss of innocence, even when it involves "dirty hands," is not the same as loss of virtue.[33] Yet it carries moral risk. We lose innocence when we become responsible through our choices for the undeserved sufferings of others or when we betray their trust, even when we make the best decision open to us under the circumstances. When we fail to live up to the responsibilities we thereby incur, as we must when we lack the means, our integrity may be compromised. We risk losing self-respect and moral motivation. Once we feel we have crossed the line of participating in the infliction of evil, we may have less to restrain us from more and worse in the future.

Privileged prisoners, Levi observed, were a minority of the camp populations. But he also claimed that "they represent a majority among survivors."[34] I do not know whether he was right about that. Presumably, many survived only because they were among the last to be deported. Luck was always a major factor. Nevertheless, how the realization that survivors included many privileged prisoners should affect survivors' attitudes toward themselves and toward other survivors were questions that troubled him profoundly and led him to draw distinctions. Regarding members of the Sonderkommando who did not kill with their own hands, he wrote, "I believe that no one is authorized to judge them, not those who lived through the experience of the Lager [camp] and even less those who did not."[35] Yet he did not refrain from all judgments of those who inhabited the gray zone. He noted that "they are the rightful owners of a quota of guilt" but also that were it up to him, he "would lightheartedly absolve all those whose concurrence in the guilt was minimal and for whom coercion was of the highest degree."[36]

Levi may seem, to some, generous in his responses to gray zone agents, even in his concession that "they are the rightful owners of a quota of guilt." Regarding absolution, perhaps he was thinking primarily of the Sonderkommando, although that was not typical even of gray zones (if we can speak of what is typical here), and it is not clear that its members were rightful owners of any guilt at all. It seems unlikely that many would have identified with persecutors who promised so little. But agents in other gray zones have had space to act on their own initiatives, more control over their options, more to gain by compliance, and more room for responsibility and for involvement with oppressors. In later years former kapos were pursued by former prisoners over whom they had authority in the camps, prisoners who were certainly prepared to hold them responsible for abuse.

Hearst was convinced by the SLA that if police found their hiding place, she would be killed in the ensuing shootout. She was right. She would have been killed in the shootout and fire, had she been in the Los Angeles hideout when police found it. For a time, the police thought they had killed her there. She was also convinced, from conversations overheard from her closet, that if she did not join them, the SLA would kill her because she knew too much. Even so, her death was less certain than that of Sonderkommando prisoners. She had some access to weapons. Hearst was her own worst victim. Like some camp prisoners, she chose to enlist in the service of her oppressors. But unlike kapos, the victims of her criminal deeds were not other victims quite like herself, not other prisoners of the SLA (although they were other victims of the SLA).

The ambivalence of the gray zone is mirrored in the ambivalence of other victims' responses to gray choices. On one hand, they may identify with the chooser, thinking, "had I the opportunity, I'd seize it, too; how could anyone not?" On the other hand, they may feel even more wronged by other victims than by their morally unambiguous oppressors, thinking to themselves, "[I]f we cannot trust even those who are as hated and despised as we, what can we hope for? Since we don't trust those who hate us, they don't really betray us. Betrayal comes from those we count on for assistance." Thus, women may feel, paradoxically, more wronged by other women than by men, even though the women who wrong them have less power to do them harm. When complicity is the price of survival, one may think, on one hand, "It's good that at least some of us will survive." But if backstabbing is the price of complicity, one may think, on the other hand, "What is the good of surviving in a world where no one is trustworthy?"

Confronted with morally gray choices, it is tempting to reason, "If I can just stay alive, there's a chance I can help, but I can't be any good to anyone dead." Similarly, one may reason, "If I can just get some power, I may be able to help, but I can't do any good as long as I acquiesce in my own impotence." Yet sometimes it is not true, as these cases show, that as long as one is alive, there is any real chance to help, or that as long as one has more power, one is in a better position to do so. For one may have little or no control over how one's life or one's power is used. Being no good to anyone is not the worst thing. Being an instrument of evil is worse.

Gray areas, whose inhabitants are at once victims and perpetrators of oppression, develop wherever the evils of oppression are severe, widespread, and lasting. There are gray areas in slavery, for example, and in the policing of and resistance to organized crime. There have been gray areas in U.S. prisons for criminal offenders, where prisoners have been used as guards, armed with weapons and able to avoid a certain measure of abuse themselves by abusing other prisoners.[37] Survivors of the Gypsy death camp Lety in Czechoslovakia told Paul Polansky about Gypsy prisoners who were sent from Auschwitz "to teach us order" and who "had to prove themselves so they wouldn't be sent back," with the result that the Czech guards, who for a time did not have to beat Gypsies themselves, "laughed about Gypsies beating Gypsies to death."[38] There are gray areas within organized crime, as in the Cosa Nostra or the mob, where women are sometimes used, with varying degrees of knowledge, as go-betweens or to arrange meetings, or where women are simply caretakers of men who are fully involved. Sociologist Renate Siebert of the University of Calabria (Italy) writes in her book on women and the mafia of mothers who raise a son to avenge the death of his father.[39] There are gray areas wherever women who are victims of severe misogyny provide essential services and emotional support to men who are engaged in conquest, exploitation, annihilation, and oppression. The labor of the oppressed in the daily workings of maintaining and operating oppressive institutions frees the energies of those on top for the joyous pursuits of cultural development. The insulation of being on top enables them to avoid confronting dirt on their own hands, thus offering many of them the illusion of innocence.

What Makes Gray Zones Gray?

Levi's gray zone has three striking features. First, its inhabitants are victims of evil. Second, these inhabitants are implicated through their choices in perpetrating some of the same or similar evils on others who are already victims like themselves. And third, inhabitants of the gray zone act under extraordinary stress. Many of them have lost everything and everyone, and they face the threat of imminent and horrible death. Although Levi does not use the term "hostage syndrome," he notes that among the oppressed who sought power were many who "had been contaminated by their oppressors and unconsciously strove to identify with them."[40]

Grayness may seem at first to be conveyed by Levi's first two features alone: being both a victim of evil and implicated in the perpetration of that evil on others. These features can be enough to confuse our need to judge. But the third feature—the extraordinary stress of extreme loss and the threat of imminent and horrible death—makes judgment even more problematic, given the frailty of human nature. Something like this third feature is also important, we will see, for distinguishing gray zones from other mixtures of good and evil in our lives.

I understand the basic idea of a gray area in such a way that the third feature, the stress feature, is satisfied when agents must choose under such conditions as intense or prolonged fear for basic security or their very lives or for the lives or basic security of loved ones. The gray areas of misogyny and racism in the developed world today may seldom, if ever, approach the extremity of death camps. They may have come close for women who participated in the slaughters of the Rwandan genocide or for those who ran brothels of "comfort women" during World War II.[41] Yet, even if few gray areas reach that extremity, widely tolerated violence against women of all ethnic backgrounds and against people of color in the United States today is such that their lives often do contain major stress and the motive of survival or fear for basic security.

Grayness has multiple sources. One is the presence of a mixture of evil and innocence. Victims undergo suffering they did nothing to deserve. They are in that sense innocent. Yet services they perform with some degree of voluntariness implicate them in perpetrating evils on others who also did not deserve to suffer and who may not be similarly implicated themselves. Still, the involvement of those who live in gray areas is not of the same order as that of perpetrators who are not also victims. Gray agents lack the same discretion and power to walk away. One would often not readily describe as "murderers" prisoners who did not kill with their own hands. At the same time, it can be difficult to draw the line that "kill with their own hands" suggests. When ghetto prisoner police, who eventually knew the finality of the destination, physically pushed others onto transport trains and bolted the door, did they or did they not "kill with their own hands"? They are both innocent and not innocent, in other words, "gray."

Grayness often suggests unclarity regarding the degree of an agent's responsibility. We may not know how to assess the power of the threats facing the agent or the agent's powers of endurance. The agent may have to make difficult, irreversible decisions quickly and in the absence of relevant information. There may be a combination of these factors. They make it unclear to observers and to choosers themselves what was avoidable and at what cost. Gray zones often lie on or at the foot of slippery slopes, and the agent's responsibility is a significant dimension of slipperiness. It is tempting to distinguish degrees of involvement in evildoing along something like the following lines. A first degree may be that of bystanders who witness evils without saying or doing anything but are not instrumentally involved. Of course, when many bystanders do nothing (else), they become enablers. A second degree may be that of unavoidably becoming an instrument of evil to others. And a third, that of participating in avoidable evildoing but only under duress.[42] The third degree, at least, can land one in a gray area. But there are also other dimensions of grayness besides degree of responsibility.

One such dimension is ambiguity in the agent's motivation. Levi finds gray persons ambiguous and "ready to compromise." He describes the moral status of prisoners in the gray zone as somewhere between the status of victims and that of custodians. Readiness to compromise is also suggested by ambiguity in the positions themselves. To function effectively, auxiliary functionaries must have some power and some discretion regarding its use. This combination of power and discretion presents the seductive thought that one may be able to use the position for sabotage. Some did. Of those involved in secret defense organizations, such as Eugen Kogon in Buchenwald and Herman Langbein in Auschwitz, Levi says that they were only apparently collaborators but in reality camouflaged opponents.[43] Even as opponents of National Socialism, however, they had to acquiesce in risking the infliction on others of torture or death in order to further their resistance efforts. Arguably, some such risks were in the interests of those whose lives were risked (who would almost certainly have been murdered anyway), as some of our interests outlive us. Yet even such activity carries the moral dangers of dirty hands.

There is sometimes a greater likelihood that those who accept a position of privilege will be able to do nothing significant to resist, that all they will manage to do is become implicated in the perpetration of evil. There is the danger of using the bare possibility of sabotage as a rationalization for saving one's skin or gaining reprieve from suffering. Levi notes that the power wielded by Kogon and Langbein was counterbalanced by the greater risks they ran in belonging to secret defense organizations.[44] Power wielded by many others, however, reduced their own risks or benefited friends without sabotaging the operation or any significant part of it.

The ambiguity in gray zone agents' motivations is sometimes matched by the difficulty of ascertaining what it would be right or wrong to do. Where evil threatens not only oneself but others and there is some chance that one can alleviate dangers for others, whereas if one fails, one may expose them to even greater evils than they already face, it can be far from clear whether to take the risk. Grayness here stems from an unclarity that may lead us to question whether "right" and "wrong" give us an adequate moral vocabulary to describe the choices the agent faces.

Thus, "gray" suggests many things. Sometimes it evokes a complex judgment whose elements are mixed, although individually they are clear enough. It may be impossible to do justice to the case with an overall summary such as "good on the whole" or "bad on the whole." At other times, "gray" evokes a deed whose very elements are morally unclear or ambiguous.

"Gray" may seem basically an epistemological concept, referring to what is unclear or ambiguous (to the agent, an observer, or both), whether it be degree of responsibility, motive, or rightness of the action. Levi is not the only writer to use "gray" to refer to what is morally unclear. Renate Siebert writes that "the thoughts, fears, desires and dreams of women who live in mafia families are still a grey area for the rest of us," apparently because we know so little.[45]

And yet the unclarity of gray zones can give rise also to questions about the *ontological* status of the choices in question. Are there really always right and wrong choices in such situations (where voluntariness is not the issue)? Are there always responsible or excusable choices (where rightness or wrongness is not the issue)? Is there always such a thing as the agent's real motive? Does our moral vocabulary fail to mark distinctions that we should want to make, to capture the ways things really are? Would gray zones cease to be gray, if we had more fine-tuned concepts? Or are some gray zones ineliminable?

One thing is clear. People who have lived under the extreme stress of gray zones have often not abandoned the categories of morality, nor ceased responding in moral ways emotionally, nor ceased entering relationships of trust and holding one another responsible. Simon Wiesenthal asked himself continually whether he was doing the right thing—in staying to listen to Karl, in remaining silent in response to Karl's plea for forgiveness, in burdening fellow prisoners with the story of that encounter and asking what they would have done. Elie Cohen, a prisoner doctor at Westerborck (later author of *Human Behavior in the Concentration Camp*), confesses his shame that he did not find the courage to continue falsely declaring people unfit for transportation after he was caught and threatened with transportation for both himself and his family. But he also insists, "One thing I was not—and I'd like to make that clear, I wasn't corrupt. I was offered plenty. Women even offered themselves to me. I'm no saint—but I never fell for that. I never declared people unfit to go on one of the transports in return for money or other things. That standard I did, evidently, maintain in Westerbork."[46] Yet he also recounts a later episode at Auschwitz in which a patient who was a professor pleaded, "Will you see to it that I'm given enough narcotics to make sure I'm no longer conscious when I go into the gas chamber?" Dr. Cohen's moral anguish is palpable when he confesses, "I didn't do it. I didn't do it. Images that haunt you. . . . Why didn't I give that professor any drugs? Well, that, of course, is a terribly sore point for me. Because I was scared to! Because I didn't want to put my own life in jeopardy unnecessarily. He was going to die, anyway. . . . I *could* have gotten those narcotics, of course . . . but I *didn't do* it. I *didn't do it*."[47]

Rudolf Vrba, later a (successful) Auschwitz escapee, tried to persuade Fredy Hirsch, a prisoner caring for the children in the "family camp" who had been deported from Terezin, that because he was held in such high esteem, he should lead a revolt in Auschwitz among the Terezin inmates. Hirsch objected that to do so would be to sacrifice the children. Vrba responded that the children would die anyway, and Hirsch replied, "but at least I won't have betrayed them."[48] Unable, finally, to embrace either option, Hirsch chose within the hour to end his life by poison. Hirsch was almost morally incapacitated. Yet he did make a choice.

Tzvetan Todorow's book *Facing the Extreme: Moral Life in the Concentration Camps*, which also discusses this episode, is filled with numerous examples of prisoners responding out of moral concern and anguish under conditions that many have assumed would make morality evaporate.[49] Skeptics may find these prisoners confused, perhaps emotionally *akratic*, in failing to recognize the limits within which moral concepts apply.[50] I prefer to respect the perceptions of agents who have actually confronted gray areas, in hopes of learning from them.

Women and Gray Choices

Women have suffered the evils of oppression globally and for millennia. And women have lived in many gray areas, including those of slavery, death camps, and ghettos. Women have been implicated in perpetrating evils not only of misogyny but also of slavery, racism, anti-semitism, classism, hatred of sexual diversity, and hatred and fear of the poor.[51] Misogyny is often an element that complicates women's choices, presenting special possibilities and temptations. Women can inhabit gray areas in relation to children (as Hedda Nussbaum did in relation to Lisa Steinberg) and in buying into male protection rackets regarding rape.[52] We are not always sensitive to the grayness of particular choices we confront. But American feminists have been aware in general at least since the lesbian/straight political battles of the 1970s that there is a serious problem here.

In her struggles to find a way out, radical feminist philosopher Joyce Trebilcot came close to using the gray area metaphor: "My life is like a muddy lake with some clear pools and rivulets—wimmin's spaces—but many areas thick, in one degree or another, with the silt and poisons of patriarchy."[53] Although she was describing her life, she did not at the time that she wrote these lines want to count as a "wimmin's space" those portions marked by oppressive practices. Yet, to count only ideal spaces as women's suggests that women interacting with women are better at resisting compromise with evil. History neither supports the view that we are nor yet sustains the hope that we might be. Women's spaces, too, must confront the challenges of grayness.

La Malinche, or Malinztin (a.k.a. Doña Martina), an Aztec noblewoman, is an ambiguous figure in the history of the conquest of Mexico.[54] She appears to me to have faced morally gray choices when she was presented to Hernan Cortés, upon his landing in Veracruz in 1519, to serve as his lover, translator, and tactical adviser. Refusal might have cost her life and perhaps the lives of others, although records left by Cortés's biographer and by one of his soldiers suggest that she served willingly and with pride.[55] (Should we trust them? Critics said the same of Patricia Hearst.) Did Doña Martina prevent Cortés from doing worse damage than he did? Did she significantly facilitate the Spanish conquest? Did she do both? How much did she know? What had she seen? How much did those who used her know of what it was like to be in her position?

And what of Sacajawea, who traveled with and translated for the explorers Meriwether Lewis and William Clark from 1804 to1806? Lewis and Clark were not Cortés; their mission was exploration, not conquest. But Sacajawea, like Doña Martina, was a slave. She was enrolled as one of his "wives" by a French Canadian, Toussaint Charbonneau, who also traveled as a translator on the expedition. He had won her in a bet with, or purchased her from, the Hidatsa raiding party, who had stolen her from the Shoshone, or Snake, people four years previously when she was ten or eleven years old.[56] We know relatively little about her contributions to the Lewis and Clark expedition. Her role, it appears, was to translate from the Shoshone so Lewis and Clark could purchase horses from them. Historians find it an exaggeration to call her a guide.[57] But Lewis's journal documents that she rescued important materials from a capsized boat. Considering how the "Lewis and Clark" explorations were subsequently used by white people, how white people had already treated Native peoples, and considering the effects on Native peoples of this "opening of the American West," as historian Stephen Ambrose calls it, Sacajawea's agency is morally unclear.

Sacajawea birthed a son shortly before the expedition, and she carried him on her back for the journey. Escape would probably have risked his life. She may not have wished to escape, as she wanted to see her people, the Shoshone, which the expedition enabled her to do. Still, she left Charbonneau later in life because he beat her cruelly. What did she know of European-Native interactions when she was fifteen? What could she have foreseen? Could she do anything for Native peoples? Could she engage in sabotage? Had she any interest? We have primarily in her case not only the testimony of white men but also the researches in 1924 of Charles Eastman, who was a Sioux Indian. Interviewing people who had known her, he researched her life and death at the request of the commissioner of Indian Affairs. Yet much about her life remains unclear. White children in the United States, who learn that she was brave and resourceful (but not that she was a slave), idolize Sacajawea. The Girl Scout camp of my Wisconsin childhood was Camp Sacajawea. But she must be an ambiguous figure for Native Americans, as she is for feminists.

Less ambiguous were slave owners' wives in the United States who managed house slaves, especially wives who did not resist slavery (which some did, covertly).[58] Although they did not live under the stress of a gray zone, their positions sometimes lay on related continua. Like kapos, they had some discretion regarding the use of their authority, and there was, effectively, no upper limit to the cruelty they could inflict with impunity. Wives who used their power to take revenge on female house slaves who were attractive to their husbands did unambiguous evil. Yet some wives' functions were analogous to those of overseer slaves. Both might both count as what Levi calls "external auxiliary functionaries," although slave overseers were far more external and under greater stress. White women were not vulnerable to being sold away and did not generally live under death threats, but they were vulnerable to marital rape and domestic battery. If marriage was not totally involuntary, the alternatives could be grim. Marriage saved upper- and middle-class white women from isolation and economic insecurity. But it saved others from the far worse outcast status of prostitution or poverty, with attendant risks of disease and early death. The latter set of options was itself an evil. Yet marrying slave owners to escape their worst alternatives implicated white women in genuine atrocities perpetrated against slaves.

A few decades ago a white woman caught in (or suspected of) a sexual liaison with a Black man could be threatened by white men with battery or worse if she refused to accuse her lover of rape. The woman who gave in and accused him might confront gray choices at the intersection of sexism and racism. She might reason correctly that if she did not, another would, and so her refusal would not save him, or that some other excuse would be found to lynch him, and so her own suffering or death would be for nothing. But if all white women refused to cooperate in lynching, public support for this atrocity might have been less. It might not have lasted so long or spread so far—as some have been tempted to say that the National Socialist killing machine might have operated less efficiently had Sonderkommando and other prisoners generally and immediately refused their assignments.[59] Levi reports, however, that at least one group of 400 Jews from Corfu who had been included in the Sonderkommando did just that—they "refused without exception to do the work and were immediately gassed to death."[60]

There is, of course, something outrageous in comparing slave owners' wives with death camp prisoners, and perhaps also, for similar reasons, even in comparing kapos and ghetto police with Sonderkommando prisoners. These comparisons ignore real and important differences in levels of stress and also in the level of control that different victims have over the consequences of their choices. Most Sonderkommando prisoners faced certain death, whatever they chose. They had so little to lose by resisting that their not resisting seems more an indication of the power of terror and the frailty of human nature than any reflection of their character. In his testimony *Eyewitness Auschwitz: Three Years in the Gas Chambers* Filip Müller (also interviewed in Claude Lanzmann's film *Shoah*) gives a detailed account of what it was like to work the furnaces on the Sonderkommando.[61] He was one of a very few to survive that experience. The position of most Sonderkommando prisoners, those who were not also kapos, was not one of responsibility and administration. The vast majority had no significant discretion or decision-making power.

In contrast, all kapos had some discretion. And the wives of white slaveowners, like administrators who have served other oppressors, often had considerable discretionary power. Incrementally and over time, they were sometimes able to raise the stakes so that although they had little to lose at first, later on they had a great deal to lose by ceasing to cooperate and much to gain by continuing.[62] Such a pattern does raise questions about character deterioration and suggests greater complicity.

In this regard, what are we to make of Gumbu Smart (1750–1820), an African slave on Bunce Island slave trading center off the African coast, who rebelled against his own masters and then became involved in the slave trade? He certainly raised the stakes for himself. He was sent out by white slavers to purchase slaves, "and because he realized what he was doing, he bought a lot of his countrymen . . . and he kept them and built up a formidable force . . . instead of enslaving them, settled them in the village of Rokon" where "leaning on their gratitude" he formed them into his personal following and rebelled against his own white masters.[63] He then cut off trade coming down the Rokel River and began to charge fees to other traders who wanted to pass upriver to buy people. Edward Ball, who recounts this story in his book *Slaves in the Family,* goes on to ask Smart's African American descendant (whom he is interviewing) whether this doesn't mean that Smart was a victim who became a tyrant, a slave trader. Peter, the descendant, admits that Smart was a "middleman" but resists judging him negatively, and Ball sums it up by saying that "Peter knew the gray areas of behavior, and although he was no apologist for the slave business, he understood why his family sold people to America."[64] Peter was more affirmative: "Our family feels just a bit lucky. I'm proud when I see his name, and I have no reason not to be proud of it."[65] Smart was a survivor. That took ingenuity. And a willingness to compromise.

There are many kinds of gray zones, some much worse than others. But if gray zones are understood so widely that they comprehend the lives of all agents who are both victims and perpetrators of evil, they will be too wide. They will include those who survive to take revenge, for example, by doing to former torturers—or to persons suspected of being former torturers—some of what was done to themselves, even though the retaliators are no longer in danger of suffering torture. This was apparently the case with former prisoners of National Socialist camps who were hired in 1945 by Russians to staff camps for German inmates who were accused or suspected of having been members of the National Socialist Party or of having served it.[66] One may wonder also whether mafia widows who raise a son to avenge the death of his father should be thought to inhabit a gray area, although cases may vary regarding continuing real dangers to the family.

Gray choices understood so widely as to include all who are both victims and perpetrators would also include those who wrong others when doing so saves them from no wrong at the hands of still others and when the wrongs they perpetrate bear no particular relation to the wrongs they suffer. (Was Gumbu Smart still in a gray area after he successfully rebelled? Was he just plain wrong to stay involved in the slave trade? What were his options?) It would include those who wrong others in order to advance their own positions when what they gain bears no comparison with what those they victimized lost or suffered. Such was the case, for example, with the thousands of white Protestant women in the United States who joined the Ku Klux Klan in the 1920s not only to promote racist, intolerant, and xenophobic policies but for a social setting in which to enjoy friendship and solidarity among like-minded women and even to safeguard white women's suffrage and expand white women's other legal rights. When she was interviewed in the 1980s by sociologist Kathleen Blee, an elderly white woman from rural northern Indiana "showed little remorse" but "remembered—with pride, not regret . . . the social and cultural life of the Klan, the Klan as 'a way to get together and enjoy.'"[67] She also insisted that she and others were "forced" to join the Klan "to defend themselves, families, and communities against corruption and immorality," citing such "dangers" as Catholicism's influence on the public schools.[68]

Such behavior is evil, not gray. It is not ambiguous. It is not even morally difficult or complex. That a person's life as a whole evokes in us a mixed emotional response—sympathy insofar as they are wrongly victimized by others but also anger insofar as they wrong others—does not imply that any of their choices possessed the moral complexity or ambiguity of a gray zone. Probably most people's lives taken as a whole would evoke mixed emotional responses. If gray zones are understood that broadly, they threaten to encompass the entire world.

There are also other choices that are in some sense gray, although not in Levi's sense. Choices may be morally unclear or ambiguous, even though their victims were not already targets of oppression. Francine Hughes of the (in)famous "burning bed" killed her batterer by pouring gasoline on him and igniting it while he slept. The morality of her deed may be unclear: given that the law had failed to protect her and her children, was it justifiable self-defense? She lived in hell, too. But the unclarity of the morality of her deed does not give us a gray zone in which the agent victimizes someone who, like herself, is already a victim or already a target of oppression.

Like Levi, I understand gray zones more specifically to result from choices that are neither gratuitously nor willfully evil but that nevertheless implicate choosers who are themselves victims in perpetrating evils against others who are already also victims, paradigmatically victims of the same evils as the choosers. Like Levi, I also resist the idea that we are all murderers or oppressors, even when we benefit from murder and oppression by others. "I do not know," Levi wrote, "and it does not much interest me to know, whether in my depths there lurks a murderer, but I do know that I was a guiltless victim and that I was not a murderer."[69] To confuse murderers with their victims, he wrote, is "a moral disease or an aesthetic affectation or a sinister sign of complicity," "service rendered (intentionally or not) to the negators of truth."[70] I agree. Not everyone is a murderer. Cases such as Levi's own may be clear. Yet, as he also saw, it is not always clear who is "a guiltless victim." Moral grayness was not confined to the camps and ghettos, even during the Holocaust. Stella Goldschlag, whose family failed to escape Germany before the war, became a "catcher" for the Gestapo, hunting down hidden Jews in wartime Berlin in exchange for a promise not to send her family to Auschwitz. She survived the war and was interviewed by Peter Wyden, a former classmate whose family did escape just before the war, who wrote a book about her.[71] If she was not a murderer, she was not a "guiltless victim," either.

Concluding Thoughts

Conditions less extreme than those of the Holocaust can produce some of the ambiguities and complexities of grayness. They set up victims of oppression to pass along oppressive practices to the next generation. The evils of everyday misogyny, racism, homophobia, and anti-semitism are not always imminent or looming in the form of well-defined events. They take shape gradually, over a lifetime or even centuries. They are less readily noticed or identified, and yet they shape our options and perceptions. They may inflict social rather than biological death, or permanent deformation, disability, or unremitting pain. They can produce self-hatred.

Two decades ago radical feminist philosopher Mary Daly wrote in *Gyn/Ecology: The Metaethics of Radical Feminism* of mothers who bound their tiny daughters' feet and of mothers who participate in the surgical imposition on very young daughters of clitoridectomy and infibulation.[72] These mothers were not under death threats. No spectacular events precipitated their action. They were not quite in a gray zone. And yet, important elements of the gray zone apply. Instead of clearly identifiable stress factors in the form of threats to their lives and basic security, their whole lives prepared them to do as they did. Their own mothers had done the same to them, and likewise their mothers before them. They acted for their daughters' marriageability, not necessarily to advance their own personal standing. They may have known no other ways to secure a tolerable future for their daughters. But those were choices that implicated them in the evils of marriage systems that deformed and immobilized women, including themselves.

Like Levi in commenting on many prisoners in the camps, Daly refused to judge mothers who did these things. She called them "token torturers." Critics rightly find that term troubling when applied indiscriminately to all women in sexist society who participate in atrocities. Daly's account could have benefited from some of the distinctions introduced by the concept of the gray zone. They would have enabled her to distinguish foot-binding mothers, who were caught up in supporting practices that were just as oppressive to themselves as to their daughters, from such sadists as Irma Griese, Ilse Koch, and other National Socialist women in the camps, who were victims of nothing quite comparable to the evils they inflicted on others and whose choices were no grayer than those of the Indiana women of the Klan.

Daly and Levi reflected on others' past choices. One's position as a potential evaluator changes as one thinks more in a forward-looking and first-personal mode, as one who might find oneself in a morally gray area. In the forward-looking first-personal mode, a refusal to judge is apt to seem too quick an abdication of responsibility. Feminists have long struggled with the question of how ethically responsible agency is possible under oppression, given that oppressive practices are coercive. Perhaps outsiders are seldom in a position to judge. Yet who is and who is not an outsider may not be obvious. Daly is no outsider to misogyny, although she is to foot binding and clitoridectomy. Levi was no outsider to death camps, but he was to the Sonderkommando. But if outsiders should ordinarily refrain from judging, some victims may be able to imagine and create new alternatives and take responsibility for their choices in relation to other victims. Some mothers refused to bind their daughters' feet. Some women became marriage resisters.[73] If bonding and trust are still possible, so, it would seem, are obligation and responsibility. We may need more distinctions to clarify what such obligations and responsibilities imply.

Moral conclusions to draw from the gray zone are not simply about its inhabitants but also about the very production of gray zones. No doubt some gray zones are produced unintentionally, although they may result from other evils that were intentional. But just as clearly, many gray zones have been produced intentionally. If action within the gray zone is not unambiguously evil, the act of knowingly *producing* a gray zone has no such moral ambiguity. Knowingly creating gray zones may be the greatest of evil deeds. Levi called the creation of the Sonderkommando "National Socialism's most demonic crime." Gray zones jeopardize, erode, and destroy the character of decent people, making physiological death a mercy. They make murder by the oppressor no longer necessary, for within the gray zone, victims often enough take their own lives (like Adam Czerniakov and Fredy Hirsch) or the lives of family, friends, and neighbors.

Among survivors, some will have identified with oppressors. Some may continue to do so, thereby developing a real potential for evil, even diabolical evil. Gray zones are one way in which evil perpetuates itself, corrupting others who will, in turn, corrupt others. But in survivors who refuse to abdicate responsibility and somehow create ways to meet the challenges of extreme moral stress and or who, like Elie Cohen, remain ashamed when they think they have failed, the chain of evil is broken.

Notes

Chapter 1

1. On the idea of "family resemblance," see Ludwig Wittgenstein, *Philosophical Investigations*, trans. G. E. M. Anscombe (Oxford: Blackwell, 1958), pp. 31–33.

2. John Rawls, *A Theory of Justice*, rev. ed. (Cambridge, Mass.: Harvard University Press, 1999), p. 5. Unless otherwise specified, further references to Rawls are to the revised edition.

3. On the Tuskegee syphilis experiment, see James H. Jones, *Bad Blood: The Tuskegee Syphilis Experiment* (New York: Free Press, 1993).

4. See Norman F. Cantor, *In the Wake of the Plague: The Black Death and the World It Made* (New York: Free Press, 2001), pp. 147–67.

5. W. D. Ross, *The Right and the Good* (Oxford: Clarendon Press, 1930), pp. 16–47; H. A. Prichard, *Moral Obligation: Essays and Lectures* (Oxford: Clarendon Press, 1957); Rawls, *A Theory of Justice*, pp. 52–56, 98–101.

6. Stanley Milgram, *Obedience to Authority* (New York: Harper and Row, 1974); Craig Haney, Curtis Banks, and Philip Zimbardo, "Interpersonal Dynamics in a Simulated Prison," *International Journal of Criminology and Penology* 1 (1973): 69–97. Milgram and Zimbardo were briefly colleagues at Yale.

7. Ervin Staub, *The Roots of Evil: The Origins of Genocide and Other Group Violence* (Cambridge: Cambridge University Press, 1989).

8. B. F. Skinner, *Walden Two* (New York: Macmillan, 1948).

9. Susan Nieman argues that the classical theological problem of evil should be just as ethically interesting to nontheists, in "Metaphysics, Philosophy: Rousseau on the Problem of Evil," in Andrews Reath, Barbara Herman, and Christine M. Korsgaard, eds., *Reclaiming the History of Ethics: Essays for John Rawls* (Cambridge: Cambridge University Press, 1997), pp. 140–69.

10. Hastings Rashdall, *Theory of Good and Evil: A Treatise on Moral Philosophy*, 2 vols. (London: Oxford University Press, 1924).

11. W. D. Ross, *The Right and the Good*.

12. Henry Sidgwick, *The Methods of Ethics*, 7th ed. [1907] (New York: Dover, 1966).

13. Rawls, *A Theory of Justice*, pp. 385–86.

14. Mary Midgley, *Wickedness: A Philosophical Essay* (London: Routledge and Kegan Paul, 1984).

15. Laurence Mordekhai Thomas, *Vessels of Evil: American Slavery and the Holocaust* (Philadelphia: Temple University Press, 1993), p. 74.

16. Hannah Arendt, *Eichmann in Jerusalem: A Report on the Banality of Evil*, rev. and enlarged ed. (New York: Viking, 1965).

17. Friedrich Nietzsche, *On the Genealogy of Morality: A Polemic*, trans. Maudemarie Clark and Alan J. Swensen (Indianapolis: Hackett, 1998), pp. 9–33.

18. For a fascinating account, see Mary Ann Glendon, *A World Made New: Eleanor Roosevelt and the Universal Declaration of Human Rights* (New York: Random House, 2001).

19. For the declaration, see Glendon, *A World Made New*, pp. 310–14.

20. Glendon, *A World Made New*, pp. 73–78; 147.

21. Primo Levi, *The Drowned and the Saved*, trans. Raymond Rosenthal (New York: Vintage, 1989); Ronald Milo, *Immorality* (Princeton: Princeton University Press, 1984); Stanley I. Benn, "Wickedness," *Ethics* (1985): 795–810; John Kekes, *Facing Evil* (Princeton: Princeton University Press, 1990) and *Against Liberalism* (Ithaca: Cornell University Press, 1997); Nel Noddings, *Women and Evil* (Berkeley: University of California Press, 1989); Robin Schott, "Philosophical Reflections on War Rape," in Claudia Card, ed., *On Feminist Ethics and Politics* (Lawrence: University Press of Kansas, 1999), pp. 173–99.

22. Jonathan Glover, *Humanity: A Moral History of the Twentieth Century* (New Haven: Yale University Press, 2000).

23. Arthur Schopenhauer, *On the Basis of Morality*, trans. E. F. J. Payne (Indianapolis: Bobbs- Merrill, 1965), pp. 120–98, and Schopenhauer, *The World as Will and Representation*, trans. E. F. J. Payne, (New York: Dover, 1969), 1: 271–412.

24. The evil status of the use of nuclear and other bombs against civilian populations remains controversial in the United States, which has never apologized for its bombings of Hiroshima and Nagasaki, nor for its fire bombing of Tokyo.

25. Gail A. Eisnitz, *Slaughterhouse: The Shocking Story of Greed, Neglect, and Inhumane Treatment Inside the U. S. Meat Industry* (Amherst, N.Y.: Prometheus, 1997); Eric Schlosser, *Fast Food Nation: The Dark Side of the All-American Meal* (New York: Houghton Mifflin, 2001).

26. For elaboration of the idea that some nonhuman primates have a degree of moral agency, see Frans de Waal, *Good Natured: The Origins of Right and Wrong in Human and Other Animals* (Cambridge, Mass.: Harvard University Press, 1996) and *Peacemaking Among Primates* (Cambridge, Mass.: Harvard University Press, 1989).

27. Roy F. Baumeister, *Evil: Inside Human Cruelty and Violence* (New York: Freeman, 1997), pp. 18–19.

28. Baumeister, *Evil*, p. 46.

29. On the role of the *Protocols of the Elders of Zion* in National Socialism, see Norman Cohn, *Warrant for Genocide: The Myth of the Jewish World-Conspiracy and the Protocols of the Elders of Zion* (London: Eyre and Spottiswoode, 1967); on the "blood libel" against the Jews, see Alan Dundes, ed., *The Blood Libel Legend: A Casebook in Anti-Semitic Folklore* (Madison: University of Wisconsin Press, 1991).

30. Levi, *The Drowned and the Saved*, pp. 105–26.

31. For a focus on perpetrator psychology, see, in addition to Staub's treatise and the Milgram and Zimbardo studies already mentioned, Erich Fromm, *Anatomy of Human Destructiveness* (New York: Holt, Rinehart, and Winston, 1973); Alice Miller,

For Your Own Good: Hidden Cruelty in Child-Rearing and the Roots of Violence, trans. Hildegarde Hannum and Hunter Hannum (New York: Farrar, Straus, Giroux, 1983) and *Thou Shalt Not Be Aware: Society's Betrayal of the Child*, trans. Hildegarde Hannum and Hunter Hannum (New York: Farrar, Straus, Giroux, 1984). On victims' responses to trauma, see Judith Lewis Herman, *Trauma and Recovery* (New York: Basic Books, 1992); Shoshana Felman and Dori Laub, *Testimony: Crises of Witnessing in Literature, Psychoanalysis, and History* (New York: Routledge, 1992); and Jonathan Shay, *Achilles in Vietnam: Combat Trauma and the Undoing of Character* (New York: Atheneum, 1994).

32. Martha Minow, *Between Vengeance and Forgiveness: Facing History After Genocide and Mass Violence* (Boston: Beacon, 1998).

33. Kekes, *Facing Evil*, p. 3.

34. He understands evil as unjustified harm "serious enough to damage its victims' capacity to function normally." Kekes, *Against Liberalism*, p. 26.

35. Levi, *The Drowned and the Saved*, p. 53.

36. *New York Times*, 15 June 1999, pp. D1, 4.

37. David Hume, *Dialogues Concerning Natural Religion*, Part 10, in *Hume's Ethical Writings: Selections from David Hume*, ed. Alasdair MacIntyre (New York: Collier, 1965), p. 315; John Stuart Mill, "Nature," in *The Philosophy of J. S. Mill: Ethical, Political, and Religious*, ed. Marshall Cohen (New York: Modern Library, 1961), pp. 468–69.

38. John Grisham's novel *The Chamber* (New York: Doubleday, 1994) is a powerful example.

39. Aristotle, *The Nicomachean Ethics*, trans. David Ross (New York: Oxford University Press, 1925), p. 38, "For instance, both fear and confidence and appetite and anger and pity and in general pleasure and pain may be felt both too much and too little, and in both cases not well; but to feel them at the right times, with reference to the right objects, towards the right people, with the right motive, and in the right way, is what is both intermediate and best, and this is characteristic of virtue," and p. 45, "For in everything it is no easy task to find the middle. . . . [A]nyone can get angry—that is easy—or give or spend money; but to do this to the right person, to the right extent, at the right time, with the right motives, and in the right way, *that* is not for everyone, nor is it easy; wherefore goodness is both rare and laudable and noble." Aristotle's critics tend to misunderstand his "mean" as a simpler, more quantitative notion, as, for example, Kant, who took Aristotle to task, arguing "What distinguishes avarice (as a vice) from thrift (as a virtue) is not that avarice carries thrift *too far* but that avarice has an entirely *different principle* (maxim)." *The Doctrine of Virtue: Part II of the Metaphysic of Morals*, trans. Mary J. Gregor (Philadelphia: University of Pennsylvania Press, 1964), footnote, p. 65.

40. Rachel Carson, *Silent Spring* (Boston: Houghton Mifflin, 1962).

41. Kristin S. Shrader-Frechette, *Burying Uncertainty: Risk and the Case Against Geological Disposal of Nuclear Waste* (Berkeley: University of California Press, 1993), p. 1.

42. Charles Larmore, *The Morals of Modernity* (Cambridge: Cambridge University Press, 1996). More specifically, his position is that we can sometimes rank incommensurable values.

43. Michael Burleigh, *Death and Deliverance: "Euthanasia" in Germany c. 1900–1945* (New York: Cambridge University Press, 1994).

44. Steven T. Katz, *The Holocaust and Mass Death Before the Modern Age*, vol. I of *The Holocaust in Historical Context* (New York: Oxford University Press, 1994).

45. Thomas, *Vessels of Evil*, pp. 9–11.

46. Ibid., pp. 7–8. On the concept of natal alienation, see Orlando Patterson, *Slavery and Social Death* (Cambridge, Mass.: Harvard University Press, 1982).

47. Hitler's so-called euthanasia program was a program of outright murder. See Henry Friedlander, *Origins of Nazi Genocide: From Euthanasia to the Final Solution* (Chapel Hill: University of North Carolina Press, 1995). The term "euthanasia" functions here as an instance of what George Orwell in his novel *1984* (New York: New American Library, 1961) called "double- think," whereby a term is used to mean its opposite. The ill and disabled murdered in the "euthanasia program" had horrible deaths, not good ones.

48. Claudia Card, *The Unnatural Lottery: Character and Moral Luck* (Philadelphia: Temple University Press, 1996), pp. 72–96, esp. 90–96.

49. In the first edition of *A Theory of Justice* (Cambridge, Mass.: Harvard University Press, 1971), see pp. 62, 92. In the revised edition, on p. xiii, as in *Political Liberalism* (New York: Columbia University Press, 1993), p. 178–90, Rawls redefined primary goods as goods necessary to the development of two moral powers: the capacity for a conception of the good and the sense of justice. The list remains roughly the same, although Rawls notes that it is expandable.

50. Thanks to Susan Bordo for noticing the differences between these formulas and pressing me to think about the significance of the difference.

51. Jeremy Bentham, *An Introduction to the Principles of Morals and Legislation* (New York: Hafner, 1948), p. 170; Anthony Flew, "The Justification of Punishment," p. 85. *Philosophy* 29, 3 (1954): 291–307.

52. For examples, see Barry Scheck, Peter Neufeld, and Jim Dwyer, *Actual Innocence: Five Days to Execution, and Other Dispatches from the Wrongly Convicted* (New York: Doubleday, 2000).

53. See Marcus G. Singer, *Generalization in Ethics* (New York: Knopf, 1961), pp. 311–18.

54. Thomas Hobbes, *De Cive, or The Citizen*, ed. Sterling P. Lamprecht (New York: Appleton- Century-Crofts, 1949), p. 79 (chap. 6).

55. Aristotle, *Nicomachean Ethics*, pp. 128–32, 134–36.

56. Kant, *Doctrine of Virtue*, pp. 79–81.

57. John Stuart Mill, *On Liberty*, in *The Philosophy of J. S. Mill: Ethical, Political, Religious*, ed. Marshall Cohen (New York: Modern Library, 1961), p. 276 (chap. 4).

58. For an instructive example, see Thomas's discussion of Rosa Parks in "Self Respect and Self Esteem," in Leonard Harris, *Philosophy Born of Struggle: Afro-American Philosophy from 1917* (Dubuque, Iowa: Kendall/Hunt, 1983), pp. 183–84.

59. Kant, *Groundwork of the Metaphysics of Morals*, 4:390, in Kant, *Practical Philosophy*, trans. Mary Gregor (Cambridge: Cambridge University Press, 1996), p. 45, and Barbara Herman, *The Practice of Moral Judgment* (Cambridge, Mass.: Harvard University Press, 1993), pp. 1–22. Kant's own understanding of evil motivation is given in his *Religion Within the Boundaries of Mere Reason*, in Kant, *Religion and Rational Theology*, trans. Allen W. Wood and George Di Giovanni (Cambridge: Cambridge University Press, 1997), pp. 57–215.

60. Malicious envy is understood by Kant in *The Doctrine of Virtue* and by Rawls, *A Theory of Justice*, pp. 464–68, as the desire that those better off suffer major harm, even if that would improve the lot of no one.

61. Arendt, *Eichmann in Jerusalem*, p. 90.

62. Gerald Dworkin and David Blumenfeld, "Punishment for Intentions," *Mind* 75 (1966): 396- 404; see also Herbert Morris, "Punishment for Thoughts," *The Monist* 49 (1965): 342–76.

63. Roughly the same distinction is made with a different vocabulary by Kant and Schopenhauer, who sometimes distinguish between motives and incentives, understanding desires as incentives and understanding a motive as the higher order choice to act on an incentive (to let that incentive determine one's more specific choice). Incentives (desires or inclinations) move us toward a range of choices but do not make the choice for us. They can exist in tension with other incentives. One can experience the attraction of evil incentives but choose not to act on them.

64. The conference, called "The Prism of Sex," was sponsored by the Women's Research Institution of Wisconsin, Inc. Many of its papers were published in *The Prism of Sex: Essays in the Sociology of Knowledge: Proceedings of a Symposium*, ed. Julia A. Sherman and Evelyn Torton Beck (Madison: University of Wisconsin Press, 1979). Mary Daly did not consent to have her presentation included in that volume. But the material she presented can be found in her *Gyn/Ecology: The Metaethics of Radical Feminism* (Boston: Beacon, 1978), pp. 107–222.

65. Jeremy Bentham, *An Introduction to the Principles of Morals and Legislation* (New York: Hafner, 1948). This book is part of Bentham's project to reform the criminal law of England. Its concluding chapters are specifically devoted to the ethics of criminal punishment.

66. Martha Nussbaum, *The Fragility of Goodness: Luck and Ethics in Greek Tragedy and Philosophy* (Cambridge: Cambridge University Press, 1986).

67. Card, *Unnatural Lottery*, pp. 97–117.

68. Simon Wiesenthal, *The Sunflower: On the Possibilities and Limits of Forgiveness*, trans. H. A. Pichler, with a symposium edited by Harry James Cargas and Bonny V. Fetterman (New York: Schocken, 1997).

69. Levi, *The Drowned and the Saved*, pp. 36–69.

Chapter 2

1. Friedrich Nietzsche, *On the Genealogy of Morality: A Polemic*, trans. Maudemarie Clark and Alan J. Swensen (Indianapolis: Hackett, 1998). My reading of the *Genealogy* is influenced by the Nietzsche scholarship of Walter Kaufmann, his student Ivan Soll, and his student Maudemarie Clark, although they are not to blame for the feminist lens through which I read. See Walter Kaufmann, *Nietzsche: Philosopher, Psychologist, Antichrist*, 4th ed. (Princeton: Princeton University Press, 1974), and Maudemarie Clark, *Nietzsche on Truth and Philosophy* (New York: Cambridge University Press, 1990). See also Clark, "Nietzsche's Immoralism and the Concept of Morality," and Soll, "Nietzsche on Cruelty, Asceticism, and the Failure of Hedonism," both in *Nietzsche, Genealogy, Morality: Essays on Nietzsche's On the Genealogy of Morals*, ed. Richard Schacht (Berkeley: University of California Press, 1994).

2. Nietzsche, *Genealogy*, p. 5.

3. Ibid.

4. Ibid., p. 51.

5. Ibid., p. 53.

6. Ludwig Wittgenstein, *Philosophical Investigations*, trans. G. E. M. Anscombe (Oxford: Blackwell, 1958), p. 32e.

7. Ray Monk, *Ludwig Wittgenstein: The Duty of Genius* (New York: Free Press, 1990), pp. 121–23.

8. "Query: Nietzsche/Mauthner/Wittgenstein," North American Nietzsche Society *Nietzsche News* 18 (Spring 1996): 6. Ludwig Wittgenstein, *Tractatus Logico Philosophicus*, the German text of *Logisch-philosophische Abhadlung*, English trans. D. F. Pears and B. F. McGuinness (New York: Humanities, 1961).

9. Aristotle, *The Nicomachean Ethics*, trans. David Ross (Oxford: Oxford University Press, 1925) [7:1148b], p. 171.

10. Nietzsche, *Genealogy*, pp. 35–66.

11. For articulate and vigorous defense of the view that Nietzsche's last six books reject his earlier skepticism about truth, see Clark, *Nietzsche on Truth and Philosophy*.

12. *Friedrich Nietzsche Sämtliche Werke Kritische Studienausgabe*, ed. Giorgio Colli and Mazzino Montinari (New York: Verlag de Gruyter, 1967), *Band 5*, p. 253.

13. Thanks to Mabel Maier, who taught me, on machines of more than forty years ago, all the sewing I know.

14. Thomas Nagel, *The View from Nowhere* (New York: Oxford University Press, 1986).

15. Thanks to Robin Schott for raising this issue in discussion of an ancestor of this chapter at the University of Copenhagen in 1996.

16. Nietzsche, *Genealogy*, pp. 28–30.

17. For Jesus' Sermon on the Mount, see Matthew 5:3—7:27; a shorter version is also in Luke 6:20–49.

18. Virginia Held, in *Feminist Morality: Transforming Culture, Society, and Politics* (Chicago: University of Chicago Press, 1994), also takes this history seriously.

19. For more on gender in ethical theorizing, see my book *The Unnatural Lottery: Character and Moral Luck* (Philadelphia: Temple University Press, 1996), pp. 49–71.

20. See Marilyn Frye, *Willful Virgin: Essays in Feminism* (Freedom, Calif.: Crossing Press, 1992), pp. 59–75, for discussion of the idea of articulating the world from women's perspectives and the problems presented for that idea by an appreciation of differences among women.

21. Clark, *Nietzsche on Truth and Philosophy*. Thanks to Paul Eisenberg for discussion in correspondence of alternative interpretations of Nietzsche's evaluation of perspectives.

22. In addition to Harriet Jacobs's narrative, cited below, see, for example, *Six Women's Slave Narratives*, ed. William L. Andrews (New York: Oxford University Press, 1988), and *Great Slave Narratives*, ed. Arna Bontemps (Boston: Beacon, 1969).

23. Nietzsche, *Beyond Good and Evil*, in *Basic Writings of Nietzsche*, trans. Walter Kaufmann (New York: Modern Library, 1968), sec. 260, p. 394.

24. Carol Gilligan, *In a Different Voice: Psychological Theory and Women's Development* (Cambridge, Mass.: Harvard University Press, 1982). For further developments, see also her "Moral Orientation and Moral Development," in *Women and Moral Theory*, ed. Eva Feder Kittay and Diana T. Meyers (Totowa, N.J.: Rowman and Littlefield, 1987), pp. 19–33; *Mapping the Moral Domain: A Contribution of Women's Thinking to Psychological Theory and Education*, ed. Carol Gilligan, Janie Victoria Ward, and Jill McLean Taylor, with Betty Bartige (Cambridge, Mass.: Harvard Graduate School of Education, 1988); and "Hearing the Difference:Theorizing Connection," *Hypatia* 10,2 (Summer 1995): 120–27, in which she acknowledges a distinction between "feminine" and "feminist," not clearly present in her earlier work.

25. Nel Noddings, *Caring: A Feminine Approach to Morality and Education* (Berkeley: University of California Press, 1984) and *Women and Evil* (Berkeley: University of

California Press, 1989); Sarah Lucia Hoagland, *Lesbian Ethics: Toward New Value* (Palo Alto, Calif.: Institute for Lesbian Studies, 1988).

26. Claudia Card, "On Mercy," *Philosophical Review* 81 (1972): 182–207.

27. Claudia Card, "Women's Voices and Ethical Ideals: Must We Mean What We Say?" *Ethics* 99 (1988): 125–35; *The Unnatural Lottery*, pp. 49–71.

28. For the view that Nietzsche indulges in victim-blaming of women and of slaves generally, see Lynne Tirrell, "Sexual Dualism and Women's Self-Creation: On the Advantages and Disadvantages of Reading Nietzsche for Feminists," in *Nietzsche and the Feminine*, ed. Peter J. Burgard (Charlottesville: University Press of Virginia, 1994), pp. 158–82.

29. Nietzsche, *Genealogy*, p. 19.

30. Nietzsche, *The Gay Science*, trans. Walter Kaufmann (New York: Vintage, 1974), p. 126; cf. Tirrell, "Sexual Dualism."

31. Nietzsche, *Beyond Good and Evil*, p. 399.

32. Nietzsche, *Genealogy* 1:8–10, pp. 17–21.

33. For a fictionalized portrayal of Jefferson's relationship with his slave Sally Hemings, see Barbara Chase-Riboud, *Sally Hemings: A Novel* (New York: Viking, 1979). For historical inquiry, see Annette Gordon-Reed, *Thomas Jefferson and Sally Hemings: An American Controversy* (Charlottesville: University Press of Virginia, 1997), and Jan Ellen Lewis and Peter S. Onuf, eds., *Sally Hemings and Thomas Jefferson: History, Memory, and Civil Culture* (Charlottesville: University Press of Virginia, 1999).

34. Milton Meltzer, *Slavery: A World History* (New York: Da Capo, 1993), p. iv: "Most of us—no matter what our color or where in the world we came from—have ancestors who at one time or another were slaves or, to put it morally, shared in the guilt of enslaving others. Many . . . were both: slaves at one time and masters at another."

35. On the "Sambo" and "Uncle Tom" controversies, see Howard McGary and Bill E. Lawson, *Between Slavery and Freedom: Philosophy and American Slavery* (Bloomington: Indiana University Press, 1992). See also Stanley M. Elkins, *Slavery: A Problem in American Institutional and Intellectual Life* (Chicago: University of Chicago Press, 1959).

36. Nikki Giovanni, *Gemini: An Extended Autobiographical Statement on My First Twenty-Five Years of Being a Black Poet* (New York: Penguin, 1976), p. 97.

37. Nietzsche, *The Gay Science*, trans. Walter Kaufmann (New York: Vintage, 1974), pp. 316- 17.

38. Bernard Boxill, "Self-Respect and Protest," in *Philosophy Born of Struggle: Afro-American Philosophy from 1917*, ed. Leonard Harris (Dubuque, Iowa: Kendall/Hunt, 1983), p. 197.

39. Robert J. Lifton, *The Nazi Doctors: Medical Killing and the Psychology of Genocide* (New York: Basic Books, 1986). Lifton argues that the Nazi doctors who worked in the camps developed two selves ("doubling"), a camp self and a family self, each with different values.

40. For the long quote from Tertullian, see Nietzsche, *Genealogy*, pp. 28–30. For Jesus' Sermon on the Mount, see Matthew 5:3–7:27.

41. Nietzsche, *Genealogy*, p. 19.

42. For careful discussion of truth and falsification in the writing and critique of history, see Richard J. Evans, *Lying about Hitler: History, Holocaust, and the David Irving Trial* (New York: Basic Books, 2001).

43. See Edward Ball, *Slaves in the Family* (New York: Farrar, Straus and Giroux, 1998).

44. Immanuel Kant, *Observations on the Feeling of the Beautiful and Sublime*, trans. John T. Goldthwait (Berkeley: University of California Press, 1960), pp. 76–96. Jean Jacques Rousseau, *Emile*, trans. Barbara Foxley (New York: Dutton, 1966), pp. 321–414.

45. Harriet Jacobs, *Incidents in the Life of a Slave Girl*, ed. Lydia Maria Child (New York: Harcourt, Brace, Jovanovich, 1973), p. 88.

46. Toni Morrison, *Beloved* (New York: Knopf, 1987).

47. Flavius Josephus, *The Jewish War*, trans. G. A. Williamson (1959; rev. ed. E. Mary Smallwood, London: Penguin, 1981), esp. chap. 23, pp. 387–408. The story is reported by Josephus to have been told by an old woman who escaped with another woman and five children by hiding in the water conduits. See Andrea Dworkin, *Mercy* (New York: Four Walls Eight Windows, 1991), ch. 10, pp. 273–307, for protest of the assumption that the women's and children's deaths were suicides.

48. Nietzsche, *Genealogy*, p. 19.

49. Ibid., p. 19.

50. Mary Daly, *Beyond God the Father: Toward a Philosophy of Women's Liberation* (Boston: Beacon, 1973), ch. 2, "Exorcising Evil from Eve," pp. 44–68.

51. Nietzsche, *Genealogy*, p. 16.

52. "The New Misandry," in *Amazon Expedition*, ed. Phyllis Birkby et al. (New York: Times Change Press, 1973), pp. 27–32.

Chapter 3

1. These are the types of theories most widely discussed in philosophy journals and most commonly taught in university philosophy departments in the United States today. For an overview, see Marcia W. Baron, Philip Pettit, and Michael Slote, *Three Methods of Ethics: A Debate* (Malden, Mass.: Blackwell, 1997), with essays on Kantian ethics, consequentialism, and virtue ethics. The standard texts for these three types of theory, available in many editions, are selections from Jeremy Bentham, *Introduction to the Principles of Morals and Legislation*; Immanuel Kant, *Groundwork of the Metaphysics of Morals*; John Stuart Mill, *Utilitarianism* and *On Liberty*; and Aristotle, *The Nicomachean Ethics*.

2. Books 8 and 9 of Aristotle's *Nicomachean Ethics*, trans. David Ross (Oxford: Oxford University Press, 1925), are on friendship. Kant discusses friendship in his *Lectures on Ethics*, ed. Peter Heath and J. B. Schneewind, trans. Peter Heath (Cambridge: Cambridge University Press, 1997), pp. 184–90, and in *The Metaphysics of Morals*, in Kant, *Practical Philosophy*, trans. Mary Gregor (Cambridge: Cambridge University Press, 1996), pp. 584–88. See also Marilyn Friedman, *What Are Friends For? Feminist Perspectives on Moral Relationships and Moral Theory* (Ithaca: Cornell University Press, 1993).

3. Jeremy Bentham, *The Theory of Legislation*, trans. from the French of Etienne Dumont by Richard Hildreth (London: Routledge and Kegan Paul, 1931), p. 2: "*Evil* is pain, or the cause of pain." Cf. Bentham, *An Introduction to the Principles of Morals and Legislation* (New York: Hafner, 1948), p. 102: "[P]ain is in itself an evil; and, indeed, without exception, the only evil."

4. Kant, *Groundwork of the Metaphysics of Morals*, in Kant, *Practical Philosophy*, pp. 73, 80.

5. Hannah Arendt, *Eichmann in Jerusalem: A Report on the Banality of Evil*, rev. and enlarged ed. (New York: Viking, 1965). See, for example, John Kekes, *Facing Evil*

(Princeton: Princeton University Press, 1990), for an account of evil influenced by Aristotle's ethics. This view is also supported by Christopher Browning in *Ordinary Men: Reserve Police Battalion 101 and the Final Solution in Poland* (New York: Harper Perennial, 1998).

6. John Rawls, *A Theory of Justice*, rev. ed. (Cambridge, Mass.: Harvard University Press, 1999), pp. 26–27.

7. For interesting discussions of Kant in relation to virtue ethics, see Marcia Baron, "Kantian Ethics," in Baron, Pettit, and Slote, *Three Methods of Ethics*, pp. 3–91; Barbara Herman, *The Practice of Moral Judgment* (Cambridge, Mass.: Harvard University Press, 1993); Martha Nussbaum, "Virtue Ethics: A Misleading Category?" *Journal of Ethics* 3 (1999): 163–201.

8. John Stuart Mill, "Utilitarianism" in *The Philosophy of John Stuart Mill: Ethical, Political and Religious*, ed. Marshall Cohen (New York: Modern Library, 1961), p. 337. Further references to Mill will cite pages in this edition, using "U" for *Utilitarianism* or "L" for *On Liberty*.

9. A prominent example is Australian philosopher Peter Singer (now at Princeton), whose concerns extend to all sentient beings. See his *Animal Liberation*, new rev. ed. (New York: Avon, 1991), and *Practical Ethics* (Cambridge: Cambridge University Press, 1979).

10. See, for example, Richard Brandt, *Ethical Theory: Problems of Normative and Critical Ethics* (Englewood Cliffs, N.J.: Prentice-Hall, 1959), pp. 364–65.

11. For a critique of this problem, see Kurt Baier, *The Moral Point of View: A Rational Basis of Ethics* (Ithaca: Cornell University Press, 1958).

12. See, for example, *Utilitarianism: John Stuart Mill, with Critical Essays*, ed. Samuel Gorovitz (New York: Bobbs-Merrill, 1971).

13. John Rawls, "Justice as Fairness," *The Philosophical Review* 67 (1958): 164–94. For the discussion of slavery, see pp. 187–93.

14. Tom Regan's "worse off" principle in *The Case for Animal Rights* (Berkeley: University of California Press, 1983), pp. 301–12, is tailored to avoid this consequence: "Special considerations aside, when we must decide to override the rights of the many or the rights of the few who are innocent, and when the harm faced by the few would make them worse-off than any of the many would be if any other option were chosen, then we ought to override the rights of the many." If we substitute "inflict harm on" for "override the rights of," the basic idea is the same.

15. It does not follow, of course, that without a leisure class there would be no poetry, music, or painting. The arts would no doubt have a different character and might not be preserved.

16. Actually, he puts his point hypothetically and in terms of pleasures, rather than in terms of a trade-off between pleasure and pain: "Of two pleasures, if there be one to which all or almost all who have experience of both give a decided preference . . . that is the most desirable pleasure. If one of the two is, by those who are competently acquainted with both, placed so far above the other that they prefer it, even though knowing it to be attended with a greater amount of discontent, and would not resign it for any quantity of the other pleasure . . . we are justified in ascribing to the preferred enjoyment a superiority in quality, so far outweighing quantity, as to render it, in comparison, of small account" (U, 332).

17. "Involuntary euthanasia" (a euphemism for murder) is not the same as *non-voluntary* euthanasia, which is not a euphemism, however controversial. Euthanasia is nonvoluntary when the person killed was unable to give or withhold consent (because

of such things as coma, brain damage, or infancy). It is *involuntary* when the person was able to consent but was not consulted or withheld consent.

18. For more on Mill's stoicism, see Marcus G. Singer, "Mill's Stoic Conception of Happiness and Pragmatic Conception of Utility," *Philosophy* 75 (2000): 25–47.

19. A classic and thorough taxonomy and critique of the varieties of utilitarianism is David Lyons, *Forms and Limits of Utilitarianism*, reprinted with corrections (Oxford: Clarendon Press, 1967).

20. Although John Rawls's "Two Concepts of Rules," *The Philosophical Review* 64 (1958): 3–32, is commonly cited and even reprinted as an example of a defense of rule-utilitarianism, Rawls's aims in that essay are more modest and more specific. He does not use the language of act and rule utilitarianism, and he does not endorse any kind of utilitarianism.

21. See, e.g., Brandt, *Ethical Theory*, pp.396–400. Marcus Singer does not regard his generalization argument (if the consequences of everyone's doing *x* would be undesirable, no one ought to do *x*) as a form of utilitarianism. See Singer, *Generalization in Ethics* (New York: Knopf, 1961). A theoretical difference between indirect utilitarianism and Kant's ethics, which it resembles, is that indirect utilitarianism appeals to the undesirability of the hypothetical consequences, whereas Kant appeals to the idea of contradiction in the will.

22. Rawls, "Two Concepts of Rules," p. 23.

23. Mill's discussion of rules occurs near the end of chapter 2 of *Utilitarianism* (U 348–52). See J. O. Urmson, "The Interpretation of the Moral Philosophy of J. S. Mill," *Philosophical Quarterly* 3 (1953): 33–39.

24. J. D. Mabbott uses the terms "direct" and "indirect" this way in "Punishment," *Mind* n.s. 48 (1939): 152–67.

25. Rawls, *A Theory of Justice*, pp. 52–58, 266–67; John Rawls, *Political Liberalism* (New York: Columbia University Press, 1993), p. 291.

26. Rawls, *A Theory of Justice*, p. 54. In the first edition, on p. 62, the first six primary goods are listed as "rights and liberties, powers and opportunities, income and wealth"; in the revised edition, on p. 54, the first five primary goods are given as "rights, liberties, and opportunities, and income and wealth"; "powers" are not mentioned. In *Political Liberalism* (New York: Columbia University Press, 1993), pp. 181–82, he adds "freedom of movement and free choice of occupation" and suggests that an expanded list might also include leisure time and freedom from physical pain.

27. Rawls, *Political Liberalism*, pp. 178–90; TJ, p. xiii.

28. John Rawls, *Collected Papers*, ed. Samuel Freeman (Cambridge, Mass.: Harvard University Press, 1999), pp. 529–72.

29. Avishai Margalit, *The Decent Society*, trans. Naomi Goldblum (Cambridge, Mass.: Harvard University Press, 1996); John Rawls, *The Law of Peoples* (Cambridge, Mass.: Harvard University Press, 1999), p. 3, n. 2.

30. Rawls, *A Theory of Justice*, pp. 251–52.

31. On the revised understanding, primary goods are not simply what anyone can be presumed to want given their other wants (whatever they may be) but goods necessary for the development of our moral capacities for a sense of justice and a conception of the good life for ourselves.

32. A. A. Long and D. N. Sedley, *The Hellenistic Philosophers*, vol. 1: *Translations of the Principal Sources with Philosophical Commentary* (Cambridge: Cambridge University Press, 1987). Further references to passages translated in this work are given in parentheses in the text with the translators' names and page number from this work.

33. *The Stoic and Epicurean Philosophers*, ed. and trans. Whitney J. Oates (New York: Modern Library, 1940), pp. 223–487. Further references to passages from Epictetus are given in parentheses in the text with the translator's name and page number from this work.

34. Martha C. Nussbaum, *The Fragility of Goodness: Luck and Ethics in Greek Tragedy and Philosophy* (Cambridge: Cambridge University Press, 1986), p. 5.

35. Martha C. Nussbaum and Jonathan Glover, eds. *Women, Culture, and Development: A Study of Human Capabilities* (Oxford: Clarendon Press, 1995).

36. Ibid., p. 377.

37. Ibid., pp. 378–79.

38. Lawrence C. Becker, *A New Stoicism* (Princeton: Princeton University Press, 1998).

39. Ibid., p. 81.

40. Ibid., p. 147.

41. Bernard Williams, *Moral Luck: Philosophical Papers, 1973–1980* (Cambridge: Cambridge University Press, 1981).

42. Rawls, *A Theory of Justice*, p. 82.

43. See Martha Nussbaum, "Political Animals: Luck, Love, and Dignity," *Metaphilosophy* 29,4 (Oct. 1998): 273–87.

44. Nussbaum, *The Fragility of Goodness*, pp. 327–421.

45. Whitney J. Oates and Eugene O'Neill, eds., *The Complete Greek Drama* (New York: Random House, 1938), 2:807–40.

46. Laurence Mordekhai Thomas, *Vessels of Evil: American Slavery and the Holocaust* (Philadelphia: Temple University Press, 1993), pp. 56–65.

47. Martha Nussbaum, "Equity and Mercy," *Philosophy and Public Affairs* 22,2 (Spring 1993): 83–125.

48. John Rawls, "The Sense of Justice," *Philosophical Review* 72 (1963): 281–305.

49. Attributed to Edmund Burke.

50. See Filip Müller, *Auschwitz Inferno: The Testimony of a Sonderkommando*, with literary collaboration by Helmut Freitag, ed. and trans. Susanne Flatauer (London: Routledge and Kegan Paul, 1979), pp. 102–11. Compare with cases offered by Becker in "Life on the Rack," *A New Stoicism*, pp. 146–47. Becker seems prepared to draw the stoic conclusion even in such cases.

51. Becker's view is less extreme, because he recognizes reciprocity in human interaction as a natural form that human agency takes.

52. For a stoic reading of Nietzsche, see Martha Nussbaum, "Pity and Mercy: Nietzsche's Stoicism," in *Nietzsche, Genealogy, Morality: Essays on Nietzsche's* On the Genealogy of Morals, ed. Richard Schacht (Berkeley: University of California Press, 1994), pp. 139–67.

53. Nussbaum and Glover, *Women, Culture, and Development*, pp. 61–104.

Chapter 4

1. Immanuel Kant, *Lectures on Ethics*, trans. Peter Heath (Cambridge: Cambridge University Press), pp. 186–89. Further references to Kant in the text cite in parentheses the page numbers and name of the translator in the Cambridge Edition English translations, preceded by pages in the Academy edition, using "G" for *Groundwork*, "CPrR" for *Critique of Practical Reason*, "MM" for *The Metaphysics of Morals* (all are found in

Kant, *Practical Philosophy*, trans. Mary Gregor, Cambridge: Cambridge University Press, 1996); "R" for *Religion within the Boundaries of Mere Reason* (found in Kant, *Religion and Rational Theology*, trans. and ed. Allen W. Wood and George di Giovanni, Cambridge: Cambridge University Press, 1996); and "LE" for the *Lectures on Ethics*.

2. Contrast, for example, his lecture on duties to oneself in the *Lectures on Ethics*: "It is already a breach of the duty to oneself if one accepts favours; for he who accepts favours creates debts that he cannot repay; he can never even the score with his benefactor, since the latter first did him the kindness of his own accord; if he returned the favour, he does it only insofar as the other preceded him in this, and thus remains forever owing thanks to him; but who will incur such debts? A debtor is at all times under the constraint of having to treat the person he is obliged to with politeness and flattery; if he does not, the benefactor soon lets him know of it, and often he has to circumvent the latter with many detours and greatly burden himself. But he who pays promptly for everything can act freely" (LE 27:341–42; Heath, 123) with his remarks on gratitude in *The Doctrine of Virtue*: "[The least degree of gratitude] involves not regarding a kindness received as a burden one would gladly be rid of (since the one so favoured stands a step lower than his benefactor, and this wounds his pride), but taking even the occasion for gratitude as a moral kindness, that is, as an opportunity given one to unite the virtue of gratitude with love of man, to combine the *cordiality* of a benevolent disposition with *sensitivity* to benevolence (attentiveness to the smallest degree of this disposition in one's thought of duty) and so to cultivate one's love of human beings" (emphasis in the original; MM 6:456; Gregor, 547).

3. In *Unnecessary Evil: History and Moral Progress in the Philosophy of Immanuel Kant* (Albany: State University of New York Press, 2001), Sharon Anderson-Gold argues that it is a mistake to read Kant's concern as simply with one's own moral purity because he is clearly concerned, in both the *Religion* and the essay "Idea for a Universal History with a Cosmopolitan Purpose" (in *Kant's Political Writings*, ed. Hans Reiss, trans. H. B. Nisbet [Cambridge: Cambridge University Press, 1970], pp. 41–53) with promoting a society in which people would not interact in ways that support propensities to evil. Still, it seems to me that his concern is fundamentally with moral purity, rather than with happiness, albeit the moral purity of an entire community, not just one's own.

4. John Silber, "The Ethical Significance of Kant's *Religion*," in Kant, *Religion Within the Limits of Reason Alone*, trans. Theodore M. Greene and Hoyt H. Hudson (New York: Harper and Row, 1960).

5. Barbara Herman, *The Practice of Moral Judgment* (Cambridge, Mass.: Harvard University Press, 1993), pp. 113–31.

6. Lawrence C. Becker, *A New Stoicism* (Princeton: Princeton University Press, 1998), p. 147.

7. Paul Taylor, *Respect for Nature: A Theory of Environmental Ethics* (Princeton: Princeton University Press, 1989); Gary L. Francione, *Animals, Property, and the Law* (Philadelphia: Temple University Press, 1995) and *Rain Without Thunder* (Philadelphia: Temple University Press, 1996).

8. For an interesting discussion of how Kant might resolve conflicts of duties (which he preferred to recognize as conflicts between the grounds of obligation), see the last chapter of Onora Nell, *Acting on Principle: An Essay on Kantian Ethics* (New York: Columbia University Press, 1975), esp. pp. 132–37.

9. Daniel Goldhagen, *Hitler's Willing Executioners* (New York: Knopf, 1996). The *Einsatzgruppen* were mobile killing units in German-occupied territories of eastern Eu-

rope during World War II, who slaughtered entire villages of Jews and other Russians, ordering victims to dig trenches, then shooting them at the edge of the trenches.

10. Christopher R. Browning, *Ordinary Men: Reserve Police Battalion 101 and the Final Solution in Poland* (New York: HarperCollins, 1998), pp. 55–70.

11. Richard Henry Dana, Jr., *Two Years Before the Mast: A Personal Narrative of Life at Sea* (New York: Penguin, 1981), p. 155.

12. S. I. Benn, "Wickedness," *Ethics* (1985): 795–810, esp. 805–10.

13. Bishop Joseph Butler, *Fifteen Sermons Preached at Rolls Chapel* (1725; reprint London: Bell and Sons, 1967), pp. 168–69.

14. Christine Korsgaard, *Sources of Normativity* (Cambridge: Cambridge University Press, 1996), pp. 250–51.

15. Jack Katz, *Seductions of Crime: Moral and Sensual Attractions in Doing Evil* (New York: Basic Books, 1988).

16. Korsgaard, *Sources of Normativity*, esp. chaps. 3 and 9, on "practical identities" and on evil.

17. Lorna Smith Benjamin, "An Interpersonal Theory of Personality Disorders," in *Major Theories of Personality Disorder*, ed. J. F. Clarkin and M. F. Lenzenweger (New York: Guilford Press, 1996), pp. 141–220; Harry Stack Sullivan, *The Interpersonal Theory of Psychiatry* (New York: Norton, 1953); George Herbert Mead, *Mind, Self, and Society* (Chicago: University of Chicago Press, 1943); John Bowlby, *The Making and Breaking of Affectional Bonds* (1979; reprint New York: Routledge, 1989), esp. pp, 126–60 and *Attachment and Loss*, vol. 1, *Attachment* (London: Hogart, 1969).

18. Compare Benn's discussion of "heteronomous wickedness" and "conscientious wickedness," pp. 800–804.

19. Robert Jay Lifton, *The Nazi Doctors: Medical Killing and the Psychology of Genocide* (New York: Basic Books, 1986).

20. Benjamin, "Interpersonal Theory," pp. 181–210. See Lorna Smith Benjamin, *Interpersonal Reconstructive Therapy (IRT)* (New York, Guilford, in press) for further development.

21. Bowlby, *Making and Breaking*, p. 129.

22. Kenneth Craik, *The Nature of Explanation* (Cambridge: Cambridge University Press, 1943), quoted in Inga Bretherton and Kristine A. Munholland, "Internal Working Models in Attachment Relationships: A Construct Revisited," in *Handbook of Attachment: Theory, Research, and Clinical Applications*, ed. Jude Cassidy and Philip R. Shaver (New York: Guilford, 1999), pp. 90–91; J. Z. Young, *A Model for the Brain* (London: Oxford University Press, 1964); Bowlby, *Attachment and Loss*, pp. 80–83.

23. Benjamin, "Interpersonal Theory," pp. 189–90.

24. For illustrations, see cases discussed throughout Lorna Smith Benjamin, *Interpersonal Diagnosis and Treatment of Personality Disorders*, 2d ed. (New York: Guilford, 1996). See also Benjamin, "Interpersonal Reconstructive Therapy for Passive-Aggressive Personality Disorder," APA Psychotherapy Videotape Series II (American Psychological Association, 1998).

25. Benjamin, *Interpersonal Diagnosis*, pp. 190–91.

26. Ibid., p. 191.

27. Thomas Hobbes, *Leviathan* (1651; reprint New York: Dutton, 1950), and *De Cive, The Citizen*, ed. Sterling P. Lamprecht (1642; New York: Appleton-Century-Crofts, 1949); Ayn Rand, *The Virtue of Selfishness* (New York: New American Library, 1964).

28. Lorna Smith Benjamin, "Every Psychopathology Is a Gift of Love," *Psychotherapy Research* 3,1 (1993): 1–24; cf. Benjamin, *Interpersonal Diagnosis*, passim.

29. This much discussed case is from Michael Stocker, "The Schizophrenia of Modern Ethical Theories," *Journal of Philosophy* 73,14 (12 Aug. 1976): 462.

30. Herman, *The Practice of Moral Judgment*, pp. 1–22.

Chapter 5

1. Shirley Jackson, *The Lottery and Other Stories* (1949; reprint New York: Farrar, Straus, and Giroux, 1982).

2. Philip P. Hallie, *Tales of Good and Evil, Help and Harm* (New York: Harper-Collins, 1997), pp. 96–99. See also Hallie, *Cruelty* (Middleton, Conn.: Wesleyan University Press, 1982) and *Lest Innocent Blood Be Shed: The Story of the Village of Le Chambon and How Goodness Happened There* (New York: Harper and Row, 1979).

3. Hallie, *Tales of Good and Evil*, pp. 93–101.

4. Harry Frankfurt, *The Importance of What We Care About* (Cambridge: Cambridge University Press, 1988), pp. 134–35.

5. Joseph Raz, *The Morality of Freedom* (Oxford: Clarendon Press, 1986), pp. 217–44.

6. Ibid., p. 235.

7. See Avishai Margalit, *The Decent Society*, trans. Naomi Goldblum (Cambridge, Mass.: Harvard University Press, 1996), for the idea that a decent society is one the institutions of which do not humiliate people but, on the contrary, manifest a certain basic respect for them.

8. See Emma Goldman, "The Traffic in Women," in Goldman, *Anarchism and Other Essays* (1917; reprint New York: Dover, 1969), pp. 177–94.

9. For an example of intolerable working conditions, see Eric Schlosser, *Fast Food Nation: The Dark Side of the All-American Meal* (Boston: Houghton Mifflin, 2001), pp. 169–90, on 1990s working conditions in U.S. slaughterhouses that supply the fast-food industry.

10. Catharine A. MacKinnon, *Feminism Unmodified: Discourses on Life and Law* (Cambridge, Mass.: Harvard University Press, 1987), pp. 32–45.

11. Martha Minow, *Making All the Difference: Inclusion, Exclusion, and American Law* (Ithaca: Cornell University Press, 1990).

12. Marilyn Frye, *The Politics of Reality: Essays in Feminist Theory* (Trumansburg, N.Y.: Crossing Press, 1983), pp. 2 ff.

13. Ibid., pp. 3–4.

14. Iris Marion Young, *Justice and the Politics of Difference* (Princeton: Princeton University Press, 1990), pp. 39–65.

15. On these elements of African American slavery, see Laurence Thomas, *Vessels of Evil: American Slavery and the Holocaust* (Philadelphia: Temple University Press, 1994).

16. I use the term "homophobia" with some hesitation, because what is usually called homophobia is a social hatred, rather than fear. See Claudia Card, "Homophobia and Lesbian/Gay Pride," in Card, *Lesbian Choices* (New York: Columbia University Press, 1995), pp. 151–68.

17. On the concept of "social death," see Orlando Patterson, *Slavery and Social Death* (Cambridge, Mass.: Harvard University Press, 1982).

18. Kathleen Barry, *Female Sexual Slavery* (Englewood Cliffs, N.J.: Prentice-Hall, 1979).

19. Edith Wharton, *The House of Mirth* (New York: Holt, Rinehart, and Winston, 1962).

20. I believe it was Paul Ziff who made this observation in the 1960s, but I have not been able to locate the passage.

21. William March, *The Bad Seed* (Hopewell, N.J.: Ecco Press, distributed by Norton, 1997).

22. See Card, "Homophobia and Lesbian/Gay Pride," pp. 151–68, for development of a similar argument regarding so-called homophobia.

23. Thanks to economist Barbara Bergmann for pressing me on this question.

24. Rawls shortens "lexicographical" (the ordering of entries in dictionaries) to "lexical."

25. Peter Unger, *Living High and Letting Die: Our Illusion of Innocence* (New York: Oxford University Press, 1996); Peter Singer, *Practical Ethics* (Cambridge: Cambridge University Press, 1969), pp. 158–81.

26. See Unger, *Living High*, pp. 24–25, for the cases he refers to as "the Envelope" and "the Sedan."

27. John Stuart Mill, *The Philosophy of John Stuart Mill: Ethical, Political and Religious*, ed. Marshall Cohen (New York: Modern Library, 1961), p. 332.

28. For a true case of nursing home multiple murder, see Lowell Cauffiel, *Forever and Five Days* (New York: Zebra Books, 1992).

29. Quoted, for example, in *Women in Sport: Issues and Controversies*, ed. Greta L. Cohen (Newbury Park, Calif.: Sage, 1993), p. 13.

30. Mary Daly, *Gyn/Ecology: The Metaethics of Radical Feminism* (Boston: Beacon, 1978); Susan Griffin, *Woman and Nature: The Roaring Inside Her* (New York: Harper and Row, 1978); Audre Lorde, *Sister Outsider: Essays and Speeches* (Trumansburg, N.Y.: Crossing Press, 1984); Andrea Dworkin, *Woman Hating* (New York: Dutton, 1974); María Lugones, "Playfulness, 'World'-Travelling, and Loving Perception," *Hypatia* 2 (1987): 3–19; Catharine MacKinnon, *Feminism Unmodified: Discourses on Life and Law* (Cambridge, Mass.: Harvard University Press, 1987), and Adrienne Rich, *On Lies, Secrets, and Silence: Selected Prose 1966- 1978* (New York: Norton, 1979).

31. Raz, *The Morality of Freedom*, p. 228. Thanks to Angelika Krebs for discussion of this distinction in personal correspondence.

32. Virginia Woolf, *Three Guineas* (New York: Harcourt, Brace and World, 1938).

33. Babylonian Talmud, Mishnah Sanhedrin, chap. 4, 37a.

Chapter 6

1. George Hicks, *The Comfort Women: Japan's Brutal Regime of Enforced Prostitution in the Second World War* (New York: Norton, 1994).

2. Ibid., pp. 152–67.

3. Human Rights Watch/Africa, Human Rights Watch Women's Rights Project, Fèdèration Internationale des Ligues des Droits de l'Homme, *Shattered Lives: Sexual Violence During the Rwandan Genocide and Its Aftermath* (New York: Human Rights Watch, 1996), p. 30.

4. Ibid., pp. 30–31.

5. Ibid., p. 27.

6. Ibid., p. 33.

7. Susan Brownmiller, *Against Our Will: Men, Women, and Rape* (New York: Simon and Schuster, 1975).

8. *Shattered Lives*, p. 32.

9. For an account of suppressed whistle-blowing regarding war crimes by U.S. officers during the war in Vietnam, see Anthony B. Herbert, with James T. Wooten, *Soldier* (New York: Dell, 1973).

10. Lt. Col. Dave Grossman, *On Killing: The Psychological Cost of Learning to Kill in War and Society* (Boston: Little, Brown, 1995).

11. Robin Schott, "Philosophical Reflections on War Rape," in Claudia Card, ed., *On Feminist Ethics and Politics* (Lawrence: University Press of Kansas, 1999), p. 188. According to Hannah Arendt, Eichmann actually did see some of the victims of Nazi murders firsthand. Still, the point remains that he was sheltered from most of it.

12. Stanley Milgram, *Obedience to Authority: An Experimental View* (New York: Harper, 1975), pp. 32–43.

13. John Conroy, *Unspeakable Acts, Ordinary People* (New York: Knopf, 2000), p. 256. The three episodes are the 1971 torture of Northern Irish men by the British, the 1988 torture of Arab men by Israeli soldiers during the *intifada*, and the 1982 torture by Chicago police of a man who killed two Chicago policemen.

14. Ibid., pp. 243–47.

15. Ibid., p. 249.

16. This feudal custom, referred to as *marquette*, was discussed from a radical feminist point of view in 1893 by Matilda Joslyn Gage, *Woman, Church, and State* (Watertown, Mass.: Persephone Press, 1980), pp. 66–93.

17. Friedrich Nietzsche, *On the Genealogy of Morality: A Polemic*, trans. Maudemarie Clark and Alan J. Swensen (Indianapolis: Hackett, 1998), pp. 38–39.

18. Carl Wellman, "On Terrorism Itself," *Journal of Value Inquiry* 13 (1979): 250–58; see esp. p. 254.

19. For graphic accounts of the classic *strappado* torture (a.k.a. "the rope"), see Jean Amery, *At the Mind's Limits: Contemplations by a Survivor on Auschwitz and Its Realities*, trans. Sidney Rosenfeld and Stella P. Rosenfeld (Bloomington: Indiana University Press, 1980), and Malise Ruthven, *Torture: The Grand Conspiracy* (London: Weidenfeld and Nicolson, 1978), pp. 3–7.

20. Claudia Card, *The Unnatural Lottery: Character and Moral Luck* (Philadelphia: Temple University Press, 1996), pp. 97–117.

21. For an exposé of fraternity gang rape, including testimony by former fraternity members who defected, see anthropologist Peggy Sanday, *Fraternity Gang Rape: Sex, Brotherhood, and Privilege on Campus* (New York: New York University Press, 1990).

22. A now classic essay on this topic, used in rape crisis training centers from coast to coast, is the first chapter of Susan Griffin, *Rape: The Power of Consciousness* (New York: Harper and Row, 1979). For more on the idea of misplaced gratitude, see Card, *The Unnatural Lottery*, pp. 118–39.

23. Alexandra Stiglmayer, ed., *Mass Rape: The War Against Women in Bosnia-Herzegovina*, trans. Marion Faber (Lincoln: University of Nebraska Press, 1993).

24. Brownmiller, *Against Our Will*, p. 33; Hyemeyohsts Storm, *Seven Arrows* (New York: Ballantine, 1972), pp. 106–9, offers a fictionalized portrayal of the rape of Native American women.

25. Brownmiller, *Against Our Will*, pp. 76–86.

26. Stiglmayer; *Shattered Lives*; Donatella Lorch, "Wave of Rape Adds New Horror to Rwanda's Trail of Brutality," *New York Times* 15 May 1995, A-1, A-4.

27. Milton Meltzer, *Slavery: A World History* (New York: Da Capo Press, 1993).

28. John Rawls, *A Theory of Justice*, rev. ed. (Cambridge, Mass.: Harvard University Press, 1999), p. 218.

29. See, for example, Mary Renault, *The Persian Boy* (New York: Pantheon, 1972).

30. Griffin, *Rape*. See also Susan Rae Peterson, "Coercion and Rape: The State as a Male Protection Racket," in *Feminism and Philosophy*, ed. Mary Vetterling-Braggin, Frederick A. Elliston, and Jane English (Totowa, N.J.: Littlefield, Adams, and Co., 1977), pp. 360–671; and Card, *The Unnatural Lottery*, pp. 97–117.

31. Nietzsche, *Genealogy*, p. 22.

32. Lorch, "Wave of Rape."

33. Achilles is said to have fallen in love with Penthesilia's corpse after he slew her, which some translators take to be a euphemistic way of saying that he raped her body.

34. Sara Ruddick in *Maternal Thinking: Towards a Politics of Peace* (Boston: Beacon, 1989).

35. For success stories, see *Stopping Rape: Successful Survival Strategies*, ed. Pauline B. Bart and Patricia H. O'Brien (Elmsford, N.Y.: Pergamon, 1985), and *Her Wits About Her: Self-Defense Success Stories by Women*, ed. Denise Caignon and Gail Groves (New York: Harper and Row, 1987).

36. Hugo A. Bedau, "Offenses Punishable by Death," in Bedau, ed., *The Death Penalty in America: An Anthology* (New York: Doubleday, 1964), p. 45.

37. A commentator on an earlier draft of this chapter suggested a suitably positioned scarlet "R."

38. On damaged identities suffered by transsexuals, see Hilde Lindemann Nelson, *Damaged Identities, Narrative Repair* (Ithaca: Cornell University Press, 2001), pp. 125–35.

39. Mary Daly, *Gyn/Ecology: The Metaethics of Radical Feminism* (Boston: Beacon, 1978); David Halberstam, *The Best and the Brightest* (New York: Random House, 1972).

40. Hicks reports, in *The Comfort Women*, that one survivor claimed that at war's end she and others killed the husband and wife who had been in charge of their comfort station. *Shattered Lives* includes testimony (p. 44) from a survivor who describes women participating in the Rwandan atrocities against other women.

41. See Robert Proctor, *Racial Hygiene: Medicine Under the Nazis* (Cambridge, Mass.: Harvard University Press, 1988), and Sheldon H. Harris, *Factories of Death: Japanese Biological Warfare 1932–45 and the American Cover-Up* (New York: Routledge, 1994).

42. Beverly Allen, *Rape Warfare: The Hidden Genocide in Bosnia-Herzegovina and Croatia* (Minneapolis: University of Minnesota Press, 1996), p. 78; Cherif Bassiouni, *United Nations Document S/25274* (cited in Allen, pp. 43–48).

43. Rezak Hukanović, *The Tenth Circle of Hell: A Memoir of Life in the Death Camps of Bosnia*, trans. Colleen London and Midhat Ridjanović (New York: Basic Books, 1996), pp. 35, 75–76.

44. Libby Tata Arcel in discussion following a symposium on martial rape at the University of Copenhagen, September 1996. See also *War Violence, Trauma, and the Coping Process: Armed Conflict in Europe and Survivor Response*, ed. Libby Tata Arcel (Copenhagen: Institute of Clinical Psychology, University of Copenhagen, 1998).

45. Marlise Simons, "For First Time, Court Defines Rape as War Crime," *New York Times*, 28 June 1996, A-1, 7.

46. Marlise Simons, "Three Serbs Convicted in Wartime Rapes," *New York Times*, 23 Feb. 2001, A-1.

47. On Lorna Smith Benjamin's theorizing about IPIRs, see chap. 4.

Chapter 7

1. Richard J. Gelles and Murray A. Straus, *Intimate Violence: The Causes and Consequences of Abuse in the American Family* (New York: Simon and Schuster, 1988), pp. 59–69.

2. See Angela Browne, *When Battered Women Kill* (New York: Free Press, 1987); Ann Jones, *Next Time She'll Be Dead: Battering and How to Stop It* (Boston: Beacon, 1994); Donna Ferrato, *Living with the Enemy* (New York: Aperture, 1991); Kathleen M. Heide, *Why Kids Kill Parents: Child Abuse and Adolescent Homicide* (Columbus: Ohio State University Press, 1992).

3. See, for example, Barry Scheck, Peter Neufeld, and Jim Dwyer, *Actual Innocence: Five Days to Execution and Other Dispatches from the Wrongly Convicted* (New York: Random House, 2000).

4. Women's Action Coalition, *WAC Stats: The Facts About Women* (New York: New Press, 1993), pp. 55–58 (sources listed on p. 58).

5. Michele E. Beasley and Dorothy Q. Thomas, "Domestic Violence as a Human Rights Issue," in Martha Albertson Fineman and Roxanne Mykitiuk, eds., *The Public Nature of Private Violence: The Discovery of Domestic Abuse* (New York: Routledge, 1994), pp. 329–30.

6. Beasley and Thomas, "Domestic Violence," pp. 326–27.

7. Denise Maupin, discussed by Hilde Lindemann Nelson in *Damaged Identities, Narrative Repair* (Ithaca: Cornell University Press, 2001), p. 140, was convicted in 1991 of aiding and abetting the first-degree murder of her two-year-old son, whom she left with her boyfriend while she went to work. Her boyfriend beat the child to death for wetting his pants. See also Dorothy E. Roberts, "Mothers Who Fail to Protect Their Children," in Julia E. Hanigsberg and Sara Ruddick, eds., *Mother Troubles: Rethinking Contemporary Maternal Dilemmas* (Boston: Beacon, 1999).

8. Quoted in Mildred Daley Pagelow, with the assistance of Lloyd W. Pagelow, *Family Violence* (New York: Praeger, 1984), p. 48; David Gil, *Violence Against Children* (Cambridge, Mass.: Harvard University Press, 1970), p. 6.

9. Marie Asch and Naomi R. Cahn, "Child Abuse: A Problem for Feminist Theory," in Fineman and Mykitiuk, *Public Nature*, p. 174.

10. Linda Gordon, *Heroes of Their Own Lives: The Politics and History of Family Violence* (New York: Viking, 1988), pp. 173 ff.

11. Pagelow, *Family Violence*, pp. 187, 191.

12. Ibid., p. 191.

13. Ibid., p. 196; Jessie Bernard, *The Future of Motherhood* (New York: Penguin, 1975), p. 67.

14. Adrienne Rich, *Of Woman Born: Motherhood as Experience and as Institution* (New York: Bantam, 1976), pp. 260–86.

15. Kate Millett, *The Basement: Meditations on a Human Sacrifice* (New York: Simon and Schuster, 1979).

16. Christina Crawford, *Mommie Dearest* (New York: Morrow, 1978).

17. Dave Pelzer, *A Child Called "It"* (Deerfield Beach, Fla.: Health Communications, Inc., 1995), first of a trilogy that also includes Pelzer, *The Lost Boy: A Foster Child's Search for the Love of a Family* (Deerfield Beach, Fla.: Health Communications, Inc., 1997) and Pelzer, *A Man Named Dave: A Story of Triumph and Forgiveness* (New York: Plume, 1999).

18. For arguments favoring distributed childcare for extremely dependent children, see Eva Feder Kittay, *Love's Labor: Essays on Women, Equality, and Dependency* (New York: Routledge, 1999). The greater need of the extremely dependent child for protection against abuse also supports her position.

19. R. M. Hare, "On Terrorism," *Journal of Value Inquiry* 13 (1979): 241–49; p. 244.

20. On the difficulties of defining terrorism, see Hare, "On Terrorism" (n. 1, supra); Carl Wellman, "On Terrorism Itself," *Journal of Value Inquiry* 13 (1979): 250–58; Grant Wardlaw, *Political Terrorism: Theory, Tactics, and Counter-Measures*, 2d ed., rev. (Cambridge: Cambridge University Press, 1982), pp. 3–17; and R. G. Frey and Christopher W. Morris, eds., *Violence, Terrorism, and Justice* (Cambridge: Cambridge University Press, 1991).

21. Tobias Wolff, *This Boy's Life: A Memoir* (New York: Atlantic Monthly Press, 1989), and Sue William Silverman, *Because I Remember Terror, Father, I Remember You* (Athens: University of Georgia Press, 1996).

22. Faith McNulty, *The Burning Bed* (New York: Harcourt Brace Jovanovich, 1980).

23. Beth Sipe and Evelyn J. Hale, *I Am Not Your Victim* (Thousand Oaks, Calif.: Sage, 1996); Charlotte Fedders and Laura Elliott, *Shattered Dreams* (New York: Dell, 1987). See note 2 above for relevant works by Browne, Ferrato, and Jones.

24. Judith Lewis Herman, *Trauma and Recovery* (New York: Basic Books, 1992), pp. 28–32.

25. Sue William Silverman, "We Must Rescue These Child POWs," *Chicago Tribune*, sec. 13, "Womanews," 6 April 1997.

26. Jones, *Next Time She'll Be Dead*, pp. 90–91.

27. The cage metaphor is from Marilyn Frye, "Oppression," in Frye, *The Politics of Reality: Essays in Feminist Theory* (Trumansburg, N.Y.: Crossing Press, 1983), pp. 4–7.

28. Kerry Lobel, *Naming the Violence: Speaking Out About Lesbian Battering* (Seattle, Wash.: Seal Press, 1986, p. 173.

29. Ibid., pp. 188–89.

30. Claire Renzetti, *Violent Betrayal: Partner Abuse in Lesbian Relationships* (Newbury Park, Calif.: Sage, 1992), p. 21.

31. Kathleen Barry, *Female Sexual Slavery* (Englewood Cliffs, N.J.: Prentice-Hall, 1979).

32. Joyce McConnell, "Beyond Metaphor: Battered Women, Involuntary Servitude, and the Thirteenth Amendment," *Yale Journal of Law and Feminism* 4,2 (Spring 1992): 207–53.

33. bell hooks, *Feminist Theory from Margin to Center* (Boston: South End Press, 1984), pp. 133–46.

34. Ibid., p. 144.

35. In defense of paying caregivers, see Kittay, *Love's Labor* and "A Feminist Public Ethic of Care Meets the New Communitarian Family Policy," *Ethics* 111,3 (April 2001): 523–47.

36. Patricia Hill Collins, *Black Feminist Thought: Knowledge, Consciousness, and the Politics of Empowerment* (New York: Routledge, 1991), chap. 6.

37. hooks, pp. 133–46.

38. Audre Lorde, *Sister Outsider: Essays and Speeches* (Trumansburg, N.Y.: Crossing Press, 1984), pp. 72–80.

39. Betty Berzon says her book *Permanent Partnerships: Building Lesbian and Gay Relationships That Last* (New York: Penguin, 1988) is about "reinventing our gay and lesbian relationships" and "learning to imbue them with all the *solemnity* of marriage without necessarily imitating the heterosexual model" (p. 7), and yet by the end of the book, it is difficult to think of anything in legal ideals of the heterosexual nuclear family that she has not urged us to imitate.

40. Mary Daly, *Gyn/Ecology: The Metaethics of Radical Feminism* (Boston: Beacon, 1978), pp. 113–72.

41. Laura M. Purdy, *In Their Best Interest? The Case Against Equal Rights for Children* (Ithaca: Cornell University Press, 1992).

42. See, for example, Kath Weston, *Families We Choose* (New York: Columbia University Press, 1991); Phyllis Burke, *Family Values: Two Moms and Their Son* (New York: Random House, 1993); and Suzanne Slater, *The Lesbian Family Life Cycle* (New York: Free Press, 1995). Berzon uses the term "partnership," reserving "family" for social structures based on heterosexual unions, as in chap. 12, subtitled "Integrating Your Families into Your Life as a Couple."

43. Richard D. Mohr, *A More Perfect Union: Why Straight America Must Stand Up for Gay Rights* (Boston: Beacon, 1994), pp. 31–53.

44. John Boswell, *Same-Sex Unions in Premodern Europe* (New York: Villard Books, 1994).

45. For examples of domestic partnership application forms, see Berzon, *Permanent Partnerships*, pp. 163–82.

46. Christine Pierce, "Gay Marriage," *Journal of Social Philosophy* 28,2 (1995): 5–16; Warren J. Blumenfeld, "Same-Sex Marriage: Introducing the Discussion," *Journal of Gay, Lesbian, and Bisexual Identity* 1,1 (1996): 77; Evan Wolfson, "Why We Should Fight for the Freedom to Marry: The Challenges and Opportunities That Will Follow a Win in Hawaii," *Journal of Lesbian, Gay, and Bisexual Identity* 1,1 (1996): 79–89; Victoria A. Brownworth, "Tying the Knot or the Hangman's Noose: The Case Against Marriage," *Journal of Gay, Lesbian, and Bisexual Identity* 1,1 (1996): 91–98; William Eskridge, *The Case for Same-Sex Marriage: From Sexual Liberty to Civilized Commitment* (New York: Free Press, 1996); Mark Strasser, *Legally Wed: Same Sex Marriage and the Constitution* (Ithaca: Cornell University Press, 1997); Ralph Wedgwood, "The Fundamental Argument for Same-Sex Marriage," *Journal of Political Philosophy* 7,3 (Dec. 1999): 225–42.

47. Mohr, *A More Perfect Union*, pp. 31–53.

48. Berzon, *Permanent Partnerships*, p. 266; Pierce, "Gay Marriage," p. 5.

49. Emma Goldman, "Marriage and Love," in *Anarchism and Other Essays* (New York: Dover, 1969).

50. Mohr, *A More Perfect Union*, pp. 49–50.

51. Boswell, *Same-Sex Unions*, note 19, supra.

52. On lesbian battering, see Renzetti; on gay battering, see David Island and Patrick Letellier, *Men Who Beat the Men Who Love Them: Battered Gay Men and Domestic Violence* (New York: Harrington Park Press, 1991).

53. See, for example, Sandra Faulkner, with Judy Nelson, *Love Match: Nelson vs. Navratilova* (New York: Birch Lane Press, 1993).

54. Pierce, "Gay Marriage," p. 13; cf. Christine Pierce, *Immovable Laws, Irresistible Rights* (Lawrence, Kans.: University Press of Kansas, 2000), pp. 105–114; Radclyffe Hall, *The Well of Loneliness* (New York: Pocket Books, 1950).

55. Claudia Card, *The Unnatural Lottery: Character and Moral Luck* (Philadelphia: Temple University Press, 1996), pp. 118–39.

56. Claudia Card, *Lesbian Choices* (New York: Columbia University Press, 1995), pp. 169–73.

57. Betty Mahmoody with William Hoffer, *Not Without My Daughter* (New York: St. Martin's, 1987).

58. Linda Lovelace with Mike McGrady, *Ordeal* (New York: Berkeley Books, 1981).

59. See Jeffner Allen, "Motherhood: The Annihilation of Women," in Joyce Trebilcot, ed., *Mothering: Essays in Feminist Theory* (Totowa, N.J.: Rowman and Allanheld, 1983).

60. John Boswell, *The Kindness of Strangers: The Abandonment of Children in Western Europe from Late Antiquity to the Renaissance* (New York: Pantheon, 1988).

61. Leslea Newman, *Heather Has Two Mommies* (Northampton, Mass.: In Other Words Publishing, 1989).

62. An outstanding anthology on the many varieties of lesbian parenting is Katherine Arnup, ed., *Lesbian Parenting: Living with Pride and Prejudice* (Charlottetown, P.E. I.: Gynergy Books, 1995). Also interesting is the anthropological study of lesbian mothers by Ellen Lewin, *Lesbian Mothers* (Ithaca: Cornell University Press, 1993). Both are rich in references to resources on both lesbian and gay parenting.

63. Kittay, *Love's Labor*, pp. 117–46.

64. Joan Williams, *Unbending Gender: Why Family and Work Conflict and What to Do About It* (Oxford: Oxford University Press, 2000).

65. Charlotte Perkins Gilman, *Herland*, in *Herland and Selected Stories by Charlotte Perkins Gilman*, ed. Barbara H. Solomon (New York: Signet, 1992); *Women and Economics: The Economic Factor Between Men and Women as a Factor in Social Evolution*, ed. Carl Degler (New York: Harper, 1966).

66. Virginia Held, *Feminist Morality: Transforming Culture, Society, and Politics* (Chicago: University of Chicago Press, 1993). Cf. Sara Ruddick, *Maternal Thinking: Toward a Politics of Peace* (Boston: Beacon, 1989); Nel Noddings, *Caring: A Feminine Approach to Ethics and Moral Education* (Berkeley: University of California Press, 1984); and Annette C. Baier, *Moral Prejudices: Essays on Ethics* (Cambridge, Mass.: Harvard University Press, 1994).

67. Held, *Feminist Morality*, p. 70.

Chapter 8

1. See *Hate Crimes: Confronting Violence Against Lesbians and Gay Men*, ed. Gregory M. Herek and Kevin T. Berrill (Newbury Park, Calif.: Sage, 1992), and the film *Boys Don't Cry*.

2. For a graphic contemporary account of surviving poverty that rivals those of Charles Dickens, see Frank McCourt, *Angela's Ashes* (New York: Scribner, 1996). For

tables on life expectancy and other interesting statistics in developing countries, see Martha Nussbaum's introduction to *Women, Culture, and Development: A Study of Human Capabilities*, ed. Nussbaum and Jonathan Glover (Oxford: Clarendon Press,1995), pp. 16–34.

3. John Stuart Mill, *The Philosophy of John Stuart Mill: Ethical, Political and Religious*, ed. Marshall Cohen (New York: Modern Library, 1961), p. 340.

4. Norman S. Care, *Living with One's Past: Personal Fates and Moral Pain* (Philadelphia: Temple University Press, 1996).

5. Bernard Williams, "Ethical Consistency," in Williams, *Problems of the Self: Philosophical Papers, 1956–72* (Cambridge: Cambridge University Press, 1973), pp. 166–86.

6. Martha Minow, *Between Vengeance and Forgiveness: Facing History After Genocide and Mass Violence* (Boston: Beacon, 1998); Carlos Santiago Nino, *Radical Evil on Trial* (New Haven: Yale University Press, 1996).

7. Nino, *Radical Evil*, p. 3.

8. John Kekes, *Facing Evil* (Princeton: Princeton University Press, 1990), esp. pp. 182–237.

9. Arthur Schopenhauer, *The World as Will and Representation*, 2 vols., trans. E. F. J. Payne (New York: Dover, 1969), and *On the Basis of Morality*, trans. E. F. J. Payne (Indianapolis: Bobbs-Merrill, 1965). Most of Nietzsche's best-known books are collected in two volumes, both translated and edited by Walter Kaufmann: *The Portable Nietzsche* (New York: Penguin, 1976) and *Basic Writings of Nietzsche* (New York: Modern Library, 1992). For his *On the Genealogy of Morality: A Polemic*, I prefer the translation of Maudemarie Clark and Alan J. Swenson (Indianapolis: Hackett, 1998).

10. For more on the theme of Nietzsche's revaluation of suffering, see Ivan Soll, "Nietzsche on Cruelty, Asceticism, and the Failure of Hedonism" in *Nietzsche, Genealogy, Morality: Essays on Nietzsche's On the Genealogy of Morals*, ed. Richard Schacht (Berkeley: University of California Press, 1994), pp. 168–92.

11. On punishment, see Gertrude Ezorsky, ed., *Philosophical Perspectives on Punishment* (Albany: State University of New York Press, 1972); H. D. Acton, ed., *The Philosophy of Punishment* (New York: St. Martin's, 1969); and A. C. Ewing, *The Morality of Punishment with Suggestions for a General Theory of Ethics* (London: 1929; reprint Montclair, N.J.: Patterson Smith, 1970). On resentment, in addition to Nietzsche, *On the Genealogy of Morality*, see Max Scheler, *Ressentiment*, trans. William W. Holdheim (New York: Schocken, 1972), and P. F. Strawson, "Freedom and Resentment," in Strawson, *Freedom and Resentment and Other Essays* (London: Methuen and Co., 1974), pp. 1–25. On praise and blame, see Joel Feinberg, "Justice and Personal Desert," in Feinberg, *Doing and Deserving* (Princeton: Princeton University Press, 1970), and Richard B. Brandt, *Ethical Theory: Problems of Normative and Critical Ethics* (Englewood Cliffs, N.J.: Prentice-Hall, 1959), or William K. Frankena, *Ethics*, 2d ed. (Englewood Cliffs, N.J.: Prentice-Hall, 1973), pp. 62–78. On forgiveness, see Simon Wiesenthal, *The Sunflower: On the Possibilities and Limits of Forgiveness*, rev. and exp., with symposium ed. Harry James Cargas and Bonny V. Fetterman (New York: Schocken, 1997); Joram Graf Haber, *Forgiveness* (Savage, Md.: Rowman and Littlefield, 1991); Aurel Kolnai, "Forgiveness," in Kolnai, *Ethics, Value, and Reality: Selected Papers of Aurel Kolnai* (Indianapolis: Hackett, 1978), pp. 210–24; and Cheshire Calhoun, "Changing One's Heart," *Ethics* 103 (Oct. 1992): 76–96. On mercy, see Alwynne Smart, "Mercy," in Acton, *The Philosophy of Punishment*; Claudia Card, "On Mercy," *Philosophical Review* 81,2 (April 1972): 182–207; and Martha Nussbaum, "Equity and Mercy," *Philosophy and Public Af-*

fairs 22,2 (Spring 1993): 83–125. On gratitude, see Terrence McConnell, *Gratitude* (Philadelphia: Temple University Press, 1993), and Card, "Gratitude and Obligation," *American Philosophical Quarterly* 25,2 (April 1988): 25–37.

12. Williams, "Ethical Consistency," p. 179.

13. Aristotle, *The Nicomachean Ethics*, trans. David Ross (New York: Oxford University Press, 1925), pp. 104- 105 (4:9; 1126b12–35).

14. Nietzsche, *On the Genealogy of Morality*, p. 39. Norman O. Brown argues that Nietzsche got it backward, that economic debts are a form taken by guilt. See Brown, *Life Against Death: The Psychoanalytic Meaning of History* (New York: Vintage, 1959), p. 268.

15. See, e.g., Claudia Card, "Retributive Penal Liability," *American Philosophical Quarterly Monograph* 7: *Studies in Ethics* (Oxford: Blackwell, 1973), pp. 17–35; also, H. L. A. Hart, "Prolegomena to the Principles of Punishment," in Hart, *Punishment and Responsibility: Essays in the Philosophy of Law* (Oxford: Clarendon Press, 1968), pp. 1–27, and Kurt Baier, "Is Punishment Retributive?" *Analysis* 4 (1952): 25–32.

16. Nino, *Radical Evil*, pp. 45–104.

17. John Rawls, "The Sense of Justice," *Philosophical Review* 72 (1963): 281–305.

18. Prisons tend to make guards worse, too. See Ted Conover, *Newjack: Guarding Sing Sing* (New York: Random House, 2000). Conover, an investigative journalist, trained and served for a year as a guard in Sing Sing in order to be able to write about conditions there.

19. See Barry Scheck, Peter Neufeld, and Jim Dwyer, *Actual Innocence: Five Days to Execution, and Other Dispatches from the Wrongly Convicted* (New York: Doubleday, 2000), and Edwin M. Borchard, *Convicting the Innocent: Errors of Criminal Justice* (New Haven: Yale University Press, 1932).

20. Minow, *Between Vengeance and Forgiveness*, pp. 25–90.

21. John Conroy, *Unspeakable Acts, Ordinary People: The Dynamics of Torture* (New York: Knopf, 2000), pp. 225–41.

22. Joel Feinberg, "The Expressive Function of Punishment," in Feinberg, *Doing and Deserving*, pp. 95–118; Nietzsche, *On the Genealogy of Morality*, p. 56.

23. Hannah Arendt, *The Human Condition* (Chicago: University of Chicago Press, 1958), pp. 236–43.

24. Henrik Ibsen, *Eleven Plays of Henrik Ibsen* (New York: Modern Library, 1935), p. 83. Introduction by H. L. Mencken.

25. How to define "genocide" is a matter of controversy, and one of the chief subjects of controversy is which groups to include. See *Genocide: Analyses and Case Studies*, ed. Frank Chalk and Kurt Jonassohn (New Haven: Yale University Press, 1990).

26. On the status of groups as ethical agents and bearers of interests and rights, see Larry May, *The Morality of Groups: Collective Responsibility, Group-Based Harm, and Corporate Rights* (Notre Dame, Ind.: University of Notre Dame, 1987).

27. Bishop Joseph Butler, *Fifteen Sermons Preached at Rolls Chapel* (2d. ed. 1729; reprint, London: G. Belland Sons, 1967). See Sermons 8–9 on resentment and forgiveness of injuries.

28. Arendt, *The Human Condition*, p. 241.

29. Ibid., p. 243.

30. Ibid., p. 241.

31. Howard McGary, "Forgiveness and Slavery," in McGary and Bill Lawson, *Between Slavery and Freedom: Philosophy and American Slavery* (Bloomington: Indiana University Press, 1992), pp. 90–112.

32. For an interesting discussion of the reparations issue for African Americans in relation to slavery, see Randall Robinson, *The Debt: What America Owes to Blacks* (New York: Dutton, 2000).

33. In *Forgiveness: A Philosophical Study* (Lanham, Md.: Rowman and Littlefield, 1991), Joram Graf Haber defends the view that "the only acceptable reason to forgive a wrongdoer is that the wrongdoer has repented the wrong she did–has had a change of heart," p. 90.

34. Immanuel Kant, *Practical Philosophy*, trans. Mary Gregor (Cambridge: Cambridge University Press, 1996), p. 574.

35. Aurel Kolnai, "Forgiveness," 215–17.

36. See Minow, *Between Vengeance and Forgiveness*, p. 23 for a similar list of responses to atrocities that fall between vengeance and forgiveness.

37. Jeffrie G. Murphy and Jean Hampton, *Mercy and Forgiveness* (Cambridge: Cambridge University Press, 1988).

38. Arendt, *The Human Condition*, p. 241.

39. Hastings Rashdall, *Theory of Good and Evil: A Treatise on Moral Philosophy*, 2d ed. (London: Humphrey Milford, 1924) 1:306–12.

40. J. D. Mabbott, "Punishment," *Mind* n.s. 48 (1939): 152–67.

41. Wiesenthal, *The Sunflower*, pp. 3–98.

42. The first symposium appeared in the 1976 edition published by Schocken; the second in the 1997 edition.

43. Wiesenthal, *The Sunflower*, p. 97.

Chapter 9

1. Claudia Card, "On Mercy," *Philosophical Review* 81,2 (April 1972): 182–207, and "Gratitude and Obligation," *American Philosophical Quarterly* 25,2 (April 1988):115–27.

2. For a thorough and sensitive treatment of the topic of pardon, see Kathleen Dean Moore, *Pardons: Justice, Mercy, and the Public Interest* (New York: Oxford University Press, 1989).

3. President Ford's pardon of former President Nixon was an exception to the general rule that pardons can be issued only after a finding of guilt. And according to Carlos Santiago Nino in *Radical Evil on Trial* (New Haven: Yale University Press, 1996), p. 38, after Chile's Truth and Reconciliation Commission's report, courts began to interpret amnesty as consistent with trials although not with punishment.

4. Peter Twambley, "Mercy and Forgiveness," *Analysis* 36,2 (1975/76): 84–90.

5. Immanuel Kant, *Practical Philosophy*, trans. Mary Gregor (Cambridge: Cambridge University Press, 1996), pp. 477–78. (This passage is from part 2 of *The Metaphysics of Morals*.)

6. Alwynne Smart, "Mercy," *Philosophy* 43,166 (1968): 345–59.

7. Card, "On Mercy," pp. 183–87.

8. See, for example, Sue William Silverman, *Because I Remember Terror, Father, I Remember You* (Athens: University of Georgia Press, 1996), on the childhood sexual abuse perpetrated against her sexually abusive father. See also Alice Miller, *Thou Shalt Not Be Aware: Society's Betrayal of the Child*, trans. Hildegarde Hannum and Hunter Hannum (New York: Farrar, Straus and Giroux, 1984), on relationships between severe corporal punishment of children and later adult violence.

9. See, for example, Alan Dershowitz, *The Abuse Excuse and Other Cop-outs, Sob Stories, and Evasions of Responsibility* (Boston: Little, Brown, 1994).

10. When the abuse has been continuous, however, the case is not so clear. For a deeply troubling case, see Gary Watson, "Responsibility and the Limits of Evil: Variations on a Strawsonian Theme," in *Responsibility, Character, and the Emotions: New Essays in Moral Psychology*, ed. Ferdinand Schoeman (New York: Cambridge University Press, 1987).

11. J. L. Austin, "A Plea for Excuses," in Austin, *Philosophical Papers* (Oxford: Clarendon Press, 1961).

12. See Card, "On Mercy," for elaboration of this idea. For an excellent exploration of connections between justice and desert, see Joel Feinberg, "Justice and Personal Desert," in Feinberg, *Doing and Deserving: Essays in the Theory of Responsibility* (Princeton: Princeton University Press, 1970), pp. 55–94.

13. Interestingly, in that case, even the apology from Germany was negotiated with representatives from Israel. See Tom Segev, *The Seventh Million: The Israelis and the Holocaust* (New York: Henry Holt, 1991), pp. 189–226.

14. Fred Berger, "Gratitude," *Ethics* 85 (1975): 298–309.

15. Richard Brandt, "The Concepts of Duty and Obligation," *Mind* 73 (1974): 374–93.

16. Sidgwick, *The Methods of Ethics*, 7th ed. (London: Macmillan, 1907), pp. 259–61.

17. Aristotle, *The Nicomachean Ethics*, trans. David Ross (Oxford: Oxford University Press, 1925), pp. 217–18 (1163a10–24).

18. Sidgwick, *Methods*, p. 261.

19. Thomas Hobbes, *De Cive (The Citizen)* (New York: Appleton-Century-Crofts, 1949), pp. 43–59.

20. Claudia Card, *The Unnatural Lottery: Character and Moral Luck* (Philadelphia: Temple University Press, 1996), pp. 118–39.

21. Hobbes, *De Cive (The Citizen)*, pp. 43–59.

22. Robert Axelrod, *The Evolution of Cooperation* (New York: Basic Books, 1984).

23. Friedrich Nietzsche, *On the Genealogy of Morality: A Polemic*, trans. Maudemarie Clark and Alan J. Swensen (Indianapolis: Hackett, 1998), pp. 36–41.

24. Nietzsche, *Genealogy*, pp. 35–66.

25. Norman O. Brown, *Life Against Death: The Psychoanalytical Meaning of History* (New York: Vintage, 1959), p. 270.

26. Sigmund Freud, *Civilization and Its Discontents*, trans. James Strachey (New York: Norton, 1961).

27. John Rawls, *A Theory of Justice*, rev. ed. (Cambridge, Mass.: Harvard University Press, 1999), pp. 405–19. See also Jean Piaget, *The Moral Judgment of the Child* (New York: Harcourt Brace, 1932).

28. Amélie Oksenberg Rorty, "Explaining Emotions," in *Explaining Emotions*, ed. Rorty (Berkeley: University of California Press, 1980), pp. 103–26.

29. Herbert Morris, "Nonmoral Guilt," in *Responsibility, Character, and the Emotions: New Essays in Moral Psychology*, ed. Ferdinand Schoeman (Cambridge: Cambridge University Press, 1987).

30. Sandra Lee Bartky, "In Defense of Guilt" in *On Feminist Ethics and Politics*, ed. Claudia Card (Lawrence: University Press of Kansas, 1999), pp.29–51.

31. Simon Wiesenthal Center: Museum of Tolerance, 9786 West Pico Boulevard, Los Angeles, Calif. 90035. www.wiesenthal.com

32. A classic conference volume on this topic is *When Medicine Went Mad: Bioethics and the Holocaust*, ed. Arthur L. Caplan (Totowa, N.J.: Humana Press, 1992). See also *The Nazi Doctors and the Nuremberg Code: Human Rights in Human Experimentation*, ed. George J. Annas and Michael A. Grodin (New York: Oxford University Press, 1995).

33. Robert L. Berger argues in "Nazi Science: Comments on the Validation of the Dachau Human Hypothermia Experiments" that the data from these "experiments" are worthless (Caplan, *When Medicine Went Mad*, pp. 109–33).

34. Kristen Moe, "Should the Nazi Research Data Be Cited?" *Hastings Center Report* (Dec. 1984), pp. 39–41; see p. 41.

35. Eva Mozes Kor, "Nazi Experiments as Viewed by a Survivor of Mengele's Experiments," in Caplan, *When Medicine Went Mad*, pp. 3–8. See also Kor (as told to Mary Wright), *Echoes from Auschwitz: Dr. Mengele's Twins: The Story of Eva and Miriam Mozes* (Terre Haute, Ind.: CANDLES, Inc., 1995). For responses by other survivors, see Nancy L. Segal, "Twin Research at Auschwitz-Birkenau: Implications for the Use of Nazi Data Today," in Caplan, *When Medicine Went Mad*, pp. 281–99.

36. G. J. Barker-Benfield, *Horrors of the Half-Known Life: Male Attitudes Toward Women and Sexuality in Nineteenth-Century America* (New York: Harper and Row, 1976).

37. Elie Wiesel, *Night*, trans. Stella Rodway (New York: Hill and Wang, 1960).

38. Paul Zielbauer, "Hartford Courant Apologizes for Sale Ads It Published in Slavery Era," *New York Times*, 6 July 2000, A22.

39. Ruth Benedict, *The Chrysanthemum and the Sword: Patterns of Japanese Culture* (New York: New American Library, 1946).

40. Gerhart Piers and Milton B. Singer, *Shame and Guilt: A Psychoanalytic and Cultural Study* (New York: Norton, 1971); John Rawls, *A Theory of Justice* (Cambridge, Mass.: Harvard University Press, 1971), ch. 8.

41. Thanks to Steve Whitton for conversations on shame sentencing and provocative reflections in an unpublished paper draft, "What's So Good About Shame?" (1999), a topic that led to his Ph.D. dissertation "Punishment and Character" (University of Wisconsin, 2001).

42. Hannah Arendt, *Eichmann in Jerusalem: A Report on the Banality of Evil* (New York: Viking, 1963).

43. On Inca culture, including sacrifice rituals, see Inga Glendinnen, *Aztecs: An Interpretation* (Cambridge: Cambridge University Press, 1991).

Chapter 10

1. Immanuel Kant, *Religion Within the Boundaries of Mere Reason*, trans. and ed. Allen W. Wood and George di Giovanni (Cambridge: Cambridge University Press, 1996), p. 83.

2. Nietzsche's philosophy, as filtered through his sister Elizabeth Förster-Nietzsche, who was married to a proto-Nazi, was popular with National Socialists during the Third Reich. On Elizabeth Förster-Nietzsche's life, see Ben Macintyre, *Forgotten Fatherland* (New York: Farrar, Straus and Giroux, 1992).

Nathan Leopold and Richard Loeb, who killed another child for sport in the 1920s in Chicago, were reportedly high on Nietzsche when they did it. See Clarence Darrow, *The Plea of Clarence Darrow: August 22nd, 23rd, and 25th, in Defense of Richard Loeb and Nathan Leopold Jr., on Trial for Murder*, authorized and revised edition with a brief summary of the facts (Chicago: R. F. Seymour, 1924).

3. Primo Levi, *The Drowned and the Saved*, trans. Raymond Rosenthal (New York: Vintage, 1989), pp. 36–39.

4. Ibid., pp. 52–53.

5. James T. Turner, "Factors Influencing the Development of the Hostage Identification Syndrome," *Political Psychology* 6,4 (1985): 705–11; Louis Jolyon West and Paul R. Martin, "Pseudo-Identity and the Treatment of Personality Change in Victims of Captivity and Cults," *Cultic Studies Journal* 13,2 (1996): 125–52; Irka Kuleshnyk, "The Stockholm Syndrome: Toward an Understanding," *Social Action and the Law* 10,2 (1984): 37–42; and Thomas Strentz, "The Stockholm Syndrome: Law Enforcement Policy and Hostage Behavior," in *Victims of Terrorism*, ed. Frank M. Ochberg and David A. Soskis (Boulder, Colo.: Westview, 1982), pp. 149–61.

6. Kuleshnyk, "The Stockholm Syndrome," p. 40.

7. Patricia Campbell Hearst with Alvin Moscow, *Patty Hearst: Her Own Story* (New York: Avon, 1988; orig. *Every Secret Thing*, 1982).

8. Kathleen Barry, *Female Sexual Slavery* (Englewood Cliffs, N.J.: Prentice-Hall, 1979).

9. Susan Lee Painter and Don Dutton, "Patterns of Emotional Bonding in Battered Women: Traumatic Bonding," International Journal of Women's Studies 8,4 (1985): 363–74; Christopher R. Goddard and Janet R. Stanley, "Viewing the Abusive Parent and the Abused Child as Captor and Hostage," *Journal of Interpersonal Violence* 9,2 (1994): 258–69. Cf. Marilyn Frye, "In and Out of Harm's Way: On Arrogance and Love," in Frye, *The Politics of Reality: Essays in Feminist Theory* (New York: Crossing Press, 1983), pp. 52–83.

10. W. E. B. Du Bois, *The Souls of Black Folk* (New York: New American Library, 1969), p. 45.

11. Larry Koger, *Black Slaveowners: Free Black Slave Masters in South Carolina, 1790–1860* (Columbia: University of South Carolina Press, 1995). Milton Meltzer also writes of slaves in ancient Rome who were themselves owners of yet other slaves. See his *Slavery: A World History* (New York: Da Capo, 1993).

12. See Mary Ann Humphrey, *My Country, My Right to Serve: Experiences of Gay Men and Women in the Military, World War II to the Present* (New York: HarperCollins, 1990), and Randy Shilts, *Conduct Unbecoming: Gays and Lesbians in the U.S. Military* (New York: St. Martin's Press, 1993).

13. Curt Gentry, *J. Edgar Hoover: The Man and the Secrets* (New York: Plume, 1992); Nicholas Von Hoffman, *Citizen Cohn: The Life and Times of Roy Cohn* (New York: Doubleday, 1988) and "Citizen Cohn" (videotape), Home Box Office, Inc., 1992.

14. George H. Weinberg, *Society and the Healthy Homosexual* (New York: St. Martin's, 1972).

15. Lorna Smith Benjamin, "An Interpersonal Theory of Personality Disorders," in *Major Theories of Personality Disorder*, ed. J. F. Clarkin and M. F. Lenzenweger (New York: Guilford Press, 1996), pp. 141–220.

16. Margaret Walker, *Moral Understandings: A Feminist Study in Ethics* (New York: Routledge, 1998), pp. 123–28.

17. Martha Nussbaum, *The Fragility of Goodness: Luck and Ethics in Greek Tragedy and Philosophy* (Cambridge: Cambridge University Press, 1986).

18. Gary Watson, "Responsibility and the Limits of Evil: Variations on a Strawsonian Theme," in *Responsibility, Character, and the Emotions: New Essays in Moral*

Psychology, ed. Ferdinand Schoeman (New York: Cambridge University Press, 1987), pp. 256–86 (quotation is from p. 272); Peter Strawson, "Freedom and Resentment," in Strawson, *Freedom and Resentment, and Other Essays* (London: Methuen and Co., 1974), pp. 1–25.

19. Ilene R. Prusher, "Arab Women: Out of the Shadows," *Christian Science Monitor*, 7 Aug. 2000, 1. Thanks to Suzanne Solensky for alerting me to this story.

20. Andrea Dworkin, *Life and Death* (New York: Free Press, 1997), pp. 51–52.

21. Ibid., pp. 53–54.

22. Levi, *The Drowned and the Saved*, p. 42.

23. "Kapo" may be an abbreviation of "KZ [Kat Zet] Polizei" (for *Konzentrationslager Polizei*) or of *Kamaradschafts Polizei*, as Miklos Niyszli suggests in a footnote to his memoir *Auschwitz: A Doctor's Eyewitness Account*, trans. Tibere Kramer and Richard Seaver (New York: Arcade, 1993), p. 43, n. 1. Levi and many other prisoners associated it with the Italian "*capo*" (head).

24. Levi, *The Drowned and the Saved*, p. 42.

25. Ibid., p. 43.

26. "Twilight zone" has been preempted by science fiction. In any case, if the only reason it might work is because of the color of the twilight, it isn't really an alternative.

27. See Elizabeth V. Spelman, *Fruits of Sorrow: Framing Our Attention to Suffering* (Boston: Beacon, 1997), for thoughtful reflection on the misappropriation of others' pain.

28. A novel based on the life of Chaim Rumkowski is Leslie Epstein's *King of the Jews* (New York: Coward, McCann, and Geoghegan, 1979).

29. See Isaiah Trunk, *Judenrat: The Jewish Councils in Eastern Europe Under Nazi Occupation* (Lincoln: University of Nebraska Press, 1996), and Raul Hilberg, *The Destruction of the European Jews*, revised and definitive ed. (New York: Holmes and Meier, 1985). Not all ghetto councils were charged with deportation tasks, and in those that were, some agonizing ethical discussions took place as council members decided how to respond.

30. Calel Perechodnik, who became a ghetto police officer in a small town near Warsaw, left a memoir recording his inner conflict over that decision and his ultimate remorse, *Am I a Murderer?* (Boulder, Colo.: Westview, 1996).

31. According to Nyiszli and Levi, there were twelve Sonderkommandos at Auschwitz.

32. See Herbert Morris, "Lost Innocence," in *On Guilt and Innocence: Essays in Legal Philosophy and Moral Psychology* (Berkeley: University of California Press, 1976), pp. 139–61.

33. On "dirty hands," see Michael Stocker, *Plural and Conflicting Values* (New York: Oxford University Press, 1990).

34. Levi, *The Drowned and the Saved*, p. 40.

35. Ibid., p. 59.

36. Ibid., p. 49, 54.

37. Joseph T. Hallinan, *Going Up the River: Travels in a Prison Nation* (New York: Random House, 2001), pp. 23–24 ff.

38. Paul Polansky, *Black Silence: The Lety Survivors Speak* (New York: Cross-Cultural Communications, 1998), p. 45. The quotations are from survivor Barbara Richterová. Many others confirmed her report about the Gypsies sent from Auschwitz to be guards at Lety and their extreme abuse. The translations are, apparently, by

Polansky, who collected the oral testimonies that fill this volume. Although prisoners were not gassed at Lety and the camp guards were not Nazis but Czech citizens, Polansky regards Lety as a death camp on the basis of evidence that thousands of Gypsies were murdered there, including babies and children, apparently for no other reason than that they were Gypsies. He has sought to have the site recognized with a monument, in accordance with the Helsinki Agreements that all death camps at the end of World War II should be so preserved. At the time his book was published, a pig farm stood on the site of the camp.

39. See Renate Siebert, *Secrets of Life and Death: Women and the Mafia*, trans. Liz Heron (New York: Verso, 1996).

40. Levi, *The Drowned and the Saved*, p. 48.

41. Human Rights Watch/Africa, et al., *Shattered Lives: Sexual Violence During the Rwandan Genocide and Its Aftermath* (New York: Human Rights Watch, 1996); George Hicks, *The Comfort Women: Japan's Brutal Regime of Enforced Prostitution in the Second World War* (New York: Norton, 1994).

42. Something like these levels of grayness were suggested in correspondence by David Weberman, who read an earlier draft of this chapter.

43. Levi, *The Drowned and the Saved*, pp. 45–46.

44. For more on resistance within the camps, see Eugen Kogon, *The Theory and Practice of Hell* (New York: Berkley Medallion, 1960), or *The Buchenwald Report*, trans. David A. Hackett (Boulder, Colo.: Westview, 1995), and Hermann Langbein, *Against All Hope: Resistance in the Nazi Concentration Camps 1938–1945* (New York: Paragon, 1994).

45. Siebert, *Secrets of Life and Death*, p. 147.

46. Elie A. Cohen, *The Abyss: A Confession*, trans. James Brockway (New York: Norton, 1973), pp. 60–61, 67. *Human Behavior in the Concentration Camp*, trans. M. H. Braaksma, was also published by Norton in 1953.

47. Cohen, *The Abyss*, pp. 93–95.

48. Rudolf Vrba and Alan Bestic, *I Cannot Forgive* (New York: Grove, 1964).

49. Tzvetan Todorow, *Facing the Extreme: Moral Life in the Concentration Camps*, trans. Arthur Denner and Abigail Pollak (New York: Henry Holt, 1996), p. 209.

50. On emotional *akrasia*, see Amelie Rorty, "Explaining Emotions," in Rorty, ed., *Explaining Emotions* (Berkeley: University of California Press, 1980), pp. 103–26. She notes that although "sometimes our emotions change straightaway when we learn that what we believed is not true," "often changes in emotions do not appropriately follow changes in belief" but "their tenacity, their inertia, suggests that there is *akrasia* of the emotions" (p. 103).

51. See, for example, Claudia Koonz, *Mothers in the Fatherland: Women, the Family, and Nazi Politics* (New York: St. Martin's, 1987).

52. On rape as a male protection racket, see Susan Rae Peterson, "Coercion and Rape: The State as a Male Protection Racket," and Susan Griffin, "Rape: The All-American Crime," in *Feminism and Philosophy*, ed. Mary Vetterling Braggin, Jane English, and Frederick A. Elliston (Totowa, N.J.: Littlefield, Adams, 1977), pp. 360–71 and 313–32. For further development, see Claudia Card, *The Unnatural Lottery: Character and Moral Luck* (Philadelphia: Temple University Press, 1996), pp. 97–117.

53. Joyce Trebilcot, "Dyke Methods," in *Lesbian Philosophies and Cultures*, ed. Jeffner Allen (Albany: State University Of New York Press, 1990), p. 17.

54. Norma Alarcón, "Chicana's Feminist Literature: A Re-Vision Through Malintzin/or Malinztin:Putting Flesh Back on the Object," in *This Bridge Called My Back:*

Writings by Radical Women of Color, ed. Cherríe Moraga and Gloria Anzaldúa (Watertown, Mass.: Persephone, 1981), pp. 182–90.

55. See Francisco López De Gómara, *Cortés: The Life of the Conqueror by His Secretary*, trans. Lesley Byrd Simpson (Berkeley: University of California Press, 1964), pp. 56–57, and Bernal Díaz del Castillo, *The Discovery and Conquest of Mexico*, trans. A. P. Maudslay (New York: Da Capo, 1996).

56. Stephen E. Ambrose, *Undaunted Courage: Meriwether Lewis, Thomas Jefferson, and the Opening of the American West* (New York: Simon and Schuster, 1996), p. 187.

57. See, for example, Ella E. Clark and Margot Edmonds, *Sacagawea of the Lewis and Clark Expedition* (Berkeley: University of California Press, 1979).

58. On Southern white women's collaboration with black women in resistance to slavery, see Adrienne Rich, "Disloyal to Civilization: Feminism, Racism, Gynephobia," in Rich, *On Lies, Secrets, and Silence* (New York: Norton, 1979), pp. 275–310.

59. The claim that lack of prisoner cooperation would have slowed the National Socialist killing machine is controversial. The *Einsatzgruppen* (mobile killing units) in the East killed very large numbers without help from victims, although those methods were abandoned as too hard on the perpetrators.

60. Levi, *The Drowned and the Saved*, p. 58.

61. Filip Müller, *Eyewitness Auschwitz: Three Years in the Gas Chambers*, literary collaboration by Helmut Freitag, ed. and trans. Susanne Flatauer (Chicago: Ivan R. Dee, 1999).

62. I owe this observation to Paula Gottlieb, who read and commented on an early draft of this chapter.

63. Edward Ball, *Slaves in the Family* (New York: Farrar, Straus and Giroux, 1998), pp. 422–23.

64. Ibid., p. 423.

65. Ibid., p. 423.

66. See John Sack, *An Eye for an Eye*, with a new preface (New York: Basic Books, 1995).

67. Kathleen M. Blee, *Women of the Klan: Racism and Gender in the 1920s* (Berkeley: University of California Press, 1991), p. 1.

68. Ibid., p. 2.

69. Levi, *The Drowned and the Saved*, p. 48.

70. Ibid., p. 49.

71. Peter Wyden, *Stella* (New York: Simon and Schuster, 1992).

72. Mary Daly, *Gyn/Ecology: The Metaethics of Radical Feminism* (Boston: Beacon, 1978).

73. On marriage resistance, see Jan Raymond, *A Passion for Friends: Toward a Philosophy of Female Affection* (Boston: Beacon, 1986), pp. 115–47.

Index

abolitionists, 13, 140
abortion, for rape pregnancies, 119–120, 130
abuse. *See* specific type
abuse excuse, 143, 193
access rights
  with cohabitation, 157–158
  to marital property, 151, 153
accountability
  in communal parenting, 147, 163
  in marriage contract, 156
  of perpetrators, 173, 175
  for self-respect, 19
action(s)
  capacity for evil, 22, 48–49
  moral worth of, 12, 20–21, 27–28, 86
  in stoicism, 73–75
  utility of, 58–59
ad hominem arguments, 29–30
affiliation, in attachment theory, 92–93
affirmative action, 106
agency
  in evil, 5, 51, 54–55
  gray zone applications of, 212–213, 225–227
  in radical evil, 79–80, 94
  of rationality, 79–82
  in stoicism, 66, 71
  in utilitarianism, 55–57, 60
aggression
  internalized, guilt association with, 199, 201
  of perpetrators, 11
akrasia, 202, 206, 227

amazons, 131, 133
ambiguity. *See also* gray zone(s)
  in denial of evil, 32, 38
  of motherhood, 160–161, 233
ambivalence
  in denial of evil, 38, 47–48, 75
  gratitude and, 74–75
  of gray zones, 223
amnesty, moral power of, 171, 190, 198
Amnesty International (AI), chart of coercion, 144–145, 153
anger, as feminism problem, 29
animal victims, 9–10
anti-Christ, 212
anti-Semitism, 21, 83, 89, 100
Anthony, Susan B., 98
apartheid, South African, 103
apology(ies)
  forgiveness and, 182, 184
  mercy and, 189–191, 194
  moral power of, 168, 172, 190
arbitrariness
  in mercy, 191–192
  in punishment, 172
  of relative well-being, 96–97, 114
Arcel, Libby Tata, 135
Arendt, Hannah, 7, 174, 176–177, 179
aristocracy
  entitlement sense of, 46
  narcissism of, 47
  valuation by, 40, 42–44
Aristotle, views on ethics, 19, 31, 50–54, 94, 170
arrogance, 47

assassinations, political, 143
assault
    to dignity, 104–105
    forms of, 146
atheism, 13, 17
Athena syndrome, 217
athletic development, inequality of,
    112–113, 115
atrocity(ies). *See also* evil(s)
    basic components of, 9, 12–13; relational
        interpretation of, 5, 16–22
    case examples, 8–9
    comparative judgments of, 7, 13–15
    cost-benefit analysis, 57–58, 71
    evils and, 9, 12–13, 102
    international interest in, 7, 167
    invisible, war rape as, 5, 8–10, 24,
        118–124
    as paradigms, 8–16, 101–102
    perpetration component of, 9–12
    research overview, 3–4, 23–26
    suffering component of, 9–11
    victim testimonies of, 10–11
attachment theory, 6, 68–69
    of child abuse, 160–161
    in radical evil, 90–94, 216
Auschwitz, 21, 70, 225, 227
autonomy, of will, 75, 78
Axelrod, Robert, 188

backstabbing, 223
bad
    ethics of, 50–51, 53
    evil vs., 46–49
    moral, evil vs., 101–102
    valuation of, 28, 33, 86
The Bad Seed (March), 101
Ball, Edward, 231
Baron, Marcia, 53
Barry, Kathleen, 145
Bartsky, Sandra, 202
The Basement (Millett), 142
battering
    forms of, 145, 153–154, 159
    spousal, 139–143, 145, 193
Baumeister, Roy, 9
beating(s), with war rape, 119, 123, 125
*Because I Remember Terror, Father, I Re-
    member You* (Silverman), 144
Becker, Lawrence, 67
benefactors

of gratitude, 196–198
    moral relationships with creditors,
        167–168
beneficiaries, gratitude of, 195
benevolence. *See* good and goodness
Benjamin, Lorna Smith, 24, 87, 90–93, 211,
    216
Benn, Stanley I., 8, 85
Bentham, Jeremy
    on justifiable harm, 57–58
    moral philosophy of, 50–54
    on punishment, 18, 23
    on slave/master morality, 40–41
    utilitarian views of, 57–58, 60
Benthamite ideals, critique of, 40
betrayal, 223, 227
Beyond Good and Evil (Nietzsche), 36, 39
bias(es), in denial of evil, 32–34
bisexuals. *See* lesbians, gay men, bisexuals,
    and transgender people (LGBTs)
blame
    ethics of, 50–51, 53
    for evil harms, 55–56
    forgiveness potential with, 205
    irrational, with guilt, 202–206
    moral power of, 102, 167, 173, 176, 190
    in war rape victims, 121
Blee, Kathleen, 232
boarding schools, 146
Bobbitt, Lorena, 134
Bobbitizing, of rapists, 134–137
bombings
    as atrocity, 8, 143
    war rape vs., 122, 125
bonding, erotic, in slave/master morality,
    40
böse, 101. *See also* evil(s)
Bosnia-Herzegovina camps
    genital crimes in, 135–136
    rape in, 24, 126, 128, 130, 137
Boswell, John, 149, 158
brainwashing, 71
Brandt, Richard, 196
Brown, Norman O., 199
Browning, Christopher, 83–84
Brownmiller, Susan, 20
burdens, of perpetrators. *See* moral burdens
Butler, Bishop Joseph, 175–176

camaraderie, soldier, with war rape,
    128–129

capital punishment. *See* death penalty
care and caring
    in communal parenting, 147–148
    as duty, 74, 82–83, 95
    as same-sex marriage focus, 154–155
    in slave/master morality, 37
    in stoicism, 66–67, 69–70, 74
    for victims, 74–75
Care, Norman, 166
caregivers
    for children (*see* childrearing)
    in same-sex marriage, 154–155, 163–164
carelessness, 14
castration. *See* genital mutilation
catastrophes. *See* natural disasters
Categorical Imperative, 21, 27, 51, 70, 74, 76
    difficulties with, 83, 87, 216
    in murder and mayhem, 79–83
character corruption, in victims, 11–12
character judgments, 51, 53
character-based ethics, 50–51
    self-interest and, 85–87
    in stoicism, 66, 68–69
chemical warfare, as atrocity, 8
child abuse
    as atrocity, 6, 8, 25, 103
    attachment theory of, 160–161
    incestuous (*see* incest)
    neglect as, 141–142, 163
    by parents, 141–142, 163
    as terrorism, 139–146, 193
child neglect
    as abuse, 141–142, 193
    revolutionary parenting as, 146–147, 163
childrearing. *See also* motherhood
    communal: advantages of, 142–143;
        forms of, 146–150, 163
    revolutionary, 146–150, 162–163, 165
choice. *See* personal choice
Christianity
    as hatred source, 40, 46, 49
    power distortions in, 34–35, 37, 40, 87
citizenship
    in decent society, 62
    guilty feelings about, 203, 206
civil court model, of mercy, 191, 194
civilian rape, 121, 125–126, 128
Clark, Maudemarie, 32, 35
clemency, mercy vs., 190
clitoridectomy, 23, 134, 233
closeted abuse victims, 154, 215–216

coercion
    Amnesty International's chart of,
        144–145, 153
    in the home, 143–146, 153
    oppression vs., 144–145, 153
    targets with torture, 124–125
cohabitation rights, 157–158
Cohen, Elie, 227, 234
Collins, Patricia Hill, 147
comfort women, in World War II, 24, 119,
        125, 129, 132
common folk
    hostility of, 47
    value distortions of, 34, 37–39, 42
communal childrearing
    advantages of, 142–143
    forms of, 146–150, 163–164
communicable disease(s), marriage and,
        155, 159
comparison, judgmental, of atrocities, 7,
        13–15
compassion, 22, 69
    forgiveness and, 177, 181–183, 189
compensation, for victims, 172, 191
complicity
    in marginalized people, 217
    in victims, 6, 11–12, 221–223
compromise theory
    of diabolical evil, 217, 221–223, 231
    of punishment, 170–171
concern. *See* care and caring
condemnation, moral power of, 167, 176,
        184
condescension
    in denial of evil, 44–45
    as men's view of women, 36–39, 43, 45,
        112, 115
condonation
    forgiveness and, 178–179
    as survivors guilt outlet, 203
confession, moral power of, 181–183, 185,
        190
confidence, in stoicism, 65, 67
conquerors. *See* victor(s)
consciousness, public, of war rape victims,
        121–122
consciousness-raising (CR), 215–216
consequentialism, 50, 52–53, 56
contempt
    in denial of evil, 44–45
    as guilt factor, 206–207

contingencies
    of identities, 88
    in stoicism, 73–74, 80
contract(s), marriage, 154–156
contrition, moral power of, 182, 184, 190
control factor
    of evil harms, 55–57
    in stoicism, 64–65, 67–69, 74
corruption, of judgment, 52, 94
cost-benefit analysis, of atrocities, 57–58,
    71
creator. See supreme being
creditors, moral relationships with benefac-
    tors, 167–168, 199
criminal court model, of mercy, 191–194
criminal justice system, as evil, 18, 63–64
criminals, habitual, 13
cruelty
    as immoral desire, 70, 84–85
    in radical evil, 85–87
Cuban missile crisis, 8
culpability
    in denial of evil, 45, 120
    dimensions of, 14, 20–21, 56
    as evil component, 3–4, 12, 102
    intolerable harm relationship to, 9, 16–22
    supreme being and, 13
cultural decimation
    as gray zone, 215
    slavery as, 119, 124, 126–128, 215
    with war rape, 119, 124, 126–127; resist-
        ance to, 134, 136

Daly, Mary, 23, 45, 113, 147, 233–234
Dana, Richard Henry, 84
danger(s)
    as judgment of evil, 33
    morality as, 28–29
Death and the Maiden, 124
death, natural vs. harmful, 63
death camps. See also genocide
    gray zones in, 212, 219–224, 227, 230
death penalty
    arguments against, 140
    as atrocity, 8, 13, 63
    compromise theory of, 170–171
    Mishnah declaration on, 116
    for rapists, 132, 135
debtor paradigm
    of gratitude, 188–190, 194–199
    of guilt, 199, 201, 205

in marriage contract, 156
    of perpetrators, 168–170, 174, 199
decency, relative well-being vs., 96–97
decent society, 62
deception, in slave/master morality,
    37–38
decision-making, power imbalance in, 35
decriminalization, 149
deed(s), intention behind, 20, 22
Deep Throat, 159
deference, lack of, 45
degradation, as evil, 103–104
demonization, 28, 49
demoralization, through rape, 119, 125
denial of evil, 27–49
    distortion in, 29, 32–33, 36–44
    entitlement concept with, 36, 44–49
    genealogies and perspectives in, 30–35
    hatred and impotence in, 28–30, 36,
        44–49
    as Nietzsche's approach, 23, 27–49
    power imbalance in, 36–44
    questioning of concepts, 27–30, 91–92
deontology, 50–53, 73
dependence
    as guilt source, 200
    heterosexual, 146, 151–152, 155, 159
    human, 69, 71
deserved gratitude, 195
deserved mercy, 193
desirability
    ethics of, 50–51, 53, 75
    self-love and, 85
detachment, emotional, 66
diabolical evil
    radical evil vs., 91–92, 94, 211
    reality of, 211–213
difference(s), as feminism focus, 99, 115
dignity
    assault vs. affront to, 104–105
    in rational agency, 81
Diogenes Laertius, 64, 65
"dirty hands," 18
disability(ies)
    marriage and, 155, 159
    from war rape, 120
disappointment, moral sense of, 102
discipline, of children, 162–163
discrimination
    racial, 103–104
    of same-sex marriage, 149–151

disease. *See* illness(es)
disengagement, in attachment theory, 91
dishonesty
    in denial of evil, 27–29, 36, 44
    in repentance, 172
distancing, in war rape, 122–123
distortion
    correcting for, 33, 45
    in denial of evil, 29, 32–33
    of evil vs. evil deeds, 48–49
    power imbalances and, 36–44
distributive justice, 57, 62, 114
divorce, 152–153
domestic violence
    alleviation of, 105, 109, 115
    as atrocity, 6, 8, 25, 139
    as coercion, 143–146
    forms of, 139–143, 171
    statistics on, 140–141
dominance
    benevolent, 99, 102
    domestic violence as, 143–146
    as feminism movement focus, 99
    genetic, 119, 124, 126, 130
    as hatred, 45–49
    morality distortions with, 36–44
    rape as symbol of, 125–126, 132; resist-
        ance to, 134, 136
    self-perceptions with, 33–35
Dorfman, Ariel, 124
double axes, 131–132
double-consciousness, 215
"doubling," 89, 91
driver's license, 159
drug testers, cost-benefit for, 57–58
DuBois, W. E. B., 215
duress, 14
duty-based ethics, 24, 27, 50–51
    perfect vs. imperfect, 82–83, 93–95
Dworkin, Andrea, 113
dynasties. *See* genealogies

economic assets, distribution of, 97,
    108–109, 194
economic security, through marriage,
    151–153
Education Amendment Act (1972), 113
education system, inequality in, 103–106,
    113, 115
egoism, attachment vs., 92–93
Eichmann, Adolph, 21, 52, 207–208

elderly
    abuse of, 139–140, 159
    unjust inequality of, 112–113
elite. *See* aristocracy; nobility; victor(s)
emotions
    as guilt supplements, 206–210
    residual, in victims, 169
    in stoicism, 65–66, 81
empiricism, in personal choice, 6, 75–76, 78
enemy, demonization of, 28
energy, hatred relationship to, 49
enjoyment. *See* joy
enrichment, involuntary unjust, guilt over,
    203, 205–206
entitlement, 36, 44–49
environmental contamination, as atrocity,
    8, 14
envy
    avoiding, 27, 36
    in denial of evil, 27, 36
    in master/slave relationship, 44–47
Epictetus, 64, 67, 70
epidemics, of fatal disease, 5, 12
Equal Rights Amendment, 113
equality
    as feminism focus, 24, 98–100, 113–115
    respect for humanity as, 48, 114–116
    as social and political value, 96–97
equality feminism, 113–114
erotic bonding, in slave/master morality, 40
esteem, ethics of, 50–51, 53, 86
ethics
    in communal parenting, 147, 164
    culpability component, 4, 12
    of evil: conceptions of, 4–5, 7, 12–13; re-
        visiting theories of, 50–54
    Kant's approach to, 75–79
    in power imbalances, 36–37
    of self-respect, 19, 210
    Stoic approach to, 69–72
    utilitarian approaches to, 51–54, 58–59
ethnicide, 126
euthanasia
    consensual, 16–17
    involuntary, 10, 15, 17, 58
Eve, as bad vs. evil, 77–78
evil(s). *See also* atrocity(ies)
    atrocity vs., 9, 12–13
    basic components of, 4, 12, 102
    degrees of, 13–14
    entitlement and, 36, 44–49

evil(s) (*Continued*)
  ethics of: conceptions of, 4–5, 7, 12–13;
    revisiting theories of, 50–54
  global concepts of, 31, 108–110, 116
  morally bad vs., 101–102
  negative valuation of, 27–30, 32–33
  Nietzsche's approach to (*see* denial of
    evil)
  ordinary wrongs vs., 3–4, 7, 12–13, 17,
    83
  philosophy of, 3–8
  prevalence and distribution of, 6
  questioning concept of, 27–30
  radical (*see* radical evil)
  reducing to unjust inequalities, 7, 18, 24,
    112
  resistance to, 6, 11–13
  self-inflicted, 19
  theological views, 6–7, 12–13
  unjust inequalities as, 96, 100, 103–105
  utilitarian approach to, 54–60
evildoer(s). *See* perpetrator(s)
exclusion, social
  career-focused, 98, 100, 105–106
  education-focused, 103–106, 113, 115
executioners, evil interests of, 83–85
experiments, medical, during war, 5, 8,
    203–204
exploitation
  forgiveness of, 174
  sexual (*see* rape)
  as social oppression, 99–100
extended family, childrearing by, 142–143,
    148–149, 161
"external auxiliaries," of oppression, 220,
    229–230

fairness, 96, 114. *See also* unjust inequali-
    ties
faith, 13, 200
family
  etymology, 148–49
  inequalities prioritization by, 106–108
  as social support, 154–155
family camp, 70
family resemblance concepts, 4, 30–31,
    149
family violence. *See* domestic violence
fantasy penalty(ies), for rapists, 132–138,
    172
fatal disease

epidemics of, 5, 12
euthanasia for, 16–17
fault, in evil harms, 55–56
favoritism, in mercy, 192, 194
fear
  hatred association with, 46–47
  as torture goal, 124
feet binding, 147, 233
Feinberg, Joel, 173
femininity, 39, 43, 45, 219
feminism movement
  anger as problem of, 29
  application and implications of, 111–114
  consciousness-raising focus of, 215–216
  in domestic violence activism, 139,
    147–148, 150, 163–165
  equality focus of, 24, 98–100, 115
  as opposition to oppression, 98–100,
    113
  power perspectives and distortions of,
    35–37
  prioritization within, 105–106
feminists
  historical, 98–99
  radical vs. social, 113–114
folk culture, power sources in, 46–48
forgiveness
  blocks to, 176–177, 180
  desert bases of, 192
  ethics of, 173–181, 189
  as goodwill, 166, 169, 182, 189–190
  group, 175
  of guilt, 206–207; blameless, 204–205
  moral power of, 167–169, 173
  nonparadigm cases of, 175
  obligation with acceptance of, 197–198
  paradigm of interpersonal, 174–175, 177,
    180, 183–184
  punishment and, 176, 179–180, 184
  reconciliation and, 179–180
  rectification and, 167–170, 173
  remorse and, 208–209
  repentance and, 175, 178, 180
  resentment association with, 175–177
  of self, 176–177
  of shame, 206
  as survival strategy, 11, 25
  Wiesenthal's dilemma with, 181–187,
    190
  worthiness and, 176–177, 180
Frankfurt, Harry, 97

free riderism, 79
free will. *See* will and willingness
freedom(s), as human right, 7, 54, 63
Freud, Sigmund, 199–200
friendship, stoic ethics of, 73–74
Frye, Marilyn, 99
functional meanings, in guilt, 31–32

Gage, Matilda Joslyn, 98
games (Wittgenstein), 30–31
gang rape, 125–126, 131
gay men. *See* lesbians, gay men, bisexuals, and transgender people (LGBTs)
The Gay Science (Nietzsche), 38–39, 41–42
gender equality/inequality
   in education system, 103–105
   as evil vs. unjust inequality, 24, 98
genealogies
   breaking up of, 43, 57, 158; with rape, 119, 124, 126
   of evil, 4–5, 22, 30–36, 38, 47; interrupting, 166–169, 177, 180
genetic imperialism, 119, 124, 126, 130
Geneva Conventions (1949), war rape and, 120
genital mutilation
   as cultural norm, 134, 233
   for rapists, 133–135, 137
   as war sex crime, 132, 135–136
genocide
   as atrocity, 4, 8, 13, 136
   cost-benefits of, 57, 71
   against Jewish people, 21, 83, 100, 221
   survivors of (*see* Holocaust survivors)
Genovese, Kitty, 123
Gilligan, Carol, 37
Gilman, Charlotte Perkins, 164
Giovanni, Nikki, 41
glass ceilings, as oppression, 99, 102
Glendon, Mary Ann, 7
global concepts. *See* international concepts
global warming, as atrocity, 8
Glover, Jonathan, 8
God, as hypermoral, 13, 74, 87
Goldhagen, Daniel, 83
Goldman, Emma, 98, 99, 152
Goldschlag, Stella, 232–233
Goldstone, Justice Richard, 120
good and goodness
   ethics of, 50–51, 53–54, 93
   gray zones of, 218–219

personal responsibility for, 77–78, 218
   in stoicism, 66–67, 73
   valuation of, 27–30, 32–34
"good dog" morality, 40–41
goodwill
   of common folk, 47
   ethics of, 51–52
   forgiveness and, 166, 169, 182, 189–191
   gratitude and, 195–196, 198–199
   motive behind, 21, 73, 86
   in stoicism, 73–74
Gordon, Linda, 141–142
gratitude
   ambivalence of, 74–75
   benefactors debt with, 196–198
   desert basis of, 196
   reciprocity with, 195–196, 198
   as unwelcome, 195
   without obligation, 195–196
gratitude obligations
   ethics of, 194–199
   as perpetrators' burden, 188–190, 194–196
   as victims' power, 11, 168–169, 174
gray areas, 221, 223
gray zone(s)
   agents' choices within, 212–213, 218, 225–227
   in death camps, 212, 219–224, 227, 230
   diabolical evil of, 211–213
   examples of, 216–224
   features of, 224–227
   good and goodness, 218–219
   of guilt, 218–219, 222
   of misogyny, 217, 219, 223–224, 228
   of morality, 217–219, 227, 234
   motherhood as, 160–161, 233
   of National Socialism, 221, 230–231, 233–234
   of oppression, 6, 34, 38, 213, 215, 217–218, 233
   within privileged prisoners, 212, 221–223, 226, 230
   of responsibility, 218, 221–227, 233–234
   of slave values, 215, 230–231
   Stockholm Syndrome, 213–216
   as theoretical perspective, 6, 26, 212
   of victims, 160, 224–227; as perpetrator, 6, 19–22, 26, 193, 212, 216
   of voluntariness, 14, 219, 225

"greater good," in utilitarianism, 57–58, 110

Griffin, Susan, 113

group forgiveness, 175

guardian(s)
    legal, for children, 142–143, 148–149
    in marriage contract, 156

guilt
    alleviation through forgiveness, 174, 184
    alternatives and supplements to, 206–210
    blameless, 202–206
    gray zones of, 218–219, 222
    guilt about feeling, 207
    as internalized aggression, 199, 201
    as moral remainder, 169–170, 173
    as perpetrators' burden, 25–26, 188–190
    shame vs., 200, 205–206
    in survivors (see survivors' guilt)
    value of, 199

Gypsy prisoners, 223–224

Hallie, Philip, 97

Hampton, Jean, 179

happiness
    as human conduct product, 8, 54, 86
    virtue vs., 74

harem politics, 217

Harlow, Harry, 92

harm(s)
    basic, 63
    foreseeable intolerable (see intolerable harm)
    justifiable, 13, 56–59, 61
    magnitude gap, 9–10, 33, 48–49
    severity of, 3, 14
    utilitarian approach to, 51–54, 56–57
    willingness to inflict, 211–212

Harris, Robert, 218–219

Hart, Barbara, 145, 154

Harvard University, 104–105

Hatikva, 70

hatred
    in denial of evil, 28–30, 36, 44–49
    motive behind, 21, 29, 49
    in powerful people, 44–45
    as waste of energy, 49

Hearst, Patricia, 214–215, 217, 220, 222, 228

Hecuba, 68

Held, Virginia, 164

helplessness, as women's atrocity, 11, 111–112

Herman, Barbara, 53, 67, 79–83

heroism, for torturers, 122–123

heteronomy, of will, 75

heterosexual dependency, 146, 151–152, 155, 159

Hirsch, Fredy, 227, 234

Hitler's Final Solution, 15–16, 83, 212

Hitler's Willing Executioners, 83

Hoagland, Sarah, 37

Hobbes, Thomas, 92, 196–197

Holocaust survivors
    comparative judgment of, 15–16, 233
    complicity in, 6, 11–12, 221–223
    forgiveness by, 181–182
    guilt in, 11, 205
    moral powers of, 166, 181–187
    self-respect of, 194

home, terrorism in, 143–146

homelessness, 105–106, 111

homophobia, 89, 100, 216

homosexuals. See lesbians, gay men, bisexuals, and transgender people (LGBTs)

honesty, questioning motives of, 27–29

"honor killing," 219

hope, 54

hopelessness, 64

Hostage Identification Syndrome, 213–216

hostage phenomenon, 213–214

hostility
    of common folk, 47
    of oppressors, 47–48, 102
    renunciation of, 166–169; 177, 180–183, 189
    to self, with guilt, 199–201

House of Mirth (Wharton), 101

human rights
    approach to domestic violence, 141
    basic, 54, 63
    Universal Declaration of, 7
    for women (see feminism movement)

Human Rights Watch, on war rape, 120

humanity, respect for, as equality, 48, 114–116

humiliation
    as evil, 104
    institutional sources of, 62
    through rape, 120, 125

identification
    of perpetrator with victim, 209–210

of victim with perpetrator, 6, 19–22, 26,
    193, 212
identity, practical, normativity and,
    87–90
ignorance, 14, 56
illness(es)
    in children, alleviation of, 108–109
    fatal, 5, 12, 16–17
    same-sex marriage support of patients,
        155
illusion(s), 72
    of guilt, 199–200
immorality
    in atrocity paradigm, 11–12, 28–30
    in philosophy of evil, 4–5, 7–8, 12, 84
    with oneself, 19
imperfection, 12–13
imperialism, genetic, 119, 124, 126, 130
Important Persons and their Internalized
    Representation (IPIR), 90–94, 216
impotence, in denial of evil, 28–29, 36,
    44–49
imprisonment
    as evil, 18, 63–64, 111
    parole with, 172–173
    for rapists, 132–134
inattentiveness, 14, 22
incest, 103, 111, 153, 160
inclinations, social, 62, 84
incommensurability, in atrocity judgments,
    14–15
incontinence, in actions vs. judgment, 52,
    202, 206
indifference, in stoicism, 67, 70
inequality. See unjust inequalities
inferiors, envy by powerful, 44–47
infibulation, 23, 134, 233
ingratitude, 197–198
injustice(s)
    ethics of, 7, 12
    guilt association with, 200, 203,
        205–206
    as inequality (see unjust inequalities)
    minor, 13
    in perpetrator obligations, 189, 191
    social, in utilitarianism, 60–64
inmates, rape of, 112
innocence, of victims, 12–13, 29
    loss of, 218, 221–222, 225
institutional sources
    of alleviation of evil, 108

of atrocities, 21–22, 102
of evil, 140, 213
of humiliation, 62, 104
of rape, 24–25, 128–129, 134, 137
insubordination, and power, 45–46, 48
insults, 45
insurance, as spousal benefit, 151–152,
    157–158
intellectual pleasures, prioritization of,
    110–111
intelligence, rational vs. empirical, 75–76,
    78–80
intention(s), evil in, 3, 20–22
interaction
    interpersonal (see interpersonal psychol-
        ogy)
    Sullivan, Harry Stack and George Her-
        bert Mead, 87
    survivors' approach to, 11
interests, radically evil, 83–85
intergenerational trauma, 19–20
international concepts
    of evil, 31, 108–110, 116
    of terrorism, 143
international doctrines, 7, 167
interpersonal psychology
    of attachment, 87, 90–93
    ethics in, 51, 73
    in philosophy of evil, 6, 14, 80–81
    self-concept in, 87, 90–91
    in stoicism, 65–66, 68–69, 71, 73
intervention, human failure of, 5
intimidation, through rape, 118–119, 125
intolerable harm, foreseeable
    as atrocity component, 9, 13
    culpable wrongdoing relationship to,
        16–22
    as evil component, 3–4, 12–13
    intentional dimensions of, 3, 20–21
involuntariness, as gray zone, 219, 225
involuntary servitude. See also slavery
    in the home, 145–146, 219
IPIR (Important Persons and their Internal-
    ized Representation), 90–94, 216
irrationality, of guilt, 202–206

Jacobs, Harriet, 43
Japanese internment camps, as atrocity, 8,
    24
Japanese military, war rape by, 119, 125,
    129

jealousy, motive behind, 21
Jefferson, Thomas, 40
Jews
    genocide against, 21, 83, 100, 221
    humiliation of, 104
    marginalization of, 100
    as prisoners, gray zones of, 212, 221–223,
        230
    Russian military conscription, 157
    as survivors (see Holocaust survivors)
Jim Crow laws, 104
Jones, Ann, 144
joy, 8
    guilt over feeling, 199, 203
Józefów, Poland, 83
Judaism, valuation in, 37, 44, 87
judgment(s)
    of bad vs. evil, 46, 48–49; moral,
        101–102, 112
    better, acting contrary to, 52, 202, 206
    of character, 51, 53
    comparative, of atrocities, 7, 13–15
    corrupt, 52, 94
    of good vs. evil, 27–30
    of oppression, 6, 34, 38, 44–46
justice. See also criminal justice system
    distributive, 57, 62
    in good vs. evil, 5, 7, 24, 53
    in slave/master morality, 37, 57
    social (see social justice)
justification(s), of harms, 13, 56–59, 61
    in the home, 143, 193

Kant, Immanuel
    ethical theory, 50–54. 73–75
    radical evil theory, 4, 24, 27, 75–79;
        solving mystery of, 85–87
    his stoicism, 23, 50–54, 59, 73–75
kapos, 221, 230
Katz, Stephen, 15
Kekes, John, 8. 11–12
kidnapping, in war rape, 119, 123, 132
killings, mass. See mass murder
Kingdom of Ends, 87
Kittay, Eva Feder, 162, 164
knowledge
    perspectivism, 31–33
    of wrongdoings, 15, 21, 56
Koger, Larry, 215
Kolnai, Aurel, 178
Kor, Eva Mozes, 204

Korsgaard, Christine, 24, 87–90, 211
Ku Klux Klan, 231–233

labor, productive, through slavery,
        118–119, 121, 125–128, 140, 194
lack of opportunity
    as inequality vs. evil, 103–105
    as social oppression, 98, 100
lawsuits, cost-benefit analysis of, 57
legal guardians
    domestic partnerships as, 157
    as motherhood alternative, 142–143,
        148–149
legal institution(s), marriage as, 139,
        147–148, 151, 154, 164
leniency, mercy vs., 190–191
lesbians, gay men, bisexuals, and transgen-
        der people (LGBTs)
    as banned from military, 156–157
    complicity in, 217
    as parents, 161–165
    partner abuse in, 154, 160
    as same-sex marriage activists, 139,
        147–148, 150, 164–165
    as targets of violence, 142–143, 166
Levi, Primo, 6, 10, 26, 212, 219–222,
        224–225, 229–230, 232–234
Lewis and Clark explorations, 228–229
LGBTs. See lesbians, gay men, bisexuals,
        and transgender people (LGBTs)
liberal society, 61–62
liberalism, 8, 11
license(s)
    driver's, 159
    marriage, 158–160
lies
    in denial of evil, 36, 42
    radical evil and, 76
life and living, survivors' approach to, 11,
        25, 166–169
Lorde, Audre, 113, 147
love
    Christian, 37, 40
    in slave/master morality, 40
    as social value, 45, 93
loyalty
    motive behind, 21
    in slave/master morality, 37, 40
Lugones, María, 113
luxury(ies), unjust spending on, 108, 110,
        114

Mabbot, J. D., 180
MacKinnon, Catharine, 99
Mafia, 212, 223–224
"magnitude gap"
    between perpetrators' and victims' perceptions, 9–10, 29, 45, 188
    in war rape, 120–121
Mahmoody, Betty, 157
maliciousness, 4
malnutrition. See starvation
maltreatment, as evil, 103–104
man-hating, 49
manipulation, in slave/master morality, 37–38
March, William, 101
Marciano, Linda, 159
marginalization
    complicity with, 217
    as social oppression, 99–100
marital rape, 25, 129, 153, 159
marriage
    as legal institution, 139, 147–148, 151, 154, 164
    military compared to, 156–157
    mutual consent in, 157–158
    as parenting support, 147–148
    as property rights, 151, 153
    same-sex (see same-sex marriage)
    social advantages of, 154–155, 229–230
    as socially controversial, 139–140, 147
    as terrorism trap, 140–141, 155–157
marriage contract, 154–156
marriage license, 158–160
Martina, Doña, 228–229
Masada, 43
mass murder. See also genocide
    as atrocity, 4, 8, 18
    comparative judgments of, 15
mass rape, as weapon. See war rape
mass starvation, as atrocity, 8, 10
master morality
    erotic bonding with slaves, 40
    power imbalances and, 36–44
masturbation stations, 132
maternal abuse, 141–142
maxims, universality of, 79–80, 87
mayhem, as radical evil, 79–83, 95
McConnell, Joyce, 145
McVeigh, Timothy, 170

meanings
    functional, 31–32
    of punishment, 30–31
medical data, experimental, guilt with use of, 203–204
medical practice(s)
    in penalties for war rape, 132–135
    in war experiments, 5, 8, 203–204
Melzer, Milton, 40, 126
men
    condescending view of women, 36–37, 39, 43, 45, 112, 115
    as domestic violence victims, 141
    as war rape victims, 128, 135–138
mercy
    civil court model of, 191, 194
    criminal court model of, 191–194
    desert bases of, 192
    ethics of, 69, 190–194
    as perpetrators' burden, 188–190
    by victims: obligation with acceptance of, 197–198; as power, 11, 25, 167, 169, 173
metaphysics
    of evil, 6–7, 12–13
    of gray zones, 226–227
    of stoicism, 52, 73–74
Midgley, Mary, 7, 11
Milgram, Stanley, 6
military
    lesbians and gay men in, 156–157
    marriage compared to, 156–157
    rape by (see war rape)
    women participating in, 131, 136–137
Mill, John Stuart
    on doing without happiness, 166
    moral philosophy of, 50, 53–54, 110
    on self-regarding vices, 19
    utilitarian views of, 58–59
mind-body dualism, in power distortions, 41–42
Minow, Martha, 99, 115
Mishnah declaration, on death penalty, 116
misogyny, 113, 115, 146
    gray zones of, 217, 219, 223–224, 228
    war rape and, 133–134, 136
mockery, 46
Moe, Kristin, 204
Mohr, Richard, 149–150, 152
monetary compensation, for victims, 172
Monk, Ray, 31

monogamy, 152
moral burdens, of perpetrators, 188–210
    gratitude as, 168–169, 174, 188–190;
        ethics of, 25–26, 194–199
    guilt as, 189–190, 199–202; alternatives
        and supplements, 206–210; blameless,
        202–206
    mercy and, 189–194
    neediness as, 181–187, 207
    release by victims, 167–168, 174, 184
    source of, 172–174
moral law. See Categorical Imperative
moral obligations. See moral burdens; obli-
    gations
moral powers, of victims, 166–187
    applications of, 25, 217–219, 227
    forgiveness and, 173–181, 207; Wiesen-
        thal's dilemma with, 181–187, 190
    for living with evil, 11, 25, 166–169
    punishment and, 170–173
    rectification and, 169–170
    remainders and, 169–170
moral relationships, of victims and perpe-
    trators, 167–168, 188
moral remainders, 201
    guilt as, 169–170, 173
    regret as, 169, 180, 208
    remorse as, 169, 185, 208–209
    repentance as, 21, 171, 208
    shame as, 169–170
morality
    of actions, 66–67, 73, 75, 87
    in bad vs. evil, 101–102
    of decency, 96–97
    in gray zones, 217–219, 227, 234
    of guilt, 199–207
    in interpretation of evil, 4–5, 7–8, 12, 77;
        clarifications for, 16–22, 48–49; ques-
        tions for, 27–30
    natural events lack of, 5, 13
    of perpetrators, 25–26, 188–210
    power imbalances and, 36–44
    radical evil and, 75–78, 83–85, 95
    of self-respect, 19
    of victims, 25, 166–187, 217–219, 227
Morris, Herbert, 202–205
Morrison, Toni, 43
mother(s), biologic vs. otherwise, 161–163
mother-child relationships, 161
motherhood
    alternatives to, 142–143, 146–150, 161

arguments for, 160–165
    exclusive responsibility, 142–143, 160,
        164–165
    as gray zone, 160–161, 233
    as sheltering abuse, 160–161
    as socially controversial, 139–140, 142
    as terrorism trap, 140–141, 160
motive(s)
    in attachment theory, 92–93
    behind hatred, 21, 29, 49
    evil dimensions of, 14, 20–22
    gray zones of, 225–226
    of honesty, 27–29
    intentions vs., 22
    of perpetrator, 3, 10–11
    radical evil and, 76, 85, 93–95
    of self-interest, 85–87, 94
movies, war rape in, 124
Müller, Filip, 230
multiple personalities, 19
murder
    mass (see mass murder)
    as radical evil, 79–83, 95
    by rapists, 120
Murphy, Jeffrie, 179
Muslim women, rape of. See Bosnia-Herze-
    govina camps
mutual consent
    for commitment to partner, 157–158
    for divorce, 152–153

National Socialism, oppressive gray zones
    of, 221, 225, 230–231, 233–234
nationality, as human right, 7, 84
natural disasters
    atrocities vs., 5, 12
    suffering caused by, 55
Nazism, 15, 28. See also Jews; Wiesenthal
    forgiveness of, 181–183
neediness
    moral, of perpetrators, 181–187, 207
    stoicism and, 69, 71
neglect, of children
    as abuse, 141–142
    revolutionary parenting as, 146–147,
        163
negligence, 14, 21
Neiman, Susan, 8
Nietzsche, Friedrich, 4, 71, 199, 212
    denial of evil, 23, 27–49, 101
nihilism, 168

nobility
    power and distortion, 37–38, 42
    reversal of values of, 44–49
    valuation of, 31–34
Noddings, Nel, 8, 11, 37
normativity, sources of, 87–90, 216
noumena (Kant), 74–75
numbers (Wittgenstein), 30–31
Nuremberg trials, 120
nursing homes, 111
Nussbaum, Hedda, 220–221, 228
Nussbaum, Martha, 64, 66, 68, 71

obedience
    in slave/master morality, 27, 37, 40–41,
        45
    as torture goal, 125
objectiveness, in right vs. wrong, 5, 56
obligation(s)
    of gratitude (see gratitude obligations)
    to oneself, 19, 210
    of perpetrators (see moral burdens)
    in rational agency, 82, 218–219
omnipotent being. See supreme being
On the Genealogy of Morality (Nietzsche),
    27–28, 30, 32, 34–35, 37–39, 44–45
ontology. See metaphysics
opportunity. See lack of opportunity
oppression
    creativity, 44
    feminist opposition to, 24, 98–100, 113
    gray zones of, 6, 34, 38, 213, 215,
        217–218, 233
    hostility among the oppressed, 47–48
    opposition to, 102
    social (see social oppression)
    survivors' testimony on, 11
origins, purposes vs., in guilt, 31–32
orphanages, 146, 161–163
ostracism
    as punishment, 171
    of rape victims, 120, 122, 125, 128, 130
othermothers, 162–163
ownership, of perspectives, 34–35
OXFAM, 110, 116

pain
    as basic evil (Noddings), 11
    as evil (Bentham), 18
    relevant wrongness of, 11, 18, 80
    revaluation of, 168–169

Schopenhauer's and Nietzsche's evalua-
        tion of, 168–169
    wrongness, relevance to (Kant), 80
Pardeeville, Wisconsin, 47
pardon(s), moral power of, 168, 171–172,
    179, 190
parental abuse
    of children, 141–142, 163
    as coercion, 143–146
    by teenagers, 139
parenting. See childrearing
pariahs, Jews as, 100
parole, 172
partner abuse, 139–143
    in heterosexual marriages (see spousal
        battering)
    in same-sex marriages, 154, 160
Pelzer, Dave, 142–144, 160
penalty(ies)
    fantasy, for rapists, 132–138, 172
    preventive vs. rectificatory, 170–172,
        179, 206–207
perception
    in denial of evil, 32–35; distortion of, 29,
        32–33, 36–44, 48–49
    in slave/master morality, 36–44
perpetration, as atrocity component, 9–12
perpetrator(s)
    freedom of, 172–173
    guilt within, 25–26
    identification with victims, 209–210
    moral burdens of, 25–26, 188–210
    moral relationship with victim, 167–168,
        188
    perception distortions, 29–30, 36–44,
        48–49, 188
    personal characteristics of, 3–4, 9, 22,
        94
    supreme being as, 13
    as victims, 6, 19–22, 26, 193, 224
    view of harm, 9–10
personal choice
    in attachment theory, 90–91
    gray zones of, 218, 221–227, 233–234; for
        women, 228–233
    intelligible vs. empirical, 75–76, 78
    in knowledge of evil, 6, 21–22, 26
    oppression impact on, 218, 221–222
    of perspectives, 33, 58–59, 74
    responsibility for, 75, 77–78
    wrongful tampering of, 71–72

personal terrorism, 143–146. *See also*
    domestic violence
personality disorders, 91
perspectivism
    in denial of evil, 32–35
    power imbalance impact on, 38–44
pesticides, 14
Philosophical Investigations (Wittgenstein),
    30–31
philosophy, of evil
    case illustrations, 5–6
    components of, 4
    empirical inquires for, 6, 75–76, 78
    historical views, 4–7
    human agents in, 5
    international interest in, 7
    interpretation of, 4–5, 7–8, 12
    metaphysical views, 6–7
    modern views, 7–8, 27–28
    moral views, 4–5, 7–8, 12, 27–29
    questions answered by, 3–4
    questions unanswered by, 6
    judgmental views, 7, 13–15
phoenix argument, 203–204
Piaget, Jean, 200
Pierce, Christine, 150, 155
pity, moral sense of, 102
playfulness
    of common folk, 47
    in slave/master morality, 40–41
pleasures, prioritization of, 110–111
points of view. *See* perspectivism
poisoning, environmental, as atrocity, 8, 14
policy(ies)
    international, 7, 167
    for relative well-being, 96–97
political assassinations, 143
political prioritization, of inequalities, 106,
    116–117
polygamy, 151
post-traumatic stress disorder, 144
poverty, alleviation of, 97, 108–109
power imbalance
    distortion and, 36–44
    hatred and impotence in, 44–49
    self-perceptions in, 33–35
powerful people. *See* victor(s)
powerlessness
    hate potential with, 46–47
    revenge and, 40
    stoic exaggeration of, 64–65, 67–68

unjust inequalities with, 111–112
"practical identity," normativity and,
    87–90
praise, ethics of, 50–51, 53, 86
predispositions, social, 62, 84
pregnancies, from war rape, 119–120, 126,
    130
prevention
    of harm: with penalties, 172, 170, 179,
        206–207; personal choice, 21–22;
        philosophical, 5–6
    of unjust inequalities, 108, 111–116
priests, 40, 46
primary goods theory (Rawls), 17, 61, 63
principles, as radical evil, 83–85
prioritization
    within feminism movement, 105–106
    of unjust inequalities, 105–111
prisoners of evil. *See* victim(s)
prisoners of war
    domestic, 144
    privileged, 212, 221–223, 226
privacy, marriage impact on, 158
privileged prisoners, gray zones within,
    212, 221–223, 226
problem of evil. *See* theology
property rights
    with cohabitation, 157–158
    with marriage, 151, 153
prostitutes
    decriminalization of, 149
    marginalization of, 100
    seasoning process of, 214
    in war rape, 118, 120
protection
    from domestic violence, 141, 154–155,
        159
    from rape threat, 126, 130
    requirements for, 47
    with stoicism, 67–68
proximity, psychic, in attachment theory,
    69, 90–91
prudence
    radical evil and, 76, 83–85
    self-interest vs., 85–87, 92
Prusher, Ilene R., 219
psychiatric illness(es), 91, 111
psychic proximity, in attachment theory,
    69, 90–91
public consciousness, of war rape victims,
    121–122

punishment
  compromise theory of, 170–171
  death as (see death penalty)
  deterrent value of, 6, 22, 30
  forgiveness and, 176–180, 184
  merciful, 191–194, 201
  moral power of, 169–173, 176
  Nietzsche's approach to, 30–31
  for rapists, 132–136
  responsibility as basis for, 15
  of self with guilt, 208–210
  for torture, 122–123
  torture as, 18
  utilitarian definition of, 17–18
purposes, origins vs., in guilt, 31–32

racism
  in education system, 103
  principles of, 83–85, 89
  in war sex crimes, 136–138
radical evil(s), 73–95
  conclusions about, 93–95
  diabolical evil vs., 91–92, 94, 211
  important persons and their internalized
    representations in, 90–93
  interests and principles as, 83–85
  Kant's theory of, 4, 24, 27, 75–79; solving
    mystery of, 85–87
  murder and mayhem as, 79–83
  normativity sources in, 87–90
  stoicism relationship to, 73–75
radical feminists, 113
radioactive wastes, 14
Rand, Ayn, 92
rape
  as domination symbol, 119, 124–129
  of inmates, 112
  institutional source of, 24–25, 112
  mass, 5, 8–10, 24, 118
  of partners, 25, 129, 153, 159
  punishment for, 132–138
  as war weapon (see war rape)
  women buying into, 228, 230
Rape of Nanking, 119
Rashdall, Hastings, 6
rationality
  intelligent vs. empirical, 75–76,
    78–80
  Kant on rational agency, 79–82
rationalization, of privileged position,
  212, 221–223, 226

Rawls, John
  ethics position of, 52–53
  on guilt, 200
  justice theory, 5, 53, 57; as response to
    utilitarianism, 60–64
  on slavery, 126–127
Raz, Joseph, 97
reciprocity, with gratitude, 195–196, 198
recklessness, 14, 21
reconciliation, moral power of, 179–180,
  184–185, 198
recovery, by victims, 3–4. See also sur-
  vivor(s)
recreational sex. See prostitutes
rectification
  moral power of, 167–170, 173
  through penalties, 170, 172, 179,
    206–207
redemption, by achievement, 207
reformists, revolutionaries vs., 102
regret, as moral remainder, 169, 180,
  208
rejection, hatred relationship to, 49
religion. See theology
remainders. See moral remainders
remorse, as moral remainder, 169, 185,
  208–209
renegotiation, in attachment theory, 91
reparation(s)
  forgiveness vs., 177–178, 181, 189
  guilt and, 200, 207, 210
  merciful, 191
repentance
  forgiveness and, 175, 178, 180
  as moral remainder, 21, 171, 208
rescue
  from punishment, 194–195, 198
  of victims, morality of, 116
resentment. See also envy
  forgiveness association with, 175–177,
    205
  moral power of, 167–168, 171
resistance
  to doing harm, 11–12
  elimination through torture, 124–125
  to evil, 6, 11–13
  to rape, 118, 124, 129, 134
resource allocation
  for basic equality, 114–116
  for equal education, 113, 115
  moral perspectives of, 97, 107–109

respect
  for humanity, equality as, 48, 114–116
  in rational agency, 81
  of self (see self-respect)
  in slave/master morality, 38, 40–42
  of survivors, 194
responsibility
  for childrearing, 142–143, 160, 163–165
  gray zones of, 218, 221–227, 233–234
  as guilt factor, 202–206
  perpetrators taking on, 11
  for personal choices, 75, 77–78
  punishment based on, 15
ressentiment, 27, 36, 40
restitution, 172, 189–191
retribution, 172
revaluation, of pain and suffering, 168–169
revenge
  as entitlement, 44–45, 85
  with power distortions, 28, 41, 231
revolutionaries, reformists vs., 102
revolutionary parenting, 146–150,
    162–163, 165
Rich, Adrienne, 113, 142
ridicule, 206
right, wrong vs., 5, 56
Ross, W. D., 5, 6–7
Rumkowski, Chaim, 221
Rwanda
  genocide, 224
  war rape in, 8, 24, 119–120, 126, 130

sabotage, 226
Sacajawea, 228–229
sadism, 10, 14, 21–22, 84, 121, 218
salvation, moral power of, 168
"Sambo" hypothesis, 41
Sanday, Peggy, 125
same-sex marriage
  as dilemma, 150–155
  discrimination of, 149–151
  legal recognition of, 139, 147–148,
    154–155, 164
  parenting and, 161–163
  social advantages of, 154–155
Satan, 212
sati, 147
schlecht, 101–102. See also bad
Schopenhauer, Arthur, 168
Schott, Robin, 8
segregation, racial, 103–104

self-absorption, with guilt, 207–209
self-blame, guilt association with, 199–200,
    203, 205
self-concept
  in attachment theory, 87, 90–91
  double-consciousness, 215
  normativity and, 87–90
  with slave/master morality, 38
self-condemnation, guilt association with,
    200–201
self-criticism, 34, 36, 38, 43
self-defense
  against murder or mayhem, 80, 84
  women's skills for, 126, 130–131,
    136–138
self-destruction, with guilt, 200–201
self-devaluation, as punishment, 170
self-forgiveness, 176–177, 205, 210
self-interest
  in attachment theory, 92–93
  in forgiveness, 176–177
  motives of, 85–87
  in radical evil, 76–78
self-judgement, with guilt, 209–210
self-love, in radical evil, 84–85
self-punishment, with guilt, 208–210
self-reliance, extreme, 71
self-respect
  as moral duty, 19, 210
  in slave/master morality, 38, 42–44
  stoic value of, 19, 61
  of survivors, 194, 213
self-worth
  entitlement view of, 44
  as feminism focus, 47, 49
  guilt impact on, 199–201
  self-forgiveness in, 176–177
sensual pleasures, prioritization of,
    110–111
separation, basic evil (Noddings), 11
Sermon on the Mount (Jesus), 34, 42
service, in slave/master morality, 40–41
servility. See submission
servitude, involuntary. See slavery
sex crimes, in war, 135–137
sex trade, 127
sexism
  global, 121
  hatred in, 49, 89
  vulnerable forgiveness with,
    174–175

sexist socialization, 146
sexual abuse
    as atrocity, 6, 8, 25, 103
    incestuous, 103, 111, 153, 160
    student risks for, 115
    as terrorism, 143–146
sexual fidelity, 152
sexual slavery. *See also* prostitutes
    as atrocity, 5–6, 8
    domestic, 118, 121, 125–126
    war rape as, 118, 120, 123, 127, 132, 137
Shakespeare, 194
shame
    guilt vs., 200, 205–207
    as moral remainder, 169–170
    reversal of, 206–207
    in war rape, 121, 123
shunning, moral power of, 171–172
sibling violence, 139
Sidgwick, Henry, 7, 196
Siebert, Renate, 223–224
silence and silencing
    moral power of, 185–187
    of war rape victims, 121–123
Silverman, Sue William, 144
Sims, J. Marion, 204
slave morality
    erotic bonding, 40
    power imbalances in, 36–44
    power sources and, 46–47
slave owners' wives, 229–230
slave revolt in morality, 40
slave values
    distortion of perspectives in, 36–44
    entitlement as, 44–49
    gray zones of, 215, 230–231
slavery
    as atrocity, 7–8
    comparative judgment of, 15–16, 44, 57
    as cultural decimation, 119, 124, 126–128
    in the home, 145–146, 151, 156
    sexual (*see* sexual slavery)
    as social oppression, 99–100
    survival goal with, 43–44, 215
    valuation of, 27, 31–34, 36, 44
    in war rape, 118, 120, 123, 127
smallpox epidemics, 5, 12
Smart, Alwynne, 192
Smart, Gumbu, 230–231
social behavior. *See* interpersonal psychology

social identity, inequalities of, 103–105
social institutions
    as controversial, 139–140, 147, 154–155
    as source of harm (*see* institutional sources)
social justice
    Rawl's theory of, 60–64, 106
    requirements of, 97
social justice movements
    evil vs. unjust inequality focus of, 24
    prioritization of evils, 105–111
social minimum, for decent society, 62
social oppression
    career exclusion as, 98, 100, 105–106
    education-focused, 103–106, 113, 115
    exploitation and slavery as, 99–100
    marginalization as, 99–100
    socialist feminism, 113–114
socialization, sexist, 146
sodomy, decriminalization of, 149
solidarity, soldier, with war rape, 128–129
Sonderkommando prisoners, 221–222, 230, 234
sports participation, inequality of, 112–113, 115
spousal battering. *See also* domestic violence
    as coercion, 145, 153
    forms of, 145, 153–154, 159
    as terrorism, 139–143, 193
spousal benefits, 151–152
spousal rape, 25, 129, 153, 159
Stalinism, 8
stalking, 153, 159, 201
Stanton, Elizabeth Cady, 98
starvation
    alleviation of, 108–110
    mass, 8, 10
stay-stitching analogy, of bias, 32, 34
Stockholm Syndrome, 213–214, 216
stoicism
    as defense against evil, 64–72, 168
    in ethics, 54, 59, 64, 73
    fundamental ideas of, 66, 95
    Kant's relation to, 4, 23–24, 50–54, 59, 73–75
    in social justice theory, 61–64
    utilitarianism vs., 71–72, 95
stranger rape, 125–126
stress, as gray zone feature, 224–227
subjectiveness, in right vs. wrong, 5, 56

submission
    in slave/master morality, 40–41
    as torture goal, 124
subordinance
    hatred and, 45–49
    morality distortions with, 36–44
    self-perceptions with, 33–35
sufferer. *See* victim(s)
suffering
    as atrocity component, 9–11
    desensitization to others', 6
    as evil component, 4–5, 11
    as human conduct product, 8, 72
    with inequality, 96–97, 114–116
    intergenerational, 19–20
    revaluation of, 168–169
    utilitarian approach to, 54–60
    voluntary alleviation of, 16–17
    willful embrace of, 17, 70–71
sufficiency doctrine, 97
suicide
    euthanasia as, 16–17
    immorality of, 74
    with war rape, 120
The Sunflower (Wiesenthal), 25, 181–187
supervision, parental, 162–163
support system(s), in attachment theory,
    91–92
supreme being
    as hypermoral, 13, 74, 87
    as nonculpable, 12–13
survivor(s)
    evildoers as, 6
    of Holocaust (*see* Holocaust survivors)
    living with evils, 3–4, 11, 25, 166–169
    self-respect in, 194, 213
    testimonies of, 10–11, 121
    of war rape, 119, 121–122
survivors' guilt, living with, 11, 25, 203
Symbionese Liberation Army (SLA), 214,
    217, 220, 222–223
sympathy, 73
syphilis experiments, Tuskegee, 5, 8, 204

talent, helping to develop, 82
tameness
    in slave/master morality, 40–41
    as torture goal, 124
targets, of torture, primary vs. secondary,
    124–125
teleological ethics, 50, 52–53

temptation, as evil, 78
Terezin, 70
terrorism
    as atrocity, 8
    domestic vs. international, 143
    in the home, 143–146
    torture vs., 124–125
    war rape as, 124–129
theology
    of evil, 6–7, 12–13
    moral challenge of, 13, 74, 87
    power distortions in, 34–35, 37, 40, 42
This Boy's Life (Wolff), 144
Thomas, Laurence, 7, 16
Three Guineas, 116
Title IX, of 1972 Education Amendment
    Act, 113, 115
Todorow, Tzvetan, 227
toleration and tolerable
    inequalities as, 96–97, 108, 114
    as normative concept, 16, 21
    of rape, 119–121, 123, 132
torture
    as atrocity, 7–8
    primary vs. secondary targets of,
        124–125
    as punishment, 18
    punishment for, 122–123
    terrorism vs., 124–125
    war rape as, 120, 122–129
transgender people. *See* lesbians, gay men,
    bisexuals, and transgender people
    (LGBTs)
transsexual surgery, compulsory, for
    rapists, 133–136
Trapp, Major Wilhelm, 83
trauma, living with effects of, 11, 25,
    166–169
trust and trustworthiness, 71, 73, 189, 197,
    223
trustee model, of marriage, 156
truth
    access to, 29, 71
    distortion of, 33, 35, 38, 42
    perpetrators' confession as, 182–187, 198
    radical evil and, 76
Tuskegee syphilis experiments, 5, 8, 204
Two Years before the Mast, 84
twoness, 215

"Uncle Tom" hypothesis, 41

undesirable, as philosophical view, 7, 18, 79
unforgivableness, 176–177, 180
UNICEF, 110, 116
Uniform Code of Military Justice, 132
Universal Declaration of Human Rights, 7
universality
    of equality, 114
    in radical evil, 79–80, 82
university students
    gender-based exclusion of, 104–105
    social perspectives of, 47–48
unjust enrichment, involuntary, guilt over,
        203, 205–206
unjust inequalities, 96–117
    application and implications of, 111–114
    decency vs. relative well-being, 96–97
    as evil, 96, 100, 103–105
    feminist perspectives in, 24, 98–100
    morally bad vs. evil, 101–102
    within oneself, 19
    opposition to, 102
    prioritization of, 105–111; political, 106,
        116–117
    reducing evil to, 7, 18, 24, 112
    respect as alleviation of, 114–116
unpleasantness, 18
usefulness. *See* utilitarianism
utilitarianism
    ethics and, 51–54, 58–59, 110
    as Kant's approach, 4, 23–24, 27, 54
    personal choice in, 58–59
    in punishment, 17–18
    in slave/master morality, 27, 37–41
    stoicism vs., 71–72, 95
    war on evil, 54–60

valuation
    of good vs. evil, 27–28, 31, 33–34
    of pain and suffering, 168–169
    with power distortions, 34, 40, 42, 46
value(s)
    in attachment theory, 91–92
    equality as, 96
    guilt association with, 200, 209
    in normativity, 89–90
    in rational agency, 81–82
    in stoicism, 66–67, 70–72, 74
vices, 52, 82, 84
victim(s). *See also* suffering
    concern for, 74–75
    as creative, 44–49

gray zones of, 224–227
human vs. animal, 9
as innocent vs. guilty, 12–13
moral powers of, 11, 25, 166–187,
    217–219, 227
moral relationship with perpetrator,
    167–168, 188
passive view of, 11–12
perceptual distortions of, 29–30, 36–44,
    48–49
as perpetrators, 6, 19–22, 26, 193, 212,
    224
perpetrators' identification with,
    209–210
recovery by, 3–4, 11 (*see also* survivor(s))
view of evil, 11
view of harm, 9–10, 15
victor(s)
    envy of inferiors, 44–47
    mockery and ridicule of, 46
    morality imbalances in, 36–44
    self-perceptions of, 33–34
Vietnam War, rape in, 8, 126
violence
    family (*see* domestic violence)
    marginalized targets of, 100, 142–143,
        166
    as oppression, 113
virtue(s)
    ethics of, 50–51
    friendship and, 73–74
    happiness vs., 74
    motive behind, 21
    in stoicism, 66–67, 69, 73
vitality
    aristocratic valuation of, 40, 46
    survival as goal of, 43–44
voluntariness
    as gray zone, 14, 219, 225
    of motherhood, 142–143
Vrba, Rudolf, 227
vulnerability, with forgiveness, 174

war and warfare
    as deliberate harm, 122
    modern, arguments against, 12
    premodern, atrocities of, 12
war crimes, sexual, 135–137. *See also* war
        rape
war rape
    castration and, 132–135

war rape (*Continued*)
    as criminal, 24, 135–137
    institutionalization of, 128–129, 134,
        137
    as invisible weapon, 5, 8–10, 24,
        118–124, 126
    male victims of, 128, 135–138
    in movies, 124
    purposes of, 128–129
    racism and, 135–138
    as terrorism, 124–129
    as torture, 122–129
    victims' testimony of, 121, 128–129, 137
    women's response to, 129–132, 137–138
Watson, Gary, 215
weakness, in radical evil, 69, 74, 82–83, 94
well-being, relative, decency vs., 96–97
white feminists, 113–114
Wellman, Carl, 124
Wharton, Edith, 101
wickedness, 8, 11
Wiesenthal, Simon, 25, 181–187, 190, 203,
    207
will and willingness
    as defense, 13, 64
    in embracing of suffering, 17, 70–71
    ethics and, 51–52, 54, 75
    intelligible vs. empirical actions of,
        75–76, 78
    in radical evil, 11, 74, 79, 211
    in self-preservation, 19
    as stoicism component, 64, 66, 70, 72, 74
    of women for dominance, 36–37, 39, 43
Williams, Bernard, 67, 167, 169
witch burnings, as atrocity, 15
witnessing, moral power of, 186
Wittgenstein, Ludwig, 4, 30–31
Wolff, Tobias, 144
"woman hating." *See* misogyny
womanliness, 39, 43, 45, 219

women
    abuse of (*see* domestic violence)
    basic respect for, 115
    career exclusion of, 98, 100, 105–106
    domination valued by, 36–37, 39, 43
    educational exclusion of, 103–105
    gray choices of, 228–233
    men's condescending view of, 36–39, 43,
        45, 112
    military participation by, 131, 136–137
    rape of (*see* rape)
    self-defense skills of, 126, 130–131,
        136–138
    view of evil, 11
women of color, as feminists, 113–114
Woolf, Virginia, 116
worker compensation, spousal benefits and,
    152
working mothers, 161, 163
World War II. *See also* Jews; Nazism
    atrocities of, 8, 10, 186, 194, 203–204
    comfort women in, 119, 125, 129, 132
worthiness
    of action, 12, 20–21, 27–28, 86
    ethics of, 50–51, 53, 67
    forgiveness and, 176–177, 180
    of gratitude, 195–196
    guilt association with, 199–201
    as self-interest goal, 86–87, 89
wrong, right vs., 5, 56
wrongdoing(s)
    culpable (*see* culpability)
    Kant's view, 76–83
    ordinary, evil vs., 3–4, 7, 12–13, 17, 83
    Stoic view, 70–72
    utilitarian approach to, 56–57
Wyden, Peter, 233

Young, Iris Marion, 99
Yugoslavia, war rape in, 8, 24, 119–120